The New York City Slave Revolt of 1712

BEN HUGHES

The New York City Slave Revolt of 1712

The First Enslaved Insurrection in British North America

WESTHOLME
Yardley

First Westholme Trade Paperback 2024

©2021 Ben Hughes
Maps by Tracy Dungan
Maps © 2021 Westholme Publishing
Originally published under the title *When I Die, I Shall Return to My Own Land: The New York City Slave Revolt of 1712*

Westholme Publishing, LLC
904 Edgewood Road
Yardley, Pennsylvania 19067
Visit our Web site at www.westholmepublishing.com

ISBN: 978-1-59416-416-3
Also available as an eBook.

Printed in the United States of America.

This slave trade and slavery spread more human misery, inculcated more disrespect for and neglect of humanity, a greater callousness to suffering, and more petty, cruel, human hatred than can well be calculated. We may excuse and palliate it, and write history so as to let men forget it; it remains the most inexcusable and despicable blot on modern human history.

—W. E. B. Du Bois, *The Negro* (1915)

Onyàmé ṅkrabea nni kwatibea.
The destiny the Supreme Being has assigned to you cannot be avoided.

—Akan proverb

Contents

Illustrations

MAPS

ILLUSTRATIONS

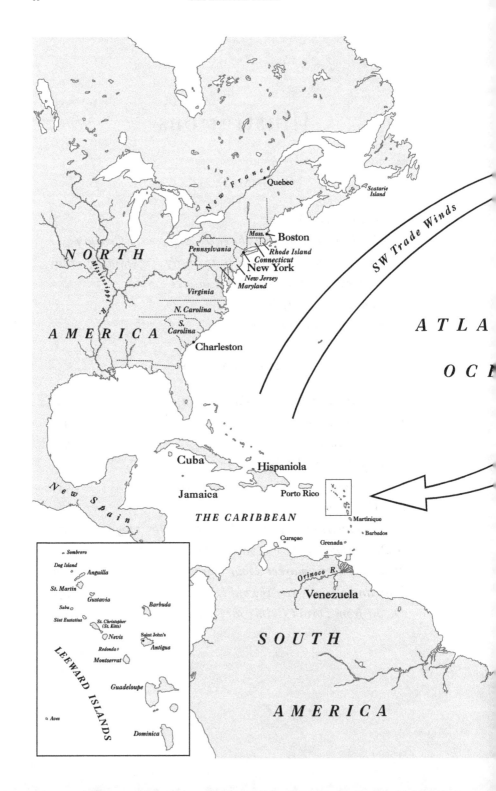

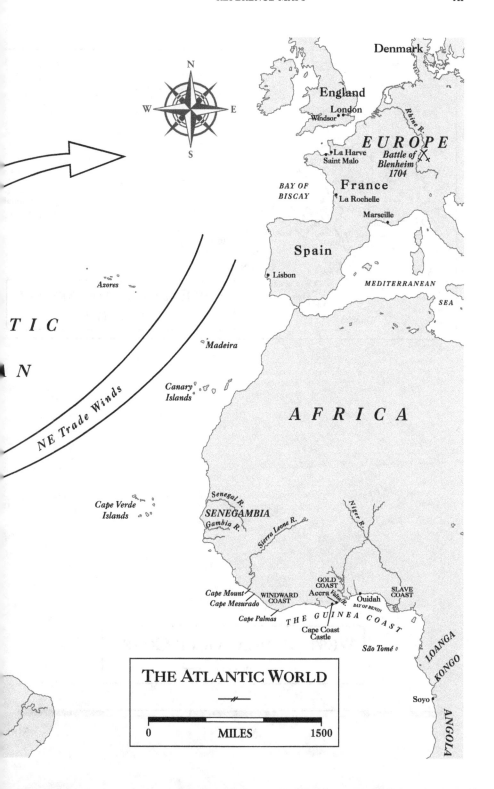

THE ATLANTIC WORLD

0   MILES   1500

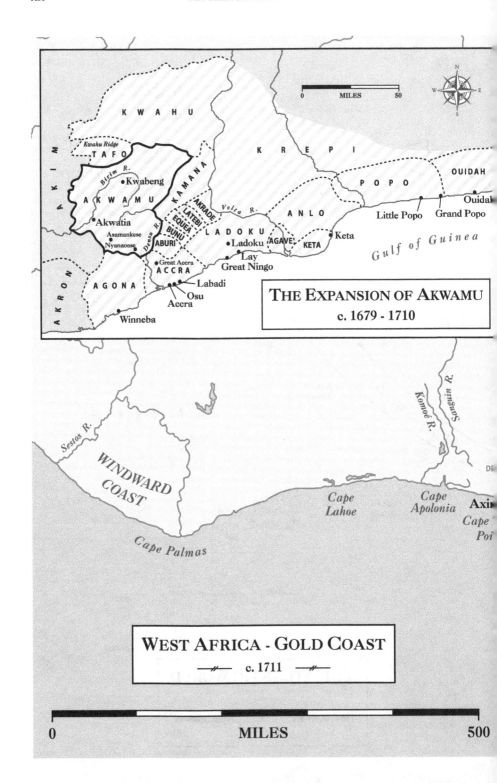

THE EXPANSION OF AKWAMU
c. 1679 - 1710

WEST AFRICA - GOLD COAST
—⚓— c. 1711 —⚓—

0   MILES   500

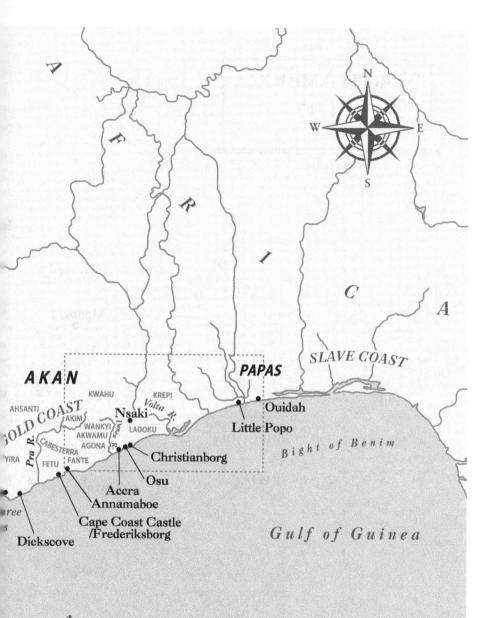

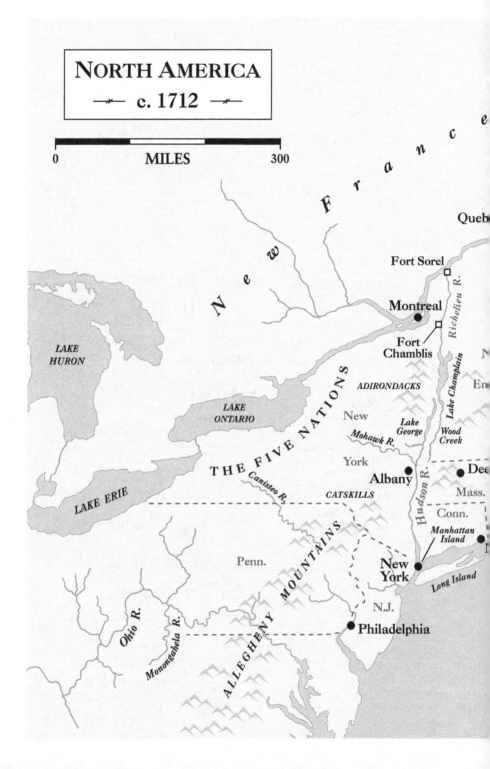

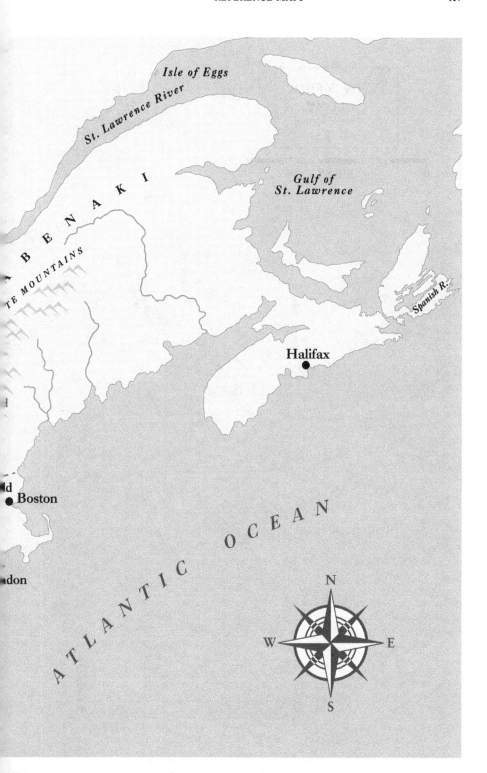

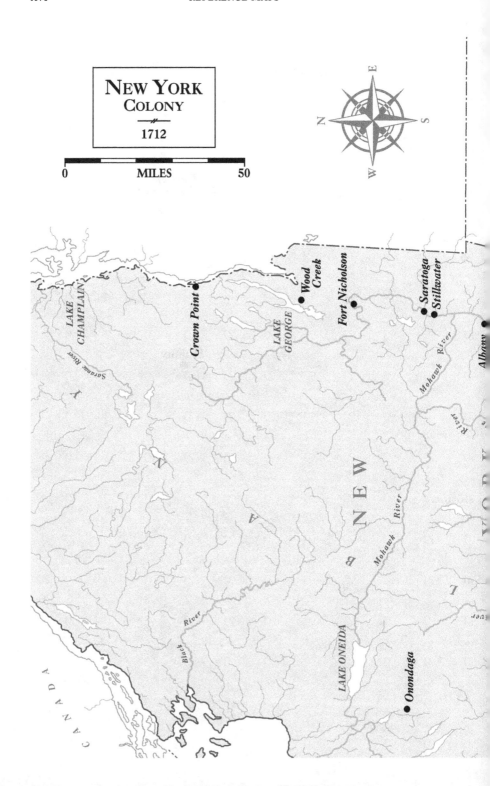

NEW YORK
COLONY
1712

0   MILES   50

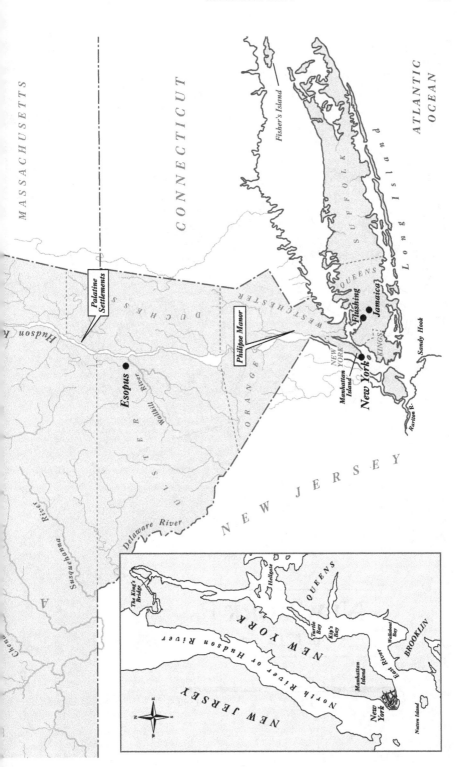

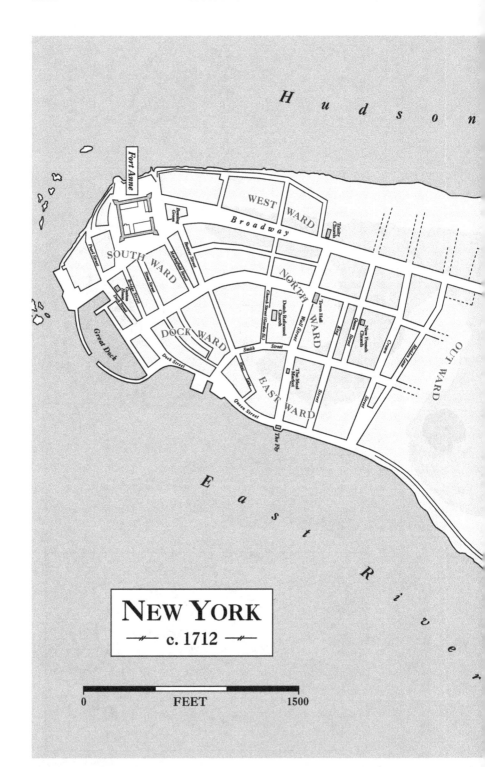

NEW YORK
— c. 1712 —

0   FEET   1500

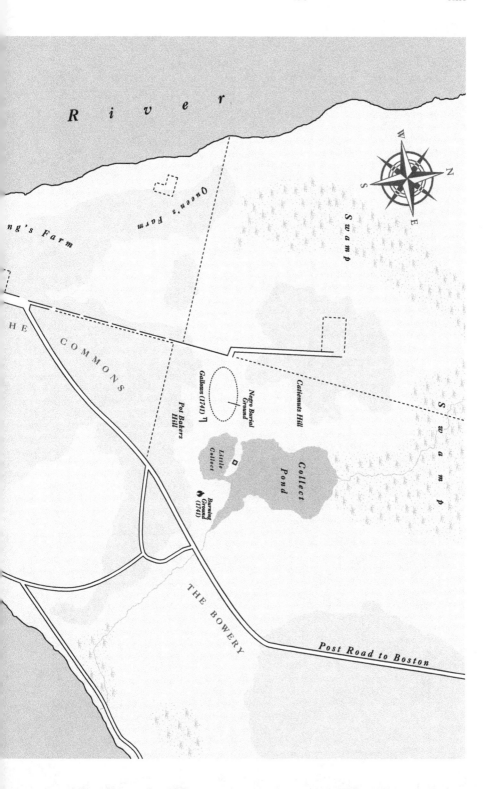

Preface

As historians, we cannot work with Euclidean standards of proof. We are obliged to interpret; to speculate not wildly but in an informed way.
—Ivor Wilks, *Forests of Gold* (1993)

Ɔkwantenni nim asɛmka, na onnim asekyerɛ.
Telling what you have seen on your journey is one thing, explaining it is another.

—Akan proverb

"When I die, I shall return to my own land" are words attributed to an eighteenth-century Akan runaway on the Caribbean island of Saint Thomas. When faced with execution he embraced what he believed to be his proximate homecoming to *asamando*, the place "where the ancestors dwell."[1] Over 1.2 million Akan, a grouping of culturally and linguistically related ethnicities from modern-day Ghana and areas of the Ivory Coast, were forcibly transhipped to the Americas from the fifteenth to the nineteenth centuries. Although representing only 10 percent of the total African diaspora of the era, the Akan, or Coromantee as they were known by the English-speaking slave-owning societies of the Americas, predominated throughout the New World in the eighteenth century in acts of rebellion and the establishment of maroon communities. This heritage is attributable to a variety of factors, chief among which are the militarization of the Gold Coast, and the stoical fatalism inspired by the Akan's spiritual beliefs.[2]

Three separate sources link the Akan to the New York Slave Revolt of 1712. The first, written one day after the revolt for the *Boston News-Letter*, states that "some Cormentine Negroes to the number of 25 or 30 and 2 or 3 Spanish Indians having conspirred to murder all the Christians here, and by that means thinking to obtain their Freedom, about two o'clock this morning put their bloody design in Execution."[3] The second is a letter written by John Sharpe, chaplain of Fort Anne, the city's principal fortification and the residence of the governor, Robert Hunter. In correspondence with an English patron on June 24, Sharpe labeled the rebels as belonging to "ye Nations of Carmantee & Pappa," the latter a reference to a number of polities situated to the east of the River Volta within the boundaries of modern-day Ghana which were established by Akan and Gã refugees in the second half of the seventeenth century.[4] Sharpe also mentioned a "free negro who pretends Sorcery [who] gave [the conspirators] . . . a powder to rub on their Cloths," as well as describing an oath-taking ceremony which involved the rebels "tying themselves to Secrecy by Sucking ye blood of each Others hands." The only "free negro" indicted with the crime in the subsequent court case was Peter the Doctor.[5] From Sharpe's description, we can deduce that Peter was an ɔkɔmfoɔ (*okomfo*), an Akan spiritualist, healer, and practitioner of *Obeah*. Such "priests," as Western sources often equivocally referred to them, typically used *hyire*, a white clay associated with rituals of spiritual purification believed to convey a divine invulnerability from an enemies' weapons in battle. Oath taking is also symptomatic of Akan cultural beliefs.[6]

The third source linking the Akan to the revolt are the minutes of New York's Supreme Court of Judicature which name all the individuals put on trial. Although the names given to enslaved people often reveal more about the whims of their masters than they do about those who carried them, they can also provide clues as to the identity of the individual. This is particularly true when it comes to the Akan, who were typically named for the day of the week on which they were born. Of the forty-seven slaves indicted in the trials that took place from April 12 to October 18, 1712, nine, or 19 percent, had Akan day names. This correlation rises to four out of nineteen, or 21 percent if we reduce the base group to include only those executed for the crime, or five out of twenty (25 percent) if we add Peter the Doctor, who,

somewhat surprisingly, was dismissed without punishment. If we include the day-named Cuffee, the rebel who escaped punishment by
turning state's evidence, and the six who committed suicide in the immediate aftermath of the revolt (an exit strategy often chosen by Akan
rebels as we shall see), we reach a figure of twelve out of twenty-seven,
or 44 percent, who either had Akan day names or displayed Akan cultural traits or behavior. The names of the remaining fifteen who were
executed tell us nothing definite. They may or may not have been
Akan, but in the court minutes they did not have Akan names.[7] There
were three Toms and two Caesars, a "mullato" named Kitto, and a
Mingo. Tom Furnis and Robin were burned at the stake. Abigail was
the only woman to be executed. Hannibal, Sam, Toby, and Titus were
hanged.[8]

Which leaves Claus. The only slave to be executed by being "broken on the wheel," Claus belonged to Alan Jarrett, New York City's
most prolific slave trader.[9] Jarrett undertook at least seven voyages to
Africa in his fifteen-year career, condemning over six hundred men,
women, and children to a life of slavery in the New World. After
working for the Royal African Company out of Antigua from 1708
to 1709, Jarrett began operating from New York as an independent
trader. The second of three voyages conducted between 1709 and 1712
saw Jarrett arrive at New York from the "Guinea Coast" with fifty-
five slaves on June 4, 1711, nine months and two days before the revolt
broke out.[10] There is no record of any other slaver arriving in New
York from Africa in the five years preceding the revolt. Furthermore,
Jarrett owned one of the executed rebels, while the man who was likely
to have been his chief financial backer, Rip Van Dam, owned two others, both of whom had Akan day names.[11] When one combines the
evidence above with the widely attested hypothesis that the vast majority of slave revolts occurring in the New World in the seventeenth
and early eighteenth centuries were carried out by recently enslaved
Africans rather than by their "seasoned" peers, it seems likely (if not
probable) that the revolt that broke out in New York City on the night
of the 6th to the 7th of April 1712 was perpetrated by Akan brought
from the Gold Coast by Alan Jarrett nine months before.[12]

The name of Jarrett's executed slave may also be significant. In
1712 New York had a diverse population. Roughly half of the free res-

idents were Dutch. The majority of the rest were British and French; many of the latter were Huguenots.[13] Although many Clauses are German, the majority are Danes, which raises the question—why did Jarrett, a French Huguenot-cum-British subject living in a city culturally dominated by the Dutch, own a slave with a Danish name?[14] There are several possibilities: perhaps Jarrett bought Claus from a Danish resident of New York City; maybe Jarrett had Danish or German connections untraceable in the extant historical record; or perhaps Jarrett, or Claus' previous owner (if he had one), merely liked (or disliked) the name. There is also another, more intriguing, possibility. The shoreline of the Gold Coast was dotted with fifty or more slave castles—wooden, stone, or brick structures erected by the various European nations engaged in the trade. The first were built in the fifteenth century by the Portuguese. Others were built by their successors, the Dutch. The English and French also built castles and trading posts along the wave-battered shore, as did the Swedish and Brandenburgers, citizens of a kingdom that went on to become Prussia.[15] Also present on the Gold Coast were the Danish, who, in the late seventeenth and first half of the eighteenth century, exported slaves to fuel their Caribbean sugar plantations from a solitary holding to the east of the region named Fort Christiansborg.[16]

At the time of Jarrett's presence on the Gold Coast prior to his return to New York in June 1711, the Danish proprietors of Christiansborg were experiencing a boom in business. This was attributable to the actions of a particular Akan polity, the Akwamu, a bellicose people originating in the "foliage entombed" interior known for their devotion to the god of war, Tutu Abo. A few months prior to Jarrett's visit, the ruler of Akwamu, King Akwonno, had defeated the neighboring polity of Kwahu, a people known for their expertise at elephant hunting and their exportation of ivory and gold, after a series of campaigns which had occupied his army for the previous four years.[17] As a result, a flood of enslaved war captives, many of whom were battle-hardened warriors, were marched to the coast and sold out of Christiansborg and at various points nearby. As the Danish slaving fleet consisted of only a handful of vessels at the time, at least two of which were busy refitting in the Caribbean, these captives were sold to "interlopers," independent traders of a variety of nations whose ships swarmed along

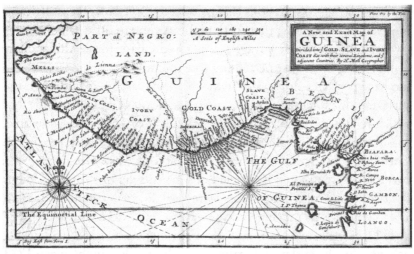

*A New and Exact Map of Guinea Divided into the Gold, Slave and Ivory Coast &
with their several kingdoms, and the adjacent Countries*, 1705. European slave castles crowd the coastline. (*New York Public Library*)

the Gold Coast despite the English and Dutch national companies'
attempts to discourage them.[18] Jarrett was among their number at the
time, and perhaps it is not too far-fetched to speculate that he was
one of the Danes' customers. This, at least, might explain the name
of his ill-fated slave. The theory is given added credence by the fact
that Jarrett was known to have traded in the area before and carried
cargoes particularly favored by the Akwamu.[19] Could it be then that
the enslaved people responsible for the New York revolt of 1712 were
originally from the Akan polity of Kwahu?

As is already no doubt evident, *The New York City Slave Revolt of
1712* involves a certain amount of speculation. "Perhaps," "maybe,"
and "may well have been" litter the pages that follow. This approach
is often forced upon the writers of histories of enslaved people. As
others have noted, the problem is the paucity of sources.[20] This is particularly true when it comes to the stories of the individual slaves involved in the New York revolt. They left no written sources behind.
As a result, any detail on those involved that has survived has been
exploited to the full in the pages that follow. Extrapolation has also
been used. Patterns of behavior and motivation evidenced by primary

sources relating to situations that parallel the 1712 revolt cast light on the events surrounding that April night. Although little evidence survives detailing Jarrett's voyage to the Gold Coast, for example, many primary accounts exist pertaining to contemporary voyages with the same purpose and similar destinations. In the same vein, although the surviving documentation concerning the revolt of 1712 is slight, that which relates to the alleged New York revolt of 1741 is considerable, as is the evidence detailing an Akan-led revolt that took place on the Caribbean island of Saint John in 1733, and an Akan/Creole plot discovered before it could be carried out in Antigua in 1736. Although the two New York-based events were very different, the records from 1741 can teach us much about the day-to-day lives of those involved in 1712, as well as about what their white owners considered plausible behavior for the enslaved. Furthermore, the similarities between 1733 and 1712 are striking, the court records from the 1736 plot also provide considerable insight. The use of such devices may not be ideal, but the alternative is even less desirable. Even though the paucity of primary evidence forces unorthodox methods, the story of the 1712 New York rebels deserves to be told.

Prologue

IF THERE WAS ONE THING the inhabitants of colonial New York City feared it was fire. Many of the houses were constructed of wood, their shingle roofs burned like tinder, and flames could leap across the narrow streets with ease.[1] By 1712, there had been many precedents of disaster: half a century before some 9,000 houses had been gutted in the Great Fire of London; in 1676 colonial Jamestown had burned to the ground; and ten years earlier seven-eighths of Bergen, Norway's largest city, had been wiped from the map by a conflagration sparked by an electrical storm. So, at 2 a.m., soon after the first tongues of flame began licking up around the walls of John Crooke's outhouse on Maiden Lane, cries of alarm shook the inhabitants from their slumber and the sleeping city came to life.

Fortunately for the 5,841 Europeans, Africans, and Native Americans then inhabiting the southern tip of Manhattan Island, the city council had long prepared for such an eventuality.[2] The watchmen shook their rattles, rapped on the doors of the nearest houses, and shouted for the inhabitants to throw their fire buckets down to the cobbled streets below. Sentries posted on the battlements of Fort Anne sounded the fire bell, and dozens of New Yorkers stumbled bleary-eyed from their beds, threw on overcoats to keep out the chill, and dashed outside. Filling the buckets from street pumps as they flowed down Broadway, Maiden Lane, and Pearl, the crowd converged around Crooke's outhouse and prepared to douse the flames.[3]

Unbeknown to the majority, the blaze had been started with murderous intent. "Twenty-four or more negro, mulatto and Indian slaves," the most miserable of New York City's underclasses, had long been plotting this moment. The laws established by the city's British administrators had enabled their masters to humiliate, beat, maim, rape, and imprison them ever since they had first been forced to stumble ashore at Manhattan. Armed with guns, six-penny daggers, swords, pistols, axes, staves, clubs, poniards, and hatchets, the slaves fell upon their masters. That night they would have their revenge.[4]

CHAPTER I

Whipped at the Common Whipping Post

NEW AMSTERDAM AND NEW YORK

1626–1705

THE HISTORY OF SLAVERY IN NEW YORK is nearly as old as the history of the European occupation itself. In 1626, just two years after the first settlers arrived, eleven enslaved men were brought to Manhattan Island. Captured at sea by privateers from an Iberian merchantman, their names reflected their African and colonial Portuguese origins. Paul D'Angola, Anthony the Portuguese, Simon Congo, Big and Little Manuel, and their companions were shackled together and put to work in gangs. Supervised by a Dutch West India Company (WIC) engineer named Cryn Fredericksen, the slaves built the first Fort Amsterdam. Two years later they were employed building dwelling houses and guard posts, cutting timber, "splitting palisades, clearing land, burning lime," and toiling on six *bouweries* or small farms which had sprung up to the north of the fort and would later give their name to the land on which they were built. Meanwhile, two Black women, one of whom was named Mayken, had been purchased and shipped in for the "comfort of the . . . Negro men." Over the next fifteen years, the population of New Amsterdam slowly grew. A trickle of African arrivals joined the ranks of the original eleven Black residents, while a number of Walloons (French-speaking protestants from modern-day

Belgium), Englishmen, Germans, and Norwegians added to the ever-increasing population of Dutch.[1]

In 1641, frontier skirmishes with the Lenape, a local Indian tribe, developed into a serious conflict. Kieft's War, named after the WIC's bumbling director whose belligerent attitude triggered it, saw the colony's slaves turned into auxiliary soldiers. "In regards to negroes," a WIC officer explained when calling for more Africans to be sent to New Amsterdam, "they ought to be stout and strong fellows, fit for immediate employment . . . , if required, in war against the savage natives, either to pursue them when retreating, or else to carry some of the soldiers' baggage." Armed with small axes and half pikes, the enslaved proved their worth. So much so, in fact, that three years into the war, eleven of them petitioned the company for an improvement in their status. With the conflict ongoing and with only forty regular soldiers based in New Amsterdam, the company agreed to negotiate, and a settlement termed "half-freedom" was arranged. While still obliged to work for the company when needed, the eleven men were henceforth entitled to wages and were free to hire themselves out when their services were not otherwise required. The contract also stipulated that they had to pay an annual tribute to the company of twenty-two and a half bushels of maize, wheat, peas, or beans and one fat hog to the value of 30 guilders. Furthermore, all children of the half-free "already in existence or hereafter born" would remain the company's property for life. Despite such clauses, the policy proved popular, offering as it did incentives to both parties, and after Kieft's War had drawn to a conclusion in 1645, the WIC granted "half-freedom" to a further two dozen enslaved petitioners as a reward for their allegiance during the conflict.[2]

In the 1650s a free Black neighborhood emerged in New Amsterdam. To the north of Wall Street, beyond the wooden palisade which marked the city limits, a settlement grew up in a fold of sunken land around the Collect or Fresh Water Pond. Domingo Antony, Manuel Trumpeter, Anthony Portuguese, and Big Manuel were among the first residents. A weekly market located near the junction of two tracks leading north to Fort Orange (the settlement known as Albany after the English takeover) and northeast to New England was at the heart of the community.[3] Meanwhile, the very nature of the colony of New

Amsterdam was changing. With revenues from the fur trade beginning to wane, the economic focus shifted to the provisions trade: supplying food, lumber, and value-added products such as beer and snuff to the European colonies in the Caribbean which were specializing in a sugar monoculture. This change was facilitated by the ever-increasing use of slave labor. Disappointed in their hopes of encouraging European immigration, largely due to the fact that the Dutch homeland was then the most prosperous of all European countries and offered far more attractive possibilities than the tough conditions prevalent in the New World, the WIC began to relax its African trading monopoly. New Netherlanders were permitted to send farm produce directly to the company's forts in Angola and "convey Negroes back home to be employed in the cultivation of their lands."[4]

In the early 1640s two slavers, the *La Garce* and the *Tamandere*, arrived in New Amsterdam. While the latter came straight from Africa, the former was a French privateer which had captured its cargo at sea from a Spanish merchantman. Although several aboard claimed to be free subjects under Spanish law, no enquiries were made by the authorities who were keen to incorporate them into the workforce. Sold as chattel along with the rest of their shipmates, these "Spanish negroes" were assumed to be slaves due to their dark skin and "wooly" hair. The burden was on them to prove otherwise, a pattern that would continue in New York under English rule. In 1652, the *St. Anthoni* reached New Amsterdam with forty-four slaves captured from a Spanish ship at sea by a Dutch privateer. Mostly Spanish-speaking Catholics, five were sold to Jacob the Miller, while ten were purchased by Peter Stuyvesant. Kieft's replacement, Stuyvesant was the last and best-known of all the Dutch West India Company's governors. He was also the largest slaveholder in the colony.[5]

The second half of the 1650s saw the slave trade increase with several vessels arriving from the Dutch-controlled Caribbean entrepôt of Curaçao. These enslaved proved particularly popular in New Amsterdam. While Blacks brought directly from Africa were considered "proud and dangerous" and difficult to control, "seasoned" Creoles, having built up an understanding of their status and having had their spirits systematically broken, were deemed by some to be less likely to threaten their enslavers. They also survived longer, having built up a tolerance to disease and having become accustomed to a European diet. In 1654, the *Witte Paert* brought a further 300 Africans into New Amsterdam by way of the Caribbean. Although most were resold to plantation owners along the Chesapeake, several remained in the colony. Five years later, with the WIC-enslaved individuals employed in fortifying Oyster Bay on Long Island to ensure it remained in Dutch hands in spite of a growing population of English Puritans who had relocated from New England, another two slavers arrived. The *St. John* brought 300 slaves into New Amsterdam. The second vessel carried a further 331. Although the origin of these slaves is unknown, the Dutch were then active in the slave trade from West Central Africa, so it is likely that the majority were from Luanda, Angola, and Congo.[6]

By the end of the 1650s New Amsterdam's governors, administrators, and courts had developed a loose legal code to regulate the ever-increasing slave population. As northwestern Europe had not seen institutionalized slavery since the end of the Middle Ages, no precedents existed, and the Dutch had to invent a system as they went along. Set alongside the draconian legal practices developed by the English, which reflected a different reality emerging in the fledgling societies of the Caribbean, the Dutch system was less harsh and restrictive. Crucially, racial distinctions were not evident. Slaves were deemed trustworthy enough to receive arms and fight the local Indians, and were even used to ensure that a number of rebellious white tenants of Rensselaerswyck (a private holding in the region of modern-day Albany established with the approval of the WIC by Kiliaen Van Rensselaer) paid their quitrents. Blacks were also permitted to get married in the Dutch Reformed Church, an opportunity that at least twelve individuals took between 1639 and 1643, including the aforementioned Little Anthony who was still enslaved when he married Lucie D'Angola on May 5, 1641. Fifty-seven enslaved and free Blacks who professed to be Christians and had attained a "right knowledge of God," had their children baptized in the church between 1639 and 1655. Blacks in New Holland enjoyed equality in the courts and were even permitted to testify against their white enslavers. In 1643, Anthony the Portuguese was awarded reparations for damage done to his hog by a white merchants' dog, while eight years later a civil action regarding the ownership of some wood was decided on the testimony of an enslaved man despite his story being contradicted by several white witnesses. Even more surprisingly for those who have studied slavery in New York in the subsequent English period, in New Amsterdam free Blacks were truly free. They were allowed to own property and even permitted to employ white indentured servants.[7]

There is also some evidence for white sympathy toward the plight of the enslaved in New Amsterdam. The government was obliged to pass three separate laws in 1640, 1648, and 1658 prohibiting whites from harboring Black runaways, while several inhabitants were moved to write a petition to the government in Holland protesting their shock and disapproval at the fact that the WIC had failed to provide religious instruction for the enslaved. Extant court cases also hint at a certain leniency compared to the brutalizing measures that would become commonplace under the English. In January 1641, when eight enslaved were charged with the murder of Jan Premero, one of their peers, "in the woods near their houses," the court determined to let God decide who should be executed for the crime. Lots were drawn and Manuel the Giant was chosen, but when the ropes securing him to the gallows broke, he was allowed to walk free. In 1664 an enslaved woman named Lysbeth Antonissen was sentenced to death for burning down the house of her enslaver, Marten Cregier. Once tied to the stake prior to strangulation, Antonissen was also granted a last-minute reprieve. Indeed, the only instance of a Black person being put to death in the entire period of Dutch rule in New Amsterdam occurred in 1646 when Jan Creoly was convicted of committing sodomy upon a ten-year-old named Manuel Congo.[8]

On August 15, 1664, the *Gideon*, the first and only WIC ship to bring slaves to New Amsterdam, arrived at Manhattan. On board were 153 enslaved men and 137 enslaved women. The *Gideon* had sailed from Amsterdam before picking up its human cargo on the Guinea and Angolan coasts. It had then sailed for Curaçao after having first stopped at Cayenne, in modern French Guiana. Seventy-three of the 421 taken on board in Africa died during the Middle Passage. Forty-seven others were sold in the Caribbean. Many of the remainder were suffering from scurvy and their health was so poor that several were replaced with seasoned slaves from Curaçao before the *Gideon* sailed northward. Ten more were to lose their lives before the vessel arrived in New Amsterdam. Forty of the remainder were bought by Governor Stuyvesant, to add to those already enslaved on his Bowery farm. A slave trader named John de Decker took another forty to sell in Albany while the majority of the remainder were transhipped to Virginia. About thirty, including a child born on the voyage from Africa, were sold to locals in New Amsterdam, bringing the Black population of the colony to 375, seventy-five of whom were free.[9]

Just eleven days after the *Gideon*'s arrival, a British flotilla of four ships sailed round Coney Island and anchored in Gravesend Bay. In anticipation of the outbreak of the second of three Anglo-Dutch wars—a series of seventeenth-century conflicts instigated by the English with the aim of establishing hegemony over worldwide trade—Charles II had decided to wrest control of New Amsterdam from his Dutch rivals. On board the flagship, the 36-gun *Guinea*, was the man tasked with carrying out his royal highness' demands—Colonel Richard Nicolls, a royalist veteran of the English Civil War. Despite being outnumbered and outgunned, Stuyvesant was determined to fight. The residents had other ideas. Having learned of the generous terms Nicolls was offering, they demanded that Stuyvesant surrender. Faced with a petition signed by ninety-three leading citizens including his own son, urging him to avert "misery, sorrow, conflagration . . . [and] the absolute ruin . . . of about fifteen hundred innocent souls," Stuyvesant conceded. Nicolls proved true to his word. Aside from changing the city's name to New York in honor of Charles II's younger brother to whom the newly won colony had been gifted, the colonel imposed surprisingly few changes: Stuyvesant was replaced by Nicolls as governor, and the English jury system was established in the colony's courts. Stuyvesant was permitted to continue residing in his farm in the Bowery, however, and many of his leading administrators retained their posts. Indeed, the colony would remain dominated by the Dutch culturally, linguistically, economically, and socially for the best part of the next half century.[10]

Over the same period the rights and privileges of the colony's Black population were systematically eroded. Just one year into Nicolls' governorship, a statute was issued bestowing legal status upon the insti-

View of New Amsterdam by Johannes Vingboons, 1664, painted the same year as the arrival of the English under Richard Nicolls. (*National Archives, The Hague, The Netherlands*)

tution of slavery, something that had hitherto only been recognized through custom and habit. On March 7, 1671, three years into the governorship of Nicolls's successor, Colonel Francis Lovelace, Domingo and Manuel Angola, "free negroes" who had lived in the Black neighborhood north of Wall Street since before the English takeover, were summoned to the mayor's court. There the Angolas were warned against continuing their habit of "entertaining sundry of the servants and negroes belonging to the Burghers and inhabitants of this city . . . on pain of forfeiting their freedom." One year later the Third Anglo-Dutch War broke out, and 1673 saw a short-lived Dutch reconquest of New York, which was briefly renamed New Orange. The following year, English rule having been reestablished by the terms of the Treaty of Westminster, the Duke of York appointed the third Englishman to be governor of New York. Like his predecessors a staunch royalist and a man of military background, Edmund Andros was to continue the established policy of regulating and restricting the colony's enslaved Africans and free Blacks alike. In 1679, Andros prohibited the enslavement of Native Americans, thus completing the policy of restricting chattel slavery only to those of African origin. The late 1670s and early 1680s also saw a spate of punishments inflicted on New York's Black inhabitants. In 1679, "a negro" John Baker was given thirty lashes at the public whipping post outside City Hall for stealing a kettle from Carston Leerson's house and "Bouy roaps and Shrowds" from Marten Cregier's sloop, while a Black man named Danielle received forty lashes for "drawing his knife agt. a Burger of this Citty & rideing in a Cart." The following year a law was issued requiring all enslaved laborers to carry passes when traveling, and Margaret Peters, a mulatto woman, was banished from New York City for theft. When she returned and continued her former practices, Peters was "Whipt at ye Comon whipen post 20 Lashes on ye bare back" and "burnt in ye shoulder" with a branding iron to ensure she would be recognized if she attempted to return.[11]

In 1682 the city's common council imposed further restrictions on Black inhabitants. Outraged by the "Rude and Unlawfull sports and Pasetimes" and other "Greate Evills and Incoveniencys . . . Done by Negros and Indian Slaues [during] their ffrequent meetings . . . in Greate numbers On the Lords Day," it was decreed that any slaves "found so doing hither forth" were to be "Severly whipped" and any person found abetting such behaviour or "P'sum[ing] to Entertaine Harbour or Conceale any Negro or Indian Slaves or buy Sell or Trade with them for any Liqours or Other Goods Whatsoever . . . shall Incurr the penalty and fforfeiture of five pounds for each Offence." Two years later the colony's slave code was tightened once more. "No Negro or Indian slaves, above the number of four," were permitted to "assemble or meet together . . . at any . . . time . . . [or] place . . . within the liberties of the city," and the carrying of "guns, swords, clubs, staves or any kind of weapons whatever" was criminalized "under the penalty of being whipped at the publique whipping-post, ten lashes, unless the master or owner of such slave will pay 6s[hillings] to excuse the same."[12]

On March 2, 1685, Cuffee, an enslaved man likely to have been of Gold Coast origin, was executed for arson. The death penalty not being considered sufficient deterrent, Cuffee's putrefying body was later disinterred and hung in chains for all his peers to see.[13] It is perhaps not too far-fetched to speculate that such a practice may have stemmed from an understanding of the Akan belief system concerning the afterlife. The natives of West Africa's Gold Coast, along with those of various polities stretching into the forested interior of modern-day Ghana, believed that after death their souls (*kra/kra*) would return to their homeland. This credence had managed to endure among those dislocated by the inhumanities of the transatlantic slave trade, albeit with one crucial caveat: those whose corpses had been mutilated after death would not be able to find their way back to Africa.[14] In light of such barbarities, it is perhaps easier to understand why this period also brought about a propensity among New York's Black residents for escape. On June 6, 1686, Jacques René de Brisay, the newly appointed governor of New France, wrote to Governor Thomas Dongan, Second Earl of Limerick, Andros's successor, informing him that two "Negro Slaves," who had run away from Schenectady and were presumed to be heading for Canada, had not been seen in that province up until that date. "I had them looked for everywhere," the Frenchman assured his Irish counterpart, "and should they turn up in the Colony . . . I will in good faith have them bound and manacled to be sent to you hoping that you will do likewise [in the event of persons enslaved by the French fleeing south]."[15]

Two years later, the Glorious Revolution swept across England. Following a half-hearted resistance, the country's final Catholic king, James II, was ousted by the Protestant Dutchman, William, and his English wife, Anne, ushering in a new era of Whig dominance and a constitutional monarchy whose authority was much curtailed by the adoption of the Bill of Rights. When the news reached the Americas, a series of revolts occurred which saw James II's largely Catholic officials overthrown by local Protestant "patriots." In Boston, the highly unpopular Edmund Andros, the former governor of New York who had since been made governor of the Dominion of New England, a union of the Mid-Atlantic and New England colonies which included New York although not Pennsylvania, was arrested by a "mob" of provincial militia and citizens; in Maryland Puritans led by John Coode revolted against the Catholic governor, Charles Calvert, Third Baron Baltimore; while in New York, a German-American merchant and militia captain by the name of Jacob Leisler seized control from Francis Nicholson, a captain in the British army whom Andros had installed as the colony's lieutenant governor. After Nicholson had sailed to England after surrendering the fort and the keys to its powder magazine to "prevent bloodshed and further mischiefe," Leisler set about consolidating his control. With considerable support from the Dutch and the city's working classes, Leisler governed New York for the next two years, a period which ushered in the beginnings of a deep-rooted political schism that would polarize the inhabitants of New York City for the better part of the next twenty-five years.[16]

In March 1691, following a series of frontier raids launched against the province by the French, who had declared war on England following James II's deposal, Colonel Henry Sloughter, William III's newly appointed governor of New York, finally arrived from England. Leisler was arrested and put on trial for treason and on May 16, 1691, he and his chief lieutenant and son-in-law, Jacob Milborne, were hanged, then cut down while still alive to have their bowels removed and burnt before them, before finally being decapitated and having their bodies "Cutt in[to] four parts . . . [to be] Deposed of as their Majties Shall Assigne." After a brief tenure, on July 23, 1691, Colonel Sloughter followed Leisler into the hereafter. His replacement, Benjamin Fletcher, was equally unsympathetic toward the pro-Leislerian rebels. The principals among them, wealthy merchants from Dutch families long-resident in New Amsterdam and New York, spent the next few years in the shadow of the scaffold. Prominent burghers such as the Beekmans, Braziers, and Gouverneurs were all forced to remain politically inactive at risk of forfeiting their lives. This subjugation of the old Dutch families and the simultaneous rise of a new breed of ambitious Englishmen, both older residents and a wave of newcomers, was neatly symbolized by the opening of New York City's first Anglican house of worship. Built with enslaved labor, Trinity Church was opened in 1698. The incumbent minister, William Vesey, a factious twenty-five-year-old native of Massachusetts and graduate of Harvard College and Oxford University, allied himself with the anti-Leislerians. One year later a new city hall was built in place of the old Stadt Huys erected in the Dock Street area in 1643. Inaugurated at the northeast corner of Wall and Nassau Streets within one block of Trinity Church, the Town Hall was another potent symbol of the political and cultural transformation of New York City.[17]

Meanwhile, the city's Black population continued to grow. As well as the occasional larger shipment arriving directly from West Africa or Madagascar, a slow yet steady trickle of slaves reached the colony from the British and Dutch possessions in the Caribbean. Crammed into the holds of small coasting vessels alongside kegs of sugar and bales of cotton, indigo, and tobacco—much of which was sold in New York for re-export to Europe—these slaves typically arrived in small groups of fewer than ten individuals. As seasoned Creoles they already spoke English, had developed resistance to American diseases, and were reckoned by some enslavers to be less prone to rebellion than their newly arrived African counterparts. As such they were quickly snapped up once put on sale. With the soil of their Caribbean home-land having lost its once fabled fertility following decades of sugar monoculture, the 1680s and 1690s also saw an influx of white Barba-dian immigrants into both New York and neighboring New Jersey. Some brought their slaves with them and set up as farmers in the hin-terland. Additionally, the period saw the arrival of hundreds of French Huguenot refugees. Forced to flee from France following Louis XIV's Revocation of the Edict of Nantes, which prohibited them from prac-ticing their Protestant faith, many established themselves in New York City. In the 1680s an unsavory alliance also blossomed between New York's Anglo-Dutch merchants and a number of pirates operating out of the Indian Ocean. Ignored by the London-based Royal African Company, which enjoyed a monopoly over the West African slave trade, New Yorkers found that government officials were willing to turn a blind eye to illegal slave imports if they originated from further afield. Loading up with food, rum, and gunpowder, the merchants sent ships to the Portuguese forts on the coast of Angola, or around the Cape of Good Hope and up the east coast of Africa, where they traded with such notorious characters as William Kidd for Malagasy slaves at the pirate enclave of Port Mary on the coast of Madagas-car.[18]

Back in New York, the slaves sold well, and the profits found their way into the hands of the city's highest officials. In 1689, one vessel captained by Edward Coats was gifted to Governor Fletcher following its return voyage. Fletcher sold the ship at auction for £800 and was given a further £1,800 for "exempting" Coats from prosecution.[19] Other prominent New Yorkers to profit from the trade were Caleb Heathcote, an English immigrant who would rapidly rise through the ranks to become mayor of New York in 1711, and Frederick Philipse, a member of Fletcher's council and the owner of Philipse Manor, a vast tract of farm land on the east bank of the Hudson River in modern-day Yonkers. On at least two separate occasions, in 1684 and 1698, Philipse colluded with Madagascar-based pirates to import several hundred slaves into New York City. "It is by negroes that I find my cheivest Proffitt," he candidly explained, adding "all other trade I only look upon as by the by." Besides selling the slaves, Philipse used at least forty to work his farmland on the Hudson.

The boom times were not to last, however. In 1697 the Treaty of Ryswick brought an end to King William's War, and the advent of peace with the French saw a reordering of colonial priorities. The East India Act of 1698, in combination with several key prosecutions in New York, brought the so-called Red Sea Trade to a halt before the turn of the eighteenth century. Foremost among the heads to roll was that of Fletcher himself, who was replaced as governor by Richard Coote, the Earl of Bellomont, and Captain Kidd, whose colorful career came to an end on May 23, 1701. Hanged at Executioners Dock in Wapping in London's East End following an extended imprisonment in both New York and London's Newgate, Kidd's body was gibbeted above the Thames at Tilbury Point for three years as a warning to others. As well as a crackdown on piracy and smuggling and the reinforcement of the Navigation Acts, Bellomont's tenure was notable for a reversal in local politics. An opponent of Fletcher's while he was in England, the earl found support in New York among the Leislerian faction. As a result, several were appointed to key positions in the city's councils and militia, and the bodies of Leisler and Milborne were exhumed from their graves near the gallows erected on an island in Collect Pond just to the north of the city limits and reburied in the grounds of the Dutch church.[20]

Meanwhile, New York's slave code continued to be tightened. In 1692, the Common Council decreed that "if any Negroe or other Slave be found playing or making any hooting or disorderly noise in the Street on the Lords day or be found in any publick houses he shall receive twenty lashes at the publick whipping post." A public whipper, appointed as a result, was to be paid "eighteen pence for every Slave so Whipt," while further restrictions were imposed upon slaves gathering at the houses of the "free negroes without the gates." Those found guilty of hosting such meetings were to be fined "Six Shillings halfe [of which was payable] to the use of the City [and] the other halfe to the Informer."[21] Such legislation was having a noticeable impact on the once flourishing free Black community north of the city's wooden palisade. At least twenty-four free adult Blacks had lived in the area in 1673, but by the turn of the eighteenth century only a handful were left. The rest had been forced to sell up and move to cheaper land in New Jersey, Long Island, and to the north along the Hudson River. Such relocations were encouraged by the authorities. The very existence of free Blacks in the city was an anathema to New York's legislators, who saw them as providing a beacon of hope and a reason for rebellion for the city's enslaved.[22] In 1702, under the mandate of an interim governor following Bellomont's death from gout in March 1701, yet more racist legislation was passed. It was made an offense, punishable by a hefty fine, to buy or sell anything to an enslaved person without the consent of his or her enslaver, an attempt to curtail a growing black market in stolen goods. Simultaneously, enslavers were awarded the right "to punish their slaves for their Crimes and Offences at discretion, not extending to Life or Member," while public gatherings of more than three enslaved were outlawed and made punishable by up to forty lashes. Any enslaved person found guilty of striking a free man or woman "professing Christianity" might be imprisoned for up to fourteen days and punished to any extent excepting death or permanent mutilation.[23]

The year 1702 saw the arrival of Bellomont's successor. Edward Hyde, or Viscount Cornbury as he was better known, reversed many of Bellomont's policies. A Tory where Bellomont was a Whig, Cornbury favored the anti-Leislerians. The New York City elections over the next eight years saw several Englishmen replace Dutchmen as mayor and aldermen of the various wards. Cornbury's arrival also coincided with the outbreak of the War of Spanish Succession, known in the American colonies as Queen Anne's War, and a series of epidemics which decimated New York's population. Hot on the heels of an outbreak of smallpox, in June 1702 yellow fever spread throughout the city. "At York they are visited with a moral distemper," announced one contemporary correspondent from Pennsylvania, "which sweeps off great numbers, tis such a visitation at that place, they say, [such as was] never knew before, carrying off eight, ten, or twelve . . . [every] day." Approximately 570 people, or 10 percent of the population, had died by the time winter brought a halt to the epidemic. While Cornbury and many others among the elite had escaped infection by fleeing to second homes in the countryside, the city's Black population, including the unseasoned new arrivals from Madagascar, proved particularly vulnerable. From an all-time high of 700 recorded in the census of 1698, the number of New York's Black inhabitants fell to 603 by 1703 despite continuing imports in the interim.[24]

War with the French saw a resurgence of privateering in New York City. Throughout the months of April and May 1703, 1704, and 1705 any resident strolling along the wharf side on the banks of the East River would have noted vessels such as the sloop *Dolphin*, the brigantine *Dragon*, and the galley *New York* watering and loading provisions, gunpowder, and round shot for such service. While the captains were often of English or Dutch descent, there were frequently a number of Black men among their crews. Judging by their names, some, such as Peter Sourinam and Jacob Swan, who sailed on privateers in 1704, were likely to have been among the city's last remaining freemen, the descendants of the "half free" of New Amsterdam. Others were escaped slaves. Keen to muster their complements in good time, privateer captains asked few questions about the backgrounds of potential recruits and were notorious for taking on runaways. Once fitted out, these ships sailed south to the warm waters of the Caribbean to prey on the richly laden Spanish merchantmen which plied the sea lanes hugging the coastlines of Cuba, Venezuela, and New Spain, before returning north to have their prizes and their cargoes condemned by New York's admiralty court. In 1704, the *Castel Del Rey*, a privateer of 18 guns commanded by the highly successful Dutch captain Adrian Claver, reaped a particularly rich harvest. While sailing along the coast of New Spain, Claver captured two Spanish ships, a settee and a sloop. Among the loot taken were 100 pipes of brandy from the Canary Islands, 30 pipes of palm wine, 900 jars of oil, 124 bales of dry goods and silks, and "30 Slaves Negroes and Indians &c."[25]

As noted above, Claver was not the first New York privateer to profit from the sale of human cargo, nor would he be the last, although such business was not without controversy. While the New York judges, accustomed to the racist code which governed slavery in England's American colonies, assumed that all dark-skinned passengers or crew captured were slaves due to their "swarthy" skin color, many among the so-called "Spanish Negroes" taken in this way protested that they were actually freemen under Spanish law and therefore the court was acting illegally in condemning them to a lifetime of slavery. The first record of such an occurrence in the English period dates to 1684, when Philip and Dego Dequae petitioned Governor Dongan for their freedom. Later, in 1700, the mayor, Isaac de Reimer, and several aldermen demanded that Governor Bellomont free an "Indian" woman, a native of Curaçao, captured under similar circumstances and sold into bondage. Among the thirty "slaves" taken by Captain Claver, at least three would use the courts of New York in an attempt to secure their freedom. Stephen Domingo, a resident of Cartagena on the Spanish Main who had been sold to a certain Mr. Perce following his capture on the high seas, petitioned the city's Common Council to aid him in his claim, while Jose and Juan, "Spanish Indians" of "swarthy" complexion, would take their case directly to the governor.[26]

Another consequence of the outbreak of war with the French in 1702 which had an impact upon New York's Black population was the increased opportunity for escape which the proximity of the enemy presented. This was evidenced by a piece of 1705 legislation issued by the city's legislative council. Entitled "An Act to prevent ye Running away of negro slaves," the bill alluded to "the fears and jealousies they have that several Negro Slaves belonging to the Inhabitants . . . have a desire to leave their respective Owners and go to the French at Canada." To prevent such an occurrence, the bill created a legal buffer zone between the two nations' colonies by prohibiting any Black slaves from "travelling Forty Miles above the City of Albany at or above a certain place called Sarachtoge." Any caught doing so were to face trial and execution. In the event of the latter, their enslavers would be compensated by the state to an amount decided upon by a committee appointed to assess their dead slave's worth. Although this act suggests that such "desertions" were relatively common, there is no record of any enslaved person actually being punished for absconding. The northern reaches of the colony of New York were sparsely populated, and the few settlements were mostly home to Mohawk and Mahigan Indians who were known for actively abetting runaways and even welcoming them into their communities. Furthermore, the wilds were vast and the lengthy frontier with New France was porous. Added to this was the fact that runaway slaves not only were economically valuable to the French but also could provide useful intelligence on conditions south of the border which might aid future French operations against the English.[27]

SUCH WAS THE SITUATION in New York City at the turn of the eighteenth century. The earlier Dutch system, which had offered enslaved persons some hope of manumission and access to various privileges, had been eroded by laws passed by a string of English governors and legislators. By 1700, the free Black community had been repeatedly targeted and its numbers much reduced, while the city's enslaved lived under a system which inflicted horrendous punishments for the most innocuous of crimes or infractions. Nevertheless, some hope remained. Black New Yorkers, enslaved and free alike, continued to express themselves culturally and socially, while a handful of moderately influential white residents had some sympathy for their plight. One in particular, a French Huguenot named Elias Neau, would offer the enslaved a spiritual escape from their physical bondage. Meanwhile, on the far side of the Atlantic, another figure was rising. The coronation of King Akwonno in the inland Akan forest polity of Akwamu was to have major implications over the next decade, not only for the inhabitants of the Gold Coast, but also for those of distant New York City.

CHAPTER 2

The Inexorable Rise
of Akwamu

The interior of the eastern Gold Coast
1677–1702

In the second half of 1702 King Akwonno succeeded to the stool of Akwamu, one of the largest and most powerful polities on the Gold Coast. Although there is no record of the coronation, it seems likely it took place at the capital of Nsaki, nestling amidst the foothills of the Akwapim Scarp, from where the coast was just visible thirty miles away "when it had rained and the air [was] . . . cleared of mist."[1] Akwonno was as fond of ceremony as he was of celebration. His coronation day would have been marked by both. We can imagine the broad, tree-lined streets of Nsaki filled with soldiers, officials, and slaves laden with tribute from the four corners of the Akwamu empire and the numerous client kingdoms beyond its borders. In the center of town, beneath the polity's banner—a black figure brandishing a sword upon a white background—was the king's palace, an impressive stone edifice, flanked by the houses of the leading families of Akwamu, the royal treasury, and shrines to the Akan deities, not least among whom was Tutu Abo, the god of war. Inside the palace, amidst a whirlwind of music, song, and dance, sat Akwonno surrounded by a heavily armed bodyguard. It seems likely that a number of European emissaries would also have been present along with a sea of courtiers, and the king's one hundred concubines, whose gold and coral jewelry would have glittered in the tropical light. Royal saber bearers stood by along with *Tie Tie*'s, or public criers. Dressed in black apeskin caps, they kept the flies off the king with swats made from rushes and the hairs from elephants' tails. A host of drummers played a frenzied beat. Horn players and trumpets added to the cacophony. Copious calabashes brimming with palm wine and bottles of American rum and French brandy lubricated the proceedings. Soon it was time for the main event—the enstooling ceremony. All eyes turned toward Akwonno as he was ritually lowered three times over the golden stool without touching it, thereby assuming the title of Akwamuhene.[2]

The polity which Akwonno thus inherited was the rising star of the Gold Coast. The new king's late father, Ansa Sasraku, had instigated the first great imperial adventure back in 1677. Triggered by a convoluted casus belli involving the unwanted circumcision of a young Akwamu prince, Sasraku had launched an attack against Accra, a major trading hub and the main city of the Gã, a people culturally and linguistically related to the Akan.[3] The king of Accra, Okia Koi, underestimated his Akwamu opponents—contemporaries dismissed them as "nothing but coarse peasants and foolish people"—but Ansa Sasraku's army proved formidable in the field.[4] Okia Koi's soldiers were defeated. Accra was burned to the ground and Okia Koi and his eldest son were beheaded, their skulls preserved as trophies of war. The king's younger son, Ofori, escaped, however, to the coastal town of Osu where he obtained the protection of the Danish trading company. The resulting Afro-European alliance was immediately put to the test. When Ansa Sasraku attacked Osu, the Danish guns of Fort Christiansborg forced the Akwamuhene to withdraw. Two years later disaster struck the Europeans. Led by a mutinous Greek-born merchant named Pieter Bolt, the garrison of Christiansborg rebelled. The Danish governor was "inhumanely murdered" and the fort was sold to the Portuguese, allowing Ansa Sasraku to renew his offensive against King Ofori, who was forced to flee once more.[5] Crossing the River Volta, Ofori took refuge in the town of Little Popo 100 miles to the east, while Osu, along with the nearby coastal settlements of Smaller Accra and Soco, where the Dutch and English maintained forts, were absorbed into the Akwamu empire.[6]

Possession of Accra brought the Akwamuhene immense wealth. The treasury swelled with rents paid by the English, Dutch, and Portuguese, taxes placed on agriculture, the manufacture of salt and the raising of livestock, and an ancient coastal trade which saw the locals exchange dried fish for gold from the polities of the interior. Money-lending was also lucrative—Akan merchants were often in need of credit. A final source of wealth was the Akwamuhene's direct involvement in the slave trade, a business which boomed each time his armies made war and enslaved their defeated opponents.[7] By the end of the eighteenth century "the King and his Nobles were so rich in gold and slaves" that the Dutch merchant Willem Bosman believed them wealthier "than all [the other kingdoms of the Gold Coast] taken together."[8] Immense riches brought immense power. Sasraku's composite army of peasant militia and professional slave warriors numbered over 10,000 men, and the mere threat of its use allowed him to expand his zone of influence.[9] Previous kings had deployed small, highly trained armies composed of professional soldiers equipped with bows and arrows, swords and spears, but the advent of European traders' sale of large numbers of muskets, a weapon which required relatively little expertise to be used effectively, enabled mass conscript armies to be raised rapidly when required then demobilized to bring in the harvest. Such *levées en masse*, long employed in Europe, were a recent development on the Gold Coast, and one not yet universally employed, thus affording the Akwamu a crucial advantage over neighboring polities, as Okia Koi had learned to his cost.[10]

The kingdom of Ladoku, to the east of Accra, was the next polity to fall under the Akwamuhene's sway. Initially, Ladoku's regent was allowed to retain a veneer of power as a client king. Soon, however, Sasraku "lord[ed] . . . it over [the people of Ladoku] so absolutely, that the[ir] slightest faults . . . [we]re often punished with death."[11] Meanwhile, on the western frontier, trouble was brewing. An alliance between Akim, Akwamu's long-standing rival, and the small polity of Agona was threatening to upset the balance of power. Ansa Sasruka attempted diplomacy, suggesting he and the queen of Agona unite their two kingdoms in marriage. Having hitherto preferred to share her bed with "a brisk jolly slave with whom she diverts herself" than share power with a husband, the queen was never likely to accept, something, one suspects, the Akwamuhene knew all along. Nevertheless, the queen's response was highly undiplomatic. She ordered Sasraku's envoys decapitated, and had their heads returned to her would-be suitor. Ansa Sasraku promptly invaded. The queen was captured, and, although she was allowed to keep her own head, her kingdom was forever demoted to the status of an Akwamu client state.[12]

The subjection of Agona was Ansa Sasraku's last act. Having been sick for some time, the king died in 1689, prompting a power struggle for succession. As a minor, Sasraku's eldest son, Addo, found himself obliged to share power with his father's principal general, a highly esteemed veteran by the name of Basua, a situation which continued until the latter's death in 1699 allowed Addo to assume full control. According to Bosman, the two men could not have been more different. While Basua was "a man of wicked, abject temper, and an inveterate enemy of the Europeans," Addo was "more intelligent and rational" and actively forged ties with the Dutch and English.[13] During this unlikely co-regency, the Akwamu finally got their revenge on the Danes. In 1683, taking advantage of a Portuguese withdrawal, the Danes had resumed control of Fort Christiansborg. Ever since, they and the Akwamu had endured each other's presence while accruing profit from mutually beneficial trade, not least of all in slaves. In 1693, however, all this changed. Learning that the Danes had come to place considerable confidence in an Akwamu trader by the name of Asameni, one of the co-regents of Akwamu, presumably the aging Basua, plotted to exploit this weakness. So it came to pass that in June that year, Asameni set up a deal to buy muskets from the Danish company. Allowed to enter the fort with eighty Akwamu "buyers," Asameni gave a signal, his men loaded the muskets with powder and shot they had concealed in their clothes, and opened fire. Although the governor escaped by leaping out of a window, the second-in-command and several others were killed. The Danes were only to regain control of the fort a year later after protracted and humiliating negotiations which saw them not only forego any pretensions toward compensation but also agree to compensate the Akwamu with fifty marks of gold.[14]

After Basua's death in 1699, Addo's first challenge as sole regent came from the west when an army from Akim, the polity which had

An Akan Warrior. The original caption, written in Danish in 1761, translates as follows: "Qvou, son of Eikoe, born in the town of Ursue, at Accra on the Guinea Coast. This illustrates the manner in which a prominent Negro is equipped when he goes into battle." (*Danish Royal Archives, Copenhagen*)

threatened Ansa Saskura in the 1680s, sacked three Akwamu border towns. Realizing that war with such a powerful enemy would result in mutual destruction, Addo paid off the aggressors. Next, he turned his attention toward the European residents of Accra, paying courtesy calls on the English and Dutch as well as his former co-regent's enemies, the Danish, before returning to the theme never far from his father's mind: imperial expansion. With the powerful polity of Akim blocking advances in the west, Addo launched an offensive eastward across the Volta River in February 1702. The campaign resulted not only in the demotion of Ladoku from client state to province, but also the incorporation into the empire of Little Popo, long a refuge for Akwamu's enemies. Not content with such successes, in May Addo pushed on toward Whydah, a major slave trading depot on the Slave Coast, which his forces entered without resistance. Due to further rumors of trouble in the west, the campaign was then brought to a premature halt. Nevertheless, it had been highly successful. Addo returned to the newly founded capital of Nsaki as the ruler of vast holdings. Stretching nearly two hundred and fifty miles from Agona to Whydah, his empire was the largest seen on the Gold Coast since before the first European arrival over two hundred years before. Addo was not to enjoy his new acquisitions for long. A mere matter of months after he returned home, he too succumbed to illness, paving the way for the succession of his younger brother Akwonno, with whom this chapter began.[15]

The new king's first act was to conclude a treaty with the Dutch, then the most influential European nation on the Gold Coast. Having entertained the Europeans' delegates at his capital with a mass execution of slaves on the occasion of the death of an Akwamu queen mother, Akwonno traveled to the Dutch fort of Crèvecoeur at Accra, where on April 3, 1703, he concluded the deal.[16] The terms were a great boon for the new king. In return for a promise to do all in his power to prevent the suspension of trade with the interior and forbidding his subjects from dealing with the interlopers on the coast, Akwonno received the promise of Dutch aid in any "just war" he might undertake. The Europeans were to send him 100 armed men, three thousand pounds of gunpowder and three hundred pounds of bullets on each occasion. The Dutch also acknowledged Akwonno's rule over Accra and agreed to continue paying the monthly rent for Crèvecoeur as well as an additional tax of an ounce of gold for every twenty ounces they traded at the fort.[17] It was a promising start for the new king who, as we have seen, had high standards to live up to. Although he would not begin campaigning for four years, Akwonno was not to disappoint. His twenty-three-year reign was to prove the most glorious in the entire history of the Akwamu empire. The wars of conquest he was to undertake would have profound consequences on the Gold Coast and the wider region of West Africa, ripples of which would pass across the Atlantic and be felt as far afield as New York.

CHAPTER 3

The Suffering of Elias Neau

FRANCE, NEW ENGLAND, AND NEW YORK

1662–1707

No man can serve two masters. —Matthew 6:24

ELIAS NEAU "had always from his tender infancy a great inclination to go to sea." Born in 1662 in Moise, Saintonge, on the French Atlantic coast, Neau "made his first trial as a cabin-boy" at the age of twelve and soon afterward became a "common sailor." At that time a wave of religious persecution was sweeping through France. Wishing to rid himself of his "heretic" Protestant subjects, Louis XIV ordered his dragoons to terrorize all those who refused to convert to Catholicism. Huguenot churches and schools were destroyed, communities were broken up, and 400,000 fled abroad. Neau was among the first to leave. He spent the next few years sailing between the Dutch and French islands of the Caribbean until the religious mania that had forced him to flee France spread to Louis XIV's possessions in the Americas. Obliged to uproot once more, Neau's next port of call was Boston, where he was naturalized in order to advance in his profession. Neau's denization papers were issued on his return to London on January 31, 1689, shortly after the outbreak of the Nine Years' War. Back in Boston soon afterward, Neau married a fellow Huguenot, Susanne Paré, with whom he would have three children. The early 1690s saw the family move to New York, where they joined the congregation of the Eglise Francoise. The following year Neau was offered his first command. Owned by the New York Huguenot Gabriel LeBoyteulx, *La Belle Marquise* was an 80-ton trading vessel bound for Jamaica.[1]

It was not a fortuitous beginning. As *La Belle Marquise* was passing Bermuda on September 8, 1692, it was captured by a French privateer. Neau was taken back to Europe and imprisoned in Saint Malo where his original nationality was discovered. With the offer of a new command under a French flag as an incentive, Neau's captors urged him to convert, but he remained true to his Protestant faith. "What is a man profited, if he shall gain the whole world, and lose his own soul?" as he later explained.[2] After four months' imprisonment, Neau was sentenced to spend the rest of his life as a galley slave. Chained together with 200 others, in May 1693 Neau was force-marched for thirty-seven days to Marseilles. There was little food and the prisoners suffered from dysentery. After arrival, Neau was assigned to the *Vieille Madame* and later to the *Guerriere*. Conditions on the galleys were appalling. Chained up with his fellow Huguenots, prisoners of war captured from the ships of the Ottoman Empire, and common criminals, Neau spent the next twelve months rowing patrols along the coastline of the Mediterranean under the lash and the relentless beating of the sun. Many galley slaves turned to self-mutilation or suicide, but Neau remained resolute. "The patience he shewed wonderfully edified all those that were witness of it," one account testified. "His pious and Christian discourses engaged the attention of the whole crew ... [and] the example he gave of an holy and religious life, attended with a sweetness which is the real character of Christianity, made him to be admired by the most wicked wretches."[3] The Catholic chaplain of the galley was less impressed, especially when Neau converted one of his fellow prisoners to Protestantism. "Looking upon him as a pestiferous and poisonous fellow," the chaplain had Neau transferred to solitary confinement in the prison at Marseilles.[4] It was May 1694, over two years since Neau's capture.[5]

Despite his continuing ordeal, Neau's faith remained unshakeable. Having irritated his jailers with his insistence on continuing to "sing the praises of God so often," in July 1696 he was transferred yet again, this time to the Chateau d'If, a fortress built upon a rocky island half a league from Marseilles later immortalized in Dumas' *Count of Monte Cristo*.[6] After fifty days' imprisonment in a tower from which he could "view the waves," Neau was thrown into a gloomy cellar for six months.[7] There he found solace in a copy of the English Bible, which he annotated with a pencil stub concealed from his guards, and in an intermittent correspondence he managed to maintain with a French Protestant pastor resident in Bergen-op-Zoom. Nevertheless, Neau "suffered . . . a great deal in this terrible dungeon."[8] The food was inadequate, and the damp settled on his lungs. The jailers, who previously had seemed to delight in Neau's sufferings, began to fear for his life and moved him to several different cells. One, which Neau described as a windowless hole, was occupied by a "babbling idiot" who died after a year.[9] Another, which he shared with three fellow Protestants, was a "ditch" filled with lice and vermin, lit only by a narrow shaft of light which shone through a crack in the door. Despite the constant "stench and nastiness," Neau slowly recovered and remained resolute in his religion.[10] "O Lord, how easy is thy yoke," he scribbled one day nine years into his confinement, "my heart bears it with abundance of pleasure. . . . My adorable Saviour promises a hundred fold to those who forsake all for the sake of his love. But I can say to his praise, that he has given me a great deal more, for he makes me prefer one moment of his presence to the longest life and the greatest tranquillity of this world without him. My prison is marvellously converted into a place of liberty."[11] Neau also learned to embrace the Anglican creed. "I . . . learned part of the Liturgy by heart in my dungeons," he later recalled, "and . . . have . . . both affection and esteem for the divine service as it is used in the Church of England."[12]

On July 3, 1698, Neau was released. His savior was William III's ambassador, Hans William Bentinck, better known as Lord Portland. Having been informed of Neau's plight by the pastor of Bergen-op-Zoom, Portland had written several letters to the French authorities asking for his release, and his efforts had finally been rewarded. Given just six weeks to leave France, Neau traveled north via Orange and Lyon to Geneva. Passing through Bern and into Holland, he was granted a gratuity of 300 florins by William Blathwayt, William III's secretary of war.[13] With the money Neau traveled to England, and a few months later embarked for New York to rejoin his wife and meet his single surviving child, Suzanne, who had been born since Neau had gone into captivity.[14]

Neau's experiences in prison made him see New York with fresh eyes. The city combined outrageous wealth with extraordinary squalor. Glittering carriages pulled by well-groomed teams of six carried prosperous merchants from their country estates to their counting houses in the city, while aging Africans abandoned by their masters were left to die alongside piles of refuse rotting in the gutter.[15] It was not so much the inequality that troubled Neau, however. What was worrying to a man of his faith was the fact that the majority of the city's Blacks were heretics and therefore barred from receiving God's grace. "On Sundays while we are at our devotions," he observed, "the streets are full of Negroes, who dance & divert themselves, for they are kept after the same manner as horses, to get from them all the work one can without any concern for their salvation."[16] In the eyes of their masters, the Africans were idolatrous and not worthy of religious instruction. The Akan, for example, commonly carried fetishes, small bundles of fur, hide, or hair, with stone or bone representations of the gods. Worn round the neck in pouches, they were treated with great reverence, thus convincing their owners' masters that these tokens were representations of the devil.[17] To make matters worse, many West Africans were polygamists, while the Creole slaves, despite the years they had spent in Christian communities, were often barred from learning about religion by masters who feared educating and therefore elevating those they exploited so cynically.[18] To rectify this problem would be a major feat, but it was one that Neau felt he was ready for. The scramble for earthly wealth was no longer enough for the devout Frenchman. A more significant test was required to give spiritual meaning to his life—the conversion of the city's enslaved was just the challenge.

Such issues had proved controversial long before Neau's second coming to New York. In 1584, Richard Hakluyt, a pioneering exponent of English colonialism, had written *A Discourse Concerning Western Planting*, in which he stated that Christians had a moral obligation to bring heathen souls into the light. While many were to agree with Hakluyt's premise in theory, the reality in the New World was more complex. If the "negroes" were baptized, could they continue to be enslaved? As stated in Leviticus 25:38, 45–46, were not all Christians free by divine right? Such arguments had brought about the beginning of the end of slavery and the rise of serfdom in medieval Europe and they continued to carry weight when the issue resurfaced in the early modern period. While the authorities generally sided with Hakluyt's premise, the majority of colonial slave owners resisted any effort to proselytize their "property" and, by doing so, bring their status into philosophical doubt. Many owners of enslaved people pointed to a biblical "justification." The postdiluvian migrations of the tribes of Noah's sons Shem, Ham, and Japheth had resulted in their attaining differing levels of civilization (or so they claimed). While those descended from Japheth founded a society based on the rule of law and the governance of political institutions, the dark-skinned sons of Ham, who bore the curse of Noah, remained "savages," an inferior category of humanity. The "fact" that they continued to dwell in spiritual darkness justified white Christians enslaving them and divesting them of their lands.[19]

Both sides of the argument gained currency in colonial New York. Dominie Jonas Michaelius, the first cleric employed by New Amsterdam's Dutch Reformed Church, showed little interest in the conversion of enslaved Africans, whom he regarded as "lazy, useless thieving trash."[20] Several of his successors were more open-minded. In 1638 a Collegiate School was established in New Amsterdam to train both whites and Blacks in Christian principles, and the following year Barent Jan Pieters became the first Black child to be baptized in the colony. In the next six years fifty-six more Blacks were baptized and fourteen marriages involving Africans took place in the Dutch Reformed Church. By 1655, however, a change in attitude can be discerned: only one Black person was baptized in the last nine years of Dutch rule. This change was a result of the fear of slave owners that their chattels would equate religion with freedom and demand their emancipation.[21] A similar reluctance persisted under British dominion. By 1686 only six Africans were members of the Dutch Reformed Church, and the following year Governor Dongan complained that, contrary to his own instructions, white New Yorkers made no effort to proselytize their slaves.[22] Indeed, some even threatened slaves who insisted on their right to religious enlightenment with transportation to one of the British plantation colonies. As this was a fate which many held to be worse than death, it proved a valuable deterrent.[23]

As the end of the century approached, the prospect of Blacks being accepted into the church deteriorated further. In 1697, the warders of Trinity Church ordered that "no Negroes be buried within the bounds & limits of the church yard."[24] The few Blacks admitted to Anglican services were obliged to occupy places so distant from the pulpit that they were often unable to follow the service, and in 1699 "a Bill for facilitating the conversion of Indians and Negroes" was rejected by the city's assembly, "they having a notion that the Negroes being converted . . . would emancipate them," as Governor Dongan observed.[25] Soon after, the issue came to the attention of the heads of the Anglican Church. In 1700 Henry Compton, the bishop of London, dispatched the Reverend Thomas Bray to investigate the state of religion in the American colonies. His report was damning. There was "little spiritual vitality" and the church was "in a poor organizational condition." As a result, the Society for the Propagation of the Gospel in Foreign Parts was established by the Royal Charter of William III. Better known by its initials, the SPG had two guiding principles: to bring Christian ministry to British subjects overseas; and to cause the evangelization of the non-Christian races. George Keith and Patrick Gordon, the first SPG missionaries to take up residence in North America, concentrated their efforts on converting the white colonists, many of whom were dissenters from the Anglican faith. Others focused on the conversion of the Indigenous inhabitants. Initially, neither had significant success, while the ever-growing African presence in the colonies was largely ignored.[26]

On July 10, 1703, Elias Neau decided to rectify the matter. "There are here," he wrote to the secretary of the SPG, "a great number of slaves which we call Negroes of both sexes & of all ages, who are without God . . . and of whom there is no manner of Care taken." He continued, "'Tis worthy of the Charity of the Glorious Body of the Society to Endeavour to find out some methods for their instruction."[27] The SPG's initial reply was far from encouraging. Having focused their efforts on the colony's Indians and dissenters, they insisted that they had no one else to send. Undaunted, in 1704 Neau converted to the Anglican Church. "I have done it," he later explained, "through a principle of Conscience, because I find more comfort in celebrating the mysteries in yor Ch[urch] and in Praying."[28] As an Anglican, Neau also had access to official backing for his previous proposal, and on August 2, 1704, he was recommended as "a Man of Piety, of sober Deportment, and serious Life" and therefore suitable as a missionary by William Vesey, the rector of Trinity Church. As a result, New York governor Lord Cornbury, one of Vesey's principal supporters, granted Neau a license to work with "children Indians, Negroes, and other persons" and awarded him a salary of £50 per year. Although the appointment would not be officially recognized by the SPG until 1705, Neau got to work "with great Diligence" and without delay.[29]

At first, Neau was obliged to go to the enslaved workers' own quarters to fulfill his remit. "From House to House," as the summer of 1704 turned to autumn, he trudged the city's cobbled streets in his attempt to win converts to the Anglican faith.[30] As it brought Neau face to face with the squalor of slavery, the method reinforced his dedication. Touring the city's "Garrets, Cellars and other nauseous places," he preached on "the principal stories of the Holy Scriptures" and read excerpts from his ever-present prayer book. "God grant them Grace to make good use thereof," Neau prayed.[31] In time his perseverance paid off. On September 15, 1704, Neau was delighted to inform the secretary of the SPG that at least a dozen enslaved persons were regularly attending his classes. "There are 3 at Mr Mayor's house, 2 at the Sheriffs, 2 at Alderman Smiths, [and] one at the collectors, besides some other[s]," he wrote in reference to slaves belonging to Mayor William Peartree, William "Tangier" Smith, and Augustus Grassett, a fellow Huguenot and the collector of the city's weigh house.[32] Neau's talent for his new role soon became evident. The secretary of the SPG observed that his adherents were "seriously persuaded that he seeks their eternal happiness by such constancy and unweariedness in his labors," while his "humility," his "sober and religious deportment," and his "bright example" aided him in his quest. The "seriousness and severity of his life," the latter imposed by his former countrymen, also worked in Neau's favor.[33] Having been a prisoner of conscience and a galley slave, Neau could empathize with the plight of his students. Many of them came to respect the Frenchman both for his commitment and for the suffering he had endured.

Nevertheless, the problems Neau encountered were legion. As well as fearing that their moral justification for enslaving their heathen chattels would be stripped from them should their slaves convert, the owners were concerned that Neau's intention to teach their slaves to read would lead them to question their station in life. The more ignorant an enslaved person was, the easier he or she was to exploit. The more educated that person became, the more likely that he or she would rebel. Another issue that Neau encountered was restricted access to his students.[34] As the secretary of the SPG observed: "a little Time in the Dusk of the Evening, after hard Labour all Day, was the whole time allowed for them for Learning." Rather than listen to Neau preach, many of his would-be converts used these precious moments for "Relaxation" or "to visit their wives and Children"—often resident out of the city or on the far side of town. Even those who did show interest in Neau's lessons "were so fatigued that their Attention could not be great. They were dull and sleepy, and remembered they must rise early the next Day, to their Labour."[35] Communication also proved a stumbling block. While many Creole slaves spoke "English, French & Dutch very well," the majority of the recently arrived Africans did not.[36] A final impediment was the fact that for many Africans their native culture and religious beliefs remained strong, despite (or perhaps because of) their geographical detachment from their homelands. Polygamy and polytheism, anathema to Christianity, were common among the Ebo, Akan, Papa, Mandingos, Angolans, and Loangans who made up the majority of New York's enslaved people.[37]

Late in 1704 Neau was given permission to hold his classes on the ground floor of Trinity Church's unfinished steeple. "The Gentlemen [who enslaved Neau's students] have promised to send their negroes every Monday, Wednesday & Friday at 4 in the afternoon . . . because 'tis the time they have least for them to do," Neau informed the SPG. Furthermore, the Frenchman was "promis'd a great many more Catechumens this Winter, because they have not so much Business as in the summer."[38] Thus, as the temperature fell and the nights drew in, more and more of the city's enslaved people began to attend Neau's classes, so much so that the small room at Trinity was soon overcrowded, obliging Neau to move the class to his own residence. The room the Frenchman chose, "48 foot in length and 22 in breadth," was "up two flights of stairs" and had "benches for the . . . [students] to sit on."[39] Typically, Neau began classes with a prayer. All his students would kneel, and those able to do so would follow the Frenchman in his recitation. Next came a discussion of the scriptures, often focusing on the Gospel of Saint John to emphasize the sufferings of Jesus, something which Neau felt the enslaved could relate to.[40] Afterward Neau administered catechisms individually or two or three at a time, depending on the numbers attending. "He took great Pains in reading to them," one observer later noted, "in making short Collections out of Books on the Catechism, and in making an Abstract of the Historical Part of the Scriptures; so that many, who could not read, could yet by Memory repeat the History of the Creation of the World, the Flood, the giving of the Law, the Birth, Miracles, and Crucifixion of our Lord, and the chief Articles and Doctrines of Christianity."[41] In this way Neau played to his African students' strengths. Brought up with the oral tradition for prayer, ritual, and storytelling, they were familiar with a call-and-response method and took an active role.[42]

By October 1705, Neau's classes were being attended by as many as thirty students. Sunday mornings, when their masters were at divine service, proved the most popular time, while on "Wednesdays & Fridays there come but Eight or Ten sometimes more sometimes less." As numbers grew, Neau began lending out catechisms and prayer books so his students could continue their studies at home. A number of peripatetic Black sailors attended irregularly. Others appeared on only a single occasion, but there were also forty-eight regular attendees. Among them was a "Mulatress" belonging to Governor Cornbury, two "Negresses" owned by Reverend Vesey, and a "Negro," property of Mr. Wilson, the city Sheriff. Four others were identified as "Indians." Eighteen were male and thirty were female. All were enslaved, and many belonged to New York's elite merchant class. The city's Anglicans were well-represented among the owners, and a number of Neau's pupils belonged to his fellow Huguenot refugees, including the merchants Peter Fauconnier and Peter Morin. Dutch owners were conspicuous by their absence. Indeed, the only prominent Dutchman on the entire list which Neau sent to the SPG in October 1705 was Rip Van Dam. A merchant by trade, Van Dam dealt in European wine and brandy, furs, and flour from the hinterlands of New York, Caribbean sugar, and African slaves.[43]

In 1706 Neau continued to make progress. Every time he held one of his candlelit classes, the Frenchmen noticed "new Faces" among his students. "That makes me believe they tell one another that we intend to instruct them," he informed the SPG.[44] The Frenchman also introduced the singing of Psalms. "[This] encourages both them and me," he wrote, "for I represent to them that God plac'd them in the World only for his Glory; and that in praying and singing those divine praises one Doth in part obey his commands." The slaves took to the addition with pleasure. "They strive who shall sing best."[45] In the first five months of 1706 several of Neau's most promising students were baptized by Reverend Vesey "against the Will and without the knowledge of their masters."[46] In response to the slave owners' continuing concerns, Neau also began lobbying Governor Cornbury to propose an act before the city's legislative council clarifying the fact that baptism did not equate to emancipation. Cornbury, who had backed Neau's mission from the start, obliged, and on October 21, 1706, "An Act to Encourage the Baptizing of Negro, Indian and Mulatto Slaves" was passed at Fort Anne.[47] Neau also persuaded the Reverend Vesey to promote his catechism classes before the congregation of Trinity Church. John Sharpe, the resident chaplain at Fort Anne, spoke in favor of Neau, and even Gaulterus Du Bois, the minister of the Dutch Reformed Church, urged his congregation to send their slaves to the Frenchman's classes. With such support, attendance increased in 1707 and by the middle of the year, Neau's Sunday sessions were drawing as many as seventy-five adherents, "8 or 9" of whom had been baptized. An "abundance of [white] people" also began to make their way to Neau's third-floor meeting room to "see and hear [the enslaved workers]" sing. Several free Blacks also attended.[48] A list compiled in 1714 included "a Free Negro woman [named] Margaret"; Ianston, "a free Indian woman"; and "Peter the Porter," a "freeman" who owned a small plot of land in the Bowery.[49]

Meanwhile, the legal status of New York's enslaved people deteriorated. Indeed, the very act that Neau himself had celebrated contained clauses that further curtailed their rights. Enslaved people were prohibited from being "admitted as a Witness for, or against, any Freeman, in any Case matter or Cause, Civill or Criminal." Even more damning, slavery, as defined by racial characteristics, was officially made an inheritable condition to be passed on matrilineally. "All and every Negro, Indian Mulatto and Mestee Bastard Child & Children who is, are, and shalbe born of any Negro, Indian, Mulatto or Mestee, shall follow ye State and Condition of the Mother & to be esteemed reputed taken & adjudged a Slave & Slaves to all intents & purposes whatsoever." Although the automatic enslavement of any offspring of an enslaved woman had long been de facto practice, its being written into law was symptomatic of the ever-worsening legal conditions.[50] Unsurprisingly, in the same period Black resistance escalated. The year 1707 would see a high-profile case of defiance brutally punished, while in 1708 the gruesome murder of an entire white household by their Black and Indian slaves would see many New Yorkers' worst fears horrifically realized.

CHAPTER 4

Akwonno's First Campaign

The Gold Coast

February 1707 to February 1708

FOUR YEARS INTO HIS REIGN King Akwonno was ready to emulate his forefathers. Having made treaties with the Europeans and grown rich through trade and usury, he would take his armies on campaign and expand the Akwamu empire. With the route to the west blocked by the powerful Kingdom of Akim, and the eastern reaches already stretched to the distant slave trading entrepot of Ouidah, Akwonno would focus on the north and northeast. His first target was the land of Krepi, a huge swathe of territory beyond the River Volta inhabited by semi-autonomous *dukou*, or small states, united by the Ewe language and cultural traits.[1] Before marching from Nsaki, Akwonno would have asked for the guidance of Tutu Abo, the Akwamu god of war; *ɔkɔmfoɔ* (okomfo)—Akan Obeah priests—were consulted to ensure the omens were auspicious. Sacrifices and divination ensued.[2] Once these ceremonies had been concluded, Akwonno made the call to arms by firing a cannon from the capital, a ritual which dated back to a time when the territory of Akwamu was so small that the sound from a single shot could be heard across the entire kingdom.[3] By 1707, however, a system of "speaking drums" was also used. By beating out a particular rhythm, one drummer passed the message of mobilization to his peers in the next town, who forwarded it to the settlement beyond, and so on until the call to arms had traveled across the entire land.[4] In each town or village, units ranging from between two hundred to four hundred militia were mustered. Bearing their own weapons and rations of dried fish, millet, yams, and rice, these detachments headed to regional hubs where they were combined into larger units, each numbering over a thousand men and commanded by a senior subordinate of the king, known as a *brafo* or *caboceer*, until the whole army, which contemporaries estimated at over twenty-five thousand strong, had mustered.[5]

Akwonno's army would have made quite a spectacle. Willem Bosman related that the "inland negroes" of the Gold Coast dressed themselves "in the richest manner possible on these occasions." Bedecked in "Ornaments of Gold, and *Conte de Terra*," a much-prized coral, they "are frequently so loaded . . . that they can scarce march."[6] Adding to the soldiers' outlandish appearance was their practice of ritual scarification. "They had on each side of their heads three incisions, one beneath the other, from the ear to the eye," explained Christian Oldendorp, a Moravian missionary who attempted to convert Akan slaves on the Danish Caribbean islands of Saint Croix and Saint John. "Their mothers made these when they were children," he explained. "The skin is cut with a knife and palm oil mixed with coal [known as *mɔtɔ*] is rubbed into it so it cannot grow shut again."[7] Another practice which marked the soldiers' appearance was the Akan habit of shaving elaborate patterns into their hair, as well as filing their teeth to points, a practice shared among many West African peoples.[8] "Thus appointed," Bosman related, "with their Bodies coloured white," their teeth filed, their faces scared, and bristling with weapons, Akan soldiers "look liker Devils than Men."[9]

Although the majority of Akwonno's army would have been equipped with muzzle-loading flintlock muskets, bows and iron-tipped arrows were also used.[10] The Akan soldiers were "so nicely dexterous" with these weapons, according to Bosman, "that in Hare-hunting they will lodge their small fine Arrows in what part of the Hare's body is desired."[11] Swords and shields were also carried. The latter were "about four or five feet long and three broad" and "made of Ossiers," as Bosman informs us. "Some . . . are covered with Gold Leather, [or] Tyger's Skins." Others, reinforced with copper plates, provided sufficient protection "to ward off . . . Arrows . . . as well as the blow of the Sabre . . . tho' not proof against a Musquet Ball." Akan swords were "shaped like a sort of chopping Knives," were "about two or three Hands broad at the extremity, and about one at the handle, and about three or four Spans long at the most, and a little crooked at the top." Bosman related, "These Sabres are very strong, but commonly so blunt that several strokes are necessary to cut off a Head." Scabbards were highly decorative. Hanging off the left side of the *paan*, a long strip of cloth which wound around the body and between the legs and was fastened with a narrow white leather belt, they were often topped by a desiccated "Tygers Head, or a large red Shell." On their heads the soldiers wore caps of woven grass or "Crocodile's skin, adorned on each side with a red Shell, and behind with a bunch of Horse Hair." They also carried "Assagayes," or throwing spears, a cartridge box, containing eighteen or twenty charges, and a pouch holding ammunition.[12] Johannes Rask, a Danish merchant resident in Fort Christiansborg in the early eighteenth century, noted that the Akwamu soldiers' bullets were made from iron bars which "they hammer out" and cut into oblong shapes "as thick as a curtain rod, or as the outermost joint of their little finger." Rask observed, "When they hit something with such a bullet, it tears a large piece of flesh, making a dangerous wound."[13]

Once all Akwonno's troops had gathered, further ceremonies ensued. Oaths of loyalty were common among the Akan. "They . . . cut themselves with a knife and drink one another's blood," Rask related.[14] Such oaths were significant. It was commonly believed that any who broke their promise would be "swelled by that Liquor till he bursts"; Bosman noted, "or if that doth not happen, that he shall shortly dye of Languishing Sickness."[15] Human and animal sacrifices were also conducted as a prelude to setting out on campaign. As previously related, Akwonno had ordered the ritual execution of several enslaved persons on the occasion of the death of one of the queen mothers in 1703, while his father, Ansa Sasraku, had a number of boys taken from various client states sacrificed to encourage the intercession of the war gods prior to the attack on Agona in the 1680s.[16] The *okomfo* would also have blessed the troops and used magic to afford them protection in battle. White clay was smeared on the warriors' skin and a brew of alcohol, grave dirt, and blood was passed round in the belief that those who drank it would be impervious to their enemies' weapons. Bullets would bounce off the warriors' skin and blades raised against them would shatter.[17]

In March 1707, after the passing of the *haramattan*, the desiccating northeast trade wind which blew in off the Sahara, Akwonno's army marched east into the territory of the client kingdom of Ladoku.[18] Although part of the empire since 1680, its rulers needed to be reminded who was in charge. By April, as black clouds darkened the horizon and electrical storms or *travados* whipped across the land, the army was ready to attack.[19] Falling upon a town near the Volta River, they destroyed it utterly, then led the inhabitants in chains westward from the smoking ruins for sale at Accra. With plantains, bananas, limes, plums, pineapples, oranges, kola nuts, and other wild foods providing a natural surplus, the army continued eastward.[20] Preceded by a host of *twafo*, or cutters, who cleared a passage through the thick bush, in July they reached the Volta. The army swept across in thousands of dugout canoes. Storks exploded into flight. Crocodiles took the unwary.[21] Akwonno then turned north, heading inland to the home of the Krepi. The inhabitants offered little resistance and their lands were incorporated into the empire as the Akwamu troops passed through. In September the *Asusuo*, or wet season, brought the campaign to a halt. Akwonno's army made camp until the rains passed in November, then advanced westward into Kwahu, recrossing the Volta somewhere north of the gorge. As renowned for their skill at elephant hunting as their prowess in mining gold, the Kwahu proved far tougher opponents than the Krepi. A series of battles ensued.[22]

When two Akan armies met in the field, lengthy preliminaries preceded the fighting. "This is chiefly owing to their Priests," Bosman recorded, "without whose Suffrage they are not easily induced to attempt a Battle; they advise them against it, under pretence that their Gods have not yet declared in favour of them; and if they will attempt it notwithstanding, they threaten an ill Issue." Once the omens proved favorable, battle commenced with opposing groups of skirmishers advancing against each other, "stooping and listening that the Bullets may fly over their Heads," Bosman observed. "Others creep towards the Enemy, and being come close, let fly at them; after which they run away as fast as they can, and as if the Devil were sure of the hindmost, get to their own Army as soon as possible, in order to load their Arms and fall on again."[23] Rask broadly agreed. "They crawl through grass and undergrowth at a remarkable speed, until they see they can successfully take a life," he noted.[24] As the battle became general, "each Commander hath his Men close together in a sort of Crowd," Bosman explained, "so that they attack the Enemy . . . one heap of Men against another." The fighting then intensified until the ranks of one side or the other had thinned to a breaking point, whereupon the losers promptly fled. "With horrible screams," the victors pursued them from the field, picking off stragglers, looting the dead, and gathering prisoners. The wounded were decapitated. The rest were enslaved, bound into coffles, and marched off for sale.[25] In the aftermath of the battle, plaudits were handed out to those who had killed most of the enemy. "[They are] called *Abringpung*," Rask related, "or *Aurangfrang*, that is, one who is accomplished in using a gun. But the one who has lost is called *Obia*, that is, a woman."[26]

As the Akwamu campaign continued, with victory following victory, the disunity of the Kwahu became increasingly apparent. According to Rask, the king's harsh treatment of his subjects and leading *caboseers* ensured that he was "helpless and hated."[27] Many were willing to help the Akwamu. Some even deserted to Akwonno's banners. Nevertheless, as 1708 dawned, the Akwamu troops grew battle weary and their supply lines were stretched perilously thin. This was the moment the king of the Kwahu had been waiting for. With his back against his western border with the Ashanti and facing imminent destruction, he rallied the troops who remained loyal and routed Akwonno's army in February 1708 in what proved to be the final battle of the campaign. Rather than risk further reverses, Akwonno returned to Nsaki to regroup. The new Akwamuhene's first campaign had had mixed results. Though the Ladoku had been taught a valuable lesson, and the lands of the Krepi had been incorporated into the empire, the Kwahu were still at liberty. Even worse, the elephant hunters had inflicted a humiliating reverse. Nevertheless, Akwonno was determined to finish what he had started. The Akwamuhene would return.[28]

CHAPTER 5

Mars, Sam, Caesar, Robin, and Will

New York City
May 1707 to June 1710

The unhappy condition of the Negro leads him naturally to detest us. It is only force and violence that restrains him . . . and if he does not visit upon us all the hurt of which he is capable it is only because his readiness to do so is chained down by terror. . . . Remove this bit, and he will dare everything.
—Nicolas Lejeune, a French planter and slave owner of Santo Domingo (1788)

MAY 1, 1707, BEGAN LIKE any other Sunday in colonial New York City. As the sun rose over the East River, churchgoers divided along denominational lines. The Anglicans headed for Trinity Church to hear the Reverend William Vesey, a "good sufficient Protestant Minister";[1] two hundred or so others made their way to the Dutch Reformed Church on Garden Street;[2] while Reverend David Bonrepos of the New French Church welcomed a hundred-strong congregation, principally Huguenot refugees.[3] Elsewhere, a number of smaller religious circles met: Scottish Presbyterians, Lutherans, Episcopalians, and a small community of much-put-upon Catholics, supposedly afforded freedom of belief by New York's policy of religious toleration.[4] At the chapel in Fort Anne, the garrison gathered to listen to the Reverend John Sharpe; while a handful of Sephardic Jews met in a rented property on Beaver Street; and a few Friends exchanged greetings at their meeting house.[5] Not all those present at church in New York that

Sunday were of European extraction. Several Black slaves shuffled in carrying hot coals in lidded pans to keep their masters' and mistresses' feet warm in the deep-shadowed interiors.[6] Standing at the back or surreptitiously taking a seat in one of the cheaper pews, a handful even chose to remain once their work was done even though they may have been too far from the pulpit to hear the wisdom of Vesey and his peers.[7]

Outside, the streets were far from quiet. Released from their routine of back-breaking work and spirit-crushing subordination, the city's Black and indigenous Indian slaves reveled in the freedom afforded them on the Sabbath.[8] An echo of the more liberal Dutch period, such weekly gatherings caused the government considerable stress. According to the city's General Court of Assizes "many Greate Evills and Incoveniencys . . . [were] Occassioned Committed and Done by Negros [at] . . . their ffrequent meetings . . . in Greate numbers On the Lords Day." The slaves "Exercise[d] . . . Severall Rude and Unlawfull sports and Pasetimes to the Dishounour of God [and caused] Breach and Disturbance of the Peace and Quiett of his Majesties Subjects." Even more worryingly, some of the city's white residents were "Drawed aside and Mislead to be Spectators of such . . . Evill Practices and thereby Diverted from the[ir] more Suitable and Pious Duty." As well as dancing, singing, and playing games, the slaves drank "spirtuous liqours."[9] To counter such behavior, in 1702 New York City's General Court of Assizes had stipulated that "Negroes and Indian slaves" caught profaning the sabbath were to be punished with a "Sever[e] . . . whipp[ing]." The law also decreed that any "person Whatsoever [who was to] . . . P'sume to Entertaine . . . any Negro or Indian Slave or buy Sell or Trade with them for any Liqours . . . without the knowledge Lycence and Aprobation of their said Mastrs . . . shall Incurr the penalty and fforfeiture of five pounds for each Offence." Even though this was a considerable sum at a time when a common laborer earned six shillings per day, neither the fine nor the threat of the lash proved sufficient deterrent. Indeed, how to prevent the slaves gathering on Sundays remained a problem throughout the colonial period.[10]

On May 1, 1707, there was a particular excuse for the revelers to enjoy themselves. That morning, the Union with Scotland Act (passed the previous July) had come into effect. England and Scotland, previously separate states despite sharing a monarch, were "United into One Kingdom by the Name of Great Britain" and would henceforth share a single parliament. Whether or not the enslaved of New York would have deemed such an event worthy of celebration is not known, but what seems certain is that they were witnesses to the revelry it inspired. Among the enslaved out in the streets of New York City that particular Sunday was "a Negro man commonly called Mars."[11] Little is known of him aside from the identity of his owner: Jacob Regnier, a native of London, who had arrived in New York in 1702 and had established himself as one of the city's premier attorneys at law.[12] Mars was probably African born and a relatively recent arrival in the New World. As a string of seventeenth- and eighteenth-century Caribbean revolts bear witness, workers who challenged the established authority, as Mars was to do that May afternoon, had normally not been enslaved for long. After a year or so of growing accustomed to their new situation, many were reluctant to challenge the status quo. They learned to fear the system. Some even formed bonds with their owners, and many began to see benefits for those who played by the rules. Enslaved persons who had recently endured the hell of the Middle Passage had no such qualms.[13]

Also present in the city that Sunday was Ephraim Pierson. As constable of the city's West Ward, the twenty-year-old Long Islander and former privateer had sole responsibility for policing the activities of over seven hundred residents.[14] That Pierson's was a difficult job, especially on days like Sunday, May 1, 1707, is abundantly obvious. In the colonial period there were over two hundred assaults by citizens against the constabulary in New York. Armed only with a staff and with little hope of back-up, the constables ran a risk every time they attempted to enforce their authority, as Pierson was about to discover.[15]

It is not known precisely when or how Mars's and Pierson's paths crossed that Sunday. What we do know is that the meeting occurred in the West Ward while Pierson was "in the due execution of . . . [his] office."[16] A law of 1684 may provide some clues as to the particulars. As part of his duties on the Sabbath Pierson was required to "walk through the Seuerall Streets, And Lanes of this Citty, with his staffe And See that . . . Ordors . . . be Duely Observed And kept." He was also required "to Enter, into all Or Any Publique houses Tapphouses or Ordinaryes" to ensure that no alcohol was being sold. Perhaps it was for a breach of one or more of these laws that Pierson attempted to arrest Mars that Sunday. Or perhaps it was for any one of a myriad of other restrictions imposed on New York City's enslaved. Mars may have been out without a written permit, or perhaps he had failed to take a lantern with him after dark. He may have been driving a cart, or perhaps he had had the temerity to gather together with two or more other enslaved.[17] It also seems possible, given the numerous precedents for such behavior, that Mars was drunk. Maybe it was this that gave him the courage to "make an assault" on Pierson and "beat [and] wound" him "with clubs staves and other weapons." Perhaps Mars was already armed—another violation of the law—or perhaps he beat Pierson with his own staff. Regardless of how it was done, we learn that the attack was made with such "evil intent" that Pierson "did despair" of his life and "grievous damage" was caused. After being on the run for five days, Mars was arrested and brought before the Court of General Sessions on May 6, the final day of its Spring sitting. Indicted for assault, he was ordered "to stand committed to the Gaol . . . 'till he be delivered by due Course of Law." Built beneath the new Town Hall on Wall Street, New York City's jail was a squalid place. Inmates complained of the cold and damp and the brutal treatment they received at the hands of the sheriff. Mars was to remain incarcerated for three months before the Court of General Sessions reconvened.[18]

Mars's trial took place on August 5, 1707. Presiding were justices of the peace Colonel William Peartree, a Jamaican planter turned privateer who had become mayor of New York in 1703 and was also commander of the city militia;[19] Captain John Tudor, Peartree's subordinate in the militia and the Recorder of the City of New York;[20] and William Merritt, a mariner turned merchant who had served as mayor from 1695 to 1698.[21] Two of the three were slave owners. In the census of 1703 Peartree was listed as owning two "male Negroes" and two "females" as well as one girl and one boy; Tudor owned a single "female," most likely employed as a domestic in his East Ward residence. Surprisingly, given his wealth and status, William Merritt did not own any enslaved people in 1703.[22] This should not be taken to

View of New York City from Long Island, c. 1717, after William Burgis. The key at the upper right reads, A. The Fort, B. The Chappel, C. Secretary's Office, D. The Great Dock, E. Part of Nutten Island (center far left), F. Part of Long Island, G. Dutch Church, H. English Church, I. The City Hall, K. The Exchange, L. French Church, M. Ship Wharfes, N. The Ferry House (lower far right), O. Cattle Pen. (*New York Public Library*)

indicate that he in any way sympathized with the city's Blacks. Indeed, the one recorded incident that explicitly ties Merritt with a slave came in 1696 when a certain Prince had the audacity to slap the then mayor in the face as Merritt tried to split up a noisy gathering of Blacks in the street one August evening. Prince was whipped to within an inch of his life for his insubordination.[23] A similar fate awaited Mars.

The acting attorney general charged with prosecuting Mars's case was an even less sympathetic character. An Englishman resident in New York since 1702, May Bickley was "a busy, waspish" man. Better known for his "voluble tongue, than a penetrating head or much learning," he would gain notoriety for using his power over the city's courts to settle "party quarrels."[24] Even worse for Mars, Bickley had a particular dislike for the accused's owner, the aforementioned Jacob Regnier. Having arrived in New York together as part of the entourage of the then newly appointed governor Lord Cornbury, Regnier and Bickley had developed an intense rivalry over the years they had spent jousting in the city's courts.[25] In 1705 Regnier had opposed Bickley's appointment as attorney general, apparently on the grounds that the posting had had less to do with Bickley's suitability for the role than the fact that he was one of Cornbury's creatures. The following June they clashed again, this time over Cornbury's ill-advised attempt to use Bickley to prosecute a traveling Presbyterian minister, Francis Makemie, despite a law protecting religious freedom in the colony. The case ended with Regnier triumphant, Cornbury accused of tyranny, and Bickley seething. Subsequently, the two attorneys' rivalry had spread to the supposedly serene interior of Trinity Church. Bickley had been appointed vestryman in 1705, a position to which Regnier acceded the following year. A final bone of contention between the two attorneys appears to have been their attitudes toward the city's enslaved people.[26] While there is reason to believe that Regnier had at least a modicum of sympathy for their plight, Bickley seems to have been of the school which maintained that the enslaved workers were treated far too leniently and should be grateful to their enslavers for the opportunity to have left the barbarity of Africa for a fresh start in the civilized world. When he learned of Mars's assault on Pierson, Bickley was no doubt secretly overjoyed. The case would provide the perfect opportunity to exact revenge on his long-standing rival.

Perhaps on the advice of Regnier, who was no doubt aware that eight out of every ten slaves accused of violent crimes in the colony of New York were convicted, Mars chose to "confesse . . . and pray[ed] . . . the Mercy of the Court."[27] Little compassion was forthcoming. Mars was sentenced to a severe whipping to be carried out at various locations around the city. At 10 A.M. the next day the sentence was executed. Led blinking into the sunlight from the shadows of the common jail, Mars was stripped to the waist and tied to the tail of a cart.[28] Shaking out his reins, the driver headed west, pulling Mars along while the public whipper, paid a stipend of six shillings a day, followed behind. At the corner of Wall Street and Broadway, the first stage of Mars's punishment began. Known as "whipping round the city," Mars's sentence would see him receive ten lashes at every street corner that the cart passed as it toured the central streets. Depending on how sadistic the whipper was feeling, and perhaps on how much or how little he had been bribed, the first ten strokes, which were delivered just outside the doorway of Trinity Church, may not even have broken Mars's skin, but as the cart proceeded south on Broadway, his back was progressively torn to shreds. At each corner, the cartman reined in his horse and Mars received another ten lashes. After Wall Street came Church Street. Another ten were administered at the corner of Beaver Street, named after the animal whose fur was the original source of New York City's wealth. Then the cart moved into the South Ward. While the red-coated soldiers of the New York Independent Companies garrisoning Fort Anne looked down from the twenty-foot-high curtain walls, a further forty lashes tore gobbets of flesh from Mars's back at the corners of Marketfield, Stone, Bridge, and Dock Streets.[29]

By the time the cart turned east and passed the city's Custom House, Mars's sufferings would have attracted a considerable crowd. Aside from regular cock fights, the residents of New York had little to amuse themselves in the way of public spectacle. Whippings and executions always proved popular.[30] Among the spectators that day may well have been several people who would go on to play key roles in the revolt of 1712. Augustus Grasset, a French Huguenot and citizen of New York since at least 1692, could have chosen to momentarily leave his duties as collector of the city's weigh house to see what all the commotion was about.[31] Rip Van Dam, one of the city's leading merchants and slave traders, may have passed by in his carriage driven by his liveried household slaves.[32] Alongside Van Dam, perhaps, was his son-in-law and fellow merchant, Walter Thong, alderman for the South Ward in 1707.[33] Other residents who may have witnessed Mars's humiliation included Isaac Gouverneur, another merchant engaged in the West Indian trade, who lived with his widowed mother alongside several other long-established Dutch families on Stone Street.[34] Perhaps Gouverneur even had one or more of his slaves with him that morning. Kitto, a "mullatto," was to hang for his participation in the revolt of 1712, while Ambrose, one of a number of enslaved Native Americans in New York City, would be dismissed after his initial indictment.[35]

With the sun nearing its zenith, Mars's punishment ground on. He was given ten more lashes at the corner of Dock Street before the cart turned north on Broad Street, skirting the western edge of the city's Dock Ward.[36] Alive with bow-legged mariners, porters, smartly dressed merchants, and peddlers hawking candied fruit and New York's famed oysters, this was the heart of the city's commercial trade. Slaves staggered by with hogsheads filled with rum, and barrels of salt pork, cheese, and beef. Balancing the goods upon their heads in the West African manner, they unloaded a myriad of merchantmen which had reached New York from Europe, North America, the Caribbean, and Africa, while sailors looked for work or spent their hard-earned money on liquor or prostitutes in one of the ward's many taverns or "disorderly houses."[37] Mars, meanwhile, received thirty more lashes at the corners of Bridge, Stone, and Marketfield Streets as the cart trundled north, leaving a trail of blood behind in its wake. Next the procession entered the North Ward where the public whipper, now no doubt sweating from his endeavors in the late summer sun, delivered Mars's final twenty lashes at the corners of Church Street and Wall Street before the cart drew to a halt outside the Town Hall at midday. Mars was cut loose, and, having paid his court fees, was allowed to stagger back to Regnier's home.[38] Unfortunately for Mars, this would not be the last time he was to appear before the justices in a New York City court. Like Ambrose and Kitto, he was to face the wrath of his white masters yet again in April 1712.

IN JANUARY 1708, eight months after Mars's assault on Ephraim Pierson, another violent crime was committed by an enslaved person in the colony of New York. This time, however, the act was premeditated, and the white victims were murdered. Somewhat surprisingly, given the underlying tensions of the bipartite society that was colonial New York, such events were extraordinarily rare. Indeed, there had only been two incidences of enslaved people murdering whites in the colony's history prior to 1708. In 1676 two women had been killed in Esopus, Ulster County, by an enslaved Black man; and twenty years later James Boyce, a blockmaker resident in the Dock Ward, was murdered by an enslaved Black woman named Mary.[39] This third murder, however, was of a different magnitude: the body count was unprecedented; several of the victims were children; and the brutality with which it was committed was to prove deeply disturbing for the colony's governing classes. As such the murder was to have profound consequences. The already suffocating law code which governed the lives of New York's enslaved people, would be further tightened and a new clause added which was to have a significant impact on the events of April 1712.

WARM INSIDE HIS FARMHOUSE in Flushing, Long Island, as the snow blown in off the nearby East River piled up against his window panes, the thirty-seven-year-old William Hallett Jr. had plenty of time to reflect on the modest rise of his family since his grandfather had immigrated to the New World from Dorset, England, over sixty years before. Seeking religious freedom in which to practice his Baptist faith, William Hallett Sr. had departed a country already slipping inexorably toward civil war and by 1649 was living in Connecticut and married to Elizabeth Fones, a double divorcee of whom the local Puritans strongly disapproved. The couple had a son, who was also called William Hallett, but were forced to leave New England soon after. By 1652, the Halletts were residents of the western tip of Long Island. Then under the administration of New Amsterdam, the island attracted many English settlers seeking religious or personal freedom. "Our habitation is by the whirlpool which the Dutchmen call the

Hellgate," Elizabeth Hallett informed her cousin in January 1653. "We have purchased a very good farm . . . [and] we live very comfortably according to our rank. In the spring the Indians killed four Dutchmen near to our house which made us think to have removed . . . yet now the[y] are quiet." The tranquility proved short-lived. In the fall of 1655, members of the Canarsee tribe, a branch of the Lenape or Delaware, burned the Halletts' farmstead to the ground. The family were forced to relocate to the nearby hamlet of Flushing and in November 1656 Hallett Sr. found himself in trouble yet again. Peter Stuyvesant, governor of New Amsterdam, had learned that Hallett had permitted William Wickendam, a Quaker from Rhode Island, to perform communion on his property "in contemptuous disobedience of published . . . placats of the . . . Council of New Netherland." What particularly upset Stuyvesant was the fact that Hallett had recently been appointed *Schout*, or sheriff, of Flushing. Not only was Hallett allowing dissenters to practice their religion in his house without permission, but he was doing so while in the pay of the state. Hallett was fired, fined £50 in Flemish currency, and banned from New Amsterdam. In 1664, however, as a result of the English takeover, the Halletts returned to their land, and by 1670 William Hallett Sr. and his sons owned plots all across the northwestern extremes of Long Island. To cap their success, a third generation of American Halletts arrived with the birth of William Hallett III, and in the 1680s William Hallett Sr. was appointed town overseer and, later, commissioner of the town court. By the time he died at the age of ninety-four in 1706, William Hallett Sr. was one of the most prosperous and respected members of the entire community.[40]

By January 1708, then, William Hallett III was a wealthy and well-established farmer and landowner, proud to add the sobriquet "gentleman" to any legal documents he signed. On his "extensive farm" at Hellsgate, he had built a brick farmhouse and sunk a well. Hallett grazed two stallions, two mares, two colts, seven cows, and a herd of twenty-nine sheep on his pastures. As well as an "extensive" list of "farming products and utensils," he possessed a silver tankard worth £7, and seven silver spoons totaling £16, 6 shillings.[41] Hallett and his wife Ruth, by whom he had already had five children, was expecting a sixth. Typically for an early eighteenth-century landowner on Long

Island, Hallett also employed enslaved workers. In 1708 he had at least two living on his property: a Native American man named Sam, whom Hallett had enslaved for four years, and Sam's "negro" wife. Both lived in an outbuilding on the Hellsgate property. At some point in early January 1708, there was a falling out after Sam and his wife had been denied permission to "go abroad on the Sabbath." Sam's wife was incensed. Over time her bitterness festered, and she eventually persuaded her husband to kill their master and his family and blame the attack on robbers. Given the fact that Native Americans had destroyed Hallett's grandfather's house a little over fifty years before, the plan may not have been quite as foolhardy as it at first appears.[42]

Sam chose January 24, 1708, to commit the brutal deed. Earlier that day, Hallett and Ruth had gone to Justice Hattely's house to visit but had returned by dark and retired to their bedroom for the night before 7 P.M. Having waited until his enslaver and his family were sound asleep, Sam took up a hatchet and crept into the house. Approaching the sleeping form of Hallett, he struck him once with the blade, then reversed the weapon and dealt him a second and fatal blow with the back of the axe. Startled awake by the first strike, the heavily pregnant Ruth Hallett barely had time to cry "murder" before she was killed with an axe blow to the head. Sam then turned his attention to the children. Seeing one "of about 7 or 8 years of age" sleeping in a box by the bedside, he killed him with his hatchet, then dragged a smaller child out from under the body of Ruth Hallett and killed him with a blow to the head. The remaining three children were similarly dispatched. Having murdered the entire family "in a quarter of an hour," Sam and his wife then sat down to discuss their next move.[43]

Early the next morning, Sam's wife ran into town. "Hoping to screen [her husband and herself] . . . from suspicion" by being "the first to announce the tragedy," she entered the nearest house and exclaimed—"Oh dear! They have killed master and missus and the children with an axe, and only Sam and I have escaped." The townsfolk were unconvinced. Seizing Sam's wife, they forced a confession from her and sent word of the crime across the East River to Governor Cornbury, who issued a special warrant for the couple's trial. Sam and his wife were held in the jail in the nearby town of Jamaica, while a court was convened. The trial was a formality. Both suspects confessed their guilt, possibly under torture, and were sentenced to death. Two other negro slaves were also implicated and duly arrested and, on February 2, "in the presence of a large concourse of spectators," the executions took place. According to one contemporary New Yorker, Sam and his wife were "put to all the torment possible for a terror to others, of ever attempting the like wickedness." Sam's wife was burned at the stake, while her husband was hung in gibbets and placed astride "a sharp iron" which sliced into his flesh as his weight bore down. According to one witness, he "lived some time in a state of delirium" before he expired. He believed "himself to be on horseback" and on several occasions "urge[d] forward his supposed animal with the frightful impetuosity of a maniac, while the blood oozing from his lacerated flesh streamed from his feet to the ground."[44]

On February 10, eight days after Sam's execution, Governor Cornbury wrote to the Board of Trade in London informing them of the "most barbarous murder," and on October 30, a new law was passed by New York's Provincial Assembly entitled "An Act for preventing the Conspiracy of Slaves."[45] It stipulated that "all and every Negro Indian or other Slave . . . who . . . shall . . . Kill unless by Misadventure or in Execution of Justice or Conspire or attempt the Death of his [or] her . . . Master or Mistress or any other of her Majesties Leige People . . . shall Suffer the paines of Death in such manner and with such Circumstances as the aggrevation and Enormity of their Crime in the Judgement of the Justices . . . shall meritt." The ambiguity regarding the punishment was quite deliberate. It enabled the imposition of the cruelest and most barbaric methods. Only by keeping the enslaved in a permanent state of fear and by enacting public and ritual suffering on transgressors would the colony's enslaved people remain subjected to the will of their white masters. The act also included a subsidiary clause: "be it further Enacted . . . that the Owner or Owners of Such Negro or Indian Slave or Slaves . . . shall be [compensated] . . . Provided the Value of such Slaves shall not exceed the price of Twenty five Pounds Lawful money of this Colony." This ensured that enslavers would not have to suffer a conflict of interests should those they enslaved be indicted under the act. If the enslavers were to be compensated, then there would be nothing to prevent them backing the full terror of the law.[46]

Passing the slave code was one of Governor Cornbury's final acts. Having made a host of enemies during his six-year tenure, his improvidence and lack of propriety had attracted considerable criticism. As well as running up debts of over £8,000 to New York's shopkeepers and merchants, Cornbury's entire administration had acquired a reputation for corruption. The Makemie case which Mars's owner, Jacob Regnier, had successfully defeated, had been the last straw. As well as prompting local accusations of tyranny and opposition to religious freedom, it also led directly to Cornbury's recall by the home government in London.[47] Above all, however, it seems that it was the rumors about Cornbury's private life that proved most damaging. "He rarely fails of being drest in Womens Cloaths every day," gossiped New York landowner Lewis Morris, "and this not privately but in the face of Sun and in sight of the Town."[48] The catechist to the enslaved, Elias Neau, had also witnessed the governor's scandalous behavior. "My Lord Cornbury has and dos still . . . expos[e] . . . himself in that Garb upon the Ramparts [of Fort Anne] to the view of ye public," he informed the secretary of the SPG in February 1709, "[and] in that dress he draws a world of spectators about him . . . especially for exposing himself in such a manner all the great Holydays."[49] On learning of the decision to recall Cornbury, and the consequential termination of his diplomatic immunity, the governor's creditors had him seized for debt by the city's sheriff and put under house arrest.[50]

On December 18, 1708, Cornbury's successor, Lord Lovelace, arrived in New York in the middle of a howling blizzard with the East River "full of ice."[51] Having endured a horrendous nine-week passage from England, Lovelace's delicate constitution was already at its limits and the New York winter proved sufficient to finish him off. The governor died on May 6, 1709, once again leaving the colony of New York without a leader, a situation which the Whig government then in power in Britain remedied by appointing Robert Hunter.[52] A Scot who had risen to the rank of general in the British army and had seen service under Marlborough at the Battle of Blenheim in 1704, Hunter would prove a far superior appointment than either of his two predecessors. Intelligent, sympathetic, determined, politically astute, and culturally accomplished, Hunter would see New York's elite, who had been factionalized ever since Jacob Leisler's bloody demise in 1691,

Robert Hunter (1666–1734), governor of New York, 1710–1719, attributed to Godfrey Kneller, c. 1720. (*New-York Historical Society*)

finally reunited.[53] Due to unfinished business in London, however, the Scot would not arrive in New York until a full year after his appointment.[54]

Meanwhile, Elias Neau's mission to bring spiritual enlightenment to the enslaved of New York City was continuing to gain ground. "I must give you an accot. of the success of my vocation since my last letter," he informed the secretary of the SPG. "Mr Vesey baptized two [enslaved people this month, and] . . . several of them are [now] able to give an account of their faith. . . . There are some . . . that seem to be affected with the Christian Truths, especially when I talk to them of the Immortality and of the rewards & punishments of another life." Encouraged by his progress, Neau had the Lord's Prayer translated later that year. As well as "Indian," presumably a reference to Kanyen'kéha—the language spoken by the Mohawks, New York colony's dominant indigenous group—Neau chose Twi, the composite language of the Akan, or Coromantee, of the Gold Coast, and Mandinka, a language spoken by the people of the Casamance region of Senegal, the Gambia, and northern Guinea-Bissau. The decision paid dividends. Three more students were baptized on Christmas day 1709, and the following Easter Sunday, April 9, after passing an examination set by William Vesey, no fewer than six of Neau's students proceeded to Trinity Church, where several free Christian Blacks "and white psons" witnessed their baptism.[55] We learn that two of the six were "negroes," one was an "Indian," and three were "Negresses." It is also probable that one of the former was an enslaved man named Caesar. Enslaved by Cornelia Van Clyff Norwood, a member of one of New York's prominent Dutch families and the widow of Benjamin Norwood, a mariner resident in the East Ward in 1703, Caesar was certainly baptized by Neau at some stage before 1712 when he resurfaces in the historical record.[56] Another enslaved person who could well have been present, although not actually baptized, was Robin, the "chattel" of Adrian Hoghlandt, "an Eminent" merchant involved in the transatlantic trade who lived with his wife and five children and three other enslaved persons in the East Ward. Robin had been attending Neau's classes for some time before 1710 when he first "Solicited his master for leave to be baptized." Perhaps concerned by the theological quandary that had previously caused Neau problems, Hoghlandt refused. Robin was adamant, and over the next two years would repeatedly request his master's permission. Each time he was denied and his resentment toward Hoghlandt grew.[57]

AROUND THE SAME TIME as Elias Neau's Easter baptism service, Jacob Regnier, the barrister and enslaver of Mars, who was whipped in the opening pages of this chapter, took on his most controversial case to date. Regnier decided to represent a "mulatto" who had brought a case against a white man, an almost entirely unprecedented occurrence in the fifty-year annals of colonial New York. The man in question was Will, or William Archer, a thirty-two-year-old butcher who was fluent in both English and Dutch. Claiming to be a freeman, Will sued his former employer, Joris, or George, Elsworth, a butcher and a resident of the city's East Ward, for unpaid wages. Elsworth retorted that as Will was actually enslaved by him and valued at £150, he would certainly not be paying him anything and added that Will had in fact been enslaved for so long that he had previously been forced to work for four different masters. Elsworth also claimed that Will had "absented himself from [his] Service" and hinted that he had stolen a considerable sum of his money. Nevertheless, Regnier argued Will's case so persuasively that Elsworth began to fear that the "Court [was] against him" and warned that "if such dealings of Attorneys at Law with Slaves be not discouraged every master may Soon be put to hazard of being sued by his own slave pretending to be free." So convinced was Elsworth that he was on the verge of losing the case that he even considered conceding, although his fears ultimately proved ungrounded. Perhaps persuaded by Elsworth's warning, or influenced by Regnier's perennial enemy in law, the attorney general May Bickley, the jury found against Will, ordering that he should be prohibited from "pretending to be free," a decision which suggests that he was handed over to Elsworth's custody. Regnier was also chastised. Leaping on the opportunity to humiliate his rival, Bickley ordered the attorney to cease taking on such cases, which he warned could only serve "to encourage [slaves] ... rising and murdering their masters (of which we have lately most deplorable Examples)," a pointed reference to the unfortunate Halletts, then less than two years in their graves.[58]

CHAPTER 6

The Kwahu Strike Back

The Kwahu–Akwamu borderlands, Gold Coast

January to July 1710

THE ORIGINS OF THE KWAHU, the Akan people who successfully resisted the advance of King Akwonno in 1708, are shrouded in mystery.
Oral tradition speaks of a people indigenous to the highlands of the
Kwahu Ridge who mixed with waves of refugees swept into the area
by conflicts farther west throughout the fourteenth, fifteenth, and six-
teenth centuries. One of the earliest known kingdoms, which was
based around the present-day town of Bepong, was called Kwaafo. Its
people were known as formidable warriors who jealously guarded the
narrow mountain paths that provided the only means of accessing
their homeland. According to legend, this fearsome reputation led to
the name Kwaafo being corrupted into "Kowo," or "you go there to
die," a warning to outsiders not to venture into the kingdom. Another
oral tradition holds that the founders of the capital of Kwahu were a
pair of royal refugees, Osei Twum and his nephew Baadu, who fled
the cruelty of the rulers of Denkyira in the mid-seventeenth century.
In the course of their wanderings, they were said to have found a
stream with a rock shaped like a stone jar. Considering it a good omen,
Osei Twum and Baadu named the place Obo-kuruwa or Bukuruwa
(stone jar). After Osei Twum's death, Baadu succeeded to the royal
stool and formed an alliance with a tribe then inhabiting the region,

perhaps the same people whose reputation was said to have given rise to the name Kwahu in the first place.[1]

The first documentary evidence relating to the Kwahu dates to 1629, when a Dutch cartographer noted that the polity was notorious for its "Rascal People" and was "Rich in gold." Jean Barbot, a French Huguenot slave trader who worked on the Gold Coast in 1678 and 1682, wrote that "nothing [is known] of the inhabitants, but that they are reputed a treacherous false people," while Willem Bosman, a contemporary of Barbot's, related that the Kwahu homelands "abound[ed] with" gold and that the inhabitants mined the metal and brought it down to the coast through the lands of Akwamu to sell it to traders at Accra.[2] Johannes Rask, a Danish merchant who arrived on the Gold Coast in 1709, added "that among the Qvahus there are truly found so-called anthrophagi, or those who slaughter people as food. I write this as it was told to me, and for my part I dare not doubt the descriptions . . . but require no one to accept this."[3] And in the mid-eighteenth century Christian Oldendorp, the Moravian missionary who attempted to convert Akan slaves on the Danish sugar islands of Saint Croix and Saint John, wrote that the Kwahu had a reputation as skilled elephant hunters who bartered ivory to middlemen from the coastal polities who then sold it on to the Europeans.[4]

In 1710 the Kwahu were to add to their already fearsome reputation. Having repulsed the Akwamu in February 1708, they endured a series of raids launched by King Akwonno over the next two years. It seems likely that these were headed by *sikadings*, heavily armed professional soldiers who launched lightning attacks with the aim of gathering slaves.[5] No doubt aggravated by such behavior, in early January 1710 the Kwahu retaliated. After receiving the blessing of Buruku, the polity's patron deity, a column of soldiers descended from the Kwahu Ridge into the heat and humidity of the lowlands, winding their way along the narrow paths that cut through the forests to the Akwamu frontier town of Kwabeng.[6] Aside from the fact that the raid resulted in the destruction of the town, no other details are known. Perhaps the Kwahu used fire as a weapon, either as a means of destroying life and property or as a way of drawing enemy troops into an ambush. Such at least was an oft-used Akan tactic. Regardless, the results are beyond doubt: the inhabitants of Kwabeng not killed in the initial assault either escaped or were executed or enslaved, while the town itself was left a ruin. Akwonno was furious. The Kwahu had been a thorn in his side too long and had to be wiped from the map. One thousand pounds of gunpowder were purchased from the Danes at Christiansborg and the army was ordered to prepare for battle. Akwonno's revenge came swiftly. By February his soldiers had set out to the north and a series of defeats were inflicted on the Kwahu forces in rapid succession. Many of their remaining troops deserted in April and May, and by July Akwonno's victory was complete.[7] Kwahu was reduced to a state of vassalage; the people were enslaved. Soon the coffles were making their way down the Volta and through Naski on their way to the coast for sale. Awaiting them were numerous European clients eager to fill their ships with human cargo, among them a man who would go on to become New York City's most prolific slave trader: a French Huguenot and peripatetic resident of the Atlantic world named Alan Jarrett to whom our narrative shall return in Chapter 8. First, however, we must go back to New York where the colony's new governor was on the verge of completing his first year in office.[8]

CHAPTER 7

The Scottish Governor

NEW YORK CITY AND ENVIRONS

June 1710 to June 1711

ELEVEN MONTHS INTO HIS TENURE as the governor of New York and New Jersey, Robert Hunter's patience had been pushed to the limit. As well as being exasperated by the infighting which seemed to come so naturally to his colonial subjects, the Scot was preoccupied by the presence of the French uncomfortably close to New York's northern border, his transient and inscrutable Indian "allies," and the host of penniless Palatine refugees scratching a living halfway up the Hudson River. "I have such variety of matter to trouble your Lordships with ... that I am at a loss where to begin," he confessed to the Lords of Trade on the night of May 6, 1711, at the start of what would be a twelve-page letter. As the sun rose over the Brooklyn Heights the following morning, Hunter was still at his desk in Fort Anne.[1] After writing to the Lords of Trade, he had dashed off a missive to the London-based Commissioners of Customs concerning a dispute over the *Santo Cristo del Burgo*, a Portuguese vessel laden with 257 tons of cocoa which had been captured by two New York privateers over a year before, before composing a note to John Chamberlayne, secretary of the Society for the Propagation of the Gospel. "I am so puzzled with the perplexed affairs here," Hunter admitted, "and the packet just a going, so I have neither power nor time to write as I cou'd wish ... Pardon this Confusion & have a little patience till the next Packet goes, and I shall make amends."[2] Signing off, Hunter dispatched a runner to carry the letters across town and out onto the East River, where the *Bristol* packet awaited. Only then did the new governor have a moment to reflect on what had been a tumultuous year.[3]

ROBERT HUNTER'S governorship had started well enough. On June 14, 1710, when HMS *Lowestoffe* had dropped anchor in the roads in the East River after a two-month passage from London, the dignitaries of colonial New York had been waiting at the newly repaired wharf to greet him. Stepping ashore, the governor paraded down Dock Street and Marketfield flanked by two files of redcoated regulars from the New York Independent companies as well as a host of city militia, who rattled out a salute on their drums and held back the crowds as Hunter proceeded to his quarters in Fort Anne.[4] The next day the governor had his royal commission read aloud outside City Hall and "was Entertained by Coll [Gerardus] Beekman, president of ye Council, at Harris's," a tavern in the East Ward named after its proprietor, city alderman Richard Harris, which was also known as the King's Head.[5] Six and a half years previously Lord Cornbury's incumbency had been marked in the same tavern with tables groaning under the weight of "beef ... cabbage ... tripe ... cow-heel ... pork ... turnips ... [a] surloin of beef ... turkey and onions ... a leg of mutton and pickles ... a dish of chickens ... mince pyes ... fruit, cheese, [and] bread," all washed down with "beer and syder" and "31 bottles [of] wine."[6] The feast had been served by "2 negroes" hired especially for the occasion. On June 16, Hunter's welcome continued. Accompanied by his armed escort, who would be ever-present throughout his tenure, the governor took his carriage to City Hall where he was presented with the city seal "inclosed in A Gold Box" by the mayor Ebenezer Wilson. The following day the attorney general, May Bickley, delivered a welcoming address in the new governor's honor. "Wee do with all humble Gratitude Acknowledge ... her [Majesty's] Royall wisdom and Goodness in Appointing Your Excellency Capt General & Governour in Chief of this Province" Bickley began. "Under ...

[your] Courage and Conduct wee [hope we] may rest secure from our Enemies abroad and . . . [your] Justice & Prudence gives us the most lively hopes of healing all our jars & divisions at home." Bickley's words bore little relation to reality. Hunter's all-too-brief honeymoon period with the City of New York was about to come to an end.[7]

Ironically enough, the new governor's most pressing problem was one that he had brought with him from London. With the War of Spanish Succession entering its ninth year, French raids along the middle reaches of the Rhine, the harsh winter of 1707 to 1708, and the resultant hike in bread prices had led to an exodus of 15,000 German-speaking, mostly Protestant, refugees. Lured by rumors that Queen Anne intended to provide them with passage across the Atlantic and land in North America, the "Poor Palatines" as they came to be known (despite originating from a variety of German principalities) traveled down the Rhine to Rotterdam, from where between 11,000 and 13,000 continued across the English Channel.[8] By June 1709 vast refugee camps had sprung up in Blackheath and Camberwell on the southern outskirts of London. Struggling to feed and accommodate the refugees and with a growing sense of resentment building against them among the locals, the British government sensed an opportunity to kill two birds with one stone and initiated a plan for their relocation to some of the more troubled regions of Her Majesty's colonies.[9] Several plans were posited, among them a scheme to transport 3,000 to New York. Among the proponents was the newly appointed governor of the colony, Robert Hunter. The Scot envisaged training the refugees in the manufacture of naval stores: pitch for caulking ships' hulls and tar for preventing ropes from rotting in the damp sea air. As Britain was currently reliant on Swedish imports for both products, the government thought the proposal a fine one. The wishes of the Palatines themselves were never considered. Hunter's plan would require them to work for several years at a trade in which they had no expertise in order to pay their passage and the initial year's subsistence with which they would be provided. Only then would they be rewarded with their own land. Nevertheless, the scheme was approved by Queen Anne and in January 1710 3,000 Palatines boarded ten transports anchored along England's southern coastline. Bad weather and poor planning resulted in a four-month delay. As winter turned to spring, the refugees' health and enthusiasm deteriorated, and it was not until mid-April that Hunter joined them with a royal navy escort of HMS *Lowestoffe* and HMS *Feversham*. Only then, with the fleet about to depart, did the Palatines learn what the government had in store for them. Sensing it was too late to turn back, their leaders reluctantly signed a contract agreeing to all terms. The first seeds of discontent had been sown. They would bear bitter fruit in America.[10]

The voyage to New York was marked by death, disease, and delay. The *Lyon of Leith*, the first of the convoy to arrive, reached New York on June 14, after a two-month voyage. According to John Sharpe, the reverend of Fort Anne, 200 of the 402 refugees onboard died during the voyage. Four more transports arrived the following day along with the *Lowestoffe*, while two others reached New York on June 16. That day Hunter wrote to Secretary Popple of the Lords of Trade. "Three of the Palatine Ships" had still not arrived, while the refugees that had done so were "in a deplorable sickly condition." Meanwhile the *Herbert* had been "cast away in the East end of Long Island" by a storm, and the goods it was carrying—including the tents intended to accommodate the Palatines—had been "much damaged." Hunter also learned that the last of the transports, the *Berkley*, had been left behind in Portsmouth for repair. It would not reach New York until late July, by then another 270 of the Palatines had died. That summer proved "excessive hot," and a further 200 expired before autumn brought some respite. Through fears that the sicknesses which the Germans had carried with them across the Atlantic would spread to the population of New York, the majority of the refugees spent their first months in America on Nutten Island, a 172-acre expanse off the southern tip of Manhattan, while Hunter sent a surveyor "with some skilful men" to the Schoharie River in what is now upper New York State to see if the area was suitable for the naval stores' project.[11]

Next, Hunter turned his attention to his principal concern as a wartime governor, the defense of New York from the French. While New England had suffered several border raids during Queen Anne's War, notably the attack on Deerfield, Massachusetts, in 1704, New York had escaped almost entirely unscathed. This fortunate circumstance owed less to the efforts of Hunter's predecessors than it did to the presence of the region's dominant indigenous group, the Iroquois

Confederacy, on the northern and western frontiers of the colony. Composed of five culturally and linguistically homogenous polities (the Mohawk, Oneida, Onondaga, Cayuga, and Seneca), the Iroquois Confederacy, or Five Nations, had risen to a position of hegemony in the northeast by trading furs acquired from the indigenous peoples of the interior to the Europeans on the coast in exchange for firearms and alcohol. By the turn of the eighteenth century, having learned that the territorial squabbling that periodically erupted between the French and British threatened both their trade and regional influence, and unsure as to which would eventually emerge as dominant, the Confederacy had settled upon an intricate diplomatic policy designed to maintain the status quo. While simultaneously promising alliances to the British in a system known as the Covenant Chain, and purporting neutrality to the French, the Confederacy was able to retain their autonomy and continue to benefit from trade with both. Ironically, this policy also suited Governor Hunter throughout his first year in office. Prevented from pursuing a more belligerent approach due to his poor defenses, inadequate troops, and limited money, the Scot had to be content with the "precarious security" afforded by the Iroquois buffer zone, while being obliged to pander to the Confederacy out of fear that they might exploit his weakness by encouraging an invasion from New France.[12]

On July 24, 1710, Hunter briefed the Lords of Trade on the latest nuances from the frontier. The Seneca, who had previously been favorable to the French despite being an integral member of the British-leaning Five Nations, had decided to switch allegiances and join the Covenant Chain, as had the Ottawa, a powerful indigenous polity from the interior whose territory stretched between Lakes Huron and Michigan. Hunter's final observation was of a less positive nature. "The French have built a stone Fort at Chamblis on the River that runs from the lake into the River of St Lawrence," he informed the Lords of Trade. "They have had lately four ships from France, two with men and two with Provisions . . . [and] have sent some small partys of their Indians toward the Frontiers of New England. . . . These advices we have from our spyes."[13] On August 3, 1710, Hunter set off upriver for Albany to meet with the heads of the Five Nations as well as the sachems of some Algonquian, or River Indian, tribes from the upper Hudson valley. Besides cementing his relationship with his indigenous allies, Hunter had a second reason for making the journey. Having learned that the land on which he had originally intended to settle the Palatines belonged to the Mohawks, the Scot needed to ask their permission for its use. The meeting took place at Albany on August 10, 1710. Brightly tattooed, heavily armed, and dressed in moccasins and buckskin breechclouts and with their heads shaven aside from a central tuft of hair dyed orange, blue, or red, the Mohawk sachems made quite an impression on the new governor. Speeches were made, toasts drunk, and presents given. As he later informed the Lords of Trade, Hunter was pleased with the outcome: "They have given assurances of their fidelity and resolution to keep the Covenant Chain bright (as they phrase it) . . . [and] have promised to receive no French Priests or Emissaries, and to acquaint me with whatsoever the French propose." Furthermore, the sachems "resolved to make a present of . . . [the lands along the Schoharie River] to her Majesty . . . I accepted with thanks in Her Name . . . and ordered them a suitable present."[14]

By August 27, Hunter was beginning to understand that the Palatines, the Native Americans, and the French were not his only concerns. "I have . . . I think a much more difficult task here," he wrote: "reconcileing men to one another and their true Interests."[15] Over twenty years since Leisler's Rebellion, New York remained deeply divided along ethnic, religious, economic, and political lines. The English merchants considered their Dutch peers clannish and haughty. They complained of the "obstructions and hinderances" put in their way by importers of Dutch descent, and resented the burghers' use of intermarriage and tight-knit family alliances to cling to their fading financial supremacy. Such tactics also fueled unfounded English suspicions that their rivals dreamed of a return to Dutch rule. The Dutch, for their part, bristled against English legalism and were angered by the advantages Anglo merchants garnered as New York increasingly looked to London as its principal trading partner to the detriment of their mercantile links with Amsterdam.[16] Further feeding conflict was the disparate range of economic interests in New York: the fading fur trade was dominated by trappers and merchants of Dutch descent and centered around Albany; the Caribbean, European, and African trades were contested between older Dutch elements and English and French Huguenot newcomers; while the long-established Dutch landowners on the Hudson valley, such as the Philipses and Van Cortlandts, competed to produce foodstuffs for export to the sugar monocultures of the Caribbean, as well as for consumption within New York City, with independent small holders on Long Island, many of whom were originally New Englanders like the Halletts who had left the stuffy confines of Boston and Connecticut for the plurality of New York.[17] Ethnic divisions were also evident in local politics. Although Dutch control was fading rapidly by the time of Hunter's arrival with the steady influx of English and French immigrants, the old pro-Leislerian block still dominated the city's North Ward where David Provoost had won seven elections as alderman in the first decade of the eighteenth century. The West Ward, by contrast, was firmly in the anti-Leislerian camp.[18] These tensions were compounded by the diversity of religion: Jews rubbed shoulders with Presbyterians, Lutherans, Anglicans, Quakers, Huguenots, and members of the Dutch Reformed Church.[19] Another bone of contention was the divide between the city's Whigs and Tories.[20] Out of a misplaced allegiance to the disgraced Tory grandee Lord Cornbury, the Reverend William Vesey of Trinity Church had taken to bad-mouthing Governor Hunter before the Scot had even arrived in the Americas. "[He] . . . had it seems . . . taken occasion to use me ill before he knew me," Hunter complained in a letter to the secretary of the SPG, "of which I was soon informed after my Arrivall, and for which reason I did all that was in the power of man by good Offices and Civilitys . . . to persuade him into a better opinion of me." Hunter's efforts would prove insufficient. Vesey, whom the governor called "a constant Caballer," would prove a thorn in Hunter's side throughout his period of office.[21]

All these tensions rose to the surface when Hunter convened the thirteenth provincial assembly in September 1710. Instructed to pass a series of bills for the financial support and military security of the colony, the governor had some initial success when an act for maintaining the colony's militia was voted through, but afterward came up against entrenched opposition. The assembly refused to consider any further bills concerning fundraising unless the responsibility for the distribution of such monies be placed in the hands of the treasurer of the province rather than with the royal representative whom Hunter had been instructed to install. The resultant impasse led to a ten-day recess, after which the assembly attempted to win the new governor around to their side with a "gift" of 2,500 ounces of silver plate. Hunter refused. The members countered by revealing that they could not pay his salary as the colony had been sunk into debt by the "mis-application of former Revenues" under the governorship of Lord Clarendon, Hunter's disgraced and corrupt predecessor Lord Corn-bury, who had recently acquired the title on his elevation to the peer-age. Compounding the difficulty the new governor faced was the fact that the assembly members had an incentive for procrastination. As each was paid six shillings per day, long sessions were profitable. So much so, in fact, that their salaries for the fall session in 1710 alone amounted to nigh on half the total government expenses for the entire year. Also strengthening the assembly's obstinacy was the fact that po-litical developments in Westminster had undermined Hunter's au-thority in New York. With the War of Spanish Succession becoming increasingly unpopular as it dragged into its tenth year, in August 1710 the Junto Whig ministry which had appointed Hunter as governor had fallen. The treasurer, Sidney Godolphin, and Secretary of War, Robert Walpole, had been forced to resign, and Lord Marlborough, once the country's darling, had also lost influence. The subsequent Tory ascendancy meant that Hunter's political currency in New York was seriously undermined. Frustrated by his lack of progress, the Scot prorogued the assembly until spring.[22]

Fortunately, by this stage Hunter was beginning to make some progress with the Palatine resettlement. Although the surveyor's as-sessment of the land on the Schoharie River was disappointing (the site proved too wet for pitch pine), a new and suitable tract was soon selected. Halfway between New York City and Albany on the east bank of the Hudson, it consisted of 6,000 acres belonging to Robert Livingston, a fellow Scot and member of the Provincial Assembly. "Besides the goodness of the soile," Hunter informed the Lords of Trade, "Ships of 50 foot water may . . . [dock nearby] without diffi-culty," and Livingston was willing to part with the land for £400 in New York currency. A second tract was acquired on the bank opposite, and in the final week of September, those Palatines well enough to travel set off for their new home. By November, 1,500 had begun work on the construction of five villages on the two sites. Too late in the season to plant crops, they remained reliant on Hunter for their subsistence, however, and with the Scot having already spent the majority of the £8,000 he had been allocated by the British government for the project, he was forced to invest his own money as well as take out loans to ensure that the "poor people [did not] starve." As the Provincial Assembly still refused to pay his salary, Hunter was soon in serious difficulty. "I must beg your Lordships assistance in setting that matter upon a right foot," he wrote on October 3, "[and] have [therefore] sent a scheme of their Past and future expence to My Lord Treasurer." Hunter's request, amounting to two annual payments of £15,000 to be received in consecutive years, would be debated by the Board of Trade at the turn of the year.[23]

Meanwhile, further tensions had arisen in New York City. The August meeting of the Court of General Quarter Sessions was dominated by cases involving the city's Black inhabitants. The widow Catherine Elbertse pleaded guilty to an indictment that she had sold alcohol to enslaved persons "for her own private and unlawful Gain," and that she "did wickedly and deceitfully receive take and convert to her own use sundry sums of money and other goods and with them the said negro slaves did then and there knowingly wilfully wickedly and deceitfully buy sell and trade to the Evil Example of Others." The next day the court heard how Elizabeth Green, the widow of a ropemaker who resided in the city's South Ward, "did suffer sundry Negro slaves to assemble and meet together to feast and Revell in the Night time and then and there did keep and maintain a disorderly house and with the said Negro slaves did . . . buy sell and trade and Receive of and deliver . . . Sundry quantities of Strong Liqours." Green was sentenced to eight days in jail. In the same session Mary Lyndsey was indicted in yet another case of Blacks and whites mixing in disorderly houses with criminal intent.[24] After the city had marked the anniversary of the foiled Gunpowder Plot, yet another case involving an enslaved man was brought to Hunter's attention. Abraham Sanntvoord, a mariner born in the New Netherlands forty-three years before, sent a petition to the governor concerning Tony, a man he had enslaved, who was "a very good sailor" and had stowed away aboard a Royal

Navy ship. As the vessel had already left the roads, there was little Hunter could do. It later transpired that Tony, with the aid of the ship's captain, had transferred to a second vessel at sea and was on his way to a life of freedom in London.[25]

As winter took hold, Hunter's financial problems became more acute. With the New York assembly still refusing to pay his salary, and the Palatines' expenses draining his dwindling private funds, the governor wrote to the Lords of Trade, suggesting that he be paid out of duties arising from the sale of prize ships condemned in New York's Admiralty Court. As fate would have it, the governor's monetary situation was being debated in London at that very moment and the man assigned the task of deciding whether his expenses should be reimbursed was none other than Lord Cornbury, now Lord Clarendon. Insular in outlook, Clarendon and the rest of his Tory peers had been opposed to the Palatine immigration from its inception, and now that the Whigs had fallen from power, the Tories were able to sabotage the plan. In early 1711 Clarendon informed the Board of Trade that Hunter's requests for funding were unreasonable and suggested putting a stop to the entire project. "It is most certain that no person that has his Limbs, and will work can starve in that country," Clarendon opined, before going on to suggest that Hunter's proposal for their government funded subsistence would merely "confirm . . . [the Germans] in that laziness they are already too prone to." Although Clarendon was considered a laughingstock following the embarrassing end to his governorship in New York, he was telling the Tory ministry exactly what they wanted to hear. Hunter's hopes of reimbursement had all but disappeared.[26]

The Palatines were growing increasingly frustrated. Having left their homes two years previously with the expectation of land and prosperity in America, they found themselves enduring a bitter winter on desolate ground under the obligation of undertaking a project in which they had little interest and for which they had even less expertise. Rumors concerning the prime farmland denied them on the Schoharie River caused further resentment. Looking back on events that winter, Hunter would write that he had "met with great opposition from many of the ill-disposed Inhabitants, who daily insinuated that there were better lands for them on the Fronteers and that they were ill used in being planted there [on the Hudson]." By early 1711, the Palatines' anger turned to resistance. They refused to prepare their plots for the spring growing season and began to direct their frustrations toward the governor. On March 6, Hunter sailed up the Hudson to meet them. He explained that the Schoharie land was unsuitable. Besides not being apt for pitch pine, the area was isolated, difficult to supply, and exposed to attack by the French and their Indian allies. Certain he had achieved his mission, Hunter returned to New York only to be overtaken by a message that the Germans were threatening mutiny. Returning upriver, Hunter called the Palatines' bluff. Ordering a deputy to read aloud the contract the Germans had signed back in London, he demanded to know if they intended to abide by its terms. "After some small deliberation they . . . resolv'd to keep their Contract," Hunter informed the Board of Trade, "Soe wee parted good Friends."[27]

Spring brought yet more problems. When the rivers first began to be free from ice, New York's enslaved Black stevedores and boatmen began loaded their masters' sloops in the East River with beef, pork, and flour destined for the sugar islands of the Caribbean, but by April swarms of French privateers had "infest[ed] the coast" ready to snap up any merchantmen brave enough to run the gauntlet. *Lowestoffe* and *Feversham*, the Royal Navy vessels which had brought Hunter from England and were assigned to the protection of New York, were ill-prepared to meet the challenge. Having been laid up all winter in Kip's Bay, some five miles up the East River, the ratings had been permitted to find work ashore in the city as tradesmen, craftsmen, or laborers. Others had deserted across the ice and disappeared into the city's back streets or into the vast American interior. As a result, Captains George Gordon and Robert Patson found themselves unable to brush aside the gathering menace.[28]

On April 24, yet another issue came to Hunter's attention. As he sat down to a meeting with his council, a petition arrived written by two enslaved men, Jose and Juan, who had been captured aboard a Spanish vessel by a privateer operating out of New York six or seven years previously.[29] "By reason of their color which is swarthy," Hunter explained, "they were said to be slaves and as such were sold [at Admiralty auction] among many others of the same color and country," along with the ships themselves and their cargo. Sold to the East Ward baker Peter Vantilborough and the merchant mariner Thomas Wenham, respectively, Jose and Juan had always maintained that they were "free men subjects to ye King of Spaine" and therefore should be treated as prisoners of war and allowed to return to their homeland. Faced with the colony's racist legal code, however, which insisted that the natural condition of all people of color in the British Americas was that of a slave, Jose and Juan had made no headway in their attempts to secure their freedom. Hunter admitted he "secretly pittyed their condition, but having noe other evidence of what they asserted than their own words, I had it not in my power to releive them." The governor did, however, propose an alternative solution. "It is ye opinion of this Board," the minutes of that morning's Council Meeting recorded, "that ye best medium that can be taken in this case . . . [is that Jose and Juan] Enter into Indentures to serve their respective Master and Mistress for such reasonable time as they can agree on and at the expiration thereof to be free." Under no legal obligation to comply with Hunter's proposal and faced with the potential loss of a hefty financial investment, Wenham and Vantilborough refused to comply. Jose and Juan would remain enslaved for the foreseeable future and their growing resentment would lead them to consider taking matters into their own hands.[30]

On May 1, 1711, a subscription was taken in New York's Trinity Church for the "finishing of the steeple." A total of £318, 5 shillings, and 10 pence was donated by 158 individuals. The list of the contributors read like a who's who of colonial New York. Governor Hunter's name was the first; the Scot donating £10 of his rapidly dwindling funds. The Reverend William Vesey gave £5; William Sharpas, the long-standing city clerk, promised £1, 10 shillings; James Neau, Elias Neau's brother, donated £1; while Adolphus Philipse, one of the colony's largest landowners and the proprietor of the rambling Philipse Manor on the east bank of the Hudson, gave £1, 2 shillings. Many of the future owners of the slaves who would be put on trial in the aftermath of the revolt of April 1712 also contributed. The merchants John Barbeire, Peter Morine, John Stuckey, Walter Thong, and Rip Van Dam—the future owners of Mingo, Caesar, Hannibal, Quacko, and Quasi, Quacko, and Tom respectively—donated between

11 shillings and £1 10 shillings each; while the widow Ruth Sheppard donated 7 shillings. The goldsmith David Lyell, the future owner of Tom, gave £1. William Walton, a former ship's captain turned carpenter and the owner of both Cuffee and Sarah, gave £1, 10 shillings; and the lawyer Jacob Regnier, Mars' master, gave £3—the fourth most generous offer after Hunter's and Vesey's and that made by Regnier's perennial competitor, Attorney General May Bickley, who donated £3, 18 shillings so as not to be outdone by his rival. Another resident whose name appears was the slave trader Alan Jarrett. Curiously, Jarrett was not in New York City at the time. With her husband navigating homeward from the Guinea Coast with the principal protagonists of the April 1712 revolt chained up in the hold of his sloop beneath him, it seems likely that it was in fact Jarrett's wife, Hannah, who made the £1 donation toward the construction of Trinity Church's steeple in Jarrett's name.[31]

May 1711 was another busy month for Governor Hunter. News of more disturbances in the Palatine villages filtered down the Hudson to New York. By this stage, Hunter was beginning to run out of patience with the Germans. As he made his way upriver, he sent word ahead to Albany asking for sixty soldiers from the town's garrison to be dispatched to meet him. At first Hunter tried to reason with the Palatines. He reminded them that Queen Anne had saved them from starvation and of the promises they had made to repay her. Hunter also reiterated that the lands on the Schoharie River, which the Germans still insisted they wanted, were unsuitable for their settlement. The Palatines had had enough, however, and the morning after Hunter's arrival, four hundred armed themselves with muskets provided for defense from the French and their Indian allies and gathered on a hillside near Livingston Manor. When they learned of the imminent arrival of the soldiers from Albany, the Palatines returned to their villages, but the next day another armed confrontation took place. This time, Hunter took the initiative. After disarming the Germans, he had the ringleaders arrested and ordered that a permanent garrison be billeted among them. Outmaneuvered and overawed, the Palatines had little choice but to comply. By the end of the month they had begun to produce the long-awaited naval stores and soon they were barking 15,000 pine trees a day.[32]

No sooner had Hunter dealt with the Palatines than he was required to meet with the Iroquois and Algonquians at Albany, a move prompted by fresh rumors of Quebec's interference in the tribes' affairs. The governor of New France, Philippe de Rigaud, the Marquis of Vaudreuil, had sent an ambassador and a troop of soldiers to the Iroquois with "a large present . . . to the Value of about six hundred pounds mostly in ammunition." Despite the Iroquois' promises to Hunter, the French were permitted to build a blockhouse at Onondaga, the principal village of the tribe of that name and the traditional meeting place of the Iroquois Grand Council. Even more worryingly for the British, the French had plans to erect a permanent fort on the site. "The neutrality that has been observed between [the French and the Iroquois], has given our enemy the opportunity of corrupting our Indians," George Clerk, Hunter's secretary, warned the Lords of Trade in a letter of May 28, 1711. "There's now nothing left to trust to but the Faith of these Savages, and how much that is shaken is but evident from these proceedings." Hunter was decidedly more positive following his meeting at Albany. The sachems assured him they would dismiss the French from Onondaga, forbid them from erecting a fort on their land, and destroy the blockhouse that had been built. "They renewed their covenant, promised punctuall obedience to all Her Majesty's commands, and at my desire broke off the designe of a war they had mediated against some of the far Indian nations, promising not to stir from home without leave."[33]

In early June, with Hunter still absent upriver, summer came to New York City. John Sharpe, the reverend of the chapel at Fort Anne, escaped the soaring temperatures to gather wild strawberries in the woods of Brooklyn and Manhattan before returning home to bottle cider. On Stone Street in the city's South Ward, the merchant Walter Thong celebrated the birth of his second child, Maria, with his father-in-law, Rip Van Dam, while in the East River a far-traveled sloop dropped anchor, its arrival heralded by a stench of sweat, fear, death, and diarrhea blown across the city by the sea breeze. In the fetid confines of the sloop's hold were fifty-five enslaved Africans purchased by its captain, Alan Jarrett, on the Guinea Coast several weeks before. As news of Jarrett's arrival spread, a crowd gathered on the quayside. Anticipation of this day had been growing for some time. Fearing capture by French privateers, no New York slavers had visited Africa since Queen Anne's War had begun. The townsfolk's excitement at the prospect of adding to the numbers of enslaved would prove ill-judged, however. Although weakened and confused following their enforced dislocation and the subsequent miseries of the Middle Passage, the Africans would regain their strength and with it a burgeoning sense of outrage. Within a year, several of those gathered on the quayside that morning would pay the ultimate price for benefitting from what was the cruelest and most inhumane of New York City's morally dubious trades.[34]

CHAPTER 8

Alan Jarrett and the
New York Slave Trade

NEW YORK CITY, THE CARIBBEAN, AND THE GOLD COAST

March 1708 to March 1711

ALAN JARRETT WAS NEW YORK CITY's most prolific slave trader. In the first two and a half decades of the eighteenth century, Jarrett made at least seven voyages to Africa, condemning well over five hundred men, women, and children to a life of slavery in the Americas.[1] No other New York–based slave trader is known to have made more than four voyages, while the vast majority of the 101 captains known to have engaged in the trade made but a single journey.[2] Slaving was a dangerous business. As Sir Dalby Thomas, the governor of the principal English fortification on the Gold Coast during the first four of Jarrett's voyages put it, those who signed up "must neither have dainty fingers nor dainty noses." Few men, Thomas continued, "were fit for . . . it. It is a filthy voyage."[3] Traveling between the pestilent tropical zones of West Africa and the Caribbean and the icy winters of northeastern America, New York's slavers needed iron constitutions. Slave ships were disease-ridden places. Their crews fell victim to malaria, yellow fever, and the "bloody flux." Others, their health ruined, were forced to withdraw from the business after one or two runs. A handful were killed in slave uprisings onboard ship, while others died at the hands of their fellow crew members. Some perished in shipwrecks, accidents, or sea battles fought against pirates or privateers. A few were even forced out of the trade by their own consciences: disgusted with the brutality and injustice of the business, they choose to retire. Bankruptcy was another risk. Although profits occasionally ran as high as 100 percent, rates of sale and purchase fluctuated wildly, and slave mortality on the Middle Passage was high. As John Newton, an English slaver operating in the mid-eighteenth century, noted, "there were some gainful voyages, but the losing voyages were thought more numerous; it was generally considered as a sort of lottery in which every adventurer hoped to gain a prize."[4]

Alan Jarrett, or Allaine Jarrat as he is also referred to in the surviving documentation, was most likely of French Huguenot origins.[5] Like the sailor-cum-catechist Elias Neau, many Huguenots were mariners by profession, and several hundred would make New York their home in the late seventeenth century.[6] Others settled in the English-speaking Caribbean, a region to which Jarrett also had strong connections. From a later reference we know that Jarrett was well-educated. In his youth he "acquired a competent Knowledge" of "the Art of Navigation." He also had a grounding in mathematics, "writeing," and "Arithmetick."[7] In terms of character, Jarrett was resourceful, innovative, ambitious, and intelligent. Judging by his later career he must also have been hard-hearted, a stranger to empathy, and capable of great brutality, violence, and cruelty, traits that defined slave ship captains throughout the period of the transatlantic trade.[8] In 1698, when Jarrett was in his early teens, he first took to the high seas. As no documents survive to give details, we can only speculate that he gained the "experience and practice" he would later boast of by serving on merchant vessels or privateers, dozens of which operated out of the Huguenot-dominated ports of Le Havre and La Rochelle on the French Atlantic coast. Jarrett's voyages took him to New York and the Leeward Islands of the Caribbean, particularly Antigua, Barbados, and Barbuda, and may also have seen him travel to the slaving castles of the West African coast. In these places Jarrett acquired business contacts and built a reputation. He was hardened to the horrors of the slave trade and gained an understanding of the profits to be made.[9]

The oldest extant reference to Alan Jarrett dates to September 21, 1703, the day on which "Allin Jarrat, Mariner" allowed his ward, the ten-year-old Edward Garnum, to be indentured to William Haywood, a New York City shipwright. The document was witnessed by William Sharpas, the Clerk of the City, and Jacobus Van Cortlandt, one of six elected aldermen and a future New York mayor.[10] Two years later Jarrett's name resurfaces. On June 20, 1705, "Jarrett, Allane" was married to Hannah Moore in New York. The union was authorized by Governor Cornbury.[11] The couple would remain married until death parted them nearly two decades later. Hannah may have been a member of the "Moor" family registered in the 1703 census. If so, she had grown up beyond the city limits in the Outward, in a house inhabited by three adults, three children, and one "Male Negro" slave.[12] Alan Jarrett may well have lived and worked with other family members in this period. A long line of "Garretts," begun by the planter Thomas, lived in Antigua from at least as early as 1673. Rene Jarrett "of the Island of Barbadoes" died in Bridgetown in 1706 heavily in debt to John Shepherd, a cooper and tax collector who lived in New York's Dock Ward, whose wife would one day enslave one of the rebels of April 1712; while William Jarrett, who could conceivably have been Alan's cousin or brother, would sell slaves in New York and Jamaica in 1719 out of the *Philipsburg*, a sloop owned by a business consortium headed by two of the city's principal merchants, Adolphus Philipse and Jacobus Van Cortlandt, the latter the same man who had witnessed Edward Garnum's indenture sixteen years before.[13]

Although he had undoubtedly worked on a slaver previously, either as a sailor or first or second mate, Jarrett's first voyage as a slave ship captain took place in 1708. His ship, the *Flying Fame*, was a 40-ton sloop operating out of St. John's, Antigua, registered to the Royal African Company, a state-sponsored enterprise established by royal charter in 1660 by King Charles II.[14] Granted a trade monopoly along the coast of West Africa, the RAC built or acquired several forts and trading posts from the mouth of the Gambia River to the Gold and Slave Coasts of modern-day Ghana, Togo and Benin. From these bases, the company's merchants, or factors, traded textiles, spirits, knives, ornamental beads, pewter bowls, metals, gunpowder, and firearms with their African counterparts for enslaved people who were loaded onto company ships and exported to British possessions in the Americas, or gold and ivory which were sent to England. Despite its advantages, the RAC endured a checkered financial history just as its short-lived predecessor, the Company of Royal Adventurers Trading to Africa, had done before it. In the late 1660s the RAC fell into debt following the capture of most of its African trading posts by the celebrated Dutch admiral Michiel de Ruyter in the build-up to the Second Anglo-Dutch War. Remerging in 1672, the company temporarily flourished, but in the 1680s began to struggle due to competition from the Dutch West India Company as well as a host of illegal, independent smugglers, known as interlopers. The Bill of Rights, introduced in the wake of the Glorious Revolution in 1689, undermined the RAC's monopoly, and in 1697 Parliament passed the Trade with Africa Act, officially opening up West Africa to the interlopers provided they pay the company a levy of 10 percent on exports. Thus, with his employer in the latter stages of a long and eventually terminal economic decline, Alan Jarrett began his career as a slaving captain.[15]

The voyage of the *Flying Fame* was a successful one. Leaving Antigua on March 23, 1708, Jarrett arrived at Cape Coast Castle two months later, and on August 3, having loaded a cargo of 120 enslaved Africans, headed back across the Atlantic. During a Middle Passage of sixty-three days, ten of the slaves died, resulting in a mortality rate of 8.3 percent, a figure which Edward Chester, the RAC's chief agent at Saint John's, Antigua, considered acceptable. The surviving slaves, seventy-eight men, twenty-eight women, three boys, and a single girl, were sold, the vast majority destined for interminable toil on the island's sugar plantations where the average life expectancy for "unseasoned" adult arrivals from Africa was seven years. Most of Jarrett's cargo fetched £40 per head, payable in hogsheads of sugar, although five "dropsical Negro males" were sold for just £10 each. Having collected his cut of £174, 19 shillings and 7 pence, Jarrett invested £30 in the only slave girl to survive the voyage. Perhaps she was intended to serve Jarrett's wife, Hannah, as a domestic in New York.[16]

On November 27, 1708, less than two months after concluding his voyage on the *Flying Fame*, Jarrett set sail for Africa once more. This time he captained the *Amiable*, a 70-ton sloop which also belonged to the Royal African Company. On board were twenty-nine hogsheads

filled with 3,000 gallons of rum, a commodity which the RAC agent
Edward Chester had been advised was much prized by the Akan on
the Gold Coast. In March 1709 the *Amiable* arrived at Cape Coast
Castle. Sir Dalby Thomas, the resident RAC governor, was unim-
pressed with the rum, which he classed as "very Ordinary," and was
annoyed that Jarrett refused to purchase slaves on the nearby Windward Coast, instead insisting that he was "obliged to buy his comple-
ment . . . between Cape Coast Castle and Whydah [Ouidah]," a major
slave trading post which lay 300 miles to the east of Sir Dalby
Thomas' headquarters which had been paying tribute to the Akwamu
since 1702. On his way up the coast, Jarrett was ordered to purchase
salt at Accra, another Akan polity subject to the Akwamu where the
Dutch, English, and Danes all had forts, and slaves were sold in abundance. By May the *Amiable* was back at Cape Coast Castle with 163
slaves and ready for her voyage home. Eighteen of the enslaved men,
women, and children on board died on the Middle Passage. Three
more succumbed while the *Amiable* was anchored at St. John's. Once
more Edward Chester was unconcerned: the profit on the survivors
was considerable. The men and women Jarrett had purchased for £10
on the Gold and Slave Coasts fetched £40 to £50 in Antigua, while
the children, bought for £6 a head, were sold for upward of £25.
Chester's commission amounted to £162, 16 shillings, while Jarrett's
cut was £218. Again, the captain chose to invest some of his profits
in his cargo—he purchased a single "Male Negro" for £50.[17]

The voyage on the *Amiable* was to be Jarrett's last for the Royal
African Company. It would also be the final time he worked out of
Antigua. From mid-1709 the Frenchman operated exclusively out of
New York City as an independent trader, one of the so-called "ten
percent men" or interlopers.[18] We can only speculate as to his motivations for the change. One possibility is that Jarrett wished to live closer
to his wife, Hannah. Another is that he may have considered Antigua
too unstable. The French, who had colonized the neighboring islands
of Guadeloupe, Marie Galante, and Martinique, the closest of which
lay under sixty miles from Antigua, were an ever-present threat
throughout the War of the Spanish Succession. A fleet of five men-
of-war had invaded nearby St. Kitts and Nevis just three years before.
Having captured over 3,000 slaves, the invaders had burned a "great

part of the canes, houses, [and] workes; [and] destroy[ed] . . . a great number of horses and cattle," causing more than £100,000 worth of damage.[19] With the war entering its eighth year, another attack seemed imminent. To make matters worse, malaria and yellow fever were rife, and there was always the threat of a slave uprising on an island where the Black inhabitants outnumbered the whites by over four to one. Just eight years before, Major Samuel Martin, one of the most prominent planters on Antigua, had been murdered by his Akan slaves. After mutilating his body, the rebels joined a growing number of runaways who preyed on the plantations from hideouts in the Shekerley Hills.[20] Another potential reason for Jarrett's move was the low moral climate prevailing on the sugar islands. Societies with economies based on enslaved labor, such as Antigua, were notoriously corrupting, and inhabitants and visitors alike frequently bewailed the slavers' decadence and wild living.[21]

If Antigua's inherent instability was not enough of a reason for Jarrett to relocate to New York, then perhaps the behavior of the island's governor, Daniel Parke, was. "A sparkish . . . gentleman" who took "quick resentment of every the least thing that looks like an affront or injury," Parke had been appointed in 1706 as a reward for his role in the Battle of Blenheim. By his own admission, the new governor soon stirred up a veritable hornets' nest largely due to his insistence on bringing the islanders to book for violations of the mercantilist Acts of Trade. Locked in an escalating dispute with Christopher Coddrington, the owner of the island's largest plantation, Parke alienated the majority of the residents to such an extent that riots broke out in 1708. The following year Parke narrowly avoided falling victim to an assassination attempt when "a negro hired for the purpose . . . shot at him and broke his arm." Among Parke's legion of enemies was Edward Chester, the island's RAC agent and Jarrett's immediate superior. Not only did Parke make "frequent and groundless seizures of [Chester's] Goods" (which may well have included items taken from Jarrett's ships), but he also had an affair with Chester's wife, Catherine, resulting in the birth of an illegitimate daughter whom Parke named Lucy after another illegitimate child he had previously sired in Virginia. In 1710, the year following Jarrett's move to New York, a mob forced its way into Government House, looted Parke's belongings, and shot the governor through the thigh, leaving him to bleed to death after he had fled to a neighboring property, an anarchic event unprecedented in the annals of British colonial history.[22]

Various economic pulls may also have influenced Jarrett's decision to relocate to New York. Having sailed to West Africa at least twice in his career, Jarrett was well aware that the trade conducted by the ten percent men was more lucrative than that overseen by the company's own merchants. Unburdened by the need to maintain costly castles and trading posts in such a hostile environment and free to deal with whomever they chose, be they African or European merchants and middlemen, the ten percenters had minimal overheads and were better able to adapt to an ever-changing business climate than the unwieldy giant that was the Royal African Company.[23] Moreover, while the Antigua slave markets were supplied by two RAC ships and as many as fifteen private traders per year, New York had not seen a single slave ship arrive direct from West Africa since 1705 when twenty-four enslaved Africans were imported by an anonymous trader.[24] New York was a sellers' market crying out to be exploited by an experienced Africa hand. The only competition that Jarrett would face would be from the merchants who imported small parcels of Creole slaves alongside hogsheads of rum and sugar from the Caribbean. Even this posed no real challenge, however, as some colonial buyers considered slaves directly imported from Africa superior to those brought from the West Indies. The latter were commonly held to be "Rogues" or troublemakers whose owners had "Ship'd [them] off for great crimes."[25] As Governor Joseph Dudley of Massachusetts put it in 1708, "the Negroes so brought in from the West Indies, are Usually the worst Servants they have."[26] An equally common problem was that slaves imported from the West Indies were often "refuse negroes"—enslaved who were sick or infirm.[27]

A piece of legislation passed by the New York City Council in September 1709 provided Jarrett with a final impetus to relocate to New York. The "Act for Laying a Duty on the Tonnage of Vessels and Slaves" could not have played more directly into the slaver's hands if he had written it himself. The act stipulated the imposition of a duty of £3 "for every Negro that shall be Imported into this Colony *not directly from Affrica*."[28] At a stroke, Jarrett's Caribbean competitors had been hamstrung, while he, as the only trader importing slaves directly from Africa, had gained a significant advantage. At first glance it appears that Jarrett was the beneficiary of good luck. If one delves a little deeper, however, another possibility suggests itself. Ten percent men like Alan Jarrett rarely, if ever, acted in isolation. Their voyages were typically funded by conglomerates of investors who pooled their capital to spread the risk (a not inconsiderable one when one bears in mind that the cost of equipping a slave ship with trade goods, paying its captain and crew, and maintaining it on a round voyage which would have lasted up to a full calendar year, would have been somewhere in the region of £7,000—perhaps as much as £1,000,000 by today's standards).[29] While no information regarding the identities of those who may have backed Alan Jarrett's New York voyages survives, by examining patterns of known investment in the period we can speculate as to who these individuals may have been. Twenty-seven merchants are known to have invested in slaving voyages operating out of New York City between 1680 and 1730. The first two decades were dominated by Frederick Philipse, the aforementioned city councilor and owner of forty slaves and the vast estate of Philipse Manor. The sole financial backer of at least seven slaving voyages from New York City between 1685 and 1700, Philipse's ships took slaves from Madagascar to New York on six occasions, while the seventh took 114 captives from Soyo, a town located at the mouth of the Congo River in northern Angola, to Barbados. After Philipse's death in 1702, the city's slave trade was financed by a diverse range of individuals, none of whom dominated the trade in the way Philipse had. Indeed, only five were involved in more than two voyages. Thomas Wenham, whose widow, Mary, owned Juan, one of the two "Spanish Indians" who would become implicated in the 1712 revolt, partially financed at least three New York based slaving vessels between 1698 and 1702; three members of the Van Horne clan, John, Garrett, and Abraham, jointly invested in three other voyages, two of which were undertaken by the *Catherine and Mary* and one by the *Dragon* between 1717 and 1718. The final member of the quintet of repeat investors in the trade was Rip Van Dam, another prominent figure in both the political and financial life of the city, and the most likely to have been Alan Jarrett's principal investor.[30]

Rip Van Dam (c.1660–1749). A prominent Dutch merchant, Rip Van Dam may well have been the principal investor in the voyage that brought the Akan rebels of April 1712 to New York. (*New York Public Library*)

Born in the Dutch enclave of Albany, Rip Van Dam was apprenticed to a New York merchant at an early age and rose to become one of the most prominent figures in the city in the first half of the eighteenth century. As well as importing rum from the West Indies and wine and manufactured goods from Europe, Van Dam was active in the fur trade. He held shares in shipbuilding yards and several of the city's trading vessels and owned the bark *John and Michael* outright. Van Dam was also politically active. A city councilor from 1702, he sat on several city boards, including the Legislative Council, and would rise to the post of acting governor in the 1730s.[31] Van Dam's first documented foray into the slave trade came in 1698 when he and five other merchants, including Thomas Wenham and the Schuyler brothers, Peter and Brands, financed the voyage of the *Peter*, a 60-ton brigantine under captain George Revelry, to Madagascar. It was an inauspicious start. The *Peter* was captured (whether by pirates, privateers, or foreign warships is unknown).[32] Van Dam's next recorded involvement in the slave trade came seventeen years later in 1715, when he and three others hired Captain Thomas Jacobs to take the *Anne and Mary*, a 40-ton sloop mounting 4 cannon, to the Gold Coast. Jacobs was successful and returned to New York 225 days later with thirty-eight slaves. Three of the four merchants involved in the *Anne and Mary*'s voyage, including Van Dam, invested in a second trip for the same ship the next year. This time she sailed under Captain John Browne and returned to New York with a cargo of forty-three slaves after a voyage of 186 days. Van Dam's final recorded involvement in the slave trade occurred in 1723 when he and three others, including his son-in-law Walter Thong, sent the *Burnet* to Africa to pick up slaves to sell in Jamaica. Crucially for our narrative, the captain of the *Burnet* was Alan Jarrett.[33]

It seems highly probable that Van Dam invested in further slaving voyages between 1698 and 1715. Unfortunately, as New York shipping records only begin in July of the latter year, no evidence is available.[34] What is certain is that Alan Jarrett conducted at least three voyages out of New York in this period as evidenced by the records of the RAC and occasional newspaper reports. Who provided the financial backing for these trips is unknown, but Van Dam seems a likely candidate: the Dutchman had been involved in the trade previously and would work with Jarrett again in the future. Furthermore, Van Dam owned three of the fifty-five slaves implicated in the 1712 revolt, more than any other owner named in the subsequent court minutes. Two of the three slaves belonging to Van Dam subsequently executed, and all three had Akan day names.[35] It is highly probable, therefore, that these rebels were brought to New York onboard the ship Alan Jarrett used for the second of his three voyages in the period 1710 to 1712. As Van Dam owned at least three of the slaves imported, it would also suggest that he may also have been financially involved in the voyage, as he had been previously and would be again in the future.[36] A final possible connection between Van Dam and Jarrett lies within the minutes of the legislative council, which reveal that the Dutchman was the driving force behind the "Act for Laying a Duty on the Tonnage of Vessels and Slaves," the very act which may have spurred Jarrett's relocation from Antigua in the first place. Not only did Van Dam lead the subcommittee charged with writing and amending the act, but he also extolled its benefits to the council, resulting in its immediate acceptance.[37] It is perhaps not too much of a leap, therefore, to imagine that Van Dam was the instigator of Jarrett's move from Antigua. It is easy to imagine the scenario playing out as follows: knowing that the slave importation act would soon be passed in council, the Dutchman contacted Jarrett, a man whom he would no doubt have known personally—the docks in New York City in the early eighteenth century being a small community—and proposed that they enter into business together. Van Dam's mercantile knowhow and capital and Jarrett's experience in the Africa trade made the pair perfect partners, while the terms of the slave importation act would allow them to undercut the competition importing small parcels of Creole slaves from the Caribbean. If Jarrett could avoid the potential pitfalls of a voyage to the West African coast, a large profit was guaranteed.

If Van Dam and Jarrett did indeed make such a deal, they moved quickly to put it into effect. Jarrett returned to Antigua from Africa on board the *Amiable* on August 3, 1709; in New York, just one and a half months later, Van Dam passed the slave importation act in the legislative council; in November "Allane Jarrat" was made a freeman of New York, a title which would enable him to work within the environs of the city; and by March 1710 Jarrett was once again at Cape Coast Castle on the Gold Coast of West Africa operating for the third time in his career as the captain of a slaver, on this occasion in command of "the Sloop *Friendship* from New York."[38] Sir Dalby Thomas mentioned Jarrett's visit in a letter to the directors of the RAC in London due to an innovation Jarrett had made which Thomas felt his employers might wish to emulate. "Captn Allne Jarrett . . . had his Corn Kiln Dryed," Thomas wrote on March 23, 1710, "and put aboard at New York & [it] is as Good [now] as when put aboard—It would be of great use to the Company if [they] could keep their corn [for as long as this]." Thomas duly requested that the next slave ship to leave London for Cape Coast should be supplied with "2000 Bricks of a sort made for that purpose and a kiln wire covering of about 16 foot square."[39] No other mention is made of Jarrett's 1710 voyage in any other source, but we do know that fifty-three "Negroes" were imported into New York that year directly from Africa, a number which tallies with the amount that a single New York sloop could supply.[40] By July 30, 1710, Jarrett was sufficiently solvent to purchase a property on Dock Street in New York City's South Ward from the city clerk, William Sharpas.[41] It was an expensive location, yet ideal for Jarrett's line of work, and by the last months of 1710 he was on his way to

Africa once more. Although it is possible that some of the "Carmantee & Pappa" rebels who would rise up in April 1712 were brought to New York by Jarrett as a result of his first 1710 voyage, it seems more probable that the majority arrived on his second New York voyage in 1711. Slave rebellions in the Americas in the seventeenth and early eighteenth centuries were generally carried out by recent arrivals, and as mortality rates were so high among unseasoned African slaves, the likelihood is that several of those who had arrived in 1710 were already dead by 1712.[42] Unfortunately, the documentary references for this second voyage are little better than those for the voyage made in 1710. To build up a picture of Jarrett's movements, therefore, it is necessary to examine each one in detail. The first, which places Jarrett at Cape Coast Castle on March 18, 1711, comes from the ship's log of HMS *Anglesey*, a 50-gun, fourth-rate ship of the line to whose quarterdeck our narrative will shift in the subsequent chapter. In September 1710 the *Anglesea's* captain, Thomas Legge, had been tasked with protecting British interests on the West African coast along with his consort, the 40-gun fifth-rate frigate HMS *Fowey* under Captain Robert Chadwick. With the entire region "much infested" with French privateers, Legge and Chadwick had plenty of work to do.[43]

CHAPTER 9

The Middle Passage

THE GOLD AND SLAVE COASTS TO NEW YORK CITY

January to June 1711

Their cup is full of pure, unmingled sorrow.
—Zachary Macaulay, abolitionist

BRITISH CAPTAINS LEGGE AND CHADWICK's "Guinea Cruze" proved most eventful. Hit by a storm in the Bay of Biscay in mid-October, just three weeks after leaving Plymouth Sound, the *Fowey* lost its main top mast and was forced to limp into Lisbon roads for a week of repairs. A month later, having left Madeira with two dozen pipes of the island's much-famed wine, Legge and Chadwick secured their first prize: a 200-ton, 26-gun French ship out of Brest bound for the Guinea Coast. With the *Anglesea* lagging behind and a high sea running, the Frenchman gave the *Fowey* a long chase. Intermittently firing his stern chasers for two days, Chadwick finally got close enough to pour two close-range broadsides into the ship, "shatter[ing] . . . hr . . . rigging" and shooting through its mainmast. Dozens of the enemy and two of the *Fowey*'s crew were killed, "several more" were wounded and Chadwick was obliged to secure his "much damaged" mizzen yard with sashes before sailing on. In mid-November, the *Anglesea* and *Fowey* reached Saint Jago roads in the Canary Islands where they remained for ten days "hogging, watering, heeling and scrubbing the ship[s]" before sailing southward with four merchantmen, the *Broughton* sloop, the *Dorothy*, the *Joseph Galley*, and the *Esperanza*, in company. The final weeks of 1710 brought "moderate gales . . . with Thunder Lightning & Rains," and on January 1, 1711, the lookout at the *Anglesea's* masthead caught sight of the African mainland: Cape Mount, rising high out of the surrounding scrubland on the westward extreme of the Windward Coast in modern-day Liberia, lay some eight leagues to the northeast.[1]

At first light on January 2, the *Fowey's* lookout sighted three "strange sails" through the haze. Chadwick fired a gun to alert the *Anglesea* and ordered his crew to give chase. Within an hour the *Fowey* was close enough to fire at the slowest of the strangers, the *Industria*, a ship of forty-five men and 12 guns from Nantes "design'd to slave upon this Coast, and from hence to Bonas Aries & Martinico." At 8 A.M., the French captain struck his colors. Chadwick sent a boat to board the prize, while the two remaining Frenchmen ran into shore with the *Anglesea* in pursuit. Soon Legge's stern gunners were "exchanging several shott" with the largest of the two, "the *Francois*, a ship of 32 Guns, [and] 150 men [which was] bound [on] the same voyage" as its consort. The chase continued until 3 P.M. when a dead calm allowed the *Francois* and its companion, "a small tender," to use their oars to escape their pursuers. At 6 P.M. night fell. The *Francois* slipped into the gloom, the English men-of-war spread out and Legge ordered his second lieutenant, John Ogilvie, to take the ship's barge out to search for the enemy. At midnight Ogilvie returned. "[He] gave me ans[wer]," the *Anglesea's* log recorded, "that . . . [the *Francois*] was soe near the *Fowey* that . . . Captain [Chadwick] Order'd him to acquaint me that I might Expect hearing of him Engag'd every minute." Chadwick's hopes were frustrated. A game of cat and mouse ensued throughout the night and into the following morning. Every time the English closed with their quarry, a calm fell enabling the *Francois* to pull away with its oars. "By Daylight [she was] above 2 leagues distant from us," the *Anglesea's* log recorded, "[but] about 8 we had a small Gale sprung up at WSW . . . [and] between 11 and 12 wee came soe near as to fire several shott, but lost her again by calms." That afternoon Legge's frustration continued. At 3 P.M. the wind picked up and by 4 P.M. the captain thought himself close enough to yawl his ship and fire a broadside, but the range proved too great and another calm allowed the Frenchman to pull away once more. In desperation, Legge ordered his men to man the boats and tow the *Anglesea* closer, but the measure proved in vain, and at dusk, with the *Francois* and its tender disappearing to the east, Legge reluctantly "made the signal for . . . leaving off [the] chase, and stood in for the land."[2]

On January 5, the *Anglesea* and *Fowey*, along with the two merchantmen remaining in convoy and the warships' two prizes, dropped anchor in fifteen fathoms eight miles off Cape Mesurado, a "reddish" headland on the coast of modern-day Liberia. A calm allowed Chadwick to "heel" the *Fowey*, exposing the keel which was scrubbed free of barnacles and *teredo navalis*, the wood-eating worms which plagued ships in topical waters. On January 8, the flotilla sailed on to the estuary of the River Sestos, a spot marked by a series of "Great rocks on the Shoar" where they were to remain at anchor for nine days. The boats were dispatched to a "large" and "beautiful" village where the locals, deemed by one contemporary traveler as a "good sort of People, [and] honest in their dealings," helped the crews fill the ships' casks with fresh water and cut wood for the galley stoves. Once Legge and Chadwick resumed their voyage toward Cape Coast Castle, the first few days proved uneventful. On January 21, they rounded Cape Palmas, the easternmost point of the Windward Coast where a reef marked by white breakers stood a mile out from the shore. Two days later Cape Lahoe was sighted. Nearby a large village inhabited by "affable and civil negroes" who dealt in high-quality "elephant's teeth" stretched a mile along a shoreline dotted with "multitudes of Coco trees."[3]

Early in the afternoon of January 24, two more sails were spotted. The strangers put on all sail and divided. One, headed in shore, was chased by the *Anglesea*, and the other was pursued out to sea by the *Fowey*. The crew of the *Anglesea* spent the day and much of that night manning the rigging, squeezing every last knot of speed out of their ship, and at "about 11 at night," they "came up with [the chase]." In the moonlight Legge and his officers identified it as the *Camwood Merchant*, an RAC slaver which had been captured on the Windward Coast by a French privateer, the *Cesar*, exactly one month before. In no state to challenge the *Anglesea*, which outgunned them by 44 cannon to 10, the French prize crew struck their colors. The *Fowey*, meanwhile, was still in pursuit of the other ship which would turn out to be the *Cesar*. At 2 A.M. Captain Chadwick engaged in a running firefight with his 6- and 9-pounders. For three hours the two ships' muzzle flashes illuminated the night. The *Fowey*'s second lieutenant, Thomas Penhallow, was killed by the *Cesar*'s shot and three sailors were wounded. At 5 A.M., as the first false light of dawn crept over the forested hills of the African coastline, the *Cesar* tacked northward toward the shore. Chadwick tacked with it. Desperate to escape, at 8 A.M. the captain of the *Cesar* tacked once more. Doggedly, Chadwick turned again, his gun crews sending round shot crashing into the *Cesar*'s hull, through its masts, sails, and rigging and across its blood-spattered deck. At 1 P.M., seeing the *Anglesea* and the rest of the flotilla approaching to join the fight, the French captain submitted. Having celebrated their success, Chadwick and his men spent the rest of the day securing the prize and repairing the damage to their ship. The surgeon tended the wounded and the next morning at 10 A.M., to the roar of a ten-gun salute, Lieutenant Pennhallow's body was committed to the deep.[4]

After the excitement of the first few weeks of January, the crews of *Anglesea* and *Fowey* had a month of relative quiet. Little broke the routine of the daily watch as the flotilla made its way eastward along the West African coast. On the night of January 26, just off the River Cobre, a man fell overboard from the *Fowey* and drowned, and at noon on January 28, the ships reached the triple hills of Cape Apolonia, a point "in all parts furnished with great and small villages," which marked the western extreme of the Gold Coast. Over the next few days, in-between being beset by a series of calms, the flotilla passed several friendly and neutral vessels. At first light on February 1 off Cape Three Points, the *Fowey* spoke two Dutch ships: a privateer and an independent slave trader. Later that morning the *Nancy*, a London-based ten percenter commanded by Captain Lowther Gale, sailed by heading toward the west. At noon the next day the flotilla reached the town of Axim, which was famed for its brisk gold trade. Later they dropped anchor a mile and a half to the southwest of Frederiksborg Castle which was run by the Brandenburgers, an independent German principality and the smallest of the European players on the

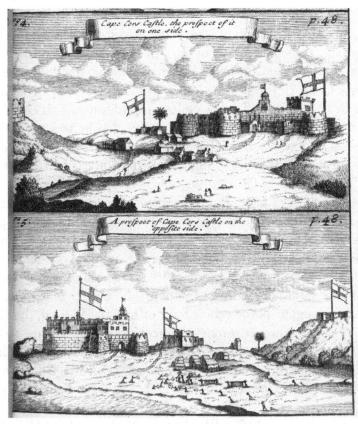

Two prospects of Cape Cors [Coast] Castle from *A new and accurate description of the coast of Guinea, divided into the Gold, the Slave, and the Ivory coasts*, published by J. Knapton, London, 1705. (*New York Public Library*)

Gold Coast. While the *Broughton, Dorothy*, and *Joseph* galley sailed on for Cape Coast Castle, the *Fowey* and *Anglesea* and their prizes remained at the fort for five days to fill their water casks. On February 6, the *Dolphin* galley and "a sloop . . . bound for England" passed by to the Windward Coast, and the next day captains Legge and Chadwick celebrated Queen Anne's birthday by issuing an extra ration of rum to the men and firing a twenty-one-gun salute. February 10 saw the flotilla reach Fort Dickscove, the westernmost trading post of the RAC, and on February 13, they arrived at the "spacious" and "strong" fortification of Cape Coast Castle.[5]

As LEGGE AND CHADWICK were about to discover, the Gold Coast was passing through a turbulent time. In late 1710 a "great mortality" had swept the region. Sir Dalby Thomas, the long-standing governor of Cape Coast Castle and the RAC's principal representative on the Gold Coast, "was seized wth a Violent inward feavour" on December 28, that "affected his head to such a degree that he was not truly in his senses from ye first day of his illness." On January 3, 1711, Thomas died. Although the most prominent of the epidemic's victims, the RAC's governor was far from the only man affected. "Not one man escaped being sick," James Phipps, Thomas' successor, recalled. Phipps himself "expected [he] had been going to make [his] Exit"; Sampson Walter, the RAC's chief merchant at Accra, succumbed on January 16; "Mr [Richard] Turner," one of three chief factors operating at Cape Coast Castle, died on February 19; Daniel Mann, the company's accountant, also fell victim to the outbreak, a particularly virulent strain of mosquito-borne yellow fever or malaria. In total, the RAC lost five factors, three surgeons, a surgeon's mate, a gardener, a ship-wright, two carpenters, a sergeant, and twenty-three soldiers to illness in a little under three months. The epidemic also affected the other Europeans on the Gold Coast. "The Dutch . . . lost a great many people," Phipps recorded, "their General Mr Adrian Schoonheydt died . . . , and a few days before [that] they buried their head [merchant Mr.] Copeman at the mine."[6]

Inter-European conflict accompanied the pestilence. Besides the encounters involving *Anglesea* and *Fowey*, several other sea battles were fought between British and French ships in 1710 and early 1711. The brig *Martha*, a ten percenter out of Bristol captained by William Courtney, was captured in late December, and on November 1, HMS *Scarborough*, a 32-gun frigate, had been taken by a French merchant-man loaded with 180 slaves bound for Martinique. "[It was] a very strange & unheard of accident . . . for a man of war to be taken by a Slaved Shipp," Phipps remarked in a letter to the RAC's board in London, especially as the *Scarborough* had outgunned its adversary by 32 cannon to 18. Phipps held the *Scarborough*'s captain, Edward Holland, responsible. In attempting to board the slaver, Holland had inadvertently exposed his ship to a close-range broadside. In the chaos that followed, Holland had been wounded in five places, while an "abundancy" of his men and most of his officers, who were then lined up "upon ye deck" in anticipation of boarding their adversary, had been killed. Holland was taken prisoner along with his surgeon and carpenter while the *Scarborough* was turned over to the surviving British sailors as a cartel. It reached Cape Coast Castle on January 14 and was still there when captains Chadwick and Legge arrived a month later.[7]

As well as fighting the French, the employees of the RAC had also been engaged in trade disputes with their European allies. In August 1710 Thomas had complained that "the Dutch are always playing underhand tricks and lately turned off some Ashantee traders that were coming to Cape Coast," while in Ouidah, on the Slave Coast, the French and Dutch factors were so enraged with their English peers for having achieved superior relations with the local king that they decided to ignore the state of hostility then existing between their two nations and joined forces against their local adversary—the RAC. According to William Hickes, the local RAC agent, the French and Dutch would have attacked the company fort in town had the king of Ouidah not threatened to intervene.[8]

A further source of conflict on the Gold Coast were the petty internal struggles which individual British merchants engaged in with the aim of furthering their own careers. A case in point concerns the relationship between Sir Dalby Thomas and his successor James Phipps. "Our late General . . . was a very good friend of mine from my first coming out with him," Phipps recalled, "but towards his later days he has been as much to ye contrary having abused me very grosly . . . his fault was for giving ear too much to a parcel of knavish rascaly fellows that was in ye castle who endeavoured what they could to breed ill blood between Sr Dalby and those next to him that they might have the opportunity of advancing themselves wch he was so blind as not to see I can impute it to nothing but the effect of his age."[9] Internal European disputes also involved African elements. At Fort Gross Frederiksborg in December 1710, the Brandenburg general was deposed by a rising led by the fort's gunner backed by prominent local Akan. The general, "a very covetous old man, who had us'd the Soldiers belonging to the Garrison very hard," was held prisoner in the interior for a few weeks before managing to escape. He found refuge at Cape Coast Castle only to succumb to the fever that had shortly before killed his English peer.[10]

Further conflict on the Gold Coast emanated from the perpetual rivalry between the ten percenters and the RAC. Resentful of the fact that their competitors were free to trade when and with whom they chose while unconstrained by the financial burdens of maintaining forts and garrisons, the company's employees realized that they could not compete. In their frustration they began to blame the independents for all their ills.[11] In November 1708, Captain Thomas Ashby of the RAC frigate *Annamaboe* summed up the situation when he wrote that "the Ten p Cent men give higher prices and are allowed to buy worse qualified negroes than the company's captain's which occasions their being quicker dispatched."[12] Two years later Sir Dalby Thomas wrote that while "some ten per cent men are civil, . . . others are not." Thomas blamed the latter for making the local traders at Annamaboe "impudent and arbitrary," while in January 1711 Phipps went so far as to claim that the ten percent men were behind the Fantes' attack on the Fetu earlier that month. "This outrage is occasioned by the ten per cent men[']s Great demand for slaves," he explained.[13] The Fante were jealous of the profits the Fetuers had made from the independent traders and wanted to ensure that they would not be able to benefit from such trade again. Regardless of the truth (or lack of it) behind such assertions, it was clear that the proliferation of independent traders, who sometimes outnumbered the company's ships on the coast by a factor of ten or even fifteen to one, had had a radical effect on the price of slaves. In the late seventeenth century RAC captains had purchased them for as little as 40 or 50 shillings per head. By the time of Alan Jarrett's 1710 to 1711 voyage, however, it was impossible to find any slaves for sale at less than £12. Prices in the West Indies, meanwhile, had also risen but by a smaller percentage. Plantation owners in Antigua, Jamaica, and Barbados who had paid £12 per head in the seventeenth century were forced to pay as much as £50 for each slave in the second decade of the eighteenth. This resulted in the slavers' profit margins falling from a sixfold mark up to a factor of just four.[14]

Such issues paled into insignificance, however, when compared with the scale of the Akan conflicts then playing out across the Gold

Coast. The early eighteenth century was a violent time, as polities struggled for primacy in conflicts fueled by imported European firearms.[15] In April 1710, the Fante, an alliance of linguistically and culturally related polities which dominated the coastal strip between the Pra and Densu Rivers, attacked the Cabesterra, a small polity immediately to the Fante's north which lay across the forest paths used by trade caravans on their passage to the coast from the interior. Outraged by the taxes the Cabesterra imposed on the passage of slaves and gold, the Fante declared war in April 1710 and by October had routed the Cabesterra in battle. They failed to follow up their victory, however, and to the minds of the Europeans observing the struggle, the Fante "gained but little by [it]."[16] The following year the Fante turned their attention to the Fetu, a tiny polity centered around Cape Coast Castle. Although nominally within the Fante alliance, the Fetu also had very close links with the RAC, a fact which aroused such jealousy and anger in the Fante that in January 1711 they attacked their weaker neighbor. "[They] kill'd and took most of the [Fetu] women and children," James Phipps noted, "but the men escaped to Cape Coast [Castle]," where Phipps afforded them sanctuary.[17]

Meanwhile, in the forested interior, even larger conflicts were raging as imperial warrior states emerged to rival the dominance of the coastal polities. Between February and June 1710, the Akwamu, the forerunner of these expansionist forest states under their king, Akwonno, destroyed their neighbors the Kwahu in a series of battles that took place near the upper Volta River; while some hundred miles to the west in mid-1711 and 1712, the Ashanti, another rising Akan forest polity whose military might would eventually eclipse that of the Akwamu and Fante alike, subjugated the territory of their neighbors, the Wankyi.[18]

All this devastation had a direct effect on the slave trade. While it made little difference to the RAC or the ten percenters where their slaves came from, what was of concern was that the supply remained constant and prices stayed low. In the short-term Gold Coast wars had a negative impact on both. As trade routes from the interior were blocked, business slowed, or ground to a halt. Prices soared on both sides of the Atlantic; RAC share prices fell; traders went bankrupt, captains and crew went unpaid; and slaveholders, from the plantations of the Caribbean to workshops in New York City, went shorthanded. Once the wars finished, trade picked up. Prisoners of war were marched to the coast, where they were sold directly to Europeans or to Akan middlemen, who in turn sold them on to the highest bidder. In such times of glut, prices fell and great profits were made. The trade was highly unstable and difficult to predict. High and lows could be extremely localized.[19] On April 9, 1710, for example, Sir Dalby Thomas complained that "Slaves . . . are hard to come by" and that prices "begin to rise and . . . will shortly be much higher." One hundred miles to the east, at Fort Christiansborg, Erich Lygaard, the chief Danish factor, was also unhappy. "The Trade is still very poor," he informed his superiors at Copenhagen on May 12, "the roads are closed everywhere, so the traders have no free passage to come down here. On the 11th February [Akwonno] . . . went to seek out his enemy [the Kwahu]. . . . As long as he is away, it is doubtful whether the trade will [improve]." Back in Cape Coast Castle at the end of May, Thomas was still lamenting that "Slaves are scarce and very dear . . . None of the ten per cent men dare pretend there to bragg of their voyages," but, less than three months later at Christiansborg, things had begun to change. "It is reported that the King [Akwonno] came home to [Akwamu] . . . on the 1st of July and has destroyed his enemy," Governor Lygaard wrote, "so the roads to the Lower Coast will now be opened . . . [and] trade will be better from now on." At Cape Coast Castle, however, business remained slow, and in January 1711 James Phipps observed that "Slaves are scarce and dear . . . they giving at Anamaboe [a port twelve miles to the east] seventeen pounds per head." Things did not pick up for Phipps until March 1711, by which time the conflict between the Fante and Fetu had been decided and the new governor noted that "the ten per cent men have great prices for slaves."[20]

With such tumultuous events going on, the activities of the New York–based slave trader Alan Jarrett passed all but unnoticed. Jarrett's former acquaintance, Sir Dalby Thomas, was too sick to make any reference to the New Yorker's voyage, while Thomas' successor, James Phipps, was too preoccupied with his various disputes. Similarly, the Danish factors at Christiansborg were mired in their own problems with King Akwono, while the Brandenburgers were also in a state of considerable flux. Indeed, the only evidence confirming Jarrett's voyage is to be found in the logbook of HMS *Anglesea,* which makes three references to his presence. On the morning of March 18, 1711, the log keeper noted that "a Sloope from New York anchored . . . at Cape Coast Castle." Five days later, with the *Anglesea* still at anchor in the roads, "ye Sloop saild to W'ward," and on April 6, 1711, by which time the *Anglesea* had sailed on to Dickscove Fort, it was noted that "at noon sailed hence a Sloope for New York."[21] The only other reference to Jarrett's second voyage as a ten percenter was written by the New York correspondent of the *Boston News-Letter* on June 4, 1711. "This morning," the report revealed, "arrived here . . . Jarrat from Guinea, who says that the *Scarborough* was taken on that coast by a French Merchant Man; and that Her Majesty's Ships the *Anglesea* and *Fowey* had taken several rich Prizes; Capt legg in the *Anglesey* took one worth 70000l. in Gold, out of which he shared 13000l."[22]

For all other details of Jarrett's 1711 voyage there is no recourse but informed speculation. We cannot even be sure of the name of the sloop which carried him to Africa, although it may have been the *Friendship,* the vessel Jarrett had used in 1710.[23] We can, however, make certain assumptions as to its nature. That it was a sloop we can be certain due to the references from the log of the *Anglesea.*[24] Indeed, all but one of Jarrett's previous and subsequent slaving voyages took place on such vessels, and sloops were consistently favored by New York slavers throughout the period. The majority of those that left the city for Africa in the first half of the eighteenth century sailed under topsails, while a minority sailed under fore-and-aft rigs. It is also safe to assume that Jarrett's sloop would have been relatively small. New York slavers prior to 1748 averaged 59 tons. The *Amiable,* the sloop that Jarrett sailed from Antigua to the Gold Coast in 1709, was a 70-ton vessel, the *Flying Fame,* the sloop he captained in 1708, was 40 tons, while the *Phillipsburgh,* the only ship-rigged vessel that Jarrett is known to have taken to Africa, was 80 tons. Considering the relatively small number of slaves it was ultimately to deliver to New York, Jarrett's sloop in 1711 was likely to have been at the lower end of this spectrum, perhaps as little as 35 tons. Such light vessels were swift and maneuverable. They could outrun or evade those that sought to capture them, while their shallow drafts permitted them to hide in coastal creeks, rivers, and lagoons where larger ships were unable to follow. These concerns were no doubt a serious preoccupation for Jarrett during Queen Anne's War, when, as has already been seen, the West African coast was frequented by heavily armed French slavers and privateers. As to armament, New York slavers prior to 1748 typically carried six cannon. These were partly intended for defensive action, but also to turn on their enslaved cargo should they attempt to revolt. The *Phillipsburgh*, the only one of Jarrett's vessels for which such data survives, carried this number, although the sloop which he captained in 1711, being in all probability considerably smaller, was likely to have had fewer guns, perhaps two or four.[25]

Jarrett's sloop would also have had various adaptations for the Guinea trade. Slavers typically had wooden platforms built into their holds enabling them to maximize the number of enslaved people that could be crammed into the limited space. They also had a series of bulkheads below deck to separate the men from the women and children, a measure intended to prevent the spread of sexually transmitted diseases, while ventilation "gratings" were cut into the ship's sides fore and aft to allow fresh air into the hold in an attempt to reduce mortality. Another telltale sign of a slaver was a series of spars jutting out from the sides of the ship a few feet below the main deck. These supported a web of intersecting ropes which formed a netting intended to prevent the slaves from committing suicide by throwing themselves overboard. Once on the African coast, slave ship carpenters built large awnings above the main deck to provide shade for the enslaved people when they were given food or exercised. A final feature particular to slavers was the *barricado*, a word taken from the Portuguese, the first of the European nations to engage in the trade and the progenitors of many of its particularities. A strong wooden barrier ten feet high, the *barricado* was constructed across the width of the ship near the main mast and extended a few feet over each side. Intended to form a defensive barrier between the crew and their cargo, it was pierced with loopholes through which muskets or small cannon could be fired into the throng in the event of that most feared of events: a shipboard uprising.[26]

The sloop Jarrett took to the Gold Coast in 1711 would have had between seven and eight crew members. Such was typical of the small

A Dutch sloop of the late seventeenth-century. This vessel may be similar to the one in which Alan Jarrett sailed between West Africa and New York in 1711.. (*Metropolitan Museum of Art*)

vessels which conducted the slave trade out of New York prior to 1748 and would have been deemed sufficient to handle the sails and rigging while also guarding the fifty-five to sixty-five slaves that Jarrett was to purchase.[27] The crew would have included a carpenter, tasked with building the platforms and *barricado*, as well as the daily maintenance of the ship. A gunner may have been present to ensure the cannon, swivel guns, and muskets were in working condition and supplied with a sufficiency of powder and ball.[28] When Jarrett sailed the *Amiable* to the Gold and Slave Coasts in 1709, he also had a doctor on board.[29] Commonly carried on African voyages, particularly those financed by the RAC, the doctor ensured the slaves were fit and healthy on purchase and remained so until sold in the Americas. Doctors received "head money" on top of their wages of a shilling for each slave to survive.[30] Although one or two of Jarrett's crew may have been landsmen or cabin boys, the majority would have been either able or ordinary seamen, professional sailors who had spent a minimum of two years at sea. Slaver crews came from a variety of nations: English, Scotch, Irish, Dutch, Danes, Prussians, Sicilians, Swedes, Germans, French,

Asians, and even Africans were employed by contemporary British slavers. Motivations for joining such a perilous voyage were various. "By far the greatest part of them go from necessity," wrote Henry Ellison, a veteran of ten slaving voyages made in the second half of the eighteenth century. Many were "the refuse and dregs" of society, scraped up from the "prisons and glass houses," the advance of two to three months' wages enabling them to escape their debts. A few "restless youth" with romantic notions were mixed among them. William Richardson, a former collier, "fell in love" with a "fine" slaver he saw at dockside in London and joined up not caring where it was bound; William Butterworth, who sailed to Guinea on a Liverpool slaver in 1786, recalled that "others had risked their lives and fortune, therefore why not might I?" Others were tricked into signing "articles of agreement" after being plied with free liquor by unscrupulous dockside employment agents, known as crimps, while a few fled the law or went on board "of hopeless passion torn" to spite a lover who had jilted them.[31]

As the nature of Jarrett's sloop in 1711 and the composition of his crew are open to speculation, so too is his itinerary. We know that Jarrett was at Cape Coast Castle between March 18 and 23, and sailed westward at the end of that period. As mentioned above, it is also documented that Jarrett was at Dickscove, the RAC's most westerly fort on the Gold Coast, on April 6. Beyond these particulars, and the fact of his arrival in New York on June 4, the only other guidance comes from the negative evidence provided by the Cape Coast Castle account books which reveal that Jarrett neither bought nor sold trade goods at the fort while he was there, a fact which may suggest that the Frenchman did not buy any enslaved people from the castle either.[32] This raises the question of where they were purchased. There are several possibilities. The majority of European slave traders bought their cargoes from a large swath of the West African coastline stretching some 4,000 miles between the Senegal River and Angola. Most of the traders based out of British territory contemporary with Jarrett, however, concentrated between the Sierra Leone River and the Bight of Benin, an area roughly 1,200 miles in length. Given that individual slave traders typically specialized in specific areas and developed long-standing relationships with the traders who operated within them, we can narrow our search further. The only areas in which Jarrett is known to have operated during his thirteen-year career were the Gold and Slave Coasts of Lower Guinea. More specifically, Jarrett traded at two regions on the Gold Coast: Cape Coast Castle and the town of Accra, seventy miles to the east. On the Slave Coast, Jarrett had previously traded at Ouidah, a town on the far side of the Volta delta 130 miles beyond Accra.[33] Supporting the possibility that the slaves Jarrett purchased in 1711 were bought in these locations is the fact that the rebels of April 1712 were said to have been Coromantee and Papa, ethnicities associated with the Gold Coast and the western parts of the Slave Coast, respectively, the very same regions in which Jarrett had expertise.[34] This hypothesis is given further weight when one considers the central role played by both Accra and Ouidah in the British, Dutch, and Danish slave trades in the late seventeenth and early eighteenth centuries. Willem Bosman, a Dutch merchant and long-term resident of the Gold Coast employed by the West India Company, remarked that "the number of slaves sold . . . [at Accra] at least equals what are disposed of on the whole coast (Annamobo not excepted;) this Country being continually in War, with some of the circumjacent Nations, who are very populous, and from whom they take a vast number of Prisoners; most of whom they sell to the *Europeans*."[35] It is also documented that contemporary slave traders commonly combined visits to both the Gold and Slave Coasts. Eric Tilleman, a Danish factor resident at Fort Christiansborg in the final decade of the seventeenth century, observed that "though one often gets slaves on the Gold Coast, and in times of war even more than one wants, yet it is not certain enough to depend on, which is why the true *Slave Coast* is always sought by everyone."[36] There is no reason to believe that Alan Jarrett's itinerary in 1711 was an exception to this rule.

Events taking place in the hinterlands of both Accra and Ouidah during the time that Jarrett was present give further reason to believe that he may have purchased enslaved people at these locations. Both regions were dominated by the expansionist Akan polity of Akwamu, whose king, Akwonno, as we have already seen, had recently returned to his capital having spent part of the last three years campaigning against the Kwahu, an Akan people whose homelands lay to the west of the middle Volta River.[37] After a prolonged resistance, the Kwahu had been reduced to a state of vassalage by July 1710. In a process known as "eating the country," the majority of the population, especially the males of military age, would have subsequently been executed or enslaved, thus ensuring that the polity would be unable to rise up against Akwamu again in the future.[38] Given that the agents of King Akwonno who were charged with selling such captives operated out of the Accra region, it seems probable that Jarrett would have been able to purchase a cargo of enslaved people there at the time of his voyage. It is also possible that they originated from the polity of Kwahu. We know from records written by Governor Eric Lygaard of the Danish company fort of Christiansborg that "many English ships" were operating at Accra at the time. That they were ten percenters is certain as no RAC ships were present. Lygaard also informs us that the Akwamu agents had "acquired a taste for Barbadis brandy" (a reference to Caribbean rum) by the second half of 1710. In fact, Lygaard complained that "they buy nothing else" and implored his European agents to add "a taste of aniseed . . . to our corn brandy, and that it be [made] black [in imitation of the Caribbean product]; otherwise no more brandy can be sold here."[39] Jarrett had favored rum as a cargo when he had worked for the RAC out of Antigua.[40] If he had continued this habit when operating out of New York, a possibility given that potent New England rum was readily and cheaply available in New York City and was even more prized by the Akan than its Caribbean equivalent, then his cargo would have been popular with the Akwamu operating on the coast around Accra in late 1710 and early 1711.[41] It would also have been around this time that the coffles of enslaved Kwahu were arriving for sale, having been marched southward from their homeland through the savanna and forest alongside the Volta, through Ladoku, and then across the coastal thickets and grassland southwest to Accra, a journey of some two hundred miles.[42] One further factor lending credibility to this theory is the fact that Jarrett arrived in New York unseasonably early. While the city's slavers typically returned from the coast of Africa in July or August, in 1711 Jarrett reached New York at the very start of June. This would suggest that the Frenchman had conducted his business swiftly in Africa, leading one to surmise that there was a glut of slaves available for sale on the coast at the time.[43]

The possibility that at least some of Jarrett's human cargo was purchased at the slave trading depot of Ouidah on the Slave Coast is also supported by contemporary evidence: as previously stated, a New York source later claimed that the rebels of April 1712 included Papa, an ethnicity associated with the town and the surrounding region; Jarrett is known to have visited Ouidah on previous voyages and although there was a shortage of slaves in Ouidah in mid-1710, by early 1711 prices had fallen so much that the RAC's agent in town, William Hickes, was able to purchase one hundred, an unusually high number for a single transaction by Hickes in this period.[44] We also learn that after waiting several months for a RAC ship to arrive to transport the slaves he had purchased to Cape Coast Castle, Hickes despaired and sold them to Captain Lovell of the *Dorothea*, an English ten percenter.[45] Although Hickes makes no mention of Jarrett, the fact that another English ten percenter was loading slaves at Ouidah at the time makes it plausible that Jarrett did likewise. It is also possible that the slaves that Hickes and others purchased at Ouidah in early 1711 may have come from Kwahu. Like Accra, Ouidah at the time of Jarrett's voyage was also overseen by the polity of Akwamu, and the prisoners of war captured following the capitulation of Kwahu may have been sold out of both ports. Although slaves purchased from Ouidah were known as Papas to traders like Alan Jarrett and may have been labeled as such by those who eventually purchased them in the Americas, this was often a reference to the place where they were purchased on the African coast rather than to the region from which they had originated, something about which most European traders knew little and cared less. Furthermore, many of the polities to the east of the River Volta, including Little Popo, the town after which the Europeans named the Papa, were founded by Akan refugees fleeing expansionist states such as Akwamu in the latter part of the seventeenth century and the first years of the eighteenth.[46] Thus, even though Jarrett may well have purchased enslaved people at two different ports on the Gold and Slave Coasts, and believed that they were of different ethnicities, the men, women, and children who ended up in the hold of his sloop may have originated from the same polity.

REGARDLESS OF EXACTLY WHERE the enslaved people Jarrett purchased came from, their initial experience of enslavement would have followed long-established patterns. Contemporary sources agree that most enslaved people sold on both the Gold Coast and the Slave Coast came from the interior.[47] The first part of their experience, therefore, long before they fell into the hands of European traders such as Alan Jarrett, consisted of a debilitating trek to the coast which could last weeks or even months. Bound together with twisted vines and animal hide rope, the enslaved were formed into human chains known as coffles. These columns marched toward the coast single file along the trade routes which twisted through the bush and scrubland of the interior. Coffles typically changed hands several times as various middlemen sold the slaves to one another.[48] Mahommah Gardo Baquaqua, a young man enslaved in the north of modern-day Benin in the early nineteenth century, for example, was sold by "7 or 8" different traders before reaching the Slave Coast.[49] Typically, coffles grew in size as they neared the sea, as new slaves were incorporated. As well as those captured in battle, debtors were sold into slavery. Some traders even pawned family members to obtain goods, while orphans or those accused of extramarital transgressions, sexual crimes, or witchcraft were also enslaved. Other enslaved people were kidnapped, either by small gangs or large state-sponsored operations, such as the *sikadings* deployed by the Akwamu. Belinda Royall, a twelve-year-old Akan from the upper Volta River, was snatched in the 1720s as her parents were praying at a nearby sacred grove; and Olaudah Equiano, a ten-year-old Igbo from the southeast of modern-day Nigeria, was taken with his sister by opportunists who snuck into their yard at some point around 1755.[50]

Many slaves died en route to the coast. According to Raymond Jalamá, a Portuguese trader of the late eighteenth century, mortality rates could rise as high as 50 percent during the journey.[51] The enslaved people suffered from hunger, dehydration, exhaustion, and psychological trauma. Any who dropped by the wayside were likely to be killed or left for wild animals. Jackals, which contemporaries claimed were "so bold . . . [as to] seize . . . and devour . . . whatever comes in . . . [their] way, whether Man or Beast," roamed the plains of Akwamu along with "droves" of "baboons" the size "of . . . large mastiff dog[s]," while hyenas were said to prey on those abandoned inland from Ouidah.[52]

Perhaps the most frightening part of the entire experience for the enslaved people was when they arrived at the coast. For many, this was their first sight of the ocean. The vast open stretch of water symbolized irreversible change. "When we arrived," Mahommah Gardo Baquaqua recalled, "I began to give up . . . [on] getting back to my home again . . . the last ray seemed fading away, and my heart felt sad and weary within me, as I thought of my mother, whom I loved most tenderly, and the thought of never more beholding her, added very much to my perplexities."[53] Once at the coast, the slaves were sold to Europeans. Some were exchanged for trade goods, the most common items being textiles made in the mill towns of northern England, which went by a host of names such as annabasses, boysadoes, and perpetuanas, each of different quality and price. Other trade goods included knives, pewter bowls, iron bars, muskets, and gunpowder. Some traders used gold or cowrie shells, a form of currency long used on the West African coast, while others, as discussed above, used rum.[54]

How many slaves Alan Jarrett bought in 1711 is open to speculation. We know that fifty-five slaves were imported directly from Africa into New York in 1711 and that Jarrett's was the only vessel recorded as making such a voyage that year.[55] We can assume, therefore, taking into account a typical mortality rate for the Middle Passage of 10 to 12 percent, that Jarrett purchased about sixty enslaved people on the Gold and Slave Coasts in the first three months of 1711.[56] A second question to consider is the proportion of men, women, and children. Documents pertaining to Jarrett's previous voyages may provide some illumination. When captain of the *Flying Fame* in 1708 and the *Amiable* in 1709, Jarrett purchased fourteen men for every five women and one child.[57] It must be remembered, however, that these voyages were made for the RAC. Furthermore, Jarrett was buying for the Antiguan rather than the New York market, and therefore required individuals better suited for agricultural duties rather than domestic and trade roles. A further piece of circumstantial evidence, however, suggests that the gender ratio of the slaves Jarrett carried to New York in 1711 may well have been similar to that of his previous voyages. According to the city censuses of 1703 and 1712, the Black population of New York grew from 630 to 972 in the period, an increase of 342. Although births and deaths would have played some role, the most pertinent factor was imports. The number recorded in the period was 233, of which 209 came directly from Africa, and all but twenty-four were transported to New York City by Alan Jarrett on the three voyages he made in 1710, 1711, and 1712. As the censuses divide the "negroes" by gender, we can also see that there were 219 more enslaved Black men living in the city in 1712 than in 1703, a figure which accounts for 64 percent of the total enslaved population increase of 342. There-fore, it seems likely that of the sixty or so enslaved people Jarrett pur-chased in 1711 on the Gold and Slave Coasts, perhaps forty were men, fifteen were women, and five were children.[58]

For the enslaved men, women, and children Jarrett purchased, re-gardless of their exact numbers, the trip from the shore to the ship, undertaken in large dugout canoes with African crews, would have been highly perilous. Violent surf characterized the shoreline of the Gold and Slave Coasts, and the canoes were frequently upset, pitching their terrified occupants into the breakers, where those not drowned were sometimes eaten by sharks.[59] For the ones who made it aboard, fresh perils lay in store. Many of the enslaved, when they first caught sight of the white men who were to be their new jailors, believed they were devils or "bad spirits" who intended to eat them. "Their com-plexions . . . their long hair . . . and the language they spoke, which was very different from any I had ever heard confirmed me in this be-lief," Olaudah Equiano recalled. "When I looked round the ship too, and saw a large furnace of copper boiling, and a multitude of black people of every description chained together, everyone of their coun-tenances expressing dejection and sorrow, I no longer doubted of my fate, and, quite overpowered with horror and anguish, I fell motionless on the deck and fainted. When I recovered, I found some black people about me who I believed were some of those who brought me on board . . . I asked them if we were not to be eaten by those white men with horrible looks, red faces, and long hair?"[60]

Having loaded his cargo, Jarrett upped anchor at some point in early March or late February 1711. Sailing westward, he reached Cape Coast Castle in mid-March. There he paused for at least eight days, most likely to fill his sloop's casks with fresh water from the cavernous tanks hollowed out of the solid rock on which the fort rested. On March 23, Jarrett upped anchor once more. Sailing westward, in early April he made his final stop on the Gold Coast—at the RAC fort of Dickscove. Perhaps his sloop had sprung its bowsprit or was in need of some other repair, or maybe Jarrett wanted to purchase corn, dried fish, palm oil, malaguetta pepper, or some other foodstuff for his captives during the Middle Passage. On April 6, or shortly afterward, Jarrett sailed from Dickscove for New York.⁶¹ From the slaver's point of view, the first stages of the homeward journey were the most perilous. As many as one in ten slave ships experienced uprisings, most of which took place within sight of the African coastline.⁶² Once their homeland was out of view, the slaves grew despondent and the likelihood of rebellion diminished. As such, security measures on board were tightest during the first few days of the voyage, as Captain Thomas Phillips, an RAC captain who carried seven hundred slaves from the Gold Coast and Ouidah to Jamaica in 1693 on the 450-ton *Hannibal*, explained. "We shackle the men two and two, while we lie in port, and in sight of their own country, for 'tis then that they attempt to make their escape and mutiny; to prevent which we always keep centinels upon the hatchways, and have a chest of small arms, ready loaden and prim'd, constantly lying at hand along the quarter deck, together with some granada shells; and two of our quarter-deck guns, pointing on the deck thence, and two more out of the steerage, the door of which is always kept shut, and well barr'd."⁶³

While Jarrett was on the West African coast in 1710 and 1711, we know that at least one shipboard slave rising occurred. The incident took place on the *Joseph Galley*, a 120-ton ten percenter commanded by Captain John Foster, an experienced slave trader with at least five successful voyages behind him who had sailed from London under convoy of HMS *Anglesea* and *Fowey*. Having purchased over 100 slaves on the Windward Coast, Foster called in at Cape Coast Castle in January 1711 before proceeding to the town of Annamaboe where he bought another 200 or more enslaved people. While the *Joseph Galley* was at anchor offshore Annamaboe the revolt occurred. Although "dangerously wounded" in the fighting, Foster recovered control of the ship. How many of his crew were killed or wounded is unknown, as is the number of slaves who lost their lives, but by the time the *Joseph* reached Jamaica at the end of April 1711, 335 of the 388 enslaved people who embarked remained alive, figures that suggest the uprising was a relatively minor one.[64] Other shipboard slave risings were more successful. In January 1685 off Grand Popo, a town on the west bank of the Volta River, the *Chartlon* was lying at anchor offshore when 100 slaves on board broke free. Seven of eight crew were killed, while the captain, John Layton, "drown'd," perhaps while attempting to escape. According to a report written by an RAC factor, the slaves "affterwards cut the cable, which occasioned [the *Charlton's*] running ashoar, and [being] staved all to pieces." The rebels escaped into the interior while the ship's gold was looted by the local "Attome people," much to the RAC's chagrin.[65]

Once slavers left the African coastline, the chances of a rising diminished, and life onboard for the crew became routine. The able seamen took it in turns to man the sails and rigging, while the ordinaries and landsmen spent their time as prison guards, herding their human cargo at gunpoint around different sections of the ship. The women and children were often allowed to spend their days on the main deck and at times were even permitted to sleep among the sailors or in the open. The enslaved men spent most of the voyage confined below deck where conditions were appalling as Equiano recalled.

I was soon put down under the decks, and there I received such a salutation in my nostrils that I had never experienced in my life; so that with the loathsomeness of the stench, and crying together, I became so sick and low that I . . . wished for the last friend, Death, to relieve me. . . . The closeness of the place, and the heat of the climate, added to the number in the ship, which was so crowded that each had scarcely room to turn himself, almost suffocated us. This produced copious perspirations, so that the air soon became unfit for respiration, from a variety of loathsome smells. . . . This wretched situation was . . . aggravated by the galling of the chains, now become unsupportable; and the filth of the necessary tubs, into which the children often fell, and were almost suffocated. The . . . groans of the dying, rendered the whole a scene of horror almost inconceivable.[66]

A report based on evidence given in 1791 by Alexander Falconbridge, a ship's doctor who made four slaving voyages to the African coast, adds more detail. "When employed in stowing the slaves," the report revealed, "[Falconbridge] made the most of the room and *wedged them in.* They had not so much room *as a man in his coffin* either in length or breadth. It was impossible for them to turn or shift with any degree of ease. He had often occasion to go from one side of their rooms to the other, in which case he always took off his shoes, but could not avoid pinching them; he has the marks on his feet where they bit and scratched him. . . . In every voyage when the ship was full they complained of heat and want of air. . . . He was never among them for ten minutes below together, but his shirt was as wet as if dipt in water." Henry Ellison, another slaver who contributed to the abolitionists' report, recalled that the heat and perspiration below decks was so intense that he often saw steam coming up through the gratings "like a furnace."[67]

While the enslaved men were below deck, the enslaved women were vulnerable to the depredations of the crew. John Newton, a slave ship captain turned evangelical preacher who found fame with the publication of the hymn "Amazing Grace," admitted such lurid details only late in life. "When the women and girls are taken board a ship, naked, trembling, terrified . . . they are often exposed to the wanton rudeness of white savages. . . . The prey is divided upon the spot. Resistance or refusal, would be utterly in vain."[68] James Field Stanfield, a slaver who sailed from the Bight of Benin to Jamaica on the *True Blue* in 1775, was equally terse. In recalling the crimes of his captain, David Wilson, who repeatedly raped "an unfortunate female slave," Stanfield confessed, "I cannot express it in any words . . . [though it was] too atrocious and bloody to be passed over in silence."[69]

At mealtimes, the enslaved men were often allowed on the main deck. On the *Hannibal*, Captain Phillips's men served "dabbadab," a mixture of ground corn, water, salt, palm oil, and malagueta pepper. All was "boil'd well in a large copper furnace; till 'tis as thick as a pudding," Phillips recalled. Two portions were doled out daily, "at 10 in the morning and 4 in the evening, which is the time they are aptest to mutiny being all upon deck," Phillips opined, "therefore all of that time, what of our men who are not employ'd in distributing their victuals to them, and settling them, stand to their arms; and some with lighted matches at the great guns that yawn upon them, loaden with partridge, till they have done and gone down to their kennels between decks." While Phillips assured his readers that the slaves on the *Hannibal* "love[d]" their food "extremely" and received it by "beating their breast . . . and crying Pram! Pram!" which means, as Phillips explained, "Very good!", other accounts tell a different tale.[70] Equiano wrote that he "became so sick and low" after being confined below deck that he "was unable to eat, nor had the least desire to taste anything." Slavers would not countenance such behavior. "On my refusing to eat," Equiano recalled, "one of [the crew] . . . held me fast by the hands, and laid me across . . . the windlass, and tied my feet, while the other flogged me severely."[71] For persistent offenders, slavers used thumbscrews to induce "good behaviour" or the application of metal tongs heated in the fire; another tool was the *speculum oris*, a metal device whose twin arms could be used to pry open a would-be hunger-striker's jaws sufficiently to allow the force feeding of a thin gruel.[72]

In another effort to maintain the slaves in good condition, captains would enforce an exercise regime. This typically took the form of "dancing," as Captain Phillips explained. "We often at sea in the evenings would let the slaves come up into the sun to air themselves, and make them jump or dance for an hour or two to our bag-pipes, harp, and fiddle, by which exercise to preserve them in health." Many captains also supplied the enslaved with rum, tobacco, and pipes in the belief that such measures would improve their health. Nevertheless, sickness was rife, particularly dysentery, or the "bloody flux," which spread with alarming rapidity in the unsanitary conditions. Unable to force their way past their fellow captives to reach the "necessary tubs," many of those afflicted chose to "ease themselves" where they lay. During one outbreak, Doctor Falconbridge found the floors below decks "so covered with the blood and mucus . . . that [the hold] . . . resembled a slaughter house. It is not in the power of the human imagination, to picture to itself a situation more dreadful," he opined.[73]

Mortality rates among slaves during the Middle Passage at the time of Jarrett's voyage were typically in the region of 12 percent to 15 percent but could rise much higher. By the time the *Hannibal* reached Barbados, two months and eleven days after leaving Africa, for example, 320 of the 700 enslaved people onboard and 14 crew had died of the "white flux." The sickness "was so violent and inveterate," Phillips complained, "that no medicine would in the least check it . . . [and] when any . . . were seiz'd with it, we esteem'd him a dead man, as he generally proved." Eight other enslaved people died of smallpox resulting in an overall mortality rate of nearly 47 percent. Phillips was most put out. "After all our pains and care to give them their messes in due order and . . . enduring so much misery and stench so long among a parcel of creatures nastier than swine . . . all our expectations [were] . . . defeated by their mortality," he complained.[74]

Such cruelty is difficult to comprehend. Nevertheless, how it came to be commonplace among those who plied the African trade can be better understood when one considers the psychology of the slaver. At the end of the eighteenth century, as the abolitionist movement gathered pace in Britain, the effects of involvement in the slave trade were studied and the resulting dehumanization of both the enslaved people and the crews who carried them were revealed. Thomas Clarkson, a young Englishman at the forefront of the abolitionist movement, observed that those sailors who only undertook one Guinea voyage "usually escaped the disease of a hardened heart. But if they went a second and a third time . . . it was impossible for them to . . . carry away men and women by force, to keep them in chains, to see their tears . . . without contracting those habits of moroseness, and cruelty which would brutalize their nature."[75] Such repeated exposure to misery hardened those involved. Equiano also recognized this phenomenon. "Such a tendency has the slave-trade to debauch men's minds, and harden them to every feeling of humanity," he declared in his 1789 memoir. "For I will not suppose that the dealers in slaves are born worse than other men—No! it is the fatality of this mistaken avarice, that it corrupts the milk of human kindness, and turns it into gall. And," Equaino was fair enough to offer, "had the pursuits of those men been different, they might have been as generous, as tenderhearted, and just, as they are unfeeling, rapacious, and cruel."[76]

ENSLAVED PEOPLE utilized various forms of resistance. One of the most common was suicide. An Akan transported with his entire family on the slave ship *Brooks* in 1784 repeatedly attempted to cut his own throat. Examining the "ragged edges" around the wound and hav-

ing noted that the man's fingers were covered in blood, Thomas Trot-
ter, the ship's physician, concluded that he had attempted to rip open
his throat with his own fingernails. While being treated, the man
stated that "he would never go with white men." He proved doggedly
resolute. His hands were bound "to prevent any further attempt," but
he "refused all sustenance, and died in about a week or ten days afterwards of mere want of food."[77] Other slaves strangled themselves with
scraps of cloth or rope-yarn, but the most common way of committing
suicide was by jumping overboard. Despite the netting and the crew's
constant vigilance, such attempts were frequent and often successful.
That this behavior was also somewhat infectious is apparent in the
following instance related by Olaudah Equiano. "One day, when we
had a smooth sea, and moderate wind, two of my wearied countrymen, who were chained together . . . preferring death to such a life of
misery, somehow made through the nettings, and jumped into the sea:
immediately another quite dejected fellow, who, on account of his illness, was suffered to be out of irons, also followed their example, and
I believe many more would very soon have done the same, if they had
not been prevented by the ship's crew, who were instantly alarmed.
Those of us that were the most active were, in a moment, put down
under the deck; and there was such a noise and confusion among the
people of the ship as I never heard before, to stop her, and get the boat
out to go after the slaves [who had thrown themselves overboard].
However, two of the wretches were drowned, but they got the other,
and afterwards flogged him unmercifully, for thus attempting to prefer
death to slavery."[78]

One of the reasons why suicide was so common was that many
West Africans, including the Akan, believed that death was a way of
returning home. No stigma was attached to suicide under such circumstances, and it was commonly held that the medium which best
facilitated the passage home of one's soul, or *kra*, was water. If the
body of a dead Akan, whether a suicide or not, was to fall into the
hands of his or her enemies, however, it was also believed that such
enemies could cause the dead person's soul great pain and distress in
the afterlife by removing the head and "mak[ing] . . . sport of it,
wip[ing] . . . their feet on their jawbone of the murdered [man],
pound[ing] on the skull, spit[ting] on it, etc.," as Ludewig Rømer, a

Danish merchant resident at Fort Christiansborg between 1739 and 1749, explained in his *Reliable Account of the Coast of Guinea.*[79] On learning of such beliefs, some slave ship captains publicly mutilated the bodies of suicides to deter the other enslaved people on board from imitating their example. This measure did not always have the desired effect, however, as Ecroide Claxton, another slave ship physician of the late eighteenth century, related. "The captain cut off the heads of those who died, intimating to [the surviving slaves] . . . that if determined to go [back to their country], they must return without the[m]." The captain then ordered his carpenter to begin striking off the heads of the dead with his hatchet, when one of those gathered to witness the event "with a violent exertion got loose, and flying to the place where the nettings had been unloosed, in order to empty the [necessary] tubs, he darted overboard. The ship brought to, and a man was placed in the main chains to catch him, which he perceiving, dived under water, and rising again at a distance from the ship, made signs, which words cannot describe, *expressive of his happiness in escaping*. He then went down, and was seen no more."[80]

The most spectacular form of suicide on board slave ships was also the rarest. In January 1773, revolting slaves on the *New Britannia* cut their way through the bulkheads of the gun room where they armed themselves and fought off the attacks of the crew for more than an hour, before setting fire to the ship's magazine. Almost everyone on board, some three hundred in total, were killed in the explosion.[81] A similar, though foiled, attempt was made on board the ship that carried Ottobah Cugoano, an Akan enslaved as a child in the mid-eighteenth century. "When we found ourselves at last taken away [from Cape Coast Castle on board a slaver bound for Grenada]," Cugoano recalled, "death was more preferable than life; and a plan was concerted among us, that we might burn and blow up the ship, and to perish all together in the flames: but we were betrayed by one of our own countrywomen, who slept with some of the headmen of the ship, for it was common for the dirty filthy sailors to take the African women and lie upon their bodies; but the men were chained and pent up in holes. It was the women and boys which were to burn the ship, with the approbation and groans of the rest; though that was prevented, the discovery was likewise a cruel bloody scene."[82]

Typically, slave resistance was less dramatic. Zachary Macaulay, an abolitionist who traveled on a Liverpudlian slaver bound for the West Indies from the coast of Sierra Leone in 1795, wrote a journal which provides a daily account of such occurrences.

[May] 7th. I observed one woman handcuffed, and inquired the cause. I found she had lately attempted to drown herself, and had been caught by the leg just as she had thrown herself over the side.... [May] 8th. The men-slaves were brought on deck for the first time since our sailing.... While the ship was on the coast they had made an unsuccessful attempt to get possession of her ... the two ringleaders are now chained to each other by the neck; besides having on the same fetters which are worn by the others.... [May] 23rd. I observed to-day, as on former occasions, several of the slaves rejecting their food. The officer on duty began to threaten and shake his cat [o' nine tails] at such as refused to eat ... the Slaves then made a shew of eating by putting a little rice into their mouths; but whenever the officer's back was turned, they threw it into the sea.

At the end of his journal, which would later serve as evidence for the abolitionist movement in Britain, Macaulay summed up his reactions to having witnessed the conditions the slaves had endured on board. "Their cup is full of pure, unmingled sorrow," he opined. "Eight died during the three weeks I was on board."[83]

What resistance occurred on board Alan Jarrett's sloop as it cut across the Atlantic toward New York City between April and June 1711 is unknown. What seems certain, however, is that the sixty or so slaves Jarrett carried formed close bonds as a result of their shared experiences. Even if they had not known each other previously, by the time they reached New York the fifty-five individuals who survived had become "shipmates"—an attachment which could endure for decades after arrival in the New World. Thomas Winterbottom, a physician who worked in the colony of ex-slaves established in Sierra Leone in the early 1790s as part of the abolitionist movement, wrote about the significance of the relationship. "It is worthy of remark," he began, "that those unfortunate people who have gone to the [Americas] ... in the same vessel, ever after retain for each other a strong and tender affection: with them the term ship-mate is almost equivalent to that of brother or sister." Having been torn from their homes in Africa and having left behind all they had known and held dear, those who shared and survived the horrors of the Middle Passage created a bond. Such a bond would be a source of unity and strength for the enslaved men and women imprisoned below decks on Jarrett's sloop once they arrived in New York. It would enable them to act in concert and resist those that oppressed them, as the inhabitants of New York were soon to discover.[84]

As SLAVERS DREW NEAR their destinations, the enslaved men, women, and children were prepared for sale. This involved an improvement in their treatment and diet and various cosmetic touches intended to enhance their appearance and therefore increase their value. About ten days before the ship's arrival, the constraints were removed from the enslaved men's wrists and ankles to allow the sores produced from the chafing of the metal to heal. The men's beards and heads were shaved; gray hairs were plucked out or dyed black. A lunar caustic was used to remove sores and extra rations were provided, often including tobacco or rum, a consideration thought to improve the slaves' health and mental well-being. Finally, just before arrival, the enslaved people were rubbed down with palm oil to give their skin a luxuriant shine.[85]

ALAN JARRETT's SLOOP reached New York City on June 4, 1711. While the Frenchman was no doubt pleased to complete yet another successful voyage, for those below deck it was a stressful experience. Their thoughts may well have been similar to Olaudah Equiano's when he first set eyes on the New World. "At last we came in sight of the island of Barbados," he wrote many years later,

at which the whites on board gave a great shout, and made signs of joy to us. We did not know what to think of this; but as the vessel drew closer we plainly saw the harbour, and other ships of different kinds and sizes: and we soon anchored amongst them. . . . We were conducted immediately to the merchant's yard, where we were all pent up together like so many sheep in a fold, without regard to sex or age. As every object was new to me, every thing I saw filled me with surprise. What struck me first was, that the houses were built with bricks, in stories, and in every other respect different from those I had seen in Africa: but I was still more astonished on seeing people on horseback.

As both brick-built multistory buildings and horses were unknown in the interior of the Gold and Slave Coasts, perhaps the slaves that Jarrett carried to New York were equally surprised.[86]

JARRETT WOULD HAVE SOLD the enslaved people he had carried from Africa soon after his arrival. Previously, the Frenchman would have allowed news of the upcoming event to circulate as well as giving the men, women, and children he had purchased a few days onshore to recover from the rigors of the Middle Passage. We know that posters were often used by slavers to promote upcoming sales, and that advertisements were placed in the city newspapers: one example announced the sale of "a Parcel of Likely Negro Men and Women also Negro boys and girls." Some included vague references as to the origin of the slaves: "imported from Africa" or "from Guinea" or "the Gambia."[87] The fact that Jarrett had purchased his slaves from the Gold and Slave Coasts would have been a major selling point and was no doubt exploited. Akan, or Coromantee as they were known in the English-speaking Americas, were highly prized. "They are . . . the best and most faithful [of all slaves]," opined Christopher Coddrington, the former governor of Antigua, "[and] grateful and obedient to a kind master."[88] Captain Phillips of the *Hannibal* agreed. "[The] gold coast negroes . . . are very bold, brave and sensible," he wrote, adding that they "yield 3 or 4 l. a head more than" other Africans. The Papa from the Slave Coast, by comparison, were thought "docile and agreeable, although not as hard working as the Coromantee."[89]

Jarrett's sale may have taken place in a number of locations. In New York slaves were sold on board ship; at brokers' offices, on the wharf; or at the Meal Market on the Wall Street slip on the bank of the East River, a location which was also appointed for the hiring of slaves by the Common Council in November 1711. Although these are the only known locations for slave sales in the city, there may have been many others. In Philadelphia, the firm of Wiling and Morris sold slaves "at

New York slave market about 1730, an early twentieth-century drawing of how a slave market along New York's East River may have appeared at the time. (*New York Public Libary*)

their store front in Front-Street," while Josiah Franklin and William Nichols held "negro auctions" in their taverns in Boston.[90]

Slave sales were carried out by various methods. "They are sold either by scramble or by vendue, (i.e.) publick auction, or by lots," British abolitionists stated in a 1791 report. Auctions were typically used to sell "the *refuse*, or sickly slaves," the report continued. "These are in such a state of health, that they sell . . . *greatly under price*."[91] In this way bargains could be picked up, such as the five "dropsical Negro males" Jarrett sold in Antigua from the *Flying Fame* in 1708 for £10 each.[92] Another source on "refuse slaves," written by RAC agents in 1680 in Barbados, noted that "[some were] Old some Poore & Blind and [there were] many burst ones, Which with the little esteeme those Negroes have here, made them ly long on our hands & goe off at low prices."[93] Although there was a risk that such slaves would die shortly after sale, some dealers specialized in their purchase, treating them until they regained their health and then selling them on for a profit.[94] In the early 1690s, the most common method of auction used by the RAC was "sale by the inch of candle." Slaves were sold individually at a previously specified time and place. The process took the form of an ascending-bid auction with the time for bidding dictated by the time it took a candle to burn down one inch. This method guaranteed a minimum amount of time for bidding and thus prevented the auctioneer from making a quick sale to a favored customer.[95]

The second method, sale by lots, was often used when enslaved people were imported directly from Africa, rather than with those who had come to North America via the West Indies. While the latter were known commodities, about whom former owners could supply information which would affect their sale price, such as whether or not they had attempted to escape captivity or if they had any specialist skills such as metal working or boat handling, virtually nothing would have been known about recent arrivals from Africa. As such they could be sold in groups and whether a buyer purchased "good" slaves or "bad" would be a matter of chance. While prices were low when enslaved people were sold in this way, the method also had certain advantages for the sellers: namely speed and expediency. Also, the less scrupulous could hide "refuse negroes" among their healthier peers.[96]

Another method, considered "the common mode in America" by the 1780s, was the scramble.[97] Potential purchasers were first permitted to examine the slaves. They inspected their teeth, felt the plumpness of their muscles, and checked their genitalia for signs of sexually transmitted disease. Another sought-after sign was callused hands, an indication that a slave was used to hard work and therefore more valuable, while Thomas Thistlewood, an eighteenth-century Jamaican overseer, maintained that the most desirable slaves had "a good Calf to their Leg and a small or moderate sized Foot." For the enslaved people themselves, such examinations were confusing and distressing as Olaudah Equiano recalled. "They put us in separate parcels, and examined us attentively," he later wrote. "They also made us jump, and pointed to the land, signifying we were to go there. We thought by this we should be eaten by these ugly men, as they appeared to us; and, when soon after we were all put down under the deck again, there was much dread and trembling among us, and nothing but bitter cries to be heard all the night from these apprehensions, insomuch that at last the white people got some old slaves from the land to pacify us. They told us we were not to be eaten, but to work, and were soon to go on land, where we should see many of our country people."[98]

After such preliminaries had been completed, the scramble took place. Doctor Falconbridge, one of the witnesses for the abolitionists' report quoted above, provided the following description. "The ship was darkened with sails, and covered round," he recalled. "The men slaves were placed on the main deck, and the women on the quarter deck. The purchasers on shore were informed a gun would be fired when they were ready to open the sale. A great number of people [then] came on board with tallies or cards in their hands, with their own names on them, and rushed through the barricade door with the ferocity of brutes. Some had three or four handkerchiefs tied together, to encircle as many as they thought fit for their purpose." Such methods were extremely frightening for the enslaved people involved. "In the yard at Grenada, where another of [Falconbridge's] ships . . . sold by scramble," the report continues, "the women were so terrified, that several of them got out of the yard, and ran about St. George's town as if they were mad"; and when a scramble took place on board the *Tryal* in 1784 we are informed that "forty or fifty of the slaves leaped into the sea."[99] Equiano provides a description from the slaves' perspective. "The buyers rush at once into . . . where the slaves are confined and make that choice of parcel they like best. . . . In this manner, without scruple, are relations and friends separated, most of them never to see each other again. I remember in the vessel in which I was brought over, there were several brothers, who, in the sale, were sold in different lots; . . . it was very moving . . . to see and hear their cries at parting."[100]

Although we do not know which method Jarrett used to sell his human cargo in 1711, we can speculate as to which purchasers were present at the sale. The most likely candidate was Rip Van Dam. As well as being the only individual who owned more than one of the slaves who would be executed in the aftermath of the revolt of April 1712, Van Dam was also the man most likely to have financed Jarrett's voyage and relocation to New York from Antigua. It seems likely that Van Dam purchased at least two enslaved men at Jarrett's sale: Quack and Quash both had Akan day names. Walter Thong was also likely to have been present. A freeman of New York since 1702, Thong had been elected alderman for the South Ward on three successive occasions from 1708 to 1712 and was an ensign in the 3rd company of the city militia. More significantly, having married Sara Van Dam prior to 1705, Thong was Rip Van Dam's son-in-law. The two merchants frequently engaged in mutually beneficial business dealings and Thong may also have been a shareholder in Jarrett's 1711 voyage. Regardless, we do know that at some stage prior to April 1712 Thong would come to own Quacko, another of the slaves implicated in the revolt. Four other city merchants, all of French Huguenot origin, were also likely to have been among the buyers that day. Peter Morin, a merchant and glazier who owned a property on Queen Street purchased an enslaved man he would name Caesar; Andrew Stuckey bought an enslaved man he would give the name of Hannibal; while John Barberie, who lived on Broadway and was a member of the governor's council, purchased a man called Mingo. All four enslaved Africans would hang in the aftermath of April 1712.[101]

Another likely purchaser was Alan Jarrett himself. We know that the slaver bought one person from each of the cargoes he had transported to Antigua for the RAC, a girl purchased for £30 from the *Flying Fame*, and a man bought for £50 from the *Amiable*. Jarrett was also the owner of one of the rebels executed in 1712.[102] That Claus was among the first to be condemned and the fact that he would be executed by the particularly brutal punishment of being broken on the wheel also suggests that he may have been one of the leaders of the revolt.[103] Another potential buyer that day was Gysbert Vaninburgh, a Dutch baker who at some stage prior to April 1712 purchased an enslaved woman he would name Abigail—the only woman to be executed for participation in the revolt.[104] A victualler named Johannes Dehonneur who owned a property on the junction of Queen and Wall Streets in the city's East Ward may also have been present. Prior to April 1712 Dehonneur acquired an enslaved man he called Tom.[105] The two other Toms who would be executed as a result of the revolt, belonged to David Lyell, a Scottish Quaker who worked as a goldsmith, and Nicholas Roosevelt, a bolter, alderman of the West Ward, and the ancestor of two future presidents of the United Sates. Both Lyell and Roosevelt may have been among the crowd at Jarrett's sale.[106] Two other possible purchasers were John Cure, a father of nine who lived in the West Ward and bought a future rebel whom he named Toby, and Ruth Sheppard, the widow of a former bolter and the owner of an enslaved man she would name Dave Furnis, one of three future rebels who would be burned to death.[107] Another likely buyer was Abraham Provoost, a minor member of an extensive and prominent Dutch family which had relocated from Albany to New York City's North and Dock Wards. Provoost, who worked as a boatman on the city's quayside, purchased Quacko, one of the three rebels who would be burned at the stake; Harmanus Burger, an "antient and lame" blacksmith, bought a boy he would name Dick; and Peter Vantilborough, a baker, purchased Cuffee, or Kofi, an Akan whose dayname indicated he was born on a Friday.[108] An enslaved woman who would come to be known as Sarah was acquired by the cordwainer Stophel Pels; Richard Ray, yet another merchant, bought an enslaved man he named Titus; and Peter Fauconnier, a fifty-two-year-old who had held the position of receiver general under Lord Cornbury, purchased an enslaved man who would come to be known as Sam.[109]

VERY LITTLE IS KNOWN of the rebels' lives in the New World between the moment of their arrival and the revolt of April 1712. We know that most were purchased by New Yorkers who lived in the East, West, and Dock Wards, and therefore would have had plenty of opportunities to maintain the bonds they had established during the Middle Passage. It is likely that these friendships, military brotherhoods, and family ties were further strengthened in the months between June 1711 and April 1712. Many of the rebels no doubt worked together, or met at the city water pumps, or by the dockside during this ten-month period.[110] They would also have interacted with the slaves Jarrett had brought from the Gold Coast in 1710. The newcomers would have informed the older hands of the news from the Gold Coast, the continuing campaigns of Akwonno and the defeat of the Kwahu, while they in their turn perhaps learned about the life of a slave in New York, or were aided in their attempts to acquire a modicum of English. At some stage, no doubt, these conversations would have turned to the subject of revenge. Aside from such speculation, little more can be said for certain about the rebels' activities in New York prior to the revolt. The chapter that follows is an attempt to bridge this gap. By exploring what is known about enslaved people in the city throughout the colonial period, by examining statistics and highlighting case studies, we can perhaps get a glimpse of the range of experiences that the rebels of 1712 may have had. We may also reach a better understanding of how their relationships developed, and of what opportunities they may have had to meet and collude, as well as gaining an insight into the reasons behind their decision to revolt the following spring.

Enslaved in New York

New York City and Environs

1703–1712

Akoa mpaw wura.
A slave does not choose his master.
—Akan proverb

SLAVERY IN COLONIAL NEW YORK CITY was marked by its diversity and contradictions. The enslaved toiled at menial, backbreaking tasks; they worked in highly skilled roles; they were abused, distrusted, and despised; they were respected and empowered in some cases despite their bondage. Slaves were beaten and murdered by their masters; they were well treated, trained, and educated, well fed and well clothed. Some whites saw New York City's enslaved people as heretics, beasts, criminals, and devil worshippers; for others they were companions, sexual objects, surrogates to their children, drinking buddies, or partners in crime. Some slaves lived in damp, dark accommodations unfit for livestock; others had private rooms, allotments where they could grow their own vegetables, and hunted and foraged for wild food. Enslaved persons in New York were subject to laws designed to control and restrict their every movement. They suffered a variety of horrendous punishments imposed by the colony's courts. Concurrently, some enjoyed considerable freedom of movement, travelled widely, and gathered with other Blacks, free and enslaved alike, to drink, sing, play music, and dance. A few slaves were barely occupied by their masters. Others negotiated their own working conditions. Some married and were buried with full religious rites. Others were forcibly separated from their families. Wives were sold away from husbands, children as young as six were torn from their mothers and sold overseas. This chapter will examine these paradoxes, beginning with one of the best documented—the working lives of enslaved people in colonial New York.[1]

Many of the enslaved in New York City worked as laborers. Trinity Church was constructed by slaves, and in 1712 the merchant Walter Thong, the owner of Quacko, one of the Akan executed following the revolt of that year, leased a slave to the city "for clearing the street by the weigh house for seventeen days," a job for which Thong was reimbursed "Eighteen Shillings and two pence."[2] Men were preferred to women for such tasks—the younger and stronger the better. On December 7, 1721, Cadwallader Colden, a future governor of New York, requested that a friend purchase some slaves for Colden's use. "Please . . . buy me two negro men about eighteen years of age," Colden wrote. "I designe them for Labour & would have them strong & well made."[3] Other slaves worked in the tanneries round the Collect Pond in the Commons, or in one of the windmills nearby. Two of the slaves executed in the aftermath of the 1712 revolt were likely to have been employed as bolters, a job which involved sifting milled flour in preparation for export to the West Indies. Tom, who was sentenced "to be burned with a slow fire that he may continue in torment for eight or ten hours," belonged to the bolter Nicholas Roosevelt, while Dave Furnis' owner, Ruth Sheppard, was the widow of John Sheppard, a former bolter who may well have passed on his business to his wife.[4] Some slaves even managed to attain positions of authority in such industries. Sam, a slave belonging to John Stevens, the owner of a city tannery in 1741, for example, worked as a foreman in charge of a three-man crew which included at least one white indentured servant.[5]

Colonial New York was a mercantile hub. Goods needed to be shifted to and from the dockside warehouses, carried to the city's fleet of small boats, rowed out to the roads in the East River, and hauled aboard ocean-going vessels. Slaves labored in all these roles. Quaco, another of the Akan executed in 1712, may well have worked as a boatman, just as his master Abraham Provoost did.[6] Indeed, Quaco may even have been purchased specifically for his skill in this task: on the Gold Coast many Akan handled small craft "very dexterously" as Nathaniel Uring, a visitor to the region in 1711, noted.[7] Somewhat surprisingly, given the opportunities such employment presented for running away, many of colonial New York City's enslaved people worked as ocean-going sailors. Several of those who attended Elias Neau's classes were seamen, and Tony, the aforementioned New York slave who stowed away aboard a Royal Navy vessel in November 1710 to his freedom, was said to be "a very good sailor."[8] Enslaved West African stevedores were another common sight. Balancing enormous loads on their heads, they traversed the slippery cobbles at speed, much to the amazement of Europeans and Americans alike. "With a Burthen of one Hundred Pounds on their heads they run a sort of continual Trot," observed Willem Bosman, a Dutch factor and long-term resident of the Gold Coast, "which is so swift that we *Hollanders* cannot keep up with them without difficulty, though not loaded with an Ounce weight."[9]

Years of performing hard labor took a heavy physical toll on the enslaved as evidenced by the skeletal remains of the 417 people unearthed in 1997 at the New York African Burial Ground (NYABG). The remains of several enslaved men evidenced degenerative joint disease and osteophytosis (the growth of bone spurs around the joints). Caused by long-term wear and tear, this condition is normally associated with individuals over sixty, but in the NYABG it was found in many who had been considerably younger: burial 23, a man interred prior to 1735, displayed lumbar osteophytosis, for example, despite being only twenty-five to thirty-five years of age. Evidence of osteoarthritis and muscle hypertrophy was also found in the elbow and shoulder joints of several male skeletons, indicating stresses brought about by heavy lifting. Burial 185, a young man who also had moderate osteoarthritis in the joints of his hand, appears to have died as early as the age of twenty-one, while the teeth of the twenty-five- to thirty-five-year-old man in burial 23 contained chemical traces suggesting that he was born in Africa. Additionally, stress fractures were common in the lower spine, as were ring fractures resulting from the collision of the spine and skull, indicative of the repeated carrying of heavy loads on the head in the West African style.[10]

A few slaves in colonial New York worked as hunters. In the backwoods beyond the settled confines of Manhattan Island, game abounded in the early eighteenth century. The fur trade made the occupation economically feasible for their masters. The meat acquired was a valuable commodity and the destruction of vermin and predatory animals was another potentially profitable role for the enslaved as evidenced by a piece of legislation entitled "An Act for the more effective preservation of Deer and other game and the destruction of Wolves Wild Catts and other vermin" passed by the New York City Council in the early eighteenth century. The act specified that "Any man or slave . . . [who] shall destroy or kill any Wolf . . . Wild Catt . . . fox . . . Squezels Crows and Blackbirds shall have . . . [a] reward." Two pounds was paid for each wolf killed; 50 shillings was offered "for a wolf cub"; 3 shillings for a wild cat; 18 pence for "catlings"; and "3 pence" for crows. Slaves taken from West African polities may have been particularly suited for such a task. Hunting was a common profession in the interior kingdoms of the Gold Coast where game formed a major part of the inhabitants' diet. Indeed, the Kwahu, many of whom were sold into slavery by the Akwamu contemporaneously with Alan Jarrett's visit in early 1711, were renowned for their skill as elephant hunters. While the wolves of New York colony no doubt posed a distinct challenge, the Akan hunters' ability to track game would have been a useful skill that may have been recognized by their enslavers.[11]

A study carried out by the historian Thelma Foote shows that as many as one quarter of New York City's enslaved were skilled tradesmen. In the mid-eighteenth century, city newspapers carried advertisements offering to sell or hire out enslaved coopers, candlemakers, masons, glaziers, plasterers, sawyers, cabinetmakers, and locksmiths.[12] Quashi, an Akan implicated in the revolt of 1712 who was enslaved by the shipwright Joseph Latham, may well have been employed in his owner's riverside yard.[13] Cuffee, whose act of arson would initiate the events of the 1712 revolt, and Juan, one of two "Spanish Indians" implicated, were enslaved by the baker Peter Vantilborough, while one of several men named Tom indicted in the aftermath was enslaved to Helena Dekey, the fifty-one-year-old widow of the former baker Teunis Dekey. Many enslavers were artisans who worked out of small workshops which doubled as retail outlets situated on the ground floor of the properties they lived in. Such individuals commonly used enslaved persons as assistants, some of whom became artisans in their own right. Jarrett, another enslaved man caught up in the 1712 revolt, was enslaved by the blacksmith Samuel Phillips, while Dick, a young man who was implicated, was enslaved to the blacksmith Harmanus Burger, a "Lame and Antient" Dutchman who lived in the Dock Ward and later claimed that he was financially reliant on the labor of his enslaved workers. One of three men named Tom executed in 1712 was enslaved by a goldsmith, the Scottish Quaker David Lyell. If Tom was an Akan, a possibility considering his fate, it is plausible that he had previous expertise in Lyell's trade and may have been chosen on this basis. The "Coromantee" were renowned for their skill as goldsmiths (*sikananfo* in Twi-Akan), particularly the manufacture of jewelry and decorative pieces. Willem Bosman, a Dutch factor resident on the Gold Coast in the early eighteenth century, noted that "the thread and texture of their hatbands and chainings is so fine that . . . our ablest European artists would find it difficult to imitate them."[14]

While enslaved artisans commonly had to give up the majority (if not all) of the money they earned, their skills at least gave them a basis for negotiating their living conditions and, on occasion, even enabled them to purchase their own freedom. Enslaved people who refused to work or deliberately produced poor quality products were of little use to their masters, some of whom took the view that it was therefore worth their while to provide an incentive for good behavior.[15] This point is illustrated by the cases of two slaves belonging to Henry Lloyd, a wealthy farmer and the owner of an estate on Long Island in the 1720s and 1730s. Jack, a skilled butcher, was permitted to "remain in [New] York as he is now," seemingly without supervision, provided he continued "to pay his Mistress [Lloyd's sister] 12 £ per annum and find himself in all things."[16] The second slave was Aurelia, a twenty-year-old textile worker, who had also been leased to Lloyd's sister. "I find Aurelia is with you in order to be forwarded to me," Lloyd wrote to an associate in the city, "but that she is obstinate in refuseing to come. I am to[o] well used to Negroes resolutions to have any regard to them. What I aim at is the complyance with my Sister Lloyds desire & interest. I have no business for [Aurelia] & had much rather she were hyred out in the City & shall be much obliged to you if you'l please to contribute towards hyreing her into some good family on as good terms as you can which will be most for my Sisters interest & by far more agreeable to me than to have her with me . . . In the mean time If she remains as she is it may be as Well."[17]

Lloyd's Aurelia was one of many enslaved women in colonial New York who worked in textile manufacture. They spent their days sewing, weaving, or working with leather. As such it is perhaps unsurprising that several of the female skeletons unearthed in the NYABG showed signs of repetitive stress injuries to the wrist and forearms.[18] Another example of a possible textile worker is Sarah, the slave who would escape the hangman's noose in 1712 by "plead[ing] her belly." One of only two female slaves convicted, Sarah was owned by Stophel Pels, a twenty-seven-year-old Dutchman residing in New York City's North Ward who was originally from Albany. Pels owned a property on the east side of Broadway where he lived with his family and at least two other slaves. As well as his lodgings, Pels' property contained a workshop where he worked as a cordwainer, or shoemaker. When one considers common employment patterns in colonial New York, it is probable that Sarah and Pels' other slaves, one "male" and one "male negro child," as well the Dutchman's wife and his four children, assisted him in his trade.[19]

The other explanation posited by the New York African Burial Ground researchers for the high incidence of osteoarthritis in the wrist joints of female slaves (as well as that found in their knees, hips, and hands), was the repeated performance of domestic chores which involved bending and kneeling.[20] The written record supports this theory. In 1734 the *New-York Weekly Journal* offered "A Young House Negro Woman," for sale. "[She is] about 20," the advert continued, "she does all sorts of House work, she can Brew, Bake, Boyle soaft Soap, Wash, Iron & Starch; and is a good darey Woman she can Card and Spin at the great Wheel, Cotton, Lennen and Wollen . . . and she is a strong hale healthy Wench . . . [and] had the small Pox in Barbads when a child."[21] In a 1723 letter Cadwallader Colden also provided an indication of the sort of work domestics would typically undertake. "Please . . . buy mee a negro Girl," he requested of his correspondent, "of abut thirteen years old my wife . . . designes her Cheifly to keep the children & to sow & thierfore would have her Likely & one that appears to be good natured."[22]

From several sources it would appear that at least some of New York's enslaved domestics held positions of relative influence and felt sufficiently empowered to talk back to their masters. In a letter written in 1718 Cadwallader Colden described a thirty-three-year-old "good House Negro . . . She . . . understands the work of the Kitchen perfectly & washes well, [and] has a Natural aversion to all strong Liqours[.] Were it not for her Alusive Tongue her sullenness & the Custome of the Country that will not allow us to use our Negroes as you doe in Barbados when they Displeas you I would not have parted with her."[23] In 1767 John Van Cortlandt, another New York merchant, described his enslaved cook as being excellent at her job, aside from "her impudence . . . [as] She is intorable sasey to her Mistress."[24] A further source is the memoir of an "American Lady" who lived in Albany and wrote toward the end of the eighteenth century about her experiences earlier in life. "[While female domestics] did their work well," she recalled, "it is astonishing . . . what liberty of speech . . . [they were] allowed. . . . They would chide, reprove and expostulate in a manner that we would not endure from our hired servants; and sometimes exert fully as much authority over the children of the family as the parents, conscious that they were entirely in their power."[25]

Many well-to-do New York households in the colonial period also had male domestics. Ukawsaw Gronniosaw, an African born in "the city of Bornou" (northeast Nigeria) in the early eighteenth century, was enslaved at the age of fifteen by an ivory trader then sold to a Dutch slaver on the Gold Coast. After a brief stay in Barbados, Gronniosaw was bought by one of the Van Hornes, a wealthy New York family, and taken to live in the city. "He dressed me in his livery," Gronniosaw later recalled, "and was very good to me. My chief business was to wait at table and tea, and clean knives." By his own account, Gronniosaw was well treated.[26] Wealthy New Yorkers chose to display their riches through the education and appearance of those they enslaved. Employed as valets, messengers, or coachmen, such slaves were well dressed and well fed so as to reflect their owners' prosperity. Some had few tasks to complete and enjoyed long periods when they were largely left to their own devices. T. J. Davis, the author of

Rumour of Revolt, a history of the events of 1741, termed such individuals "spoiled slaves," while Daniel Horsmanden, the chief justice responsible for the multiple prosecutions which followed the alleged conspiracy, argued repeatedly in court that some of New York's enslaved had far too much leisure time. "His master was frequently absent from home for days and weeks together, which left him too much at liberty," Horsmanden wrote of Jack, a slave belonging to Gerardus Comfort, while he thought Cuffee, an Akan owned by Adolphus Philipse, "a fellow of general ill character; his master being a single man, and little at home. . . . Cuff had a great deal of idle time, which, it seems, he employed to very ill purpose, and had acquired a general bad fame."[27] Some of the slaves caught up in the revolt of 1712 would perhaps have fitted into this category. Andrew Stuckey's Hannibal, Jacob Regnier's Mars, Peter Fauconnier's Sam, John Barberie's Mingo, Rip Van Dam's Quacko and Quashi, Isaac Gouverneur's Kitto, Walter Thong's Quacko, William Walton's Cuffee, and Peter Morin's Caesar all belonged to wealthy men who may well have employed their slaves as pawns in an expensive game of one-upmanship.[28]

The 1703 New York census, the most detailed undertaken in the city prior to the revolt of 1712, provides a wealth of information regarding New York City's enslaved people. A total of 799 Blacks and 3,592 whites lived in the city that year. There were 298 enslaved Black men, 276 enslaved Black women, 124 enslaved Black boys, and 101 enslaved Black girls. Unlike Britain's plantation colonies, such as South Carolina and Jamaica, where slaves often lived in large, all-Black villages, in New York they normally resided in white households, on occasion without any other Black companions, or, more typically, in small groups of two or three. Nevertheless, some New York residents had many more slaves on their properties. Rip Van Dam, the owner of two of the Akan executed in 1712, kept six slaves on his Stone Street property in the South Ward in 1703, for example. Another fact that emerges from the census is that enslaved Blacks in New York were far more likely to live in the wealthiest households and neighborhoods. The ratio of males to females in each ward also varied considerably. In the East Ward, an area known for its merchants, ships' captains, publicans, and itinerant mariners, 96 of 212 households contained enslaved people, of which there were a total of

214, or a little under 27 percent of the city's Black population. Of these, approximately half were adult males, reflecting the residents' need for physical labor to transfer goods from their warehouses to the ocean-going ships on the East River. In the Dock Ward, the city's most affluent neighborhood and one which was dominated by the multistoried homes of prosperous merchants, nearly 70 percent of households contained at least one slave, and 105 of the ward's total enslaved population of 197 were women or girls, indicative of the merchant households need for domestic servants. Across town in the North Ward, the least affluent in the city, only 58 of the ward's total population of 848 were enslaved Blacks, the majority of them owned by the neighborhood's artisans, while the sparsely populated West Ward, where many white male residents worked as tenant farmers on plots leased from Trinity Church, had a population of 622, of whom under 15 percent were slaves, most probably living in the more built-up areas of the ward to the southern end of Broadway. Examples are John Barberie's Mingo, Peter Fauconnier's Sam, and John Cure's Toby, all of whom would be hanged in 1712. Beyond the city limits at Maiden Lane, the Out Ward had only 339 residents in 1703, 72 of whom were enslaved Blacks. Of these 42 were men or boys, reflecting their owners need for farm laborers.[29]

NEW YORK CITY'S SLAVES lived in a variety of accommodations. Those owned by the city's elite often resided in "negro kitchens," spaces on the top floor of two-story outbuildings, the lower of which was given over to cooking.[30] Occasionally, such quarters could be relatively commodious. The 1778 will of Tunis Convert reveals that his "negro man Tom" lived in "the kitchen room," and also had "the privilege of [a] one acre" plot of land "for him to plant and till for himself," while Caesar, a former slave belonging to the Nicoll estate in Bethlehem, New York, spent his old age in a room on the ground floor of the kitchen extension. It had an outside entrance, a stoop, and a large open fireplace.[31] The majority of slaves, however, lived in quarters which were cramped and uncomfortable. Unheated in winter, they were airless and sweltering in summer. They were commonly shared by several enslaved Blacks and, on occasion, a number of white indentured servants as well. One account describes a poorly lit, third-floor attic dormitory where thirty Black and twenty-six white servants lived. Their personal spaces divided by thin partitions, they slept on "rude plank floors."[32] Other slaves were even less fortunate. John Sharpe, chaplain at Fort Anne, noted in 1713 that many of the slaves visited by Elias Neau lived in "garrets, cellars, and other nauseous places," while the former slave Sojourner Truth recalled in later life that Charles Hardenbergh of New York's Ulster County kept fourteen slaves in a single room in his cellar. They slept "like the horse," Truth noted, "with a little straw and a blanket" laid on loose boards which were often saturated with water.[33]

Enslaved persons owned few possessions. Those they had were sometimes hidden in their living quarters, to prevent discovery by their masters or theft by their peers. During the trials following the alleged revolt of 1741, it was revealed that a slave named Caesar had cached several stolen plates and pieces of linen in a hole dug beneath the kitchen floor of the property where he resided, while several New York City sites investigated by the archaeologist Diana Wall contained caches buried in pits lined with barrels or baskets under ground-floor spaces associated with the enslaved.[34] A hoard found on a site formerly occupied by the King's House Tavern contained twenty bottles and numerous tobacco pipes, while three separate caches buried between 1660 and the 1690s beneath the floor of a house on Broad Street belonging to the Van Tienhovens, a Dutch family who owned at least six slaves during this period, contained fifty-four glass beads, five marbles, three pieces of mica, a fragment of coral, various quartz and quartzite flakes, a jawbone, several iron nails, a pin, a thimble, a lead fishing sinker, a needle fragment, and two pieces of lead shot.[35] Such items have been discovered at various sites associated with slavery across the Americas and when buried together they are often referred to as "conjuring bundles." Believed to have belonged to West African spiritualists, such items, many of which are either associated with death (such as animal bones) or have the ability to reflect light (such as mica and quartz), are thought to have been used in divination and protection rites, as well as in ceremonies involving the diagnoses of illnesses and the control of souls which had left their bodies after death.[36]

UNSURPRISINGLY, colonial New York City's slaves suffered from a variety of health issues. Elias Neau, in a letter written to the SPG in 1709, noted that "the constitution of . . . the Blacks, dos not agree with our Climate many of 'em dye and very few live to the age of sixty years."[37] As well as the harsh New York winters, there were several other factors which were responsible for enslaved people's poor health. Foremost among them were overwork and a susceptibility to the region's infectious diseases. The situation was exacerbated by inadequate shelter, poor diet, insufficient clothing, and cramped living quarters. Many fell victim to whooping cough, "violent fever[s] and fits of shivering from ague."[38] Unsanitary living conditions led to parasitic infections and diarrhea, while others died of smallpox, measles, or yellow fever—an epidemic of the latter killed 10 percent of the city's enslaved people in 1702.[39] The poor health of the enslaved was also reflected in the findings of the researchers who worked on the African Burial Ground. Evidence of rickets, anemia, scurvy, and malnutrition was found in the skeletal remains. Burial 202, a girl who died prior to 1735 and was between twelve and eighteen years of age, showed femoral and tibial bowing associated with rickets, while high frequencies of tooth rot among the infants buried at the site is thought to be indicative of chronic malnutrition combined with periodic, seasonal rehabilitation, perhaps representing winter food shortages followed by summer gluts.[40] As a result of all these factors, slaves in New York had a short life expectancy. One sixth perished as babies, one third died before the age of five, and only 6 percent reached the age of fifty-five, a milestone surpassed by one third of the white New Yorkers buried in Trinity Church in the same period. The mean age of death of the 301 bodies examined in the NYABG was 22.3, while the life expectancy of African slaves arriving in New York between the ages of twenty to twenty-four was judged to be roughly another twenty years.[41]

As well as enduring poor physical health, enslaved people in colonial New York suffered from a variety of psychological traumas. Suicide was common. As discussed in Chapter 8, enslaved people sometimes chose to take their own lives during the Middle Passage, either by throwing themselves overboard or starving themselves to death. Similar cases of slaves choosing death are evident in colonial New York.[42] In 1677 "a Negro Slave" belonging to John Cooley, a New York blacksmith, refused to do "the Least Chore . . . nor use the Least motion for his Bodely health; In soe much that the Physicians told . . . [Cooley] if he did not constreine or force his said Negro speedily to use or fall to some bodily Exercise, hee would immediately and of necessity dye." Cooley's solution was to beat his slave into obedience. This "Lawfull Correction" doled out by Cooley, deemed "propere for Such a Slave in his present State and Condicion" by the judges in the subsequent court case, was delivered with such vehemence that "the said Negro dyed the 9th day after his Chastisement." There is no evidence of Cooley being punished for his part in the man's death.[43] Another apparent example of the mental stresses of slavery prompting extreme behavior is the case of Diana, an enslaved woman belonging to David Machado. Said to have been "in a passion, because her mistress was angry with her," Diana "took her own child from her breast" one winter's night in January 1741 "and laid it in the cold, [so] that [the baby] . . . froze to death."[44]

One cause of mental health issues was the difficulty enslaved people had maintaining meaningful bonds with family members. Unlike plantation slaves, who lived in large all-Black communities and sometimes resided in nuclear or extended family groups, enslaved families in New York often belonged to several different owners and lived in various locations across the city.[45] When enslaved women became pregnant, their male children were often sold on, sometimes as young as the age of six. These factors meant that the likelihood of slaves living with family members was low. Nevertheless, the fact that enslaved people desired to form and maintain family relationships is abundantly documented.[46] A report on slavery in New York written by the secretary of the SPG prior to 1728 noted that "a little Time in the Dusk of the Evening, after hard Labour all Day, was the whole Time allowed them for . . . Relaxation, and to visit their Wives and Children." The same report noted that "their Marriages were performed by mutual Consent," while John Bartow, an SPG missionary in the colony, noted in 1725 that "[slaves] marry after the heathen way."[47] John Sharpe, the chaplain at Fort Anne and an eyewitness to the events of April 1712, wrote at some length about "negro marriages" in New

York. After noting the prevalence of polygamy among the city's slaves, Sharpe remarked that "the husband and wife seldom happen . . . to belong to one family" and that frequently relationships were broken up when "one of the married parties [was] sold at some hundred miles distance where they can never hope to meet [their spouse and children] again."[48] While some enslavers chose to support their slaves' wishes to maintain family relationships, others deliberately impeded them. Susannah Pierson's 1715 will stipulated that the enslaved who lived and worked on her estate in Sag Harbor, near Bridgehampton in New York's Suffolk County, were "to be sold altogether, for I would not have them parted," whereas Cadwallader Colden, the future governor of New York, decided to separate a mother from her children, by selling the former to an acquaintance in Barbados and retaining the latter in New York. "I could have sold her here to good advantage," he wrote, "but I have several other of her Children which I value & I know if she should stay in this country she would spoil them."[49]

The enforced break-up of enslaved families was one of several common causes of friction between Blacks and whites. In Horsmanden's account of the trials of 1741 we learn of a man enslaved to John Roosevelt named Quack who was married to the governor's enslaved cook who worked in Fort George. On one occasion when Quack attempted to visit his wife, he was denied permission to enter the building by an armed sentry. "Quack was resolute," the report reveals, "and pushed forward . . . and said he would go in." The soldier "bid him take what followed, and clubbed his firelock, and knocked [Quack] . . . down . . . then Quack got up again and collared the [sentry] . . . and cried out murder; and the [sentry] . . . was going to strike him again, and the officer of the guard hearing a bustle . . . forbid [the sentry from] . . . striking him any more; and Quack then run in a-doors into the governor's kitchen, and they went and fetched him, and turned him out of the fort."[50] Enslaved people who were separated from spouses or children occasionally ran away from their masters to reunite with their families. Sojourner Truth spoke about her husband Tom's attempt to find a previous wife from whom he had been separated when he was sold to new owners who lived outside the city. "He . . . tramped the rutted dirt roads and wet swamps," Truth recalled, "sleeping in the woods at night, dodging behind trees to avoid the wagons that rolled past. . . . On reaching the city, Tom . . . hid . . . out for a month in those dark alleys that sheltered many runaways. But he never found his wife. Instead, the slave hunters . . . found Tom and returned him to Dumont. The scars on his back were what remained of his master's greeting to him that day."[51] Another case concerned an enslaved man named Dick who ran away from his master to be with his wife in 1697. Caught on the property of his wife's owner by a city constable who had been sent to apprehend him, Dick wounded three of his assailants with a knife before he was taken into custody.[52]

THE ATTITUDES OF NEW YORK'S WHITES toward the city's Black residents were as diverse and contradictory as the rest of the facets of this "peculiar institution." Many saw them as a subhuman underclass. Accursed by God, Blacks were perceived as "sons of Ham," "barbarians," "heathens," and "savages." They were believed to practice cannibalism, infanticide, idolatry, and witchcraft, and were thought to be incapable of human emotion. Whites in the colonial period commonly equated blackness with evil, guilt, and sin. As such, or so many whites believed, the Blacks deserved all that was coming to them. Other New Yorkers, while looking on their slaves with some fondness, considered them to be intellectually inferior and incapable of making moral judgments. John Romme, one of the whites executed in the aftermath of the 1741 revolt, referred to a group of enslaved men as being "a parcel of good children." Others thought of their Black slaves in the same way they thought of domesticated or farmyard animals, a view evidenced by the names many were given—Daisy, Sox, and Little Betty being common examples, and the fact that some enslaved persons were branded with "earmarks" in the same way as cattle. Other whites thought their enslaved fortunate regarding their lot in life and opined that they should be grateful to their masters.[53] In a speech made during the 1741 trials, Horsmanden claimed that the members of "the black tribe" accused of participating in the "revolt" had showed "monstrous ingratitude" considering the good treatment they had received.

Their slavery among us is generally softened with great indulgence; they live without care, and are commonly better fed and clothed, and put to less labour, than the poor of most Christian countries. They are indeed slaves, but under the protection of the law, none can hurt them with impunity: they are really more happy in this place, than in the midst of the continual plunder, cruelty, and rapine of their native countries; but notwithstanding all the kindness and tenderness with which they have been treated amongst us, yet this is the second attempt of the same kind, that this brutish and bloody species of mankind have made within one age.[54]

Although Horsmanden's claim that enslaved Blacks were "commonly better fed and clothed . . . than the poor of most Christian countries" is impossible to assess quantitatively, substantial qualitative evidence exists which could be used to support the assertion. The clothes worn by Ukawsaw Gronniosaw and other liveried domestics of the city's most affluent classes, for example, were considerably finer than those worn by the peasants of contemporary Europe, while a "Young Negro . . . Wench" advertised for sale in the *New-York Weekly Journal* in 1734, was described as being "well clothed."[55] Runaway notices posted in early seventeenth-century colonial newspapers, such as the *Boston News-Letter*, also provide a wealth of information regarding slaves' attire. In 1704 a "Negro Woman, called Penelope, about 35 year of Age," absconded from Captain Nathaniel Cary of "Charlstown." Among her "several sorts of Apparel" was "a flowered damask Gown."[56] In the same year a "Negro man" who "call[ed] . . . himself Sambo" and was "supposed to be Runaway" was dressed in a "gray Jacket, grey homespun kersey breeches, [and] a Souldier's cap," but had "no stockings" and only "an old pair of shoes."[57] In 1705 "a Negro Man-Slave named Peter, aged about 20" fled from "his Master William Pepperil Esqr. at Kittery in the Province of Maine." Peter was wearing "a mixt gray home-spun Coat, white home-spun Jacket and Breeches, French fall Shoes, sad coloured Stockings, of a mixt worsted pair, and a black Hat." George Robinson Carver's Jo was dressed in "a sad coloured Jacket, white Shirt, and Leather Breeches" when he ran in 1705.[58] From the above it would appear that Horsmanden may have been correct—some slaves in the northern colonies were not badly dressed when compared with "the poor of most Christian countries."[59] All this is circumstantial, however, while a final reference goes some way to contradict the lawyer's argument. On July 3,

1716, Hannah, "a mulatto," confessed to stealing several items of clothing from the premises of John Newkirke, a silversmith of New York's Dock Ward. In her defense, Hannah claimed "she stole the goods because she was almost naked, and her mistress would give her no clothes."[60]

As to slaves' diet, again the evidence provides a mixed picture. Peter Kalm, an explorer and botanist who was commissioned by the Royal Swedish Academy of Sciences to travel to the North American colonies in 1747, noted that "the Negroes . . . are treated more mildly, and fed better than those of the West Indies. They have as good food as the rest of the servants, and they possess equal advantages in all things."[61] Kalm's point regarding white servants' food requires some elucidation. In 1736 New York's poorhouse provided "bread and beer, milk porridge, or beef broth and bread for breakfast; pork and peas porridge or fish and peas porridge for dinner; and bread and cheese." A rare example of an enslaved person's diet, which will serve as a comparison, is given in the autobiography of John Jea, an African born in 1773 near Calabar on the Slave Coast. After being shipped to New York City, Jea was provided with daily rations of three-quarters of a quart of "Indian corn pounded or bruised and boiled with water . . . and about a quart of sour buttermilk poured on it" with "about three ounces of dark bread . . . greased over with very indifferent hog's lard." This was supplemented with a weekly ration of a half-pound of beef and a half-gallon of potatoes.[62] Tom, Tunis Convert's slave who was mentioned above, had "the privilege of [a] one acre' plot of land" on which he presumably grew fruit and vegetables to supplement his diet.[63] It is also probable that New York's slaves would have hunted or fished whenever possible as well as foraging for wild food including the oysters which were abundant in New York's bays and rivers. It would seem, then, that while adequate in terms of quantity, and no doubt comparable to the diet of contemporary, poor whites, the food eaten by colonial New York's enslaved people lacked vitamins and nutritional value. It was heavy in carbohydrates and light in fresh fruit and vegetables. This conclusion is supported by the research carried out at the New York African Burial Ground. Archaeologists noted that poor diet was a contributory factor to ill health, had an impact on dental decay, and restricted subadult growth and development.[64]

Horsmanden's point regarding New York's slaves being "under the protection of the law" and his claim that "none can hurt them with impunity" are easy to dismiss. Many slaves were subject to arbitrary punishment and despite rare exceptions such as the case of the legal pioneer William Archer which was discussed in Chapter 5, the vast majority of slaves had neither the ability nor the opportunity to take recourse to the law. The inventory of the estate of Adolph Philipse, one of colonial New York's largest landowners and the owner of fifteen enslaved people, including eight children, features an entry for "2 Cats of nine tails," a whip specifically designed to inflict pain on the human body. In Horsmanden's own account of the events of 1741 and 1742, another incidence of cruelty arises. Sam, the enslaved man previously mentioned due to his position as foreman of one of New York City's tanneries, was whipped by his master, John Stevens, for concealing a double gold doubloon.[65] Far more sinister was the case of a slave who was flogged so severely by his owner, John Van Zandt, as a punishment for absenting himself without permission, that he died shortly afterward. The case was assessed by the Coroner's Jury who decided that the slave's death was not attributable to his master's actions but instead was caused by the "Visitation of God."[66] Some of the skeletons discovered in the New York African Burial Ground also provide evidence of brutal punishment. A man aged between forty-four and sixty interred in lot 171 suffered a premortem fracture of the left clavicle and twenty-two other fractures distributed around the body at, or shortly before, the time of his death. Burial 205 was of a woman who had no less than thirty-two perimortem fractures, while the woman in Burial 25, a twenty- to twenty-four-year-old, "had a musket ball lodged in her rib cage, blunt-force trauma to her face, and a spiral, or oblique, fracture to the lower right arm above the wrist caused by twisting and pulling."[67]

Two more elements concerning the relationships between Blacks and whites in colonial New York are pertinent. The first concerns accusations of unfair competition that whites leveled against enslaved people working in the same jobs as they were, thus undercutting the wages whites could demand for their services. In 1686 the licensed porters of New York City complained to the Common Council that the use of enslaved labor had led to their "discouragement and [finan-

cial] loss." The council passed an ordinance to protect the porters' interests, but it would seem this had little effect, as in 1691 the porters
protested that competition from enslaved people had "so impoverished
them that they could not by their labours get a competency for the
maintenance of themselves and families." Similar disputes arose
among skilled workers and artisans. In 1737, the coopers of New York
City claimed that "great numbers of Negroes were invading their
trade" and protested "the pernicious custom of breeding slaves to
trades whereby the honest and industrious tradesmen are reduced to
poverty for want of employ." Although the lieutenant governor,
George Clarke, supported the coopers, the assembly refused to act, as
to do so would have financially prejudiced many of its members.
"Breeding slaves to trades" was so profitable for the elite that they had
no desire to ban the practice.[68]

Paradoxically, there is also some evidence of cooperation between
enslaved Black people and members of the white working classes in
colonial New York. When slaves ran from their masters, a relatively
common occurrence throughout the colonial period, they were occasionally accompanied by white indentured servants. The two groups
had several things in common. Although indentured servants' period
of service was finite (normally lasting from three to ten years), they
were unpaid and subject to restrictive and discriminatory laws, and
there is evidence that they were, on occasion, physically mistreated by
their masters.[69] One example of this mutual absconding occurred in
the spring of 1754 when "a White Man . . . named Joseph Heday" ran
away from his master George Mumford of Fisher's Island in company
with three enslaved men, one of whom, a man named Fortune, was
"mark'd in the Face or scar'd with a knife in his own country," indicating that he may well have been an Akan bearing so-called "country
marks."[70] Whites and enslaved Black people were also drawn together
when participating in criminal activity which was often conducted in
illegal taverns known as "disorderly houses." Judging by the amount
of legislation which the authorities enacted against such establishments, they were common in colonial New York, so much so that although many establishments were well known and the proprietors
barely bothered to disguise their business, the authorities had insufficient manpower to close them down.[71] The best documented example

is that belonging to John Hughson, one of three whites executed for their alleged involvement in the "Great Negro Plot" of 1741. When "reproached" by his neighbor, Francis Silvester, Hughson did not deny the fact that he ran such an establishment, explaining that it was his wife's idea and that he had been forced into the business to avoid penury.[72]

A few descriptions of how enslaved people behaved in disorderly houses may be of interest. The following was narrated by John Roosevelt's Quack, a slave of Akan origin, and concerns a meeting of the alleged conspirators of 1741.

> Another time . . . [Quack] went to Hughson's by himself, and met the three same Negroes as before; Cuffee was playing on the Violin; they had one Tankard of Egg-Punch, and another of Water, Sugar, and Rum; they sat in the Parlour; Vaarck's Caesar called for a Pack of Cards; they played a considerable Time, and Quack won two or three Bowls of Punch, which Mrs. Hughson maid, and Peggy [a white servant in Hughson's household] paid for: They got pretty merry with drinking; Judge Phillipse's Frank came in and called for A Mugg of Beer, but did not stay, his Boat being at the Dock just by.[73]

Other descriptions included in Horsmanden's account reveal that as many as "twenty or thirty negroes [would gather at Hughson's] at one time," and that drinking, dancing, and gambling often went on until two or three o'clock in the morning.[74] Disorderly houses also doubled as brothels. Margaret Sorubiero, a prostitute in her early twenties who also went by the aliases of Peggy, Kerry, Sailing-burgh, and "the Newfoundland Irish beauty," lodged at Hughson's in 1741. "She was a person of infamous character," Horsmanden wrote, and "a notorious prostitute, and also of the worst sort, a prostitute to negroes."[75] Another white prostitute who sold her services to enslaved Black men was Elizabeth Martin, "a very Low Notorious Wicked Woman of Evil Life Conversation and Behaviour" who was ordered out of New York City in 1738. When she refused to leave, Martin was given thirty-one lashes and banished for life.[76]

Moralists saw the disorderly houses as having a destabilizing effect on society. Horsmanden thought that the proprietors of such places were "guilty not only of making negro slaves their equals, but even their superiors, by waiting upon, keeping with and entertaining them with meat, drink and lodging."[77] Perhaps the most famous critic of disorderly houses was Daniel Defoe. "Those wretched places . . . are the Nurseries of Thieves," he explained in a pamphlet published in London in 1731, "for the people who keep those Houses, nourish the worst of Rogues, and encourage them to commit all these Robberies and other Disorders of the Night. These receive and entertain them when they have done; with these they share their Booty, and from these they receive constant Loans and Contributions when they have miscarried, or come home without Success."[78] This link between disorderly houses and organized crime was well established. Many white proprietors of disorderly houses in New York City fenced stolen goods supplied by enslaved people.

While John Hughson is the most documented example, several other instances emerge from the transcripts of New York City's courts. In 1718 Mary Holst was accused of receiving stolen gold and silver rings from an enslaved man named Pompey and of entertaining "negro slaves" in her house.[79] Fourteen years earlier, the tavern keeper Anne White had been indicted for "receiving stolen goods from the slave of Capt. Peter Matthews and for succoring aiding harbouring and entertaining the said slave."[80] Another white woman, Mary Smith, was charged with receiving stolen money from a slave named Somerset, while the activities of Peter Mellott, a white New Yorker, were brought to the attention of the city's courts no less than three times. In 1694 Mellott was arrested for "entertaining" enslaved people in his home; and three years later he admitted purchasing a parcel of iron from a "Negro [sailor], who spoke Spanish and Dutch." Although the sailor "claimed to be a free [man] . . . belonging to Capt. Daniell's ship which had taken a French prize with iron on it," it transpired that he was actually a slave and the iron he was selling had been stolen. Mellott was fined £5 but was back in court just three months later. On this occasion, one of Mellott's own slaves, a man named Fortune, was sentenced to be whipped round the city for stealing a bag of money from a Dutch merchant named Adrian Hoghlandt. Coincidentally, Hoghlandt was also the owner of Robin, a slave who attended Elias Neau's classes who would be executed for his alleged involvement in the revolt of 1712.[81]

Another point of contention between whites and Blacks in colonial New York was miscegenation. While interracial sexual relationships were criminalized in 1630 in Virginia due to the preponderance of white males relative to white females and the associated fear of the growth of an empowered mulatto class, in New York no such gender imbalance existed and no legislation was deemed necessary.[82] That is not to say that no such relationships occurred, or even that they were not common, but as miscegenation was taboo yet not specifically illegal, it is difficult to gauge with what frequency it occurred. Some idea may be garnered, however, from a study appearing in Thelma Foote's *Black and White Manhattan*. Of 164 enslaved children advertised for sale in New York City's newspapers in the colonial period, 21, or 13 percent, were identified as "mulattoes." As slavery was a legal condition inherited from one's mother, the majority of the couplings from which these children arose would have involved white men and Black women. Anecdotal evidence is also available.[83] In his 1711 will Joseph Baker, a mariner of New York, requested his executors "to take especial care of my negro girl, named Elizabeth, free born, in my house May 20, 1706, and christened and registered in January 1710." Baker made provision for Elizabeth to "be taught to read" and left her a house on the corner of King Street and Pearl Street in the city's East Ward as well as a pension of "three shillings a week during her life," all of which suggests a far closer relationship that that of master and slave.[84] The previously mentioned memoir of an "American Lady" also provides an example of miscegenation. The account concerns the Schuylers, a prominent Dutch New York family, one of whom owned an enslaved man implicated in the 1712 revolt.

Though, from their simple and kindly modes of life, . . . [whites in colonial New York] were from infancy in habits of familiarity with their negroes, yet being early taught that nature had placed between them a barrier, which it was in a high degree criminal and disgraceful to pass, they considered a mixture of such distinct races with abhorrence, as a violation of her laws. This greatly conduced to the preservation of family happiness and concord. An ambiguous race [children born of Black and white parents], which the law does not acknowledge, and who (if they have any moral sense, must be as much ashamed of their parents as these last are of them) are certainly a dangerous ... degraded part of the community. How much more so must be those unfortunate beings who stand in the predicament of the bat in the fable, whom both birds and beasts disowned?... of a mulatto born [in the colonial period] ... I only remember a single instance; and from the regret and wonder it occasioned, considered it as singular. Colonel Schuyler, of whom I am to speak, had a relation so weak and defective in capacity, that he never was intrusted with any thing of his own, and lived an idle bachelor about the family. In process of time, a favourite negro-woman, to the great offence and scandal of the family, bore a child to him, whose colour gave testimony to the relation. The boy was carefully educated; and when he grew up, a farm was allotted to him well-stocked and fertile, but "in depth of woods embraced," about two miles back from the family seat. A destitute white woman, who had somehow wandered from the older colonies, was induced to marry him; and all the branches of the family thought it incumbent on them, now and then, to pay a quiet visit to Chalk, (for so, for some unknown reason, they always called him.) I have been in Chalk's house myself, and a most comfortable abode it was; but I considered him as a mysterious and anomalous being.[85]

Relationships between white women and Black men in the colonial era were also documented. In 1699 Wynkey Lawrence was put on trial by the Supreme Court for "having A Bastard Child by a Negro."[86] Nine years later Jonathon Taylor of Woodbury, New York, petitioned the Court of Assistants for the right to divorce his wife, Hannah, on the grounds that she was cohabiting with Joseph Allyn, "a negro servant of Mr. Sackett, of the province of New York."[87] Another case involved Jonnoau, an enslaved Black man, who was acquitted for the attempted rape of Anne Carr, his master's wife, in 1737 due to a lack of evidence. A week later an announcement paid for by William Carr, Anne's husband, appeared in the *New York Gazette*: "Whereas Anne ... Carr of the City of New York, has behaved herself in an indecent and Wicked manner, by being too familiar with a Negro Man ... whereby she has broken the Marriage Contract; and he [William Carr] being informed, that he is not under any Obligation to live with or support her in her wickedness and also drinking to excess. [This is] ... therefore to desire all shop-keepers Publick-House-keepers, and all other Persons, not to Trust nor to Give the said Anne Carr Credit on the said [William] Carr's account."[88]

Not all relationships between whites and Blacks in colonial New York were quite so fraught. Indeed, there are several examples of concern shown by enslavers toward their enslaved workers. Numerous accounts exist of enslaved people being treated by doctors at considerable expense. Several enslaved people belonging to the Lloyd family of New York were given various treatments in the early 1730s. Opium, an enslaved man who had been with the family for a staggering fifty-five years by 1732, was administered both "Purging Physic" and "Cooling powders" on the advice of Doctor George Muirson, while Jupiter, an enslaved man who was suffering from "Pains in his Leggs, Knees, and Thighs, ascending to his Bowels" in the spring of 1730, was prescribed "Purges . . . boluses . . . powders and some Diet Drink, made with Equal Parts of Horse Reddish Roots, the Bark of Elder Roots, Pine Budds, or the Second Bark, wood or Toad Sorrel . . . [, and] some oyntment."[89] While such cases may indicate nothing more than the owner's wish to protect a financial investment, other instances are harder to assign to purely economic motives. In 1698, for example, Dyrck Vandenburgh, a bricklayer resident in the North Ward, paid the courts a surety of £300 (at a time when a laborer earned just £6 a year), to have his slave Jack, who had been found guilty of committing burglary, transported out of the colony rather than being executed.[90] Another case of an emotional bond between slave and master is related in Daniel Horsmanden's account of the trials of 1741 when a slave named Scipio explained how he had unwittingly fallen into a life of crime, a path that would ultimately lead to his execution.

As soon as Scipio was brought before Mr. Nicholls and Mr. Lodge to be examined, he was asked who his master was, and what was his name? He answered, master, don't you know me? I am Scipio, belonging to Mr. Robert Bound, and formerly belonged to Dr. Nicols; and it being then demanded of him, how he came to be concerned in the conspiracy (he being a fellow that did not want sense, and had had a better education than most of his colour) he answered, it is true, sir, I ought to have known better; my first master, Dr. Nicols, brought me up from a child, sent me to school, and taught me to read; he intended to give me to his son, who was bred a merchant, for which reason he put me to a cooper to learn that trade, but his son going to live in the country, he had no use for me in that business; my old master therefore sold me to my present master, Bound, who has likewise been very kind to me; but it was with me as it is with all my colour, who are never easy till they get a dram, and when they have one they want one more; this was my case on my meeting with Comfort's Jack, who carried me to Hughson's, where from drinking one dram I drank more, till I was bewitched with it.[91]

Two issues raised by Scipio's story are worthy of further comment. The first is the perceived prevalence of alcohol abuse among slaves in colonial New York. From court records to private letters to Horsmanden's reports of 1741, there are constant references to the drinking habits of the enslaved.[92] The city's Common Council issued laws prohibiting the sale of alcohol to enslaved persons within the city in 1681, 1684, 1691, and 1703. A man named Dick was drunk when he wounded three men with a knife in the kitchen of his enslaver's wife in 1697; and several of the skeletal remains unearthed in the NYABG showed traces of lead poisoning, a condition associated with the consumption of alcoholic beverages fermented in pewter vats.[93] In 1745 Robert Livingston, one of the colony's major slave holders, wrote to his brother explaining that he had been forced to sell his domestic because "here there are so many Little Dram Shops that ruin half the Negroes in town."[94]

That enslaved people were given alcohol while working is also documented. In the papers of the city's Common Council there is an invoice which includes an entry for "negro hire, cartage, hire of ladders, [and] ropes . . . with liquor to carpenter and negros," while a bill of expenses submitted for the repair of the City Ferry House included the hire of at least four Black men and a charge for "Liqour at Sundry times for all the workmen."[95] West Africans arriving in New York would have been somewhat accustomed to such behavior. That the Akan made liberal use of alcohol, both as a social lubricant and for various spiritual and ritual practices, was noted by Jean Barbot, a French slaver active on the Gold Coast in the 1720s, while Willem Bosman, the previously quoted Dutch factor of the West Indies Company, wrote that "the Negroes [are] . . . so besotted to strong Liqours and Tobacco [another extremely common vice in Colonial New York City], that you may equally entrust Bacon to a Cat, as either of them within their Power."[96]

The second point raised by Scipio's story is the fact that some enslaved people in colonial New York had considerable free time. As we have already seen, on Sundays in particular "the streets . . . [were] full of Negroes, who dance & divert themselves."[97] Some enslaved people came into the city from as far afield as King's County, Long Island, a trend which was viewed with such concern by the authorities that in 1690 a bill was passed prohibiting slaves from riding the New York-Brooklyn ferry on Sundays "without leave of service from their masters." This ordinance failed so completely that it was reissued in 1697.[98] Even after this date slaves traveled into the city when they were not required to work as evidenced by the Hallett's slaves' anger at being refused leave to travel shortly before the family's murder.[99] The enslaved used the time away from work in a variety of ways. New Yorkers, "from clergy down to negro slaves," according to a late nineteenth-century publication entitled "Old Colonial Days," enjoyed bowling on the green.[100] Others gathered to drink or play cards, such as Dundee, who, when tasked with fetching water from one of the city pumps by his owner, Robert Todd, one day in 1741, chose instead to play "papa" at the house of Gerardus Comfort with three other enslaved people—Jack, Cook, and Jenny. After Dundee had lost "about two shillings in pennies," Jack invited him to go for a drink. In the summer months, slaves swam in the Hudson, and at night some slipped out of their masters' houses to attend impromptu parties, or "frolics," held at the houses of the "free negroes" in the Bowery. As many as forty slaves would gather at such events to sing and dance and play the fiddle into the small hours.[101]

On public holidays such as Whitsunday, Easter Sunday, New Year's Day, and the monarch's birthday, enslaved persons were often not forced to work. On such occasions they gathered on the Commons, a wild, open triangular space just to the north of the city limits at Maiden Lane, with hills, a ravine, swampland, and woods. There, beyond the prying eyes of their masters, the enslaved celebrated their own festivals and African cultures.[102] The most famous was Pinkster, the Dutch word for Pentecost. Originally brought to New Amsterdam by Dutch settlers in the 1620s, the festival was celebrated in the week following Whitsunday and commonly featured special church services, including baptisms and confirmations. Neighbors visited each other and children dyed eggs and made gingerbread. Dutch families would also mark the event by giving their slaves a few days off. Each year the gathering on the Commons grew and in time it began to attract enslaved people from up the Hudson River valley and from neighboring Long Island. By the time of the English takeover, Pinkster had changed from being a purely Dutch celebration to one which blended Northern European and West African traditions. During the eighteenth century, Pinkster was entirely appropriated by the colony's enslaved population, and in several aspects began to resemble contemporary festivals or carnivals held by the enslaved across the Americas, most notably in the Caribbean and Brazil.[103]

A handful of contemporary accounts describe Pinkster in the colonial period. Written by an anonymous contributor who refers to himself as "the Spy," the first appeared in the *New-York Weekly Journal* in 1736. It relates the author's "discovery" of the celebrations taking place on the Commons and begins with his noticing his landlord's slave tuning "his Banger," or drum, one morning. When asked "the Meaning . . . of his being so merry," the enslaved man is said to have answered: "Massa, to day Holiday; Backerah no work; Ningar no work; me so savvy play Banger; go yonder, you see ningar play Bangar for true, dance too; you see Sport to day for true . . . Massa, you savy the Field, little Way out a Town, no Houses there, grandy Room for dance there." Keen to learn more, "the Spy" accompanied his informant to the Commons, which was "partly covered with Booths, and well crowded with Whites, [while] the Negroes [were] divided into Companies, I suppose," the Spy speculated, "according to their different Nations." Some of the slaves were "dancing to the hollow Sound of a Drum, made of the Trunk of a hollow Tree, others . . . to the grating rattling Noise of Pebles or Shells in a Small Basket, others plied the Banger, and some knew how to joyn the Voice to it." The Spy also reported that he "saw several Companies of the Blacks, some exercising the Cudgel, and some of them small Sticks in imitation of the short Pike."[104] An account from 1810 describes celebrations held in Albany and refers to Pinkster as "the carnival of the African race." The event featured a "King of the Blacks," a venerable old man known as "Charley of Pinkster Hill" who had been brought up as an Angolan prince before being sold into slavery. Elected as "king" for life, Charley was dressed as "a British brigadier" with an "ample broadcloth scarlet coat, with wide flaps" which "almost reach[ed] . . . to his heels," blue stockings, and a "three-cornered cocked hat."[105]

One of the most interesting points to arise from the descriptions above is the apparent ignorance of the average white New Yorker regarding the festival. Even though Pinkster had been going on for a century by the time the report appeared in the *New-York Weekly Journal*, its author still felt the event's African dimensions newsworthy. This tallies with the general impression gained when reading the sources regarding the average white colonial New Yorker's lack of interest in African and African American culture. While slave owners and those involved in the slave trade were experts in all areas which could directly affect their finances, and knew, for example, that a Coromantee could fetch a higher price than an Angolan, they were almost entirely unaware of how their slaves occupied their time while not working.

Another point of interest concerns the debate prevalent among historians of the Atlantic World regarding the extent to which Black culture in the Americas was African in derivation, or whether it was something that developed independently, something original, something American. Previously, the idea that African cultural elements were destroyed by the stresses of the Middle Passage and the slaves' assimilation into the New World was widely believed. Historians such as Sidney Mintz and Richard Price theorized that few traces of true African culture survived relocation to the Americas. In the last two decades, however, the West African roots of various Black American cultural elements are beginning to be better understood. This is not to say that scholars such as Linda Heywood and John Thornton deny the existence and development of African American culture, but rather that they see specific African origins in such movements. The reference made in the *New York Weekly Journal* to the slaves at Pinkster dancing with "Small sticks," for example, has been interpreted as an American reimagining of the Kongolese practice of *nsanga*, a military dance performed by warriors prior to battle and somewhat related to the Afro-Brazilian martial art Capoeira. *Nsanga*, or *Sangamento*, as it was known to a number of Portuguese priests who witnessed the dance in Maola in 1610, involved "600 armed men . . . with plumed heads, chest and arms painted red, running, leaping, and making war-like representations." The "dance" also involved mock combat intended to develop the warriors' martial prowess.[106]

Another interpretation of the Pinkster "stick dance" is that it was derived from an Akan practice known as the *Ikem*, or shield dance, the particulars of which were recorded in a report compiled in the aftermath of an abortive Akan-led slave rebellion in Antigua in 1736:

It is the Custom in Africa, when a Coromantee King has resolved upon a War with a Neighbouring State, to give Publick Notice among his Subjects, That the Ikem-dance will be performed at a Certain Time & Place; and there the Prince appears in Royal habit, under an Umbrella or Canopy of State, preceeded by his Officers, called Braffo & His Marshall, attaended by his Asseng (or Chamberlain) & Guards, and the Musick of his Company; with his Generals & Chiefs about him. Then he places himself up an advanced Seat, his Generals setting behind him upon a Bench; His Guards on each Side; His Braffo and Marshall clearing the Circle, and his Asseng with an Elephants Tail keeping the flies from him; The Musick playing; and the People forming a Semicircle about him. After some Respite, the Prince arises, distributes Money to the People; Then the Drums beating to the Ikem-beat, he with an Ikem (i.e) a Shield composed of wicker, Skins and two or three small pieces of thin board upon his left Arm, and a Lance, and the several gestures by them used in Battle. When the Prince begins to be fatigued, The Guards run in and Support him; he delivers the Ikem and Lance to the Person who next Dances; then is lead Supported to his Chair, and is seated again in State . . . Then the Same Dance is performed by Several Others, . . . Then the Prince Stepping into the Area of the Semicircle, with his Chief General, and taking a Cutlass in his hand, moves with a Whirling motion of his Body round a Bout, but dancing and leaping up at the same time from one Horn or point of the Semicircle, quite to the other, so as to be distinctly viewed by all.[107]

The Pinkster "stick dance" may have combined elements of both the Kongolese and the Akan practices. New York was home to enslaved peoples of both origins and the fact that West and Central Africans had a long history of cultural assimilation would also have enabled the process. Borders in West and Central Africa were fluid and forced migrations were common, particularly in the era of the transatlantic slave trade, and as polities, especially in West Africa, were so small, inhabitants would often have had direct experience of several, without having had to travel more than a few dozen miles from their homes. Such cultural blending also occurred in the Americas. Indeed, the process was actually facilitated and accelerated by the Africans' enforced relocation to the New World. Africans of various ethnicities had more in common with one another than they did with the Europeans, while the establishment of a common front which could be used against their masters was a pressing need. That these enslaved people also continued to recognize their own distinct cultural heritage is evidenced by numerous references to slaves dividing themselves into "nations," such as in the Pinkster celebrations described above.

Thus, in New York City at the time of Alan Jarrett's arrival in June 1711, Black society was made up of several different layers. Although all but a handful of the city's original African inhabitants, the Angolans, Congolese, and Luandans brought in by the Dutch in the mid-seventeenth century, had died, their descendants remained. Some were freemen living in the Bowery, others the domestics of long-established Dutch households. The second layer of the city's Black society consisted of the Madagascans brought in by Captain Kidd and the other pirates operating out of the Indian Ocean in the 1680s and 1690s. In the first decade of the eighteenth century, as we have seen, a few hundred Akan had been added to the mix, while a steady trickle of slaves had come to New York throughout the entire period via the Caribbean. Some of these had Akan or Senegambian origins, while others were originally from the Slave Coast (modern-day Benin) or were Creoles born in the West Indies of African parents. As such, New York's Black society was highly diverse. Despite such apparent divisions, however, these "nations" were far more inclusive in the Americas than they would have been in Africa. An Angolan and an Akan, for example, would have thought of each other as distinctly "foreign" had they happened to meet in their home continent. Were they to encounter one another in colonial New York, however, especially after having lived there for a number of years, they would perhaps be as aware of the cultural similarities between them as they were of the differences. Thus the process of African-Americanization began.[108]

As well as being the site where Pinkster was celebrated, the New York Commons played other roles in the social lives of the city's Black population. Of particular importance was the New York African Burial Ground, then known as the Negro Burial Ground. Located in "a desolate unappropriated spot" on the Commons, it spread over several modern-day city blocks round Centre, Duane, Lafayette, Baxter, Pearl, and White Streets and was situated in a low-lying ravine just to the south of the "Collect" Pond, a body of fresh water consisting of two pools divided by a small spit of land overlooked by Potbakers and Catiemuts hills. In prehistoric times the site had been a significant one for the Lenape Indians who used to sit by the pond and shuck and smoke oysters, forming over centuries the "large shell heap" which so intrigued the earliest Dutch settlers. Although it seems likely that the New York African Burial Ground was in use at least as early as 1697, the first surviving reference dates to 1713, when John Sharpe, the reverend of the chapel in Fort Anne, noted that "[enslaved Blacks] are buried in the Common by those of their country and complexion . . . [and] Heathenish rites are performed at the grave." A clerk, reminiscing in 1865, added that in "both the Dutch and English colonial times . . . many of [the Blacks who participated in burial ceremonies at the site] . . . were native Africans, imported hither in slave ships, and retain[ed] . . . their native superstitions and burial customs, among which was that of burying by night, with various mummeries and outcries." Further evidence is provided by New York's early law codes. A 1722 *Law for Regulating the Burial of Slaves*, prohibited burials after "Sunsett, under the Penalty of ten Shillings for Every Offence," and a 1731 amendment added that "Not more than twelve Slaves [were] to be [permitted] at A Funeral" and "No Pawl [was] to be allowed . . . nor Pawl Bearers."[109]

Other details regarding the burial rites of enslaved peoples in the Americas in the early modern period are revealed by contemporary Jamaican sources. John Taylor, a visitor to the island in the late 1680s, described the grave goods left by Jamaican slaves, many of whom were Akan. These included "roasted fowles, sugar, rum, tobacco, and pipes. . . . This they doe (as they say and follishly imagine)," Taylor explained, "in order to sustaine [the dead man] . . . in his journey beyond these plesant hills in their own country, whither they say he is now goeing to live at rest. After this they fill up the grave, and eat and drinck theron, singing in their own language verey dolefully, desiring the dead corpse (by ciseing the grave) to acquaint their father, mother, husband and other relations of their present condition and slavery, as he passeth thro' their country towards the plesant mountains."[110] Another seventeenth-century Jamaican source, the physician Hans Sloane, noted that grieving slaves "make great lamentations, mournings and howlings . . . and at the . . . Funeral throw in Rum and Victuals into their Graves, to serve them in the other world."[111]

Several of the graves unearthed in the New York African Burial Ground contained such grave goods. Burial 340, for example, held the remains of a woman who had died prior to 1735. She showed signs of lower-limb periostitis, nutritional stress, and osteoarthritis of the hip and shoulder. The researchers conjectured that the woman was probably of African origin on the basis of strontium-isotope analysis and the fact that her teeth had been sharpened. Around her waist the woman had 112 glass beads, one translucent red amber bead, and seven cowrie shells—a common currency in West Africa. She also had what appears to have been a bracelet on her right wrist consisting of alternating blue-green and yellow beads.[112]

The New York African Burial Ground may well have also served other ritual purposes for the early Akan residents of New York City. Akan sacred groves are areas preserved against the clearance of the land believed to be the dwelling places of gods and ancestral spirits. They were frequently located in and around hills, at burial sites, on land overgrown with thick brush and tall trees, and in areas near running or standing water, which was believed to be the medium by which spirits and the souls of the dead could travel. The beings believed to inhabit such places were thought to reside in rocks, trees, or bodies of water. They could be consulted as oracles, provide protection from enemies, avert famines, droughts or epidemics, heal the sick, aid childbirth, and provide guidance on military, domestic, or financial affairs. Sacrifices were made or offerings given to ensure the god's compliance. Although there is no evidence in the written record to suggest that the area around the Collect Pond was a sacred grove, it shared many attributes with such sites. Perhaps the area's swampland, vines, and trees were somehow evocative of the "sombre unlit depths" of the primordial forest from which the Akan ancestral forefathers were said to have emerged. As such they would have served the spiritual needs of New York City's Akan well.[113]

AT SOME POINT between September 1711 and March 1712, rumors of an impending revolt began spreading among New York City's enslaved people. The whisperings originated with the Akan and Papa who had arrived in 1710 and 1711, before passing on to those who had been resident for years or generations. Bitter about "Some Hard Usage" received at the hands of their masters, the Akan were intent on rising. Many of the Creoles, however, were no doubt afraid.[114] They thought the Akan cause was doomed, and the whites were certain to exact a terrible price for resistance to their rule. Any who doubted need only look at the fate of the Hallets' slaves on Long Island. Other Creoles considered throwing in their lot with the would-be rebels. What did they have to lose? As fall turned to winter, the rumors of revolt intensified. Enslaved persons spoke of the plot in hushed tones at the city's water pumps; clandestine meetings were held in the disorderly houses, at the Burial Ground, and in the homes of the few remaining free Blacks in the Bowery. Slowly, the idea gained currency, but the time was not yet right—the newly arrived Africans were suffering from the cold and were yet to fully recover from the horrors of the Middle Passage. Soon, however, they would have their revenge.

CHAPTER II

A Backdrop of War

NEW YORK CITY AND CANADA

July 1711 to April 1712

Owo n̈ka onipa kwa.
A snake does not bite a man without a cause.
—Akan proverb

ON JULY 11, 1711, TWO MILITARY TRANSPORTS dropped anchor in the East River. On board were thirty British and Irish officers selected for "their experience in military affairs." In return for promotion and a promise to double their pay overnight, these veterans of Marlborough's army had volunteered to participate in what was to be the largest British military expedition that North America had ever seen—an attempt to wrest control of Canada from the French. The plan had first been mooted back in April when the death of Joseph I, the warmongering Holy Roman Emperor, had threatened to bring the War of Spanish Succession to an untimely conclusion. Queen Anne's new secretary of state, Henry St. John, knew that he would have to move fast if he were to secure a bargaining chip for the peace talks which were sure to follow. New France made an ideal target. Not only would its capture demonstrate the effectiveness of the Tory's Blue Water Strategy (a policy which prioritized colonial campaigns over the commitment of large-scale land forces in mainland Europe), it would also appease the grievances of the American colonists. Ever since the raid on Deerfield in 1704, when one hundred and sixty men, women, and children had been killed or captured by French regulars and their Abenaki and Iroquois allies, Westminster's North American subjects had lived in fear, while complaining that their wishes to counterattack their northern foes were habitually ignored by the powers that be.[1]

By mid-1711 St. John had gathered an impressive invasion force. The main attack aimed at Quebec would be led by Brigadier General John Hill. Under Hill were 7,500 British marines, colonial militia, and volunteers, accompanied by 6,000 sailors manning nine ships of war, two bomb vessels, and over 60 transports and store ships. Led by Admiral Hovenden Walker, a competent naval officer, albeit one who lacked experience in command of large operations, the fleet was to proceed down the Saint Lawrence River before landing Hill's troops for a formal siege of Quebec. Meanwhile, a second division, a mixed force of colonial militia and Indian auxiliaries strengthened by the thirty recently promoted veterans from the European theater, would sail up the Hudson from New York and cross Lakes George and Champlain. After "reduc[ing] . . . [Forts] Chambly and Sorel," they were to advance northward up the Saint Lawrence to Montreal, "which place being [defended only by a palisade] may be taken sword in hand, [or] at least blocked up until the affair of Quebec is determined." While the plan appeared sound on paper, combining as it did the regulars' expertise at siege warfare with the colonials' aptitude for skirmishing in the North American wilderness, it had been inadequately prepared and rushed into effect. Only three months' provisions had been loaded on board the fleet even though the operation was likely to last at least twice as long and was to project a large force thousands of miles from their supply lines. Furthermore, Admiral Walker lacked pilots with experience of navigating the Saint Lawrence, a river notorious for its hidden rocks and shoals and dangerous winds and currents. An even more pressing factor was time. Having left England in mid-summer, Walker and Hill had the narrowest of margins to fulfill their aims before the Canadian winter closed in.[2]

With the arrival of the thirty sergeants in New York, preparations for the expedition against Montreal began in earnest. On June 16, Governor Hunter swore Rip Van Dam, John Barberie, and the rest of his counselors "to the utmost secrecy" before informing them of the plan, then issued instructions to the "officers of Customs [not to] . . . clear any vessel or vessels going out of this province unless small boats to Jersey till further notice" to ensure that sufficient river- and ocean-going vessels would be available to transport the troops. The counselors were ordered to raise money to pay the wages of the 600 militiamen the city was required to contribute, as well as providing for the expenses of the independent companies along with the money needed to pay for the troops' clothing, provisions, and supplies. On June 17, Hunter departed for New London, Connecticut, for a meeting with Colonel Francis Nicholson, the commander of the Montreal wing of the expedition. The governors of Pennsylvania, Connecticut, and Rhode Island also attended. By June 22, Hunter was back in New York, writing to the landowner and colonel of the Albany militia, Kiliaen Van Rensselaer, with instructions to receive the troops bound for Montreal. "Impress all the carpenters [in Albany]," Hunter commanded, "and set them to work immediately to make batteaus and send proper persons [into the woods] to find knees for them." Rensselaer was ordered to "buy up all the canoes and other boats [which he] judged fit for this expedition" and to send missionaries and translators to the Iroquois villages to request that their sachems gather "all their fighting men with their arms" and "march [them] down to [the rendezvous at] Albany." "Cannon, mortars and other arms" were stockpiled, along with gunpowder and ammunition; "all ye ship carpenters in New York" were impressed "to work on ye battoos for her majesty's service"; an embargo on exporting grain was introduced; Garret Viole was ordered to go to Long Island to recruit as many Indian scouts as possible; and "the justices of ye peace" in Westchester, Ulster, and Duchess Counties were commanded to "enquire what quantity of bacon and other provisions there are in their . . . districts and to send an acct thereof to his Excellency."[3]

On July 1, "about 5 in the evening," there was "a violent storm." "Terrible Claps of thunder & lightning" were heard, and "Hailstones . . . as big as . . . gooses eggs" fell across the colony.[4] By now word of the expedition had leaked to the general population. Many were worried about the city being exposed to attack by the French or their Indian allies. A petition arrived in Hunter's office insisting that the militia not required for the expedition should be paid full wages for the duration they were expected to serve as the temporary garrison in Fort Anne.[5] The mention of pay must have been particularly distressing for the governor: Hunter had still not received any wages since his arrival in New York, and his ability to access credit was diminishing. "It is not in my power to find ready money here as you desire," Hunter wrote to Brigadier General Hill on July 9, 1711, "for it is with much difficulty that I find provision for bills on the treasury and the little ready money I have been able to procure for keeping the carpenters and other tradesmen at work I am forced to take at 30 percent."[6] Nevertheless, Hunter was tireless in his preparations. When not dashing off to Connecticut and the Jerseys for further meetings, he made plans to evacuate New York City's "women, children and public records in case of invasion," and had two hundred bullocks and six hundred sheep driven from New York to Albany. Hunter also ordered signal boats to "cruise off Sandy Hook" to watch for French privateers, had "several armed sloops" fitted out "for the defence of the coast," and ordered beacons erected "both on Long Island and the Jerseys" to be set ablaze at the first sign of a French invasion.[7]

Toward the end of July Hunter's preparations were beginning to bear fruit. "All our Battoes are finished," the New York correspondent of the *Boston News-Letter* announced. "Several of them [were] gone to Albany last week with Several Indians. And this day the Regular forces here, the [30] British Officers, and Some Country Companies go up with several battoes, Stores & c." More good news came from Albany. "Several Cannoo's with French Indians and their Families are come thither," the *News-Letter* reported, "And 'tis said all the French Indians will desert them which will greatly facilitate the Expedition on this side."[8] The same day Hunter received another petition. Signed by several leading merchants and sailors of New York City including the slaver Alan Jarrett, the letter begged the governor to lift the embargo on exports thus allowing vessels to sail for the Caribbean. "The time of year requires them to be gone," the petitioners pleaded, "and if they . . . cannot saile by the first of Auguste next they shall be disappointed of their return by the approaching winter; to their great damage." As several ships had already been permitted to sail from Boston, Rhode Island, and Philadelphia, Hunter complied.[9] On July 23, Captain Abraham and David Schuyler, Hunter's Indian agents, arrived at Albany. "[They] give us an account of the readiness of those Nations ... tho' with great difficulties & gifts and that a very considerable number of them shall be ... in [Albany in] a few days," the local commander reported.[10] On July 31, repairs were carried out to New York City's fortifications, cannon were mounted at the batteries along the East River, and the entire "city [was] drawn out in arms." "None [were] excepted that were able," the *Boston News-Letter* reported. "His excellency [the governor] designs frequently to exercise them himself."[11]

On August 5 General Nicholson arrived from Boston and four days later he and Hunter traveled up the Hudson.[12] The majority of the troops destined for Montreal had already gathered in Albany by the time the commanders set off from New York. Totaling 2,400 men, the division was comprised of four separate bodies: Colonel Richard Ingoldseby, a former deputy governor of New York, commanded a regiment of 300 men drawn from the city's Independent companies including their chaplain, John Sharpe, 100 Palatine volunteers, and 200 Jersey militiamen. The second regiment, led by Colonel Peter Schuyler of Albany, comprised 350 New York militia, 100 Palatine volunteers, 50 Long Island Indians, and 40 "Sea Coast Indians ... [who were] of great use for managing batteaus and canoes and all other hard laboure." Colonel William Whiting commanded the third regiment of 360 "Connecticut levys." The final element was a body of 800 of "ye Five Nations with their Allies."[13] By the time Hunter arrived at Albany, several elements of Nicholson's command had already headed north. The vanguard had penetrated as far as Wood Creek, more than 125 miles away, while others were spread out between Saratoga, Fort Nicholson (later renamed Fort Edward), and Stillwater, where the general held a parade on August 31. "Nicholson was received with a triple huzza" by the "Christians," one witness reported, while the Indians loosed "a running fire" of arrows, a stray shot of which flew across the Hudson and struck "a private sentinel belonging to Col. Ingoldsby's regiment in the shoulder."[14]

By September 1, Hunter was back in New York City. Awaiting him was a letter from Admiral Walker, the naval commander of the Quebec-bound division. The fleet of seventy-seven vessels was "in good condition" and had enjoyed "a faire wind" which had carried it to the mouth of the Saint Lawrence by August 14. As both the provisions and specie that Walker had sailed with from London would soon be exhausted, Hunter was asked to supply more. Accordingly, the governor commanded the captains of the *Neptune, Mary*, and *Joseph* transports to load with "a thousand . . . barrills of pork, and as much bread, flower, butter, pease rum and tobacco as they can carry." Meanwhile, HMS *Feversham* was loaded with £568, 12s, 6d in specie and all were ordered to "saile for Quebeck [by] the first wind that offers." As Captain Paston's frigate was "almost unmann'd by death desertion & sickness" following a year on the American station, Hunter proposed to "borrow" some crew members from "ye Masters of [the] shipps and sloops embargo'd here . . . upon promise to restore them upon the returne of the [frigate from Quebec]." The majority of the masters agreed, but Mr. Foy, "the Supercargoe of a brigantine just come in from Bristoll," armed his crew with "hand spikes" and ordered them to repel the soldiers that Hunter sent on board. In the ensuing scuffle, Private Moore was knocked to the deck by a man who had been "soe drunk and troublesome [earlier in the day] that [his crewmates] had been obliged to bind him." On regaining his feet, Moore shot his assailant who died of his wounds the next day.[15] On the morning of September 18, as Moore was put on trial for manslaughter, the *Feversham* and its transports sailed for Quebec. A few hours later HMS *Hector* arrived in the East River. On board were Hunter's young wife, the "well educated and charming" Elizabeth Orby (also known as Lady Hay), and the couple's only child, the two-year-old Charles, whom Hunter had never seen before. It would be the last good news that Hunter would receive for some time.[16]

That evening, Hunter learned that Admiral Walker's fleet had "met with a violent storm" on the Saint Lawrence River.[17] On August 23, a heavy fog had descended, leaving the three divisions of the fleet sailing blind. Strong currents and Walker's pilots' inadequate knowledge of the river added to the danger. By evening the fleet had drifted forty-five miles off course and was dangerously close to the northern shore of the river at a point where the Saint Lawrence narrows from seventy-five to twenty-five miles, close by the Isle of Eggs. To his credit, Walker remained calm and guided the *Edgar* back to the center of the river, but seven troop transports, a store ship, and a sutler's sloop were wrecked. A total of 705 officers and men from Seymour's, Windress's, Kane's, and Clayton's regiments were drowned. Thirty-five women were lost, as were 150 sailors, and a number of children—drummer boys and the sons and daughters of the troops. A volunteer from New England wrote that "the shrieks of the sinking, drowning, departing souls" carried to him through the night, and it wasn't until 2 A.M., after the gale had subsided, that the remains of the fleet were able to stand off from shore. The admiral spent the next two days looking for survivors—almost 500 were picked up from the wrecks. On August 25, a council of war was convened on board the *Windsor*. Several of Walker's captains refused to take responsibility for what might happen should they continue upriver and his pilots admitted that they were out of their depth. His men's confidence shattered, Walker abandoned the mission and sailed for Spanish River.[18]

Hunter was devastated by the news. "My heart is too full . . . that I know not what to write," he confessed in a letter to General Nicholson, while he spoke of his "confusion" in a letter to Joseph Dudley, the governor of Massachusetts Bay.[19] When they learned of the disaster in their encampment at Lake George on September 19, Nicholson's troops were also badly affected. The Reverend John Buckingham, attached to the Connecticut militia, lamented the boost it would give to their "anti-christian and pagan enemies . . . Oh, what will those say," he mused, "how will they triumph and blaspheme, reproach and deride."[20] As word spread, a melancholy air settled over all the British colonies. New Yorkers feared that the governor of New France, Philippe de Rigaud, the Marquis of Vaudreuil, would send raiders across the frontier or even launch a full-scale invasion. In late September their worst fears appeared to have materialized when "Several French Indians" crossed Lake George "and carried away a prisoner [from] within a few miles of Albany."[21] On October 1, Governor Hunter warned General Hill that they needed to "be very alert" as "we are already threatened."[22] A week later Hunter returned to Albany to maintain the support of the Five Nations, who he was informed believed the recent disaster was evidence that "God . . . [wa]s against [them]." The governor oversaw "the defence of the Frontiers . . . [and] put them in the best posture . . . that mey be." That day, with the embargo on exports from New York City lifted, several merchantmen set sail from the East River despite the net of French privateers cruising off Sandy Hook. Among them was Alan Jarrett, the slaver who had brought the Akan from the Gold Coast that June. Having sold his last cargo, Jarrett "cleared out . . . for Guinea" on October 8.[23]

THE PARANOIA AND HYSTERIA in New York increased with news of a massacre on the frontier. A war party of twenty French Indians had attacked an isolated cabin belonging to Dutch settlers eighteen miles north of Albany on October 21. The details were widely publicized. David Ketelhuyn had been shot and killed on answering a knock at the door of his property. A stand-off had ensued, with Ketelhuyn's brother, his sixteen-year-old son, Daniel, and three soldiers who happened to be present at the time, holding off the encircling Indians by firing through loopholes in the walls. The Indians set fire to the property, forcing the besieged to make a break. One of the soldiers was the first to emerge. He was shot twice and fell dead in the doorway. The second soldier was also killed, while the third was taken prisoner as he attempted to escape across the snow drifts along with two "negro boy[s]." After making a brave defense, Daniel Ketelhuyn was shot through the shoulder and forced to surrender, while a third slave, "an Indian boy," was shot "thro the left side of his breast and thro the fleshy part of his arm" yet managed to conceal himself in some bushes. The last to leave the burning property were Ketelhuyn's wife, Johanna, her sister-in-law, and her infant nephew. "So bigg with child that she could scarcely walk," Johanna "ask[ed] . . . for quarter" but was cut down a short distance from the house. Stripped naked, she suffered "several wounds," including a fatal axe blow to the neck. The Indians scalped Johanna then dashed her nephew's "brains out against an [nearby] oak." Having hung the boy's body up "by the neck in the cleft of the tree," they scalped the other two soldiers and partially flayed David Ketelhuyn's body before marching back to New France with the surviving Ketelhuyn women and children.[24]

The news struck fear into the heart of every New Yorker. Indian attack was one of their most persistent terrors. The other, the dread of a slave revolt, was also brought to the fore in the second half of 1711 with news of a rash of lawlessness in South Carolina.[25] In May

the colony's acting governor, Robert Gibbes, had warned "how insolent and mischievous the negroes are become," and in June he wrote
that "there is scarce a day passes without some robbery . . . committed
by them in one part or other of this province." Later that month "several Negroes runaway from their Masters arm'd" themselves and began
"robbing & plundering houses & Plantations & putting ye Inhabitants
. . . in great fear and terrour." A posse was "prepare[d]" in Charles
Town "to . . . hunt . . . the runaway Negroes & . . . a number of Indians
[were hired] to assist them." In Autumn further details emerged. The
widow, Elizabeth Dutch, had had her "House & all her Substance"
burned to the ground by the maroons, while an Indian slave belonging
to Sarah Perry was killed by their leader, a "Spanish Negro" named
Sebastian. Governor Gibbes offered "fifty pounds" for his capture,
"dead or live," and £5 for the apprehension of "any other Negro [who
had been a] runaway [for] forty days." His actions brought rapid results. By October 11, Sebastian had been "took & killed" by "Indians."
The governor ordered them paid in full "for th[e] . . . Publick Service"
rendered.[26]

Back in New York, Governor Hunter had received yet more bad
news. On October 7, the *Feversham* and the three transports it had
been escorting to Quebec had been wrecked. Half a day from Spanish
River, Captain Paston had become disorientated by a strong current
and a "hard gale of wind" and the *Feversham* was driven onto the
rocks surrounding Scatarie Island on the easternmost point of Nova
Scotia. Hearing the tremendous splintering of oak that signaled the
disaster, the captains of the transports, which had been following in
single file, tried to steer clear, but each struck the rocks in succession.
While the *Mary* and *Joseph* were "bilged . . . but standing on their
keels," the *Feversham* and *Neptune* had been holed below the water-
line. "Beat all to pieces in half an hour," they broke in two and sunk
to the bottom. Captain Rouse of the *Neptune* and four of his seven
crew were drowned along with 100 of the *Feversham*'s 150 men. Captain Paston, Mr. Hyde, the ship's chaplain, and many of those who
had been reluctantly pressed aboard the undermanned frigate just before it had set sail from New York, were among the dead. The survivors managed to scramble onto Scatarie Island. Without food or
dry clothing and trapped on an inhospitable coast, over the next few

days they built signal fires and tried to salvage what they could. They hauled some provisions ashore, along with "powder and arms" and several hundred pounds worth of currency. Three days later, Captain Paston's body washed up and was buried and one of the ships' boats was saved. Four men set sail in it and were intercepted by a French privateer whose captain agreed to return to Scatarie and carry the rest of the survivors to New York in exchange for £200 of salvaged gold and silver.[27]

By November, morale was rock bottom in New York City. "Since the fatal miscarriage of the intended expedition our frontiers have been infested . . . by the French Indians," Hunter wrote to the Earl of Dartmouth on November 12. "I Have putt them into the best posture I can in such poor circumstances, and shall do my best in that and everything else for H.M. service."[28] Food shortages caused further discomfort.[29] With the grain reserves requisitioned by General Hill and Nicholson, bread prices rose. Urban protests followed. Even those in the rural hinterland began to feel the pinch. "There is a great crying among the wives and children that . . . [they] have no bread," one witness reported from the upper Hudson.[30] To make matters worse, it was bitterly cold. On November 26, the day the majority of the officers in Nicholson's division returned to New York City from Albany, it "snowed hard," and at the end of December the temperature plummeted. While the poor struggled to fill their bellies, New York City's more affluent inhabitants enjoyed the cold snap. The day after Christmas John Sharpe, the reverend of the chapel in Fort Anne, "went out in a slae" and on New Year's Eve he repeated the outing with his wife.[31]

In January the cold spell intensified. "We have abundance of snow, and . . . very severe frost, which has filld our rivers full of ice," the New York correspondent of the *Boston News-Letter* reported. While the Hudson froze every winter, the East River's high salt content meant it rarely did so, but the winter of 1711 to 1712 proved an exception. HMS *Lowestoffe* was frozen in at Turtle Bay, five miles to the north of Fort Anne by the Beekman estate, while Jacob Hall, the master of a sloop bound for Antigua, was caught by the encroaching ice sheet near Jersey. The sloop's hull buckled under the pressure, and Hall and his crew barely made it to shore alive.[32] As a result, no fresh supplies reached New York that winter. With the roads devoid of shipping, sailors, merchants, and stevedores lacked work, shopkeepers bemoaned their empty shelves, and the city's economy ground to a halt. Meanwhile, there was no sign of improvement in the weather. "We have a deep snow on the ground, and a severe frost," the New York correspondent of the *Boston News-Letter* reported on January 15, "and hitherto the hardest winter we have known."[33]

It was the city's poor who suffered most, none more so than the enslaved who had arrived with Alan Jarrett the previous June. Accustomed to the heat of the Gold Coast, where temperatures rarely fell below seventy-five degrees, and with no natural immunity to the New World's contagious diseases, their immune systems grew progressively weaker. Poor diet and the stresses brought on by enforced translocation exacerbated the situation.[34] Many, no doubt, fell victim to measles or the whooping cough, "violent fever and fits of shivering from ague."[35] Their quarters were unheated, and their workload showed little sign of diminishing. Despite the abundant snowfall, enslaved people were sent to the Commons to gather wood for their masters' fires, a chore which could result in frostbite.[36] Peter Kalm, a Swedish visitor to New York who later published an account of his travels, recorded that enslaved persons' frozen limbs "broke in the middle, and dropt entirely from the body, together with the flesh on them. Thus it is," Kalm concluded, "the same case with men here, as with plants which are brought from the southern countries, and cannot accustom themselves to a colder climate."[37] Indeed, the winter proved so detrimental to a slave's health, that sales of enslaved people in New York ceased almost entirely from December to February as potential purchasers feared that any they might acquire would die before the spring.[38]

As well as dealing with the freezing weather, poor diet, overwork, and exposure to new diseases, the newly arrived Akan were subjected to "some hard usage ... from their masters" that winter. Exactly what Governor Hunter meant by this ambiguous phrase, written several months later by way of explaining the revolt of April 1712, is difficult to say.[39] Compared to the form of slavery the Akan would have been familiar with on the Gold Coast, where the lines between the enslaved and the free were more fluid than those established by the racist law code of colonial New York, Jarrett's slaves must have considered the conditions under which they labored in the Americas intolerable.*

Another factor which could have triggered the rebellion was the poor rations the Akan slaves would have received in late 1711 and early 1712, exacerbated by the grain shortage. This, at least, was one of the factors which would prompt the Akan revolt on Saint John in 1733 after hurricane and drought had devastated the island's crops.[40] Likewise, the abortive Antigua revolt of 1736 was preceded by a period of drought, punctuated by earthquakes, hurricanes, and outbreaks of sugar cane pestilence and epidemics which caused economic turmoil as well as high mortality rates.[41] Another potential cause of the discontent in New York that winter was physical abuse. We could

---

*On the Gold Coast the enslaved fell into four distinct categories. The *akyere* was a convicted criminal who served as a slave in the period between their conviction and their execution, a ceremony normally performed as part of the funeral rites of a monarch or other dignitary, or to win the favor of the gods in the prelude to war, examples being the sacrifices ordered by Ansa Sasraku prior to his attack on Agona in the 1680s or those commanded by King Akwonno on the occasion of the death of a queen mother in 1703. Above the *akyere* in terms of status were the *odonko*, foreign-born slaves without free family members on the Gold Coast who could therefore be sold or traded. The *awowa* was a native-born Akan who had been temporarily sold into slavery to pay off a debt or as a type of reparation for civil or military crimes. Sometimes the *awowa* were subsequently redeemed by the clan which had sold them into slavery, but if this did not come to pass, they were reduced in status to the level of the *odonko*, although referred to by the distinct term *akao pa*. In Gold Coast society both the *akoa pa* and the *odonko* were entitled to hold and work parcels of land and could keep or trade the crops they produced. The Akan proverb *Akoa onim som di ne wura ade*, "A slave who knows how to serve succeeds to his master's property," indicates that these slaves could and did inherit land and, although an *odonko*'s children would inherit their parents' status, some second- and third-generation *odonko* were adopted into their enslavers' families and became free men and women as a result. This last illuminates the essential difference between slavery in the Americas and slavery on the Gold Coast. While in the former, Blacks—even those who had gained manumission—would always be second-class members of society; in Akan culture there was a possibility of the enslaved being fully reincorporated into society on an equal basis. Some have speculated that it could have been the realization of their inferior status among the colonists, that led the New York Akan to rebel. See Foote, "Some Hard Usage," *New York Folklore*, 18 (2001), 152--154.

speculate that one or more of the Akan was beaten, raped, or murdered by their enslavers. Several of the whites who would be killed or wounded during the uprising of 1712 were well-known to the Akan slaves who attacked them, raising the possibility that they may have been specifically targeted for wrongs committed. Augustus Grassett was the master of the city's weigh house, a place frequented by enslaved stevedores; Johannes Dehonneur, an East Ward victualler who would also be among the casualties, was the owner of Tom, one of the rebels executed in the aftermath of the revolt; while Henry Brasier, a twenty-seven-year-old turner who would be killed, had leased one or more slaves in the months preceding the revolt from Gysbert Vaninburgh, a South Ward baker who owned, among other enslaved people, a certain Abigail, the only woman who would be executed in the aftermath of the revolt.[42]

A further question which needs to be considered is how the rebels prepared for the revolt that winter. As the 1712 conspiracy was kept "so secret, that there was no Suspicion of it, till It came to the very Execution," little evidence resulted.[43] The copious literature produced in the aftermath of the events of 1741, however, may provide some clues as to the genesis of its predecessor. According to Attorney General Daniel Horsmanden's account, the 1741 plotters were recruited along "national" lines. The white publican, John Hughson, who Horsmanden later alleged was the ringleader of the plot, "employed some . . . head negroes as agents under him" each of whom was instructed to solicit only those of their own ethnicity. Thus, Akan recruited Akan, Congolese targeted fellow Congolese, and Creoles were recruited by Creoles. Potential recruits were taken to Hughson's disorderly house and plied with alcohol as a preliminary to sealing the deal. "Hughson always gave then drams till they were intoxicated," Horsmanden alleged, "and then the conspiracy was proposed to them . . . [to which] they generally consented without much difficulty." On the other hand, "if they were unwilling to engage, they were terrified by threats of being murdered, till they complied; then . . . were . . . sworn [to secrecy] . . . and . . . commissioned to seduce others."[44] Such details raise far more questions than they answer in regard to the events of 1711 and 1712: Was recruitment carried out in the same manner? Were threats used to bully the unwilling into compliance? Did the plot spread across national lines, or did it only involve the Akan? And, if the former was the case, who coordinated the plot?

That the 1712 plot was led by Akan is certain. That they were the same individuals who had been brought to New York City by Alan Jarrett in 1710 and 1711 seems highly probable. Slave revolts were normally instigated by recent arrivals and Jarrett was the only slaver to arrive in the city from the Gold Coast since 1705.[45] That the April 1712 New York plot also involved, to a lesser extent, Africans of other nations and some Creoles is also possible. That it was diverse is suggested by the ethnicities of those indicted in the aftermath—some of them appear to have been Creole, and several had been resident in New York prior to 1710.* This hypothesis is supported by two primary sources. The *Boston News-Letter* of April 21, 1712, contained a dispatch from New York dated the fourteenth of the month, which stated "tis fear'd that most of the Negro's here (who are very numerous) knew of the Late Conspiracy to murder the Christians."[46] The second source is a letter written by the Reverend John Sharpe concerning Robin, the would-be catechumen who had been enslaved in New York for at least two years before the revolt broke out. After Robin had been hanging in chains without sustenance for three days as punishment for his alleged involvement, he was to tell the reverend that he "knew of ye Conspiracy but was not guilty of any bloodshed in the tumult."[47] If Robin's death-row confession was true, and Sharpe certainly believed it was, then how and from whom did Robin learn of the plot before it was hatched? Had he been recruited only to renege on his commitment at the last moment? If so, who recruited him? While the Akan and Papa who had arrived with Jarrett were likely to have been close-knit, militarily capable, and well disciplined, they were unsuited to such a role. Due to linguistic barriers, the new arrivals would have been unable to communicate unequivocally with

---

*Mars enslaved by Regnier had been in New York since at least 1708 (see Chapter 2), while Caesar enslaved by Van Norwood was likely to have been resident in the city since at least the beginning of April 1710. Kitto, enslaved by Ruth Sheppard, is called a "mullato" in the Court of Quarter Sessions Minute's Memorandum for April 14–15, 1712, meaning it was highly unlikely that he was Akan. Also, Juan and Jose were also certainly not Akan (see Chapter 7).

the disparate elements that made up the slave community in colonial New York, let alone unite them in a plot which would almost certainly end in their deaths should they fail. If it was not the Akan who arrived in 1711 who recruited Robin, who, then, could have fulfilled this role?

The most obvious candidates would be the surviving slaves from the shipment that Jarrett had brought to New York from the Gold Coast in 1710.[48] They were likely to have been Twi speakers and, having spent a year in the city, at least some of them would have picked up sufficient English to communicate with New York's Creole slaves. Perhaps Claus who belonged to Alan Jarrett might fit the bill. As previously discussed, the fact that Claus was among the first to be condemned and was the only rebel to suffer the horrendous punishment of being broken on the wheel suggests that he had may have been a leader among the New York Akan. This also makes credible the possibility that he was involved in recruitment the previous winter.[49] Another possibility is that the intermediary was Kitto, "a mulatto man slave" who belonged to Isaac Gouverneur and would hang in the aftermath of the revolt.[50] Although "mulattos," or those of mixed race, were found on the Gold Coast in the period of Jarrett's voyages as a result of the long-term presence of Europeans in the region, it is much more probable that Kitto was born in New York or the Caribbean. If his mother was Akan and had taught her son to speak Twi, then he would have been in an ideal position to act as a go-between. A final candidate is Peter the Doctor. A "free Negro" laborer resident in New York's East Ward since at least 1703, Peter would have been a well-known figure among the city's Black community by the winter of 1711 to 1712. That he was involved in the plot is evidenced by his subsequent indictment and by the fact that he was to play a key role at the only recorded meeting of the rebels prior to the revolt which took place on New Year's Day 1712 (March 25 in the old-style Julian calendar). That Peter had the desire to host gatherings of Blacks is evidenced by his conviction by the city's Court of Quarter Sessions in 1715 for "Entertaining . . . Negro Slaves . . . in his dwelling house at the East Ward . . . without the privity or knowledge of their masters." Two further factors make Peter eminently suitable for the role. He was of Akan origin, therefore suggesting that he would have been able to communicate with the rebels who had arrived with Alan Jarrett in

June 1711. He was also an Obeah practitioner, or Akan priest, whose functions would have included presiding at seances, burials, weddings, and divinations, including those carried out prior to war.[51]

Alternatively, there may have been no need for coordination. The plot could have been an entirely Akan affair and Robin's prior knowledge coincidental. An Akan revolt was foiled in 1675 in Barbados when a conspirator discussing the plan was overheard by a Creole slave who then informed her master. This led to the arrest of the ringleaders before the revolt could be put into effect.[52] The 1736 Antigua plot was discovered in the same manner.[53] It seems plausible, therefore, that Robin also overheard some conspirators in an unguarded moment. Perhaps Robin was Akan by birth or had Akan parents and therefore spoke or understood Twi. This, at least, would explain how Robin "knew of ye Conspiracy but was not guilty of any bloodshed."[54] Presuming, for argument's sake, that Robin did indeed overhear a careless conversation, why did he not report his discovery to the authorities? Given his status as a slave the question may seem unnecessary, but in the two cases cited above (Barbados 1675 and Antigua 1736), along with many others around the Americas, this is precisely what happened. "Loyal" slaves who informed on their peers were typically rewarded for doing so and Creoles sometimes felt a need to protect their masters, with whom they may have lived since birth.[55] We do know, however, that Robin had reason to resent his master, and therefore a potential motive for holding his tongue. Adrian Hoghlandt, the "Eminent" merchant who owned him, had repeatedly refused Robin's requests "for leave to be baptized" by Elias Neau, whose classes Robin had been attending since at least 1710. Perhaps, therefore, Robin decided to withhold his knowledge of the impending revolt, as a way of taking revenge on those who had denied him this opportunity.[56]

Meanwhile, for New York City's white community the daily routine ground on as winter gave way to spring. On February 7 the garrison at Fort Anne fired a twenty-one-gun salute to mark Queen Anne's birthday, and on March 1 Trinity Church's steeple was finally completed.[57] Three days later the Reverend John Sharpe took a morning walk with his friend Elias Neau before celebrating Shrove Tuesday with a visit to his favorite tavern, the Fighting Cocks.[58] On March 9,

Andrew Stuckey, a Huguenot merchant and enslaver of Hannibal, one of the men who would be executed in the aftermath of the revolt, had his baby daughter, Anne, baptized in the French Church, and the following day HMS *Lowestoffe*, which had been trapped in the frozen East River since November, finally broke free of the ice. Accompanied by three merchantmen bound for Lisbon and Amsterdam, Captain Gordon set sail for Britain without delay.[59] That Gordon was wise to do so became evident on March 14 when the bitter weather returned. "We had a mighty storm of snow and wind . . . which . . . has done considerable damage [in New York]," the *Boston News-Letter* reported. "A prodigious tide" blown in off the Atlantic "fill'd most of the cellars by the waterside, [and] broke most of the Wharffs. Two or three Sloops were blown clear out of the roads from their anchors," and at Cape May two whales were washed ashore.[60]

On March 25, as the inhabitants of New York City celebrated New Year, twenty-five or more of its Black residents gathered for a clandestine meeting. As discussed above, Peter the Doctor's house in the East Ward was a possible venue, while a letter written by the Reverend John Sharpe provides some details of the event. "The Conspirators tyi[ed] . . . themselves to Secrecy by Sucking ye blood of each Others hands," he recorded, "and to make them invulnerable as they believed a free negro who pretends Sorcery gave them a powder to rub on their Cloths which made them . . . confident [of victory]."[61] There seems little doubt that the "free negro" was Peter the Doctor, while both ceremonial elements are recognizably Akan in origin. The "powder" was *hyire*, a white clay associated with victory, used for purification or to symbolize a transition to a more highly elevated spiritual state.[62] As Sharpe correctly states, the powder was also believed to convey protection from an enemy's weapons. "One is rendered secure from gunshot" by its application, one source informs us, "and if a knife is raised against one, the blade will shatter."[63] The reference to the exchange of blood also has Akan roots. In a culture in which the written word was unknown, verbal oaths were vital. Blood, at times mixed with gunpowder, was commonly used to seal the deal, particularly when oaths were taken prior to warfare.[64]

Exactly who attended the meeting is less certain. Most of the Akan brought to New York on Jarrett's sloop in June 1711 were probably present. Among them were at least two persons named Quacko, one owned by the merchant, Rip Van Dam, and the other by Van Dam's fellow merchant and son-in-law, Walter Thong. Van Dam's Quash was also likely to have been there, as was Quaco, an enslaved man belonging to the boatman Abraham Provoost, Cuffee, an Akan belonging to Peter Vantilborough, and the "slave boy" Dick, owned by the "Lame and Antient" blacksmith Harmanus Burger. Alan Jarrett's Claus, Gysbert Vaninburgh's Abigail, Kitto, the "mulatto man slave" who belonged to Isaac Gouverneur, Ruth Sheppard's Furnis, Peter Morin's Caesar, and John Barberie's Mingo were other probable attendees, while two Toms, one owned by Nicholas Roosevelt and the other by the Quaker goldsmith David Lyell, might also have been present, along with a woman who was by that time noticeably pregnant, Stophel Pels' Sarah. We can also imagine Robin, the would-be Catholic convert, lurking in the shadows, perhaps already regretting his involvement. Another two individuals who may or may not have been present were Jose and Juan, the "Spanish Indians" who had recently been frustrated in their attempts to petition Governor Hunter for their freedom. If they did indeed attend the meeting, they must also have entertained doubts about the wisdom of participating. With their magic and blood pacts, the Akan must have seemed a desperate bunch to their Creole peers. Outnumbered and outgunned and with no safe haven and little to no hope of support, the Akan were in all likelihood doomed to failure. If such defeatist sentiments did exist, they may even have been voiced that night. Even so, the doubters remained in the minority. The Akan would not be deterred.

CHAPTER 12

The Revolt

NEW YORK CITY
April 6–7, 1712

Aprile 6—I preached St. Math. 26.75. In the night abt 2 the Negroes set
fire to a house and being armed designed to murder all yt came to quench
it—in this Massacre many suffered.

—Journal of the Reverend John Sharpe, April 6, 1712

Obarima, woye no dom āno, na wonyé no fie.
A man is made in the forefront of battle and not (by remaining) at home.

—Akan proverb

SOON AFTER THEIR MEETING AT NEW YEAR, the New York rebels decided on the time and date that they would initiate the revolt. The
night of April 6 was by no means a random selection. For the Akan
the timing of such events was governed by whether days were deemed
"good" or "bad," *Soesje* days, or unlucky days, were inappropriate for
important activities, the commencement of which was normally reserved for *amgbene*, lucky days, or *kenle kpole*, "great days."[1] Also significant was the fact that April 6, 1712, was a Sunday. Many of the
rebels would be able to pursue their own agendas while their masters
spent the day with their families. Furthermore, the night of April 5
to 6 was the first night of the new moon.[2] For the Akan the day following the crescent's first appearance was characterized by the obser-
vance of religious rites and rituals concerning the dead.[3] Ludewig
Rømer, a Danish factor at Fort Christiansborg, witnessed such a cer-

emony. "They talk to . . . [the moon]," he wrote, "and shake their limbs as if they wanted to throw off their arms and legs. They finally take a firebrand and hurl it, as if they wanted to throw it up to the moon, and with that the ceremony is over."[4] One of the most important gods of the Akan pantheon was Ngame, the moon-goddess. The Akan believed she gave newly born humans their souls by shooting lunar rays into them with her new-moon bow, while for the Gã of the eastern Gold Coast the new moon signified rebirth and the continuation of life.[5] Perhaps the New York rebels believed the event would signify the beginning of their new lives as freemen, or usher in their deaths and passage to the afterlife, or perhaps the first night of the new moon was chosen for more pragmatic reasons: the darkness would add to the whites' confusion and allow the rebels to slip away into the night.

With the time and date decided, the rebels chose their point of rendezvous: an orchard in the East Ward belonging to the cooper John Crooke. The site was centrally located and two of the slaves later brought to trial, Lilly and Jack, were Crooke's property, therefore their presence would not arouse suspicion.[6] The orchard was also within a few dozen meters of many of the plotters' homes, and the trees would provide cover for the first to arrive while they waited for the rest to gather.* With the rendezvous selected, the rebels then acquired weapons. Daggers, axes, clubs, poniards, pistols, hatchets, and muskets

---

*Possible residences for seventeen of the nineteen rebels subsequently executed for their roles in the revolt can be identified. Of these, four (Caesar, enslaved by Norwood, Tom, enslaved by Dehonneur, Caesar, enslaved by Morin, and Kitto, enslaved by Gouverneur) had enslavers who lived in the East Ward. Furthermore, as discussed in Chapter 7, Abigail, the only woman executed in the aftermath of the revolt, may well have been hired out by the East Ward resident Henry Brasier at the time of the revolt. Four others (Quacko, enslaved by Thong; Furnis, enslaved by Sheppard; Robin, enslaved by Hoghlandt; and Tom, enslaved by Lyell) had enslavers who lived in the nearby Dock Ward; three (Toby, enslaved by Cure; Sam, enslaved by Fauconnier; and Mingo, enslaved by Barberie) had enslavers who lived in the West Ward; four (Quacko and Quashi, enslaved by Van Dam; Hannibal, enslaved by Stuckey; and Tom, enslaved by Roosevelt) had enslavers who lived in the South Ward; and just one (Titus, enslaved by Ray) was in the North Ward. Rothschild, *New York City Neighborhoods*, 184–204; *Census of the City of New York*, in O'Callaghan (ed.), *Documentary History of the State of New York*, volume 1, 395–405.

would all be used.[7] The majority were likely to have been stolen from their masters. This, at least, is what was said to have happened in the 1741 "revolt." When questioned by Attorney Daniel Horsmanden, Ben, a slave belonging to a captain of the city militia, recalled that he "could find a gun, shot and powder, at his master's house, that his master did not watch him," and that "he could go into every room." Cuffee, enslaved by Adolph Phillipse, claimed to have "a key of his master's things," and that "he could come at what he pleased," including "some of his master's swords and guns." Weapons might also have been purchased in one of the city's disorderly houses with the collusion of the white criminal underclass. In 1741 an enslaved man named Caesar was said to have given John Hughson "twelve pounds in silver Spanish pieces of eight, to buy guns, swords and pistols." According to Horsmanden, the publican "went up into the country; and when he returned, . . . brought with him seven or eight guns and swords . . . a bag of shot and a barrel of gunpowder."[8]

APRIL 6, 1712, began like any other Sunday in colonial New York City. As the church bells tolled that morning, those of a religious persuasion set off to join their respective congregations. The Reverend William Vesey presided at Trinity Church, and John Sharpe "preached St Math. 26.75" in the chapel in Fort Anne. "Then Peter remembered the words Jesus had spoken," Sharpe pronounced, "Before the rooster crows, you will disown me three times."[9] In the Dutch Reformed Church, the minister Gaulterus Du Bois baptized Jacob, the newborn son of Cornelius Jacobze and his wife, Jenneke Peers, while down at the East River docks, stevedores hurried to load cargoes bound for ports around the globe.[10] Captain Tynes set sail for St. Thomas; Captain Broadbank "Clear'd out" for Madeira; Captain John Tudor, the former slaver who had served as a Justice of the Peace at Mars's trial five years before, sailed for Rhode Island; and the *Eagle* brigantine arrived from Barbados. The *Eagle's* captain, "Mr. Butler," brought good news. "[Our] Men of War Cruising off [Barbados] . . . have taken about 14 or 15 Sayle of the Martinico Fleet from France, [and] Drove two a shore," he informed the New York correspondent of the *Boston News-Letter*. As a result, the French garrison on Martinique was "in great want of provisions."[11] All in all, it seemed the war in the Caribbean was going well. After sunset, New York's white working classes and the city's enslaved took advantage of the time afforded them on the Sabbath to "dance and divert themselves." The streets were full, and the disorderly houses did good trade.[12]

Amidst the hustle and bustle that Sunday night, twenty-five or so slaves slipped out of their masters' homes up cellar steps or through back doors and open garret windows.[13] Passing through the shadows of the cobbled streets, they gathered at Crooke's orchard in the East Ward. Most had only a few blocks to travel. Tom, enslaved by Johannes Dehonneur, and Caesar, enslaved by Peter Morin, came from Queen Street facing the East River. Kitto, enslaved by Isaac Gouverneur, lived in nearby Sloat Lane. Peter the Doctor, the Obeah man who had prepared the *hyire* white clay and other charms to provide the rebels with supernatural protection, also came from the East Ward, as did Cuffee, the Akan who belonged to the baker Peter Vantilborough. Quacko, enslaved by Walter Thong, and Tom, enslaved by David Lyell, made their way to the orchard from the Dock Ward, along with Furnis, enslaved by Ruth Sheppard. From the South Ward came Hannibal, enslaved by Andrew Stuckey, and Abigail, her clothes perhaps still stained with flour from the bakery of her master, Gysbert Vaninburgh; Tom emerged from his owner Nicholas Roosevelt's house on Bridge Street; while Quacko and Quashi slipped out of Rip Van Damme's imposing premises on adjacent Stone Street, then headed north and east to the rendezvous. Titus traveled east down Wall Street from his master Richard Ray's house in the North Ward, or perhaps kept to the shadows of the back alleys to avoid the main thoroughfare. Among those with the farthest to travel were Toby, enslaved by John Cure, and Sam, enslaved by Peter Fauconnier. Both came from the West Ward, along with Mingo who slipped out of his master John Barberie's home on Broadway and made his way across town.[14]

By "about twelve or one of ye clock in the night" the rebels had gathered.[15] Weapons were handed out, firearms being allocated to the Akan leaders.[16] Under the beneficence of the new moon, final ceremonies were perhaps performed. Supervised, no doubt, by Peter the Doctor, the Akan rebels smeared fresh *hyire* on their faces, torsos, and limbs to ward off the bullets that were soon to be fired against them;

final oaths were uttered, sealed with bloody handshakes and the drinking of potent brews of blood, rum, and grave dirt.[17] It seems likely that the new moon ceremony described by the Danish factor Ludewig Rømer or something similar was also performed, with much shaking of limbs, and the sacrifice of fowls or other farmyard animals.[18] Only then, having checked the edges of their axes, knives, hatchets, and swords, sharpened the points of their daggers and poniards, and loaded their pistols and muskets with powder and shot, did the rebels "put their bloody design into execution."[19] At 2 A.M., "about the going down of the moon," Cuffee snuck out from the orchard and made his way to his master's bakery on Smith Street one block from City Hall.[20] Having taken a flame, perhaps from the ovens or sparked from his own tinder and flint, Cuffee set fire to an outhouse. Once the flames had taken hold, licking up the wooden walls and throwing shadows about the sleeping town, he returned to Crooke's orchard where the rest of the rebels were waiting. According to Hunter's later report, they then "all sallyed out togeather with their arms and marcht to the fire."[21] The rebels divided into sections, each of which was assigned a position. "Plant[ing] themselves in several streets and lanes leading to" Vantilborough's bakery, which by now was completely ablaze, they "stood prepared . . . to kill everybody that approached to put [it] out."[22]

Slowly at first, the sleeping city began to awake. Seeing the shadows of the flickering flames and smelling the smoke billowing up from Vantilborough's outhouse, several residents got dressed and made their way toward the fire to douse the flames. Others, having spent the night indulging themselves in one of the city's many taverns or disorderly houses, spilled out onto the streets to join them. The night watchmen shook their rattles; the lookouts on the battlements of Fort Anne rang the fire bell.[23] Augustus Grassett, a seventy-year-old French Huguenot and master of the city's weigh house, who had once been accused of using "a false beam" to trick the city's merchants out of a shilling or two, was among the first to react.[24] Another who made his way to Vantilborough's outhouse was Adrian Hoghlandt. The young Dutch merchant who had refused to allow Robin to be baptized by Elias Neau was accompanied by his fifteen-year-old nephew, Henrick. Nearby was Adrian Beekman, the son of Geradus Beekman, the former acting governor of New York. The merchant Lawrence

Reade was also amidst the growing throng, as was the turner Henry Brasier, a thirty-seven year-old shoemaker named William Echt, the carpenter Johannes Low, and Lieutenant John Corbet. One of the thirty former sergeants involved in Francis Nicholson's abortive attempt on Montreal, Corbet had returned to New York in September and had been drawing his pay in the city ever since.[25]

It seems highly probable that there were also several enslaved people mixed in with the crowd that night. Rather than risking their own lives, the slaves' owners would no doubt have wanted their chattels to undertake the potentially dangerous task of firefighting for them. In the confusion, which was only to get worse once the killing had begun, many of those later called upon to testify in court would mistake these innocents for those involved in the rebellion. Among those unfairly implicated in this way we can perhaps count Adrian Hoghlandt's Robin as well as Jose and Juan, the two "Spanish Indians" who had petitioned Governor Hunter for their freedom. Cornelia Van Clyff Norwood's Caesar may also have been involved in this way.[26] At least three of these four had sound alibis for being out that night. As his master would be among the rebel's victims and was therefore clearly in the vicinity, Robin's presence is easy to explain.[27] It is also likely that Jose's owner, Mary Wenham, was present as she would later be called upon as a witness for the prosecution; while Juan belonged to Peter Vantilborough, the owner of the property that Cuffee had set on fire to trigger the rebellion in the first place.[28]

When the head of the crowd emerged into the light of the blazing outhouse, the Akan rebels fired a volley, then charged with their swords, daggers, axes, and cudgels drawn.[29] Perhaps having recognized him from time spent working as stevedores on the dockside, Toby, Walter Thong's Quacko, Lilly, Tom, Cuffee, Hannibal and Peter Morin's Caesar surrounded Augustus Grassett. The Frenchman threw up his arms in self-defense, but the rebels sliced through his fingers and caused "him several wounds about his Neck and head." The fatal blow was struck by Toby with a "dagger of six pence" which cut three inches into Grassett's neck.[30] Nearby, Henry Brasier, the twenty-eight-year-old East Ward merchant, was attacked by Furnis, Kitto, Mingo, Rip Van Dam's Quacko and Quasi, and Abigail, the enslaved woman whom Brasier may well have hired in the months leading up to the revolt. Amidst the frenzy of blades and cudgels battering Brasier's body, perhaps Abigail managed to exact some measure of personal revenge. Hefting an axe "of the value of eight pence," Furnis brought it down upon Brasier's neck inflicting "a Certain mortal wound" three inches across and "four inches" deep. Brasier was nearly decapitated by the blow.[31] Elsewhere, Lieutenant Corbet, the English-born veteran of Marlborough's campaigns in Flanders, fell under a flurry of blows; Johannes Low was killed; the twenty-one-year-old Joris Marschalck was dispatched with a dagger to the chest; while William Echt, the shoemaker, was surrounded and beaten with clubs and staves before being "mortally wound[ed] in three several places under his right breast and . . . [in his] throat."[32] Adrian Hoghlandt was set upon by Claus and Abraham Provoost's Quaco and killed by a dagger blow to the back as he attempted to flee; his fifteen-year-old nephew, Henrick, was wounded.[33] Adrian Beekman, the son of the former acting governor of New York, was shot through the chest with a "ten shilling" handgun by Nicholas Roosevelt's Tom. According to one account, Beekman managed to stagger back to his East Ward home where he "died in the arms of his wife," Lucretia DeKey.[34] At least seven other New Yorkers were wounded. Thomas Stewart was bludgeoned, cut, stabbed, or shot in the melee, as was John Troupe, a Huguenot barber and periwig maker, and Johannes Dehonneur, the East Ward victualler. Whether Dehonneur was attacked by his own slave, Tom, is unclear. George Elsworth, the East Ward butcher who, it may be remembered, had tangled with Jacob Regnier in the city courts over the fate of his slave Will two years before, was also wounded, while Lawrence Reade, a prosperous merchant and slave owner who lived on Smith Street, and David Coesart, a wealthy stone mason whose properties stretched across the state and into New Jersey, were so seriously wounded that many thought they would die before the night was out.[35]

When word of the uprising reached Fort Anne, Governor Hunter had one of the "great guns" fired "from the ramparts" to "Call . . . up the Inhabitants in arms." While the townsfolk gathered, Hunter sent "a detachment [of the New York Independent companies] from the fort under a proper officer to march against" the rebels. On their approach the slaves were "easily scattered" and thereafter it seems they split into two groups.[36] The Reverend John Sharpe recalled that some "hid themselves in town," while Hunter wrote that the rest "made their retreat into ye woods."[37] Another account added that the second group withdrew so "as fast as they could . . . being closely pursued," presumably by the detachment of the independent companies, and that some fled into the Commons and "concealed themselves in barns, and others sheltered in the swamps or woods" around the Negro Burial Ground. We also learn that "in their flight they also killed and wounded several white people" and that "some of them in their flight shot themselves, [and] one shot first his wife and then himself."[38]

One plausible interpretation of this seemingly conflicting information would be that the rebels divided along "national" lines. The Creole participants, such as Kitto and Sam, and the other slaves caught up in the events of that night without actually having been directly involved, such as Jose, Juan, Robin, and Cornelia Van Clyff Norwood's Caesar, fled in disorder once the soldiers appeared. Knowing that the troops were likely to presume that all Blacks out on the streets that night were rebels and fire on them indiscriminately, they hid themselves in town. Meanwhile, the Akan retreated in a more measured fashion, killing or wounding some whites as they did so. With the benefit of the military experience they had gained on the Gold Coast, the Akan were able to remain disciplined despite the stresses of the situation. Perhaps they had even planned their retreat to the Commons and set out on a predetermined route. As a well-known refuge for the city's Blacks, it was also a place where they might have presumed that pursuing whites would have been reluctant to venture. That several of this group chose to commit suicide by shooting themselves while "in their flight" also points to likely Akan origins.[39] As previously discussed, suicide under such circumstances was not deemed dishonorable by the Akan. It is also known that enslaved Akan rebels would kill their wives before taking their own lives.[40] References in three sources to the fact that the suicides were committed with firearms may also be significant.[41] According to an account by Ludewig Rømer some 4,000 Akim warriors committed suicide in this way following defeat in battle in 1742. "They killed themselves by holding their own muskets to their throats and firing with their toes, so that the entire shot went through their heads," the factor recorded.

The method was chosen according to Selena Axelrod Winsnes, an authority on such behaviors, "lest the head be taken by the enemy and subjected to soul-damaging treatment."[42] As previously mentioned, the mutilation of the decapitated heads of one's enemies was believed to cause "great pain" and "torment" to the souls of the dead and even prevent their passage to *asamando*, the place where the ancestors dwell.[43]

FOR THE REMAINDER OF THE NIGHT of April 6–7, 1712, New York was in turmoil. According to the *Boston News-Letter*, the townsfolk were in "no small Consternation," and spent the next twenty-four hours "under Arms."[44] The troops of the independent companies set up a perimeter around the Commons to prevent the rebels' escape, the wounded were attended to, and the dead were carried to the workplace of the city coroner, Henry Wileman, who would conduct "inquisitions" on the bodies over the next two days. In the East Ward the fire at Vantilborough's outhouse was extinguished, while in Fort Anne, Governor Hunter began planning his response to the rebellion.[45] Meanwhile, the perpetrators gathered at the Negro Burial Ground, and the innocents caught up in the chaos of the night who had hidden themselves in barns, cellars, and garrets throughout town no doubt reflected on what fate lay in store for them. In 1741 the attorney Daniel Horsmanden learned that some of the slaves accused on that occasion had believed themselves too valuable to be executed. "Many of these wretches buoyed themselves up with the notion, that their masters would at all hazards save them from the gallows or transportation, if they could, especially such of the slaves as had been bred up to trades or handicrafts."[46] Some of the rebels of April 1712 may also have harbored such delusions. As a result, they could have counseled surrender. The realists, however, would have warned that death by execution was their only possible plight. There were a number of examples in recent memory to back up their argument, not least the fate of William Hallett's slaves, who were "put to all the torment possible for a terror to others, of ever attempting the like wickedness" in 1708.[47] Perhaps the rebels of April 1712 were also aware of the law passed in response to the Hallett's murder, "An Act for preventing the Conspiracy of Slaves" stipulated that "all and every Negro Indian or other Slave ... who ... shall ... Kill ... or attempt the Death of his [or] her ... Master or Mistress or any other of her Majesties Leige People ... shall Suffer the paines of Death in such manner and with such Circumstances as the aggrevation and Enormity of their Crime in the Judgement of the Justices ... shall meritt." Perhaps they even knew that the act included a provision for the compensation of the masters of executed slaves to the value of "Twenty five Pounds."[48]

On the morning of April 7, Governor Hunter convened a special council at Fort Anne. The commanders of the independent companies and the town militia were present along with the civilian councilors, many of whom owned slaves who had participated in the rebellion. Rip Van Dam, the master of Quacko and Quashi, was present, as was Mingo's master, the merchant John Barberie. All three slaves were still at large and would be executed within a fortnight. Whether the president of the council, Geradus Beekman, attended is less certain. Considering the recent death of his son, Adrian, the one-time acting governor of New York may well have been excused. Hunter's response to the crisis was swift and comprehensive: Captain Edward Blagg, the commander of the 6th company of the city militia, was ordered to take his men on a patrol of the woods to the north of the city, "drive ye island" and "apprehend ... all .... vagrant negroes and slaves"; a rider was dispatched to Westchester to command Captain Joseph Hunt "to keep a guard of ... twenty men at King['s] Bridge" to prevent the rebels fleeing Manhattan; while a letter was sent to warn governor Joseph Dudley in Boston of the possibility that some of the rebels were making their way to Massachusetts "by that means to escape Justice." Several other militia companies were ordered to carry out "strict searches in the Town." The move caused considerable panic among the city's enslaved people, some of whom "Cut their own throats" as the militiamen came to "Apprehend them."[49] Others were captured on April 8, and soon the jail beneath city hall was filled with "about 70" slaves rounded up in this manner. Although the majority were innocent, by April 9 Governor Hunter was satisfied that "all [those] that [had] put the designe in execution" were under lock and key. The revolt was over. The trials and executions were about to begin.[50]

Now that the events of April 6 to 9, 1712, have been examined, it is worth pausing to consider what the rebels had hoped to achieve. When one considers the goals of other Akan rebels in the Americas throughout the era of the Atlantic slave trade, two patterns emerge. In Jamaica and Antigua, particularly in the seventeenth century, Akan rebels often sought to escape from the areas of European control and to establish independent (or maroon) communities in the islands' wild interiors. One example occurred in Saint Ann's Parish, Jamaica, in 1673 when a group of "about 200 . . . Coromantines" rose up and killed their master, Major Sebly, "and about 12 white people besides." The rebels then plundered several smaller plantations in the neighborhood, seizing "arms & amunition," and "retired to the Mountains & secured themselves in difficult places betwixt the parishes of Clarendon, St. Elizabeths and St Annes." The first party of island militia to go after them was "nearly destroyed," and over the coming decades the rebels were joined by numerous other runaways.[51]

In 1690 a similar event occurred on Major Sutton's plantation in Clarendon Parish. Having risen up "upon some disgust," unspecified in the account written by Governor Inchiquin, four hundred slaves killed the overseer and as many as seven other white workers, Sutton himself being absent in Spanish Town. The rebels equipped themselves with the contents of the plantation's armory, among which were over "160wt" of gunpowder and several small cannon which they loaded with nails and prepared to receive the militia they knew would be sent against them. The first attack was repelled, but the second forced the rebels to withdraw. Setting fire to the sugarcane as cover, they retired to the mountains after their leader had allowed ten men and several women and children to surrender. The remainder joined the survivors of the earlier rebellion at Sebly's and together they formed the nucleus of a group known as the Leeward Maroons.[52]

A third and final example of this type of rebellion occurred in 1701 on Major Samuel Martin's plantation in Antigua. Having killed Martin and decapitated his corpse but left his wife and several other workers unmolested, the "Coromantee" rebels fled into the hills. All three events share several particulars. All were committed by Akan; they shared the relatively modest aim of setting up independent communities in the wilds; and they killed their masters or overseers before fleeing.[53]

The second type of Akan revolt, the first example of which took place in Barbados in 1675, was much more ambitious. Unlike Jamaica, and Antigua prior to 1720, both of which contained areas of wildernesses in which escaped slaves could hide, Barbados had very quickly been stripped of its natural vegetation to make room for sugarcane. Would-be Barbadian slave rebels could not hope to find sanctuary and therefore had to aim for conquest. The 1675 revolt, which was discovered before it could be put into effect, was the work of a number of "Cormantee" who had been plotting over a period of years. According to a contemporary account entitled *Great Newes from the Barbadoes*, "An ancient Gold-Coast Negro" called Cuffee was to be crowned in an elaborate enstooling ceremony as a signal that the rebels should rise and "fire the Sugar-Canes, and . . . run in and Cut their masters the Planters Throats." There was some disagreement between the rebels as to whether all the whites should be killed or if they should "spare the lives of the Fairest and Handsomest women . . . to be converted to their own use." This disparity of purpose as well as the antipathy of several Creole slaves toward a general massacre, led to the plot's discovery when a domestic slave overheard a Coromantee conspirator discussing the particulars with an accomplice. The domestic confronted the plotters and persuaded them to confess. Martial law was declared and the ringleaders arrested. Forty-two were executed. Five others committed suicide in jail, and seventy were either deported or flogged severely before being returned to their masters.[54]

Another example of an Akan rebellion aimed at regime change occurred on the Danish colony of St. John, Virgin Islands, in November 1733. The protagonists, no more than 100 of the island's enslaved population of 1,087, were largely Akwamu and had been enslaved en masse following the polity's collapse in 1730 as a result of civil war and invasion by the neighboring kingdom of Akim, their age-old enemies. The aim of the rebellion, which was at least temporarily successful, was to establish an autonomous regime. The rebels were highly organized and led by former officials of the Akwamu state, principal among whom was King June, or Kong Juni, who appears to have been a former military commander. The rebellion was preceded by a series of natural disasters including drought, hurricane, and a plague of insects, all of which led to a famine, the main victims of which were the island's enslaved. Once begun, the rebellion spread rapidly. By the end of the first day the only fortification on the island, Frederiksfort, had been captured and the garrison killed. The rebels then used the warning signal employed by the Danish authorities against their former masters. By raising the flag and firing the fort's cannon, they drew the island's planters toward them into a series of ambushes. Simultaneously, the rebels sent out armed units to seize the main plantations, which had been left unguarded by their owners who were then blundering into the traps laid around the fort. The rebels grew in numbers with each liberated plantation, gathering arms and ammunition as they went, and soon the entire island, barring a single plantation where a number of whites and loyal Blacks were put under prolonged siege, was under Akwamu control.[55]

In contrast to the first category of rebellion outlined above, at St. John no damage was done to the island's infrastructure, a policy which the authorities later learned was quite deliberate. "These rebels had plotted to retain the island and had divided the plantations among themselves, according to the rank and position which each was to hold," a French planter from the neighboring island of St. Thomas explained. "The Negroes from other nations were to be provided to them to do their labors and were to belong to them as slaves. This is the reason why they preserved all the sugar factories and other buildings." The planter also learned that the Akwamu planned to spread the rebellion to St. Thomas with the aid of Akan there with whom they were in contact. The plan was not to come to fruition. In late November a French force sent from St. Thomas relieved the besieged Durlo plantation and recaptured Frederiksfort. Nevertheless, the majority of the island remained under Akwamu control and several Danish and English relief forces, dispatched from St. Croix and Tortola and St. Kitts, respectively, were defeated by the rebels. Indeed, it was not until the end of May 1734, six months after the revolt had begun, that the Danish eventually regained control with the aid of another French force of three hundred well-armed men from Martinique. Throughout May, as it became clear their cause was doomed, thirty-six of the Akan, including most of the principal leaders, committed suicide. The majority of the remainder were captured throughout May and June, although the last holdouts were only caught in August. Some were decapitated on the spot. Others were put on trial and later executed.[56]

Having examined contemporary parallels, we will now return to the topic at hand. What did the New York rebels intend in 1712? Did they aim to conquer the colony, in what has been called a "Systematic or Rational Revolt";[57] or was their intention to escape captivity and establish an independent settlement far from the reaches of their masters? The possibility that they intended to effect regime change in New York is easy to dismiss.[58] The New York rebels totaled no more than twenty-five and would surely have known that they were hopelessly outnumbered. By the time of the revolt, the Akan had been in New York for at least ten months and therefore had had plenty of time to acquaint themselves with the reality of their situation. In the midst of the War of the Spanish Succession, the city was highly mobilized with large numbers of regular troops and militia frequently passing through. In addition, a number of warships were often present in the harbor. Furthermore, unlike the Caribbean islands, where the Black population outnumbered the white (often by a factor of five to one), in New York City the opposite was the case. The census of 1703 recorded a total population of 5,841 of whom 965 were enslaved. In the colony as a whole, the preponderance of whites was even greater, with 2,425 enslaved in a population of 22,608. Surely men with military experience, as the New York rebels undoubtedly were, could not have thought they stood any chance of overcoming such odds.[59]

The second possibility, that the rebels intended to escape New York and establish an independent polity beyond the reach of their masters, is somewhat more plausible. New York contained vast areas of wilderness in which would-be maroons could hide. The climate was considerably less favorable than that of the Caribbean, however. New York winters were harsh and while West Africans used to tropical climates would have found some recognizable flora and fauna in Jamaica and Antigua, some of which would have helped them survive, the plants of the colony of New York would have been unrecognizable, while the animals, at a time where wolves, bears, and wildcats were far more common than today, would have posed a considerable threat.[60] Nevertheless, some maroon communities did exist in contemporary North America. One, which appeared in South Carolina in the second half of 1711, has already been discussed. Although its leader had been killed by the time the New York rebellion took place, some holdouts remained, and it is possible that the New York Akan may have been inspired by their exploits.[61] Another settlement which housed maroons in the colonial period was located closer to the city. The first reference dates to 1690 when the French explorer Sieur de Villiers encountered a "village of log houses, large and well made, several score in number" while travelling south from Lake Ontario through the Canisteo River Valley. "A more worthless lot of renegades and villains who had no hope of heaven or fear of hell, we never saw," de Villiers reported. The inhabitants included "Indians of many different tribes, footpads and highwaymen from most of the coast colonies, runaway slaves from Maryland, Yankees who fled from Connecticut leaving the gallows behind them, [and] renegade Frenchmen."[62] If escaped slaves from Maryland had learned of this settlement and had reached it by 1690, it seems plausible that slaves in New York also knew of its existence, given the number of enslaved seamen who would have encountered news from elsewhere. But the real question is—did the rebels of 1712 intend to escape there?

On balance, I believe that the New York rebels of 1712 neither hoped to establish themselves as the leaders of a new Akan colony, nor intended to escape to a maroon community in the wilds, or even to set up their own settlement. The former is hardly plausible, while the latter does not tally with the evidence available. Although the authorities took several precautions to prevent the rebels from escaping, it seems that these measures were unnecessary. There were no reports of slave rebels attempting to slip away to the wilderness to the north or northwest. Instead they were found in houses in the city, or made their way to the woods and swamplands of the New York Commons, perhaps to seek spiritual solace in the Negro Burial Ground and the sacred Akan groves that may have been established there. But if they did not aim either to escape or to effect regime change, what was their goal? The fact that several of the rebels' victims were high-ranking New Yorkers with connections to the slave trade may have been significant. The rebels might have been motivated by a desire to take revenge on their masters and, in some small way, on the system which had caused them to be kidnapped from their homelands and translocated across the Atlantic. To achieve this they would attempt to take their masters' lives and destroy their property. While it was assumed by the whites that the rebels' decision to initiate the revolt by starting a fire was intended to draw the inhabitants into an ambush, there may have been another intention. As well as taking the opportunity to launch a surprise attack and kill as many of their masters or their masters' family members as possible, the rebels may also have intended to destroy the city by fire, or at least as much as they could before they were overwhelmed, a seemingly achievable goal when one considers the contemporary precedents for such disasters.[63]

This theory is supported by the primary sources. On June 23 Hunter informed the Lords of Trade that the rebels had intended "to destroy as many of the inhabitants as they co[u]ld," and that they "had resolved to revenge themselves for some hard usage they apprehended to have received from their masters"; in his journal the Reverend John Sharpe recorded that the rebels "designed to murder all," and in a letter written in June he wrote that they "[had] plotted to destroy all the Whites"; on April 14, the *Boston News-Letter*'s New York correspondent stated that the rebels "[had] conspired to murder all Christians here"; while Daniel Horsmanden, when writing of the intentions of the alleged rebels in 1741, claimed that their aim was to "burn the houses of them that have the most money, and kill them all, *as the negroes would have done their masters and mistresses formerly.*"[64] Unfortunately, the source which would have given the definitive account of the rebellion is now lost. On June 23, Elias Neau, the Huguenot catechist whose close and regular contact with New York's enslaved people over a period of at least eight years meant that he, more than any of the other sources quoted above, had real insight into the city's Black society, wrote a letter to John Chamberlayne, the London-based secretary of the Society for the Propagation of the Gospel, in which full details of the plot were given. Although the letter has not survived, in Neau's subsequent message to Chamberlayne he makes a brief reference to the contents of the missing document, an allusion which may provide a further clue concerning the rebels' aim. "My last to the Honble Society was by the Harley pacquet in June 1st," Neau informed his sponsor, "by wch I did give to Mr Chamberlayne a full information of the Horrid plot of Some Negroes in this City *against their Masters*." Perhaps the reference is a general one—the term "masters" could be taken to indicate the white population of the city as a whole, but it could also be read as a specific reference to the individuals who owned the rebels concerned.[65]

To my mind, the New York rebels, or at least the leading faction within the group, had one other aim beyond killing as many of their masters as possible and destroying as much property as they could. Like the Akan rebel captured in the aftermath of the revolt in Saint John in 1734, who stated "When I die, I shall return to my own land," the New York rebels of 1712 desired to travel to *asamando*, the place "where the ancestors dwell." One suggestion for this lies in the fact that the revolt was deliberately initiated on the first day of the new moon. As we have seen, this was a time of ritual and spiritual importance and was connected with death and rebirth. When the principal leaders committed suicide in the immediate aftermath of the revolt, just as the Akwamu leaders would do in Saint John in 1734, they not only robbed their enemies of the satisfaction of their capture, trial, and subsequent execution, but also achieved their own Akan spiritual ideal. After death their souls would travel across the ocean to their homeland, perhaps to a place high up on the Kwahu Scarp where breezes blew in from the distant Gold Coast. There, they would be reunited with their ancestors, and with family members killed in warfare and raids. For those who had not managed to take their own lives, either through a lack of courage or a lack of opportunity, the same ultimate fate awaited. First, however, imprisonment, trial, and brutal public execution awaited.

CHAPTER 13

Broken on the Wheel

NEW YORK CITY
April to June 1712

It is considered by the court that the defendant be carryed from hence to
the place from whence he came & from thence to the place of execution and
there to be broke upon A Wheel & so to continue languishing until he be
dead and his head and quarters to be at the Queen's disposal.
—Minutes of the New York City Court of Quarter Sessions, April 11, 1712

Onyankōpon hyε wo na ọdasāni (ọtesefo) kum wo, wuṅwu.
If the Supreme Being does not kill you but a human being kills you, you do
not die.

—Akan proverb

IN THE SECOND WEEK OF APRIL 1712 the prison beneath New York
City Town Hall was filled far beyond its capacity. According to the
Boston News-Letter over "70 Negro's" had been detained.[1] Although
few details of the rebels' incarceration survive, a plausible picture can
be pieced together with contemporary evidence. A document entitled
"instructions for the keeper of the jail and public prison," issued in
New Amsterdam in 1658, informs us that on admittance to the jail
the name of each prisoner was noted down along with "what cloaths,
money, [and] goods they brought with them." The sheriff was required
to search inmates for "knives, irons, rope or other instruments [they
could use] to break out or to injure themselves." Prisoners were separated by gender and crammed into basement cells. No visitors were
permitted, although passers-by could crouch down and speak to pris-

oners "through the grating" which faced out onto the street. Weekly rations of three pounds of beef and one and a half pounds of pork, as well as a daily "can" of beer were doled out to each detainee. We also learn that some were "placed on bread and water" only.[2] It seems likely that the latter was the rebels' fate. According to Governor Hunter, they were kept "in a woful condition and suffer'd more than death."[3] Contemporary prisoners' accounts shed further light on the rebels' plight. One noted that he had "nothing but the bare floor to lay upon—no covering" and "was almost devour'd with all kinds of Vermine and [had] no refreshment of Apparel." Another "suffered Daily for want of the Common necessities of Life" and believed he would "perish for want of food and Raiment." Inmates were bound in fetters, food was scarce, the cells were unheated, and prisoners were permitted but a single candle every two days which had to be extinguished before 8 P.M. Colonial New York jailers were infamous for their cruelty. In April 1694 the sheriff was indicted for stabbing a prisoner; on another occasion an inmate was locked in irons without respite for fourteen days; one prisoner complained of being "grossly used"; another was "Close Confined and locked up alone"; and in June 1769 a prisoner named Stephen Porter was driven to suicide.[4]

Meanwhile, in the offices directly above the jail, Henry Wileman, the New York City coroner, was busy conducting nine "inquisitions" on the bodies of the dead. On April 9, he examined the shoemaker William Echt, and Augustus Grassett, the former master of the city's weigh house. Wileman recorded his findings in front of a jury of twenty-five, selected by Sheriff Harrison, who were "tried charged and sworn to Enquire how when and after what manner the [victims] ... came to ... [their] death[s]." The jurors' verdict was unanimous: "diverse ... Negroes and Indian slaves" had "beate[n] and mortally wound[ed]" the victims, from which blows they had "then and there Instantly Dyed." Although the jury failed to identify "twenty four or more" of the perpetrators, fourteen others thought to have committed the murders were named. On the list were Peter Vantilborough's Cuffee, Peter Fauconnier's Sam, Dick, the "Boy Slave" of the blacksmith Harmanus Burger, Abraham Provoost's Quacko, Alan Jarrett's Claus, Mary Wenham's Jose, Peter Vantilborough's Juan, and Jacob Regnier's Mars. The remaining six listed would be found not guilty. These were

John Crooke's Jack, two Toms, one belonging to Nicolas Roosevelt and the other to Jacobus Varick, Joost Lyn's Quacko, Samuel Phillips' Jarret, and Ambrose, an "Indian man slave belonging to" Isaac Gouverneur. As well as compiling the report and taking the evidence of the jurors, Wileman examined the wounds of the dead. Echt had been stabbed "in three several places under his right breast and [in] the throat," while Grasset had suffered "several wounds about his Neck and head and fingers." Once signed and sealed by Wileman and all twenty-five of his jurors (or at least the twenty-two who were literate enough to do so), the document was handed to the attorney general, the "waspish" May Bickley, who prepared his case without delay.[5]

That same day, as the Reverend John Sharpe recorded in his journal, "Eight funerals of the murdered" were held.[6] Following a tradition carried to the New World by the first immigrants from the Netherlands, the Dutch families employed *aanspreeckers*, or inviters, to spread the word. Accompanied by the tolling of the church bells, they walked the streets with streamers of black crepe paper fluttering from their hats, knocking at the doors of the friends and relatives of the victims. That afternoon eight hearses or open wagons carrying coffins and followed by trains of mourners crisscrossed the city heading for the Dutch, French, and English churches. After the services had been conducted, and the coffins buried, the mourners retired to the houses of the deceased for the postfuneral dinner. These were ostentatious affairs. Wine, rum, and beer were served, pipes and tobacco were provided, and "mourning rings" and silver "mourning spoons" commemorating the dead were handed out.[7] As night fell and the alcohol flowed, the attendees' fear, shock, and sadness turned to anger and a thirst for revenge. In their cups and with their judgment clouded by prejudice, many New Yorkers pointed the finger at the enslaved people taught by the French priest Elias Neau. "A great Jealousie was . . . raised," one contemporary account recorded, "and the common Cry was very loud, against instructing the Negroes."[8] The city's Dutch residents in particular had long opposed the idea of baptizing slaves. Education would make the "Negroes" more difficult to subjugate, they argued, and would rouse in them ambitions to better their station in life. It now seemed that these fears were justified. "The school was charged as the cause of the mischief, the place of conspiracy," the Reverend Sharpe recorded, "and [the people claimed] that instruction had made the . . . [slaves] cunning and insolent." With passions running high, Neau was forced into hiding. "[He] durst hardly appear," Sharpe reported, and the "clamour . . . had a full run for many days."[9]

Two of Neau's former students would bear the brunt of the people's ire: Adrian Hoghlandt's Robin and Cornelia Van Clyff Norwood's Caesar. Why the latter was chosen is unclear. Robin, however, was thought to bear a grudge against his master for not allowing him to be baptized.[10] Hoghlandt had been one of the victims of the revolt, and at least one witness questioned by Coroner Wileman's jurors was certain that they had seen Robin at the scene of the crime, even though it would later emerge that he was almost certainly innocent of the allegation that he had killed his master.[11] The second group of innocent scapegoats were the so-called "Spanish Indians," sailors captured by New York privateers during Queen Anne's War and subsequently sold into slavery as a result of their "swarthy" complexions and New York's racist slave laws. These individuals were blamed for several reasons. It was well-known that they were unhappy with their situation. They had long protested that they were free Spanish subjects and should be repatriated as prisoners of war.[12] This, or so the argument would have it, provided the Spanish Indians with a motive while the fact that they were Christians and not savages like the majority of the city's enslaved people, meant that they were capable of "having . . . [the] understanding to carry on a plot," as Sharpe put it.[13] Corroborating the theory, at least three "Spanish Indians" had been identified in Coroner Wileman's report. Whether "Ambrose" (Ambrosio), "Hosey" (Jose), and "John" (Juan) were actually present can never be known.[14] What is evident, however, is that they were not guilty of *participating* in the revolt—this at least is what both the Reverend Sharpe and Governor Hunter would subsequently and sincerely believe. Nevertheless, several influential people in New York did think that they were responsible, and in the weeks that followed this was the belief that would most influence the courts.[15]

Between April 9 and 10, Attorney General Bickley worked tirelessly on the case for the prosecution. Having interviewed dozens of witnesses (eighty-one would be called during the trial), Bickley drew up a list of forty-three suspects out of the seventy or more enslaved people and Black freemen who had been detained in Harrison's jail. These would be put on trial in the Court of Quarter Sessions of the Peace under the terms of the Act for Preventing Suppressing and Punishing the Conspiracy and Insurrection of Negroes and other Slaves. The remaining detainees would never face the judges. Of Bickley's forty-three accused, thirty-nine would be indicted for murder or as accessories to murder. The remaining four would be indicted for assault with intent to kill.[16] The difference as far as the defendants were concerned was academic. Both charges were punishable by death, "in such manner and with such Circumstances as the aggrevation and Enormity of their Crime in the Judgement of the Justices . . . shall meritt."[17] At some point in the second week of April Bickley made a deal with two of the accused. Realizing that the prosecution's case would be facilitated by insider witnesses, he convinced the "Slave Boy" Dick, the property of the blacksmith Harmanus Burger, and Peter Vantilborough's Cuffee, the Akan who had lit the fire at Crooke's outhouse, to turn state's evidence in exchange for an assurance that they would receive the lesser punishment of transportation.[18] According to Sharpe, it would be the testimony of these "Infidel Evidences" that would "fix the guilt" of the accused.[19] Hunter agreed. "Without [Cuffee and Dick]," he attested, "very few co[u]ld have beene punished."[20]

May Bickley was not merely motivated by the desire to seek justice. As well as a wish to instill such terror into the hearts of New York's slaves that no such rebellion could ever take place in the city again, the attorney general sought to settle a number of private scores. Governor Hunter believed the proceedings were influenced by "a party quarrel" which meant that some of the accused, rather than being judged according to their guilt or innocence, "far'd just as the people stood affected to their masters."[21] Exactly what "quarrel" Hunter was referring to is difficult to ascertain: it may have been the twenty-year-old struggle between the pro- and anti-Leislerians, or possibly a Tory–Whig divide.[22] The second bias which affected the trial is more transparent. In another letter, Hunter would mention a "private pique of Mr. Bickley's against Mr. [Jacob] Regnier."[23] As previously related, the attorney general had a long-standing feud with Regnier, the barrister with whom he had competed professionally and personally ever since both men had arrived in New York over ten years before. Chief

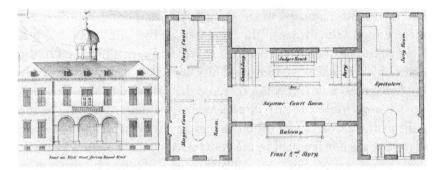

"Plan and elevation of the old City Hall . . . by David Grim," 1855. This image shows the court room where the trials of the enslaved rebels took place in 1712. More than seventy prisoners were imprisoned in the building's basement jail, some for well over a year. (*Columbia University Library*)

among Bickley's gripes was the humiliation he had endured in 1706 when Regnier had sealed the acquittal of the traveling Presbyterian minister Francis Makemie, whom Bickley had been prosecuting under the auspices of the then governor of New York, Lord Cornbury. While Bickley had already secured some measure of revenge in 1707 when he had sentenced Regnier's slave, Mars, to be whipped through the city streets, and yet again in 1710 when he had defeated Regnier's attempt to defend William Archer, the Black butcher who had used the court to sue for his freedom against his alleged owner, George Elsworth, it is apparent that Bickley was not one to bury the hatchet.[24] The Akan rebellion would provide him with yet another opportunity to see Regnier suffer. By adding the names of no less than three of his enemy's slaves to the list of the indicted, Bickley aimed to cause Regnier emotional as well as financial loss.[25]

"THE TRIAL OF NEGRO AND INDIAN SLAVES" opened at 8 A.M. on Friday, April 11. Crammed into the Supreme Court room on the second floor of the city hall were dozens of people. The five justices of the peace, wearing the long black robes required of their position, occupied the "Judger Bench" opposite the windows which looked out onto the crossroads of Broad and Wall Streets. Caleb Heathcote, the mayor of New York City, sat alongside the aldermen, Edward Blagg, the captain of the 6th company of the militia, Walter Thong, a prominent merchant and the owner of the rebel Quaco, the land owner Samuel Bayard, and Jacobus Kip, a wealthy brewer and agriculturalist. On the east side of the hall were the grand jury, twenty or more wealthy free-holders whose task it was to prosecute the case under May Bickley's supervision, while the jury of twelve charged with determining the guilt of the accused filled the benches to the west. Although their identities are not revealed in the court documents, we know that the juries were composed of "free and lawfull men" of property with estates worth at least £60, and that Governor Hunter thought them "of the most credible and substantial of the inhabitants" in New York. The balcony on the north side of the hall was open to the public.[26]

Once the foreman, Abraham Vanhorne, had hushed the crowd, the grand jurors were sworn in. They then proceeded to the bench to bring an indictment against the first group of slaves to be put on trial: Robin, Claus, Abraham Provoost's Quaco, and Peter Fauconnier's Sam. All were charged with the murder of Robin's master, Adrian Hoghlandt. The four stepped forward in custody of the sheriff, Francis Harrison, to be arraigned.[27] Claus, Robin, and Quaco pleaded not guilty. Sam remained silent. The rest of the morning was taken up with the testimony of four witnesses. Deborah Bratt, wife of Isaac Bratt the baker, was the first to take the stand. As she lived in the East Ward, Bratt may well have been able to give a firsthand account of the events of the night of April 6. Next came Cuffee and Dick, the rebel slaves whom Bickley had convinced to turn state's evidence. Finally, Katherine Mercier, the daughter of a ship's carpenter who lived on Broadway, gave evidence.[28] Over the course of the four testimonies, the jury heard how Robin, acting "traytourously" and with "malice forethought," had sunk a six-penny dagger five inches into Hoghlandt's body, and how, after Hoghlandt had fallen mortally wounded, Claus, Sam, and Quaco had "kill[ed] and murder[ed]" the merchant with a flurry of blows. As Robin would later swear he "was not guilty of any bloodshed," he may well have voiced his innocence on the day of his trial. If so, his complaints went unheeded. When given the opportunity of changing their pleas after the witnesses had finished, the slaves refused, and the jury found all four guilty "in manner and form as in the . . . indictment. Thereupon," the court minutes continue, "the said Clause Robin

Quaco and Sam were severally asked if they or any of them know or had anything to say for themselves why the Court here to Judgement and Execution against them upon the premises ought not to proceed." The slaves said nothing "but as before they have said." Following a brief deliberation with his fellow justices of the peace, Heathcote passed sentence. "It is considered by the Court," he pronounced, "that the aforesaid Clause be broke alive upon a wheel and so to continue languishing until he be dead, and his head and quarters to be at the Queens disposal. That . . . Robin be hung up in chains Alive, and so continue without any sustenance until he be dead. That . . . Quaco be burnt with fire until he be dead and consumed and that . . . Sam be hanged by the neck until he be dead." How the slaves reacted is unrecorded. It is quite possible that Claus and Quaco did not even understand enough English to realize their fate.[29]

While Sam would be put on trial again on Saturday, April 12, and Quaco and Claus's executions would be delayed by a day, Robin's punishment proceeded with immediate effect.[30] Although the sources do not reveal where the execution was carried out, when a enslaved man named Caesar was gibbeted in 1741 the punishment took place "on the island near the powder-house," a reference to a spot on the New York City Commons.[31] Perhaps this was also where Robin met his end. From the city hall he would have been carried on a cart to the site through a large crowd of onlookers, both Black and white, then locked inside a cage made of metal hoops which fit closely to his body.[32] The cage was then hauled into the air and suspended by an iron hook from a wooden gallows from which Robin was suspended "without any sustenance" until he died of dehydration or exposure.[33] We know from contemporary accounts that the cages used sometimes contained a wooden plank upon which the victim could stand and that those punished in this way could survive for several days. One example is provided by the fate of Kingston and Fortune, two enslaved men gibbeted in Kingston, Jamaica, following Tacky's Revolt of 1760. Guarded by a detachment of militia to ensure they could not be rescued, Kingston and Fortune "diverted themselves all day long in discourse with their countrymen, who were permitted, very improperly, to surround the gibbet," a local planter observed. Fortune died after seven days. Kingston, who treated all white onlookers with "hardened insolence," died after nine when a fit of convulsions shook his entire body.[34] We do not know whether Robin was guarded but we do know that he survived for at least five days.[35]

On Saturday, April 12, the trials continued. At 8 A.M. five slaves were charged with the assault of Adrian Beekman, the son of the former acting governor. Among them were Jacob Regnier's George and Tom; and two of the "Spanish Indians," Juan and Jose. The grand jury also indicted four slaves for murder: Sam, the "mulatto man slave" who had been convicted of murdering Adrian Hoghlandt the day before; Nicholas Roosevelt's Tom; Mars, the enslaved man who had been "whipped round the city" in 1707 and also belonged to Jacob Regnier; and Johannes Dehonneur's Tom. Brought to the bench, Sam, Mars, and both Toms pleaded not guilty. The jury was "sworn and charged" then heard the testimony of twenty-three witnesses. Among those to take the stand were Dick and Cuffee, the two rebels turning state's evidence; Jacobus Kip, the North Ward alderman who was also serving as a justice of the peace that day; the wheelwright, John Horne; William Shackerly, a baker and innkeeper; the cordwainer, Arout Schermerhoorn; Lucretia Dehonneur, a relative (presumably) of Johannes Dehonneur, the owner of one of the two Toms who stood accused before her; and Jacob Regnier, the aforementioned barrister and owner of three of the accused. Although the court minutes do not specify if each of the witnesses gave evidence for or against the defendants, it seems certain that Regnier was called by the defense. On a later date we know that he acted in this capacity, and, as all three of his slaves would be found not guilty at the end of the day's proceedings, it seems likely the barrister was in some measure involved.[36]

Regnier's task was far from simple. Besides being confronted with a jury prejudiced by fear and paranoia and motivated by the desire to avenge the deaths of their friends and family, Regnier found himself faced by his old adversary, May Bickley. The sparse court minutes do little justice to the events that unfolded. All we know for certain is that the case proved considerably more contentious than that which had preceded it the day before, when Robin, Claus, Quaco, and Sam had been indicted, arraigned, tried, found guilty, and condemned to death before lunchtime. By the same point on April 12 no verdict had been reached. "The jury not agreeing" on the fate of Mars, Sam, and Tom, the "Court Adjourn'd till three a clock [in the] afternoon." After lunch the proceedings continued, but at the end of this second session of the day, the outcome still remained in doubt. "The jury not agreeing," the minutes relate, the "Court Adjourn'd till six a clock." By the time the third and final session of the day had ended, the jury finally came to an agreement. Having heard of how Roosevelt's Tom had shot Adrian Beekman through the chest with a "hand Gun of the value of ten shillings," the jury found him guilty as charged, as they did his namesake, and Peter Fauconnier's Sam. Tom, Mars, and George, Regnier's three slaves, were found not guilty, however.[37] Governor Hunter later deemed Bickley's evidence against them "very defective," while the attorney general's "negroe witnesses," Tom and Cuffee, had both "wholly acquitted" Mars "of ever haveing known anything of the conspiracey."[38] Loath to be beaten by Regnier and despite the testimony of his key witnesses, Bickley insisted that Mars, Tom, and George all be recommitted for the murder of Augustus Grasset, which would be addressed the following week. As the court had not had sufficient time to hear their cases, Jose and Juan were also recommitted, as were Fauconnier's Sam, and Roosevelt's and Dehonneur's Toms for their alleged involvement in the murder of Henry Brasier. Sheriff Harrison led all eight to the overcrowded cells in the building's basement. The jurors, the justices of the peace, the witnesses, and the day's spectators, drifted home for the night.[39]

Elsewhere, two executions had taken place that day. "[April] 12.— One negro rackd. Another burned," Sharpe tersely recorded in his journal.[40] The "rackd" slave was Alan Jarrett's Claus. Bound to a broad iron wheel "about two feet in diameter," Claus would have been raised above the ground so that the crowd could bear witness to his suffering. The executioner would then have delivered a series of blows to Claus' arms and legs, breaking each in turn. Only much later would he have finally been put out of his misery. Perhaps the fullest contemporary account of such an execution is provided by a French cavalry officer, Le Fualde Conte, who witnessed the death of a merchant from Toulouse named Calas who had been found guilty of murdering his own son. "[On] the magistrate's signal," Conte related, the executioner lifted a club of iron, and with it struck the extended limb of his victim. . . . You cannot conceive the intense suffering depicted through the heaving trunk and on the convulsed features [of the victim], by this bruising between iron and iron. The blow took effect at the knee-joint, and, though given with force, was not intended quite to break the leg, but merely to try the spirit of the sufferer, and to give a specimen of what was to follow. . . . The second blow fell with a heavy hand. I had turned away, not equal to the sight, when the din of the iron against the bone, and the groan which followed, convinced me it had been more violent than the first; in truth, it had completely broken the leg at the tibia; so exquisite was the torture, that he fainted instantly, but as quickly recovered. He uttered no articulate complaint, and it was only by the painful compression of his lips, and the starting of his eye-balls, that the agony of his spirit could be discerned. . . . The blows occurred at regular intervals of fifteen minutes, with such direful effect that, after the eighth stroke, every joint in his body was dislocated, and every bone broken. He frequently fainted, and was as often recovered by the diabolical skill of his tormentor.

Finally, the magistrate signaled that "the Coup-de-grace" could be delivered and the executioner "again heaved his weapon. The weight of the iron and the force of the blood burst at once all the arteries of the stomach, and crushed the vertebrae; the blood gushed in torrents from his eyes, his mouth, his ears—a gasp convulsed his frame—a groan—one gasp more—and he had ceased to suffer." While Claus' execution "was two hours in the acting," some victims of the wheel lingered on for up to four days after their bodies had been broken. It can only be hoped that Claus' sufferings were not so prolonged.[41]

The enslaved man burned alive that afternoon was Abraham Provoost's Quaco. Although no details of his last moments survive, there are several accounts of slaves who suffered the same punishment in colonial New York. One man, executed in 1734, whose name is not recorded, died "in the presence of a numerous Company of Spectators, great part of which were of the Black Tribe." The anonymous "negro slave . . . shewed not the least sign of Repentence, but died like a Wretch harden'd in iniquity, for he was hardly heard to Complain, [and] only call'd for Water."[42] A second account relates the executions of two Akan slaves named Quack and Cuffee in 1741. As with the previously quoted example, "the spectators . . . were very numerous," but otherwise the execution differed in several particulars. "About three o'clock" in the afternoon, we are informed, "the criminals were brought to the stake, surrounded with piles of wood ready for setting fire to, which the people were very impatient to have done, their resentment being raised to the utmost pitch against them. ... The criminals shewed great terror in their countenances, and looked as if they would gladly have discovered all they knew of this accursed scheme [a reference to the alleged plot of 1741], could they have had any encouragement to hope for a reprieve." Both Quack and Cuffee made last-minute confessions, whereupon "the sheriff [was asked] to delay the execution until the governor be acquainted therewith, and his pleasure known touching their reprieve; which, could it be effected, it was thought might have been a means of producing great discoveries; but from the disposition observed in the spectators, it was much to be apprehended, there would have been great difficulty, if not danger in an attempt to take the criminals back ... for these reasons the executions continued."[43] A third account details the execution of Will, another enslaved man allegedly involved in the plot of 1741. "The pile being kindled, this wretch set his back to the stake, and raising up one of his legs, laid it upon the fire, and lifting up his hands and eyes, cried aloud, and several times repeated the names, Quack Goelet and Will Tiebout, who he had said had first brought him into this plot."[44]

THE NEXT DAY, April 13, was a Sunday: no trials were held. While Robin endured his third day gibbeted on the commons, the bells of the Dutch Reformed Church rang out to celebrate a triple baptism. Among those welcomed into the fold was young Hilletje Hulst, whose mother, Aaltje, was a relative of Abraham Provoost, the owner of Quaco, the Akan rebel who had been burned alive on the Commons the day before.[45] Down at the docks, Captains Tynes and Rivers were fitting out for a voyage to Saint Thomas; Captain Adolph was preparing to sail to Philadelphia; and dozens of enslaved stevedores were loading the produce of the colony's hinterland on board the vessels of Captains Newbald and Tucker who would soon set sail for Jamaica.[46] Despite the apparent normality of the scene, the residents of New York were still reeling. The events of the night of April 6 had left deep psychological scars which would need time to heal. Elias Neau was not yet able to walk the streets without being accosted, and many residents believed the violence was not yet over. "'Tis fear'd that most of the Negro's here (who are very numerous) knew of the Late Conspiracy to murder the Christians" wrote the city's correspondent for the *Boston News-Letter*. If close to two thousand conspirators remained at liberty, as the article suggested, surely another outbreak of slave violence was imminent. Meanwhile, in the jails beneath City Hall, the inmates were close to revolt. With "about 70 Negro's in Custody," the sheriff, Francis Harrison, "apprehended they would attempt to make their escape."[47] Adding to Harrison's worries was the fact that the Attorney General May Bickley appeared to be determined to recommit suspects such as Regnier's Mars, George, and Tom, even though their innocence had been attested by key witnesses in court. Harrison's fears were not without justification. According to one authority, "the prisons of the colony were never sufficiently secure to effectively detain suspects awaiting trial," and the surviving legal records of the northern colonies attest to numerous examples of prisoners who "broke gaol."[48] If such men were able to escape confinement, then perhaps the host of rebellious and desperate slaves packed into the cells under city hall would also make a bid for freedom.

On Monday, April 14, the trials continued. At the opening of the morning session at 8 A.M., Sheriff Harrison made a formal request, "moveing ye Court for the discharge of such as were or should be soe acquitted by reason he had soe many in his custody." Harrison explained he feared a gaol break. Bickley was unmoved. The attorney general "opposed . . . [the sheriff's] motion," explaining that he "should have something further to object" against Mars and the others who had been acquitted, "and therefore prayed he might not be discharged." With Harrison's motion dismissed, the day's proceedings got under way. Dave Furnis, the enslaved man belonging to Ruth Sheppard, was indicted for the murder of Henry Brasier; and five others were indicted as accessories for the same crime: Rip Van Dam's Quacko and Quasi, Mingo, Kitto, and Cornelia Van Clyff Norwood's Caesar, the latter the only enslaved person indicted who had been baptized by Elias Neau. Dick and Cuffee, once again the principal witnesses, were joined on the stand by a potbaker, a cordwainer, a bricklayer, a shipwright, and a ship's carpenter. The jury heard how Furnis had used an axe to strike Braiser in the neck, inflicting a mortal wound to "the depth of four inches" of which Brasier "instantly and immediately dyed." All six defendants were found guilty, and the following day, Nicholas Roosevelt's Tom and Peter Fauconnier's Sam, both of whom had been convicted of Adrian Beekman's murder on April 12, were also found guilty of involvement in Brasier's death.[49] According to John Sharpe, Caesar, the slave Elias Neau had baptized, was almost certainly innocent. "[He] was Condemned on Slender Evidence," the reverend opined, "in ye heat of ye Peoples resentment," while one of Sharpe's colleagues, the Reverend Thomas Barclay, was later informed by Governor Hunter that Caesar was "convicted . . . unjustly."[50] None of the eight had anything further to add to their defense on learning of the verdict, and the sentences were duly pronounced. Furnis was "to be burned with fire until he be dead and consumed to ashes"; Mingo, Quasi, Quacko, Kitto, Dehonneur's Tom, and Caesar were to taken "to the place of execution and there to be Hanged by the neck until dead." The most horrendous punishment was reserved for Nicholas Roosevelt's Tom, the man who had killed Adrian Beekman with a hand gun. "It is considered by the court," the minutes record, "that he be . . . burned with a slow fire that he may continue in torment for eight or ten hours & Continue burning in the said fire until he be dead and consumed to ashes."[51]

April 16, 1712, saw the largest number of executions to take place on a single day in the entire history of New York City. "[April] 16.— 7 negroes hanged & 2 burnt," John Sharpe recorded.[52] Peter Fauconnier's Sam, Johannes Dehonneur's Tom, Kitto, Mingo, Rip Van Dam's Quasi and Quaco, and Cornelia Van Clyff Norwood's Caesar were hanged. Ruth Sheppard's Furnis and Nicholas Roosevelt's Tom were burned alive, the latter being kept "in torment for eight or ten hours until dead and consumed to ashes."[53] A similar execution carried out in Jamaica in the late 1680s was witnessed by Hans Sloane, a doctor, botanist, and member of the Royal Society. "By nailing [the slave rebels] . . . down on the ground with crooked Sticks on every Limb, and then applying the fire by degrees from their Feet and Hands," Sloane observed, "[they are] burn[t] . . . gradually up to the Head, where by their pains are extravagant."[54] Another late seventeenth-cen-

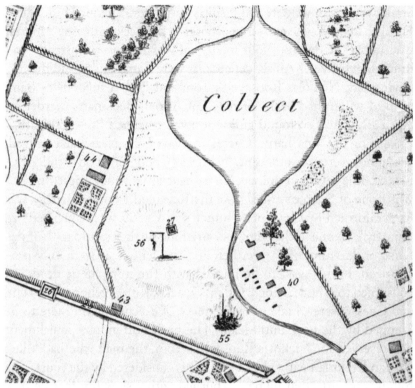

Detail from a map drawn by David Grim in 1813, depicting New York City as it was in 1742–1744. He recalled the locations (nos. 55-56) where slaves who rebelled in 1741 were hanged or burned at the stake. The same locations may well have been used for the executions of the 1712 rebels. (*New York Public Library*)

tury traveler to Jamaica also left an account of "burning by degrees." "Negroe slaves died . . . obstinately," John Taylor noted, "not semeing in the least concern'd therat, for when they were burnning, or rather roasting at the stake (for the fier was made at some distance from the stake to which they were chained and all round soe that they roasted or burnt by degrees) they would sing and laugh and by noe tortur would they ever confes . . . And soe their torment seem'd in vaine."[55]

Although we do not know if Tom displayed such stoicism, we do know something of the death of another of the slaves executed in New York that day. The Reverend John Sharpe recorded that Cornelia Van Clyff Norwood's Caesar, the enslaved man formerly baptized by Elias

Neau, "dyed protesting his innocence." Later that day Sharpe "went to" see Robin, the would-be catechumen who had been "hanging [for] five days" in the gibbet. Although Robin "was often delirious by long continuance in that posture, thro hunger, thirst and pain," when Sharpe asked him if he was responsible for the crime, "he declared to me he was innocent" and showed "a seeming concern for his master's misfortune. . . . He . . . answered directly to what I enquired," Sharpe recalled, "and called me by my name so that I might conclude he had some intervals of the exercise of his reason." The reverend's account is the last we hear of Robin. He must have died soon after.[56]

Meanwhile, the trials went on. With the nine slaves named above being hung and burned alive on the Commons, the jury heard the evidence of seven more witnesses. As well as the ever-present Dick and Cuffee, an enslaved woman named Diana testified regarding the murder of the Huguenot city weighmaster, Augustus Grasset. Over the next three days, of the eleven slaves accused of the crime, seven were found guilty. John Cure's Toby was said to have dealt the Frenchman the fatal blow, a gash of three inches depth delivered to his neck with "a dagger of six pence." Peter Morin's Caesar, Richard Ray's Titus, David Lyell's Tom, William Walton's Coffee, Walter Thong's Quaco, and Stophell Pels' Sarah were also found guilty. All seven were sentenced "to be hanged by the neck until they be dead" although it was by no means clear that Coffee had actually taken part in the revolt as Governor Hunter later learned. John Crooke's Lilly and three others were acquitted of the crime and ordered to "be discharged from their imprisonment [after] paying the fees of their prosecution." On Saturday, April 19, Jacob Regnier's Mars and George were brought back before the court to be retried as accessories to the murder of Adrian Beekman. Both were found not guilty, but were recommitted for a second time following yet another appeal by Attorney General Bickley, who "acquainted the Court that he Cannot now safely come to trial some of the queen's evidence being out of the way." Once again, Bickley's personal vendetta was indulged and the third trial of Regnier's slaves was arranged for "Tuesday Morning next [April 22] at eight a clock."[57]

April 21, 1712, saw the last mass execution to take place in New York City for over twenty-nine years.[58] John Cure's Toby, Peter

Morin's Caesar, Titus, Walter Thong's Quacko, and David Lyell's Tom were all "hanged by the neck until . . . dead."[59] Although she was believed to be "privy to the conspiracy" according to Governor Hunter, Sarah escaped the hangman's noose by "pleading her belly." Her sentence was suspended, and she remained in the jail under city hall along with William Walton's Tom, whose execution had also been delayed due to doubts over his guilt expressed by the judges.[60] The following day, Jacob Regnier's George, Tom, and Mars came before the court once more, this time to be tried for the murder of Augustus Grasset. Eighteen witnesses were called, including the ever-present Cuffee. Another who gave testimony was Anne Webb, who, along with her husband, John, would be found guilty in November of that year of running "a disorderly tipling house or Alehouse" where "Negro slaves" were entertained. Jacob Regnier also appeared, presumably to act in the defense of his enslaved as he had done nine days previously. Regnier's contribution may well have been vital: Mars, Tom, and George were acquitted once again. While Tom and George were allowed to go free, however, Mars was recommitted for a third time on Bickley's recommendation.[61]

 With the acquittal of Regnier's slaves on April 22, the "blind fury" of the people of New York began to abate.[62] Aside from a few individuals, May Bickley chief among them, the city's desire for revenge seems to have been quenched by the blood of the seventeen enslaved men already executed. In May the trials were held with diminishing frequency; fewer convictions were made; Elias Neau, who had previously been all but housebound for fear of the mob, was able to walk the streets in relative safety; and the thoughts of the city elite turned from retribution to ensuring the specter of slave revolt would never threaten the streets of New York City again.[63] It was with such sentiments in mind that Hunter sent a message to the General Assembly on May 7, advising "that . . . some good Law [should] be passed, putting slaves under a better regulation, and to encourage the importation of white servants [instead]."[64] The assembly resolved to "bring in" a far more reactionary piece of legislation than Hunter desired, however, an intent reflected in its proposed title—"a Bill for the better preventing, suppressing and punishing the Conspiracy and Insurrection of Negro and other Slaves." Meanwhile, between May 20 and 30, the

Court of Quarter Sessions sentenced three more slaves to death. Andrew Stuckey's Hannibal was found guilty of murdering Augustus
Grasset; Gysbert Vaninburgh's Abigail and Rip Van Dam's Tom were
deemed culpable of assisting him in the act. The execution of Tom's
sentence was delayed, again due to the judges' doubt as to his guilt,
but Hannibal and Abigail were hanged forthwith. The latter had the
distinction of being the only woman to be executed.[65]

With the deaths of Hannibal and Abigail, the involvement of the
Court of Quarter Sessions came to a close. As they did not "design
. . . to sitt againe," Bickley had the remaining cases transferred to the
city's Supreme Court where, "by some fetch of law," as Governor
Hunter put it, the attorney general contrived to find "a jury [more]
tractable to his purpose."[66] And so it proved. Over the course of three
sessions, held between June 4 and 7, the new jury not only convicted
Mars of Henry Brasier's murder, but also found Jose and Juan, the two
"Spanish Indians," guilty of committing assault against Adrian Beekman. By this stage the trial had become highly politicized and several
key figures gave evidence. Cuffee and Dick once again strengthened
Bickley's case, as did Johannes DePeyster, a former mayor of New
York, Monthel Noel, the son of another former mayor, and Mary
Wenham, the owner of Jose, while Jacob Regnier took the stand for
the defense yet again, as did Thomas George, another attorney—and
the future organizer of the first bar association of New York, David
Provoost, another former mayor, and Henry Wileman, the city coroner who had carried out the initial enquiry into the revolt on April 9.
Three others also gave evidence for the defense, making a total of
seven, the highest of any of the trials so far. Perhaps the most emotional testimony was given by Kate, identified in the records as the
wife of Juan, the "Spanish Indian" then on trial. Nevertheless, Bickley's
jury gave the attorney general the result he desired. Despite the evidence against both Jose and Juan being "presumptive," as John Sharpe
would later put it, and that against Mars being insufficient according
to Governor Hunter, all three were found guilty and sentenced to
hang, the punishment to be carried out on June 11.[67]

Over the four days that separated Mars, Jose, and Juan's sentencing
from the date of their execution, various forces mobilized in their defense. "Convinced in his conscience" that Mars was as innocent "as

the child unborne," Hunter "thought fitt" to override the jury's verdict
and "reprieve him till H.M. [her majesty's] pleasure be known
therein." Hunter also dismissed May Bickley as attorney general and
removed him from the city's common council. Meanwhile, George
Clarke, the secretary of the Province of New York and a future governor, took it upon himself to bring about the release of Jose and Juan.
On the very day of their execution, Clarke appealed to Mary Wenham, Jose's owner. Seemingly having undergone a change of heart
since her appearance as a witness for the prosecution on June 7, the
widow sought out the governor "to beg for a reprieve."[68] Hunter was
only too willing to intervene, although time was running out for the
two Spanish Indians, as John Sharpe recalled. "I visited them in
Prison, and went with them to the Gallows," the reverend recalled
two weeks later. "After they were tyed up they declared their Inno-
cency of what was laid to their charge and behaved themselves as became Christians, while I was at prayers with them Interest was made
with the Governour for their Reprieve."[69] By this stage the people of
New York had seen too much blood spilt and their lust for revenge
had been replaced by pity: as Hunter later wrote, "ye whole town
seemed to acquiesce in their innocence and approve of the reprieve."
With the hangman's nooses already around their necks, Jose and Juan
were given a last-minute stay of execution and led back to the jail beneath city hall. Along with Mars, Tom, and William Walton's Coffee,
they would have to wait some time to hear the ultimate word on their
fate, which was to be given by none other than Queen Anne from her
residence in Windsor Castle, some 3,500 miles away across the Atlantic.[70]

CHAPTER 14

Reprieve

NEW YORK CITY
June 1712 to August 1741

ON JUNE 26, 1712, THE *Harley*, a packet ship that ran the mail from Bristol to New York, upped anchor in the East River and set sail across the Atlantic.[1] On board, along with at least two other letters describing the recent slave rebellion, was a plea written by Governor Hunter asking the Lords of Trade to seek a royal pardon for Jose, Juan, Mars, Tom, and Coffee. Unknown to Hunter, the *Harley* was also carrying a petition written by the former attorney general, May Bickley, the aim of which was to undermine the governor's own request. Determined to have revenge on Hunter for his dismissal from his post, Bickley had spent the previous two weeks secretly gathering signatures to block Mars's pardon. By pretending that it was actually "an Address for a law to punish negroe slaves," an act which was then being debated by New York's general assembly, Bickley managed to gather the signatures of "many hands . . . [and] several gentlemen" who only later discovered "that they knew nothing of the [actual] contents." According to Hunter, who would learn of Bickley's plan from friends in London, the petition's purpose was twofold: "to confirm some people in the beleife of what hee and his associates give out that I have neither creditt or favoure at home, . . . [and] to give creditt to his own infamous proceeding in [the trial of the slaves]." Bickley was to be aided by his long-term patron, the former Lord Cornbury, Hunter's cross-dressing predecessor who was now resident in London.[2] Since his disgrace in New York in 1708, Cornbury had gone some way to reestablishing his reputation. On his father's death he had inherited the title of the Earl of Clarendon and with it a peer's right to parliamentary immunity, thus saving him from the indignity of being prosecuted for the debts he had accrued in New York. Queen Anne had since awarded Clarendon a pension and lodging at the royal palace of Somerset House and he had also landed the post of first commissioner of the admiralty. With such well-positioned enemies ranged against him, it would seem that Hunter's request was doomed to fail.[3]

Joseph Palmer, the *Harley*'s captain, made good time across the Atlantic. One month and two days after leaving the East River, he arrived at Bristol where he handed the mail to a dispatch rider who set off post haste for London.[4] Although the details of the high-level intrigue that transpired once Bickley's and Hunter's letters arrived are unclear, Hunter later learned that the Earl of Clarendon took "much trouble to obstruct the pardon," and it was perhaps as a result of this that it was not until August 27, some six weeks after they had first received Hunter's letter, that the Lords of Trade wrote to the Earl of Dartmouth, a political moderate known to have the confidence of the sovereign, asking him to put Hunter's request directly to Queen Anne.[5] "We inclose to your Lordship an extract [of the governor's] . . . letter," they explained, "wherein your Lordship will find . . . an account of one Mars a Negroe, who had been twice try'd and acquitted, but condemned upon a third trial, and whom the Governor had reprieved, together with one Hosea and one John (Spanish Indians also under condemnation). . . . We are of the opinion," the letter concluded, "that the Governor had good reason for his granting the said reprieve, and we humbly offer that Her Majesty be graciously pleas'd to grant a pardon to the said Negro and Spanish Indians, they now ly in prison at their Masters charge."[6] Despite his peers' recommendation, Dartmouth's subsequent stalling suggests he also had second thoughts as to the wisdom of pursuing the governor's plea with Clarendon still working behind the scenes. Nevertheless, Dartmouth eventually assented and on October 20, 1712, Queen Anne granted "royal pardon to Mars, a negroe, Hosea and John, two Spanish Indians."[7] Neither the queen's document nor the letter written by the Lords of Trade in August make any mention of Tom and Coffee. Somewhere amidst the chain of official correspondence that had linked New York, Westminster, and Windsor over the previous three months, Rip Van Dam's and William Walton's slaves had somehow been forgotten.

Long before Hunter learned of the queen's pardon, the last of the New York slave trials had also concluded. On August 6, Peter the Doctor, the "free negro labourer" and practitioner of Obeah who had blessed the rebels' preparations on March 25, was indicted for the murder of Joris Marschalck. With Bickley's dismissal, however, the impetus of the prosecution had dissipated and the public's thirst for revenge had been quenched.[8] Nevertheless, the remaining defendants could not simply be allowed to walk free. On August 6, the court adjourned without making any progress and Peter the Doctor was returned to the jail under city hall where he would remain, alongside Tom, Coffee, and the now heavily pregnant Sarah until October 14 when he was finally recalled before the court. Peter's exasperation with the delay was evident. "The defendant being in Custody prays that he may come to his Tryall or be discharged," the minutes record. Still the judges procrastinated, and the court was adjourned once more until eventually, on October 18, the jury found "ye defendant not guilty of ye Murthers whereof he stands indicted." Peter was discharged after paying his court fees having spent six months in jail.[9]

On December 10, 1712, the slave act that New York's general assembly had been working on since June was ready for publication. "An Act for preventing Supressing and punishing the Conspiracy and Insurrection of Negroes and other Slaves," added two new clauses to the colony's slave legislation. The enslaver was henceforth permitted to punish his or her enslaved "for their Crimes and Offences at [their own] Discretion." Any punishment deemed suitable could be inflicted providing it did not "extend . . . to Life or Member." While the first clause merely reinforced a law passed in New York in 1701, the second would have much more profound consequences. "Whereas it is found by Experience, that the free Negroes of this Colony are an Idle slothfull people and prove very often a charge on the place where they are," it began, "BE IT therefore further Enacted . . . that any Master or

Mistress, manumitting and setting at Liberty any . . . Slave, shall enter into sufficient Security unto her Majesty . . . with two Sureties not less than the sum of Two hundred pounds." In other words, whereas masters had previously been allowed to free their slaves at their own discretion, they would henceforth have to pay handsomely for the privilege. Furthermore, owners were also required to pay a yearly stipend of £20 directly to the manumitted slave to ensure that he or she would not become a burden on the state. This effectively made it impossible for all but the wealthiest of slave owners to free their slaves, a habit which had previously been relatively common, especially as part of an owner's last will and testament. Indeed, the new act specifically targeted this fashion. "If such . . . Slave shall be made free by the Will . . . of any person deceased," the bill pronounced, "[then] the Executors of such person" could either choose to ignore the deceased's request or be made responsible for the payments.[10] That the former option would inevitably be chosen was exemplified in 1715. As Governor Hunter related in a letter to the Lords of Trade, when a New York butcher named Norton attempted to manumit a "faithfull and diligent" slave who "had helpt to gaine most part of his master's wealth," his executor had "absolutely refused to enter into ye security directed by ye Act by which means the negroe [was] . . . deprived of his liberty." Hunter thought the act both "cruell" and dangerous. "[By] cutting off all hopes from those slaves who by a faithfull . . . discharge of their duty may at last look for ye reward of a manumission, . . . [the new law] will make 'em not only careless servts.," he opined, "but [also] excite 'em to insurrections more bloody than any they have attempted [thus far] seeing that by that Act death is made more eligible than life, for ye longer they live, the longer they are slaves."[11]

New York was not the only colony to pass new laws in reaction to the revolt. On June 7, 1712, Pennsylvania and South Carolina also tightened their slave codes as a direct result of the "divers plots and insurrections . . . by negroes . . . an instance whereof we have lately had in our neighbouring colony of New York." The Pennsylvania bill imposed a duty on the importation of slaves into the colony of £20 per head in an attempt to encourage the use of white indentured labor. The law also gave the authorities the power to "break open any house or place suspected of harbouring negroes or Indians illicitly imported."

In South Carolina "An Act for the better Ordering and Governing of Negroes" declared that "any slave [who] shall tempt or persuade a slave to leave the service of his master . . . upon conviction, shall suffer death," while whites found guilty of the same crime were subject to a fine of £25 and could be executed themselves if they were caught aiding the slave "in the act of escape."[12]

IN MID-JULY 1713 Hunter finally received word from the Council of Trade and Plantations that Mars, Juan, and Jose had received the royal pardon. The governor was greatly relieved. "[This] will enable me to struggle cheerfully with all other difficulties," he wrote to the council on July 18, "for indeed the notion that a faction here had spread that I was disregarded at home, and consequently speedily to be recalled had gain'd soe much credit, that the friends of ye Government cool'd whilst ye others triumph'd."[13] If Hunter was pleased, the feelings of Mars, Juan, and Jose can only be imagined. Having spent fifteen months in the jail under city hall "in a woful condition," they were finally released into the custody of their masters.[14] Hunter appears to have momentarily overlooked the fact that the pardon failed to make any mention of the other imprisoned slaves for whom he had also requested pardon, and it wasn't until September 10, 1713, that he finally got around to addressing the issue. "I believe there was an omission in the Pardon of the Negroes," he wrote to Secretary Popple, "for besides the three which Her Majesty has been pleased to pardon there were other two Vizt: Tom a negroe belonging to Rip Van Dam Esq; and Coffee a negro, belonging to Mr Walton, who were recommended by the Bench itself as proper objects of Mercey, there being no manner of convincing evidence against them." In the same letter Hunter took the opportunity to make a further recommendation for clemency. "There is likewise a Negro woman," he wrote in reference to Sarah, "who was indeed privy to the conspiracy but pleading her belly was reprieved. She is since delivered [of the child]," Hunter continued, "but . . . has suffer'd more than death by her long imprisonment, if their Lordsps think fit to include her [in the pardon], I should be much pleased, for there has been much blood shed already on that account, I'm afraid too much, and the people are now easy."[15] Whether or not their Lordships did "think fit" to take pity on Sarah, or if they ever got around to making good on their omission to request the pardons of Tom and Coffee, is unknown. No further reference to the case survives. Perhaps none was ever written. Even if they did deem the plight of a few enslaved worthy of the queen's attention for a second time, Hunter would not have received word of their assent for at least another year judging by the infrequency of the New York packet. Perhaps Sarah and her peers died in prison before word of the queen's mercy could arrive. There is a chance, however, that the last of the enslaved prisoners persevered, and after more than two years in prison, were finally released to their enslavers. This theory is reinforced by the fact that Stophel Pels Sarah's enslaver, did not receive any compensation when, in 1718, the New York Assembly finally reimbursed the enslavers of the nineteen slaves executed in the aftermath of the revolt as laid down in the 1708 Act for Preventing the Conspiracy of Slaves. Sixteen received "the Quantity of Fifty Ounces of [gold] Plate"; Rip Van Dam, as the only individual to have enslaved two of those put to death, was paid "One hundred Ounces"; while the money due to "Adrian Hoogland deceas'd", Robin's former enslaver, was paid to his "Executors or Administrators."[16]

ANOTHER LOOSE END centers on the fate of Dick and Cuffee, the two rebels persuaded to turn state's evidence by May Bickley in the buildup to the trial in the second week of April 1712. In exchange for a promise that they would be transported rather than face execution, the pair had served Bickley well. Not only had they appeared as prosecution witnesses in the trials of their peers on no less than nine occasions between April 11 and June 4, 1712, but they had also given such damning evidence that they had "fix[ed] the ... guilt" of a number of those indicted, as John Sharpe testified.[17] Hunter agreed. "Without [Cuffee and Dick]," the governor had attested, "very few co[u]ld have beene punished."[18] What became of the pair after Bickley had finished with them on June 4 is less clear. The only clue is a single allusion imbedded in the account of the trials of 1741 written by Bickley's eventual successor, Daniel Horsmanden. When discussing the evidence given by Sandy, a "negro boy of about 16 or 17 years of age" who was enslaved to the vintner Thomas Niblet, the attorney general revealed that the grand jury offered the young man a pardon, "[even] though he had been cancerned [concerned in the alleged revolt]," on condition that he make "a free and ingenuous confession." At first Sandy did not believe the jury would stick to their offer as "the time before . . . [,]" hinting at the conspiracy in 1712, as a footnote conveniently informs us, "after . . . the negroes told all they knew, then the white people hanged them." Once the jury had "assured" Sandy that this rumor "was false, for the negroes which confessed the truth and made a discovery, were certainly pardoned, and shipped off," Sandy went on to make the full "confession" as requested and was ultimately transported to the Spanish Caribbean colony of Santo Domingo on Hispaniola. Other enslaved persons sentenced to transportation in the aftermath of the trials of 1741 were sent to such diverse locations as the French colony of Cape François in what would become Haiti, Suriname, Newfoundland, Portugal, the Dutch Caribbean colonies of Statia (Sint Eustatius) and Curaçao, and the Danish island of Saint Thomas. As no record of Dick and Cuffee's destination survives, we can only presume that they suffered a comparable fate, most likely being transported to a plantation in the Caribbean, a region where new arrivals rarely lasted more than seven years before succumbing to disease or dying of exhaustion brought on by malnourishment or overwork.[19]

Only one further reference to any of the individual rebels occurs in the surviving documentation. On February 1, 1715, "a Negro Man Called Peter of the City of New York Labourer—otherwise Commonly Called Doctor Peter," presumably the same Peter the Doctor who had assisted the rebels in their spiritual preparations on New Year's Day 1712, "Did . . . Receive Harbour and Entertain Diverse Negro Slaves . . . in his dwelling House at the East Ward . . . without the . . . Knowledge of their Masters." The Court of General Sessions punished Peter with a fine of £10.[20] Whether he was able to raise the funds to secure his release is unknown. Perhaps Peter saw out the rest of his days as a debtor in the jail beneath city hall.

Of the white principals associated with the revolt of April 1712 more can be said with certainty. Robert Hunter continued as governor of New York until 1719, making his period of service longer than all but one of his predecessors. According to his biographer, Mary Lou

Lustig, the Scot was "perhaps the most highly regarded [governor] in American colonial history."[21] A less partial measure of Hunter's aptitude may be gleaned from his next overseas appointment. In 1728, after a period as Comptroller of Customs, he was made governor of Jamaica, a colony which contributed more to the British coffers than any other.[22] As Jamaica was embroiled in the first of two Maroon Wars to take place over the course of the eighteenth century, the posting proved even more problematic than New York. The descendants of escaped slaves, the maroons operated out of fortified bases in the mountainous interior of the island from where they attacked isolated plantations and used guerrilla tactics suited to their mastery of the island terrain to resist all Hunter's efforts to dislodge them. To make matters worse, the maroons received constant reinforcements in the form of runaways and were kept abreast of the militia's movements via a network of informers.[23] "[The maroons] are grown to the height of insolence," Hunter warned the Assembly in June 1730. "[The] frontiers . . . are no longer in any sort of security, [and] must be deserted, and then the danger must spread and come nearer [to the main areas of white settlement]." Of further concern were the rumors of Spanish collusion. In return for military aid, it was said that the maroons were planning to turn over the colony to the governor of "Cracas." By 1731 Hunter was warning that the maroons' numbers had reached 10,000. Although it may have been an exaggeration, the figure is indicative of how serious the situation had become. London reacted by dispatching two regiments of regulars from Gibraltar, but the redcoats fared little better than the island militia. Although they torched several maroon settlements and killed and captured some stragglers, they failed to achieve a decisive breakthrough while suffering frequent defeats themselves. In 1734 Hunter died in office "after labour[ing for some time] . . . under a Complication of Distempers." The situation in Jamaica was measurably worse than it had been on his arrival six years before.[24]

THE POST REVOLT CAREER of Alan Jarrett, the Huguenot slaver likely to have brought the majority of the rebels of April 1712 to New York, is also of interest. As previously stated, in October 1711 Jarrett had set sail for the Gold Coast on his fifth recorded African voyage. As a result, Jarrett was absent when the revolt broke out, but when he returned to the city on June 23, 1712, with a cargo of seventy-seven slaves, the trials were still running.[25] There is reason to speculate that the slaver felt a modicum of guilt for his involvement. In late June or early July 1712, just a week after his return, Jarrett addressed a "Humble Petition" to Governor Hunter. After outlining his "experience and practice of the Art of Navigation and other parts of the Mathemats for the space of fourteen years," Jarrett went on to bemoan "how much the youth brought up on this citty are at a loss in goeing to sea without a sufficient Instruction. . . . Having now some leisure time," he continued, "[I] Humbly beg . . . yor Excellency's Lycence to teach Writing, Arithmetick, Navigation and . . . Mathematicks." One interpretation is that Jarrett had had enough of slaving and wanted to turn his hand to more laudable pursuits. Whether or not the events of April 1712 had any part in this decision is impossible to know, although the timing of Jarrett's petition makes the theory plausible. Having returned to New York to discover that the slaves he had brought back from the Gold Coast had risen up and killed and wounded fifteen of his friends, business associates, and neighbors, Jarrett may have thought it was time he made a more positive contribution to society. Hunter, for his part, was only too happy to accede. "Being assured of yor experience and Knowledge," the governor wrote on July 4, 1712, "I doe hereby authorize and Impower you to Teach."[26]

Whether or not Jarrett ever embarked upon his new career is unclear. Either way, it would seem that there was insufficient demand for his services or that he realized that teaching was not as lucrative a business as his former profession, as within five years he was back on the quarterdeck of a slaver heading for the African coast. On March 7, 1717, the *Phillipsburgh*, "Allen Jarratt master," was among a number of ships "cleared for Africa" by London's Custom House. A six-gun ship with eighteen crew, the *Phillipsburgh* belonged to Adolphus Philipse, one of New York's most prominent businessmen. Jarrett purchased 150 slaves in an unspecified African port. Seventeen died during the Middle Passage, 128 were sold in Barbados, and the remaining five were brought back to New York. The three-legged voyage took 284 days and was the longest Jarrett ever undertook.[27] The Frenchman's next recorded voyage to Africa would also be his last. In 1722, Jarrett set sail on the sloop *Burnet*. Among the five investors in his voyage were Rip Van Dam and his son-in-law, Walter Thong, both of whom it will be recalled had owned slaves executed in the aftermath of the revolt of April 1712. Eighty-three slaves were embarked on board the *Burnet*, sixty-nine of whom survived the Middle Passage and were sold in Jamaica, but by the time the *Burnet* returned to New York, Jarrett was no longer on board. A newspaper report from Philadelphia written on August 29, 1723, provides the only details. "By Capt. Stockin who arrived here last Week from Barbadoes, we have advice that a Sloop belonging to New York, was arrived from Guinea, and that the Captain died on that Coast." With these words, Alan Jarrett passed into history.[28] He had probably fallen victim to the "bilious fevers" that killed so many Europeans in West Africa, or perhaps he was killed in an onboard ship rising. Having profited from the enforced translocation of over 500 African men, women, and children over a career which had spanned fourteen years and seven voyages, Alan Jarrett's luck had finally run out.

CONTEMPORANEOUSLY TO JARRETT'S DECLINE, the Akwamu, the Akan polity that may well have been the Frenchman's principal suppliers, continued to go from strength to strength. Following the campaigning of his youth, which had seen his kingdom rise to a position of regional hegemony, King Akwonno had spent the decade since the conquest of Kwahu consolidating his hold on his newly acquired territories and developing their economic potential. European demand for the slaves Akwonno supplied was greater than ever, in the port of Accra trade was booming, and even the threat from Akwonno's western neighbor, the ever-dangerous polity of Akim, seemed to have diminished. Akwonno had gained considerable influence over Ashanti, the new regional power which had risen in the forest country to Akim's north, and the threat of an Akwamu-Ashanti alliance held Akim's ambitions in check. Thus the status quo continued into the opening years of the reign of Akwonno's successor, Ansa Kwao, who succeeded to the polity's stool in 1725. Two years later, however, the balance of power shifted. As Ansa Kwao was conducting an official visit to Accra, rumors spread of an Akim plot to purchase Ashanti neutrality, thus allowing them to crush Akwamu once and for all.[29]

For a "gift" of five hundred slaves, the Ashanti king, Oppoccu, agreed
to give Akim five months to complete the conquest. On learning of
the deal, Ansa Kwao raised an army and marched against Akim, meeting his foes in battle, as we learn from the Danish factor, Ludewig
Rømer, "in territory that was unfamiliar to [his men]." The Akwamuhene's impetuosity was to prove his undoing. "In the first battle,"
Rømer wrote, "the Akims overwhelmed the [Akwamu] . . . and took
many thousand prisoners—and the heads of [the king] . . . and all the
Big Men." Within days, the Akwamu state had disintegrated and their
former subjects fell on them with glee. "The Adampes, the Mountain
Negroes [a possible reference to the Kwahu], and the Accras seized
as many [captives] as they . . . cared to . . . You can well imagine what
they did with them," Rømer continued, "as long as they could get a
pott of brandy [from the Europeans] for [each one]."[30] Many of the
Akwamu thus enslaved were transported to the Danish Caribbean
colony of Saint John where, as discussed in Chapter 12, they attempted to wrest control of the island and establish their own plantation economy with the island's non-Akan slaves as labor. The
attempt failed, however, and the would-be rulers of Saint John committed suicide or ended their days swinging from the hangman's
noose, much as many of their former enemies had done after being
transported to New York by Alan Jarrett over twenty years before.[31]

MEANWHILE, in 1741 a rash of paranoia swept through the city which
would eventually bring about the judicial execution of thirty-four. The
incident began with a burglary in February of that year. Two Black
slaves seen with a hatful of coins in a disorderly house shortly after
the theft were arrested, and the owner of the tavern, John Hughson,
was detained for questioning but released after a search of his premises
failed to turn up anything sufficiently incriminating. The case may
well have ended there had it not been for the intervention of a sixteen-year-old white indentured servant of Hughson's named Mary
Burton. Burton accused Hughson, his wife, and his daughter, Sarah,
along with a prostitute who lived at the tavern named Peggy Kerry, of
receiving stolen goods from the two slaves previously implicated. A
second search was conducted with Burton directing the constables,

and a cache of stolen goods was found buried under the tavern floor. Fate then intervened and blew the incident out of all proportion. While Hughson and his accomplices languished in jail, a rash of fires broke out. Arson was suspected and when a slave was caught looting one of the burning buildings, the people's fear of the enemy in their midst—dormant since 1712—rose to the surface. A city-wide slave plot was imagined, and the council offered a reward of £100 "for the discovery of the villainous conspiracy."[32]

In such a climate, Mary Burton's finger pointing took on a whole new significance. When she appeared in court to give evidence about the burglary committed back in February, Burton hinted at a link between the crime and the fires then occupying the city's attention. It was exactly what the judges wanted to hear. Further prompted, Burton was only too happy to accuse the Hughsons, Peggy Kerry, and two Akan slaves named Quack and Cuffee of a plot to burn the city to the ground, massacre the inhabitants with the aid of a slave army and enthrone Hughson as the king of New York. Hard as it is to imagine that such sensational claims were taken seriously, that is precisely what happened. Faced with such overwhelming sentiment, no city lawyer dared take on the Hughsons' defense, while the prosecution, led by Attorney General Daniel Horsmanden, employed tactics which would otherwise have been prevented. In just one such manifestation of these underhanded practices, a convicted thief named Arthur Price who was placed in the jail to spy on Quack and Cuffee gave evidence that he had overheard the pair admitting their guilt. This was sufficient to see Quack and Cuffee convicted even though their enslavers insisted both had been home when the fires had started. From that point on the pace of the convictions accelerated. Just before Quack and Cuffee were burned to death on the Commons, they accused Hughson and his wife of being the ringleaders of the "plot" as well as implicating Peggy Kerry. All three were hanged within a week of the conclusion of their trial.[33]

Spurred on by Mary Burton's ever more fantastic accusations, Attorney General Horsmanden filled the jail beneath city hall with over one hundred suspects, each of whom was then induced to turn evidence themselves. Thus, the web grew ever wider until so many of the city's enslaved people had been caught up in the alleged plot that the prosecutors found themselves unable to process the weight of "evidence" that had begun to accumulate. After dozens had been burned alive and hanged in the Commons, a sense of perspective was gradually regained. Just when it seemed that the madness was over, however, the arrival of an inflammatory letter from Governor Oglethorpe of Georgia gave fresh impetus to the prosecution. Plagued by Spanish raiders who attempted to incite Georgia's slaves and Indians to revolt, Oglethorpe warned that all the crown's colonies in North America were in imminent peril. Normally, such a missive would have been ignored in New York—the Spanish were less of a threat than in Georgia, but with the War of Jenkins's Ear in full swing the idea appeared plausible enough, especially when combined with the people's fears of a slave revolt. The letter breathed new life into the prosecution's desire to press on until every last individual caught up in the ever-more-convoluted plot had been successfully brought to trial.[34]

The resulting hunt for a Spanish agent led to the arrest of a schoolmaster named John Ury. Although Ury was adamant that he was an adherent of the Church of England, his recent arrival in New York and consequent anonymity in the colony, combined with his fluency in Latin and love of theological debate, had raised suspicions and prompted his arrest. Mary Burton was only too willing to denounce Ury as a Catholic priest and the real ringleader behind the conspiracy. Even though these latest developments could in no way be reconciled with the evidence Burton had given against the Hughsons and Peggy Kerry, Attorney General Horsmanden chose to proceed. Turning to Sarah Hughson, the executed landlord's adolescent daughter, Horsmanden offered her a pardon if she corroborated Burton's story. The young girl accepted, and her evidence sealed Ury's fate. He was hanged on August 29, 1741. With Ury's death, the prosecution once again lost momentum. Having seen dozens of their valuable slaves executed, the city's principal residents began to voice their criticism of the trials. Burton's ramblings were becoming ever more deluded, and when she began to accuse prominent whites of complicity, she was perceived as an embarrassment to the prosecution. Even Horsmanden admitted that her pronouncements "staggered one's belief." Thus, the trials ground to a halt. In all thirty Blacks and four whites had been executed. Twenty-one had been hanged. The remainder were burned at the stake, while seventy other Blacks were transported to the sugar plantations of the Caribbean and seven whites were banished from the city for life.[35]

Epilogue

THE YEAR 1741 WAS THE LAST TIME a slave revolt shook New York City. Nevertheless, the fear that another rising could occur remained a concern. This insecurity fostered an increasingly negative attitude toward slavery as an institution and contributed to the first calls for abolition voiced in the colony's newspapers in the 1760s.[1] Slavery also came under attack for being a violation of natural rights, an idea gaining currency as the philosophy of the Enlightenment spread. In March 1760 an editorial printed in the *New York Weekly Post-Boy* described "negro" slaves as "poor pagans whom Christians have thought fit to consider cattle," and as Americans began to demand political freedom for themselves some found the concept of slavery increasingly hard to justify. In the 1770s almost all the leaders of the Revolution denounced slavery and made calls for its gradual abolition, despite the fact that the vast majority were slave owners themselves. Thomas Jefferson's first draft of the Declaration of Independence condemned the practice; Maryland politician Luther Martin held that slavery was "inconsistent with the principles of the Revolution"; and in New York John Jay wrote that if America was unwilling to emancipate its slaves then "her own prayers to Heaven for liberty will be impious."[2]

The outbreak of war with Britain brought further changes. In 1779 Sir Henry Clinton, the commander-in-chief of the occupying forces, actively encouraged slaves to flee their patriot masters and seek asylum in the British enclave in southern New York. Thousands took up Clinton's offer. A Black exodus out of patriot territory ensued. The fear of insurrection became widespread throughout northern New York and New England, forcing the leaders of the revolution to make similar concessions to their slaves. Having originally opposed the idea of enlisting Blacks, George Washington was forced to change policy. Enslaved people were offered their freedom in return for their service, and by the end of the war more than four thousand had joined the Continental army. Many served with distinction, such as Colonel Christopher Greene's regiment which fought at Points Bridge in 1781, one of the most closely contested engagements of the war. With the end of the conflict, the British remained faithful to their pledge and in 1782 over three thousand former slaves sailed away with the departing redcoats despite patriot pressure for all runaways to be returned. Many of those that left with the British took up residence as freemen in Nova Scotia. Others would eventually sail to the newly established colony of Sierra Leone.[3]

The post independence movement toward abolition was fueled by economic and social factors. With a rapid increase in immigration into New York State between 1771 and 1786 the white population increased by 47 percent. Consequently, the necessity for slave labor declined. While both the purchase and maintenance of slaves was a heavy financial burden, casual employment of free white laborers who could be discarded when not required was relatively cheap. Thus, slavery was becoming economically obsolete. Combined with the growing realization that bondage was immoral, this financial incentive accelerated the demise of the institution, and in 1785 a bill for gradual emancipation was passed through the New York Assembly. Exactly how such a policy was to be enacted caused considerable disagreement, however, and the resulting divisions led to a stuttering and gradual erosion of slave laws rather than outright abolition. In 1788 trading in slaves was outlawed, but it was not until 1799 that the gradual emancipation first mooted fourteen years earlier was given definite and enforceable shape. The Gradual Manumission Act promised to free all children born to enslaved women after July 4, 1799. The boys would become free at twenty-eight years old, the girls at twenty-five.

In 1809 slave marriages were given legal recognition, thus legitimizing children born in wedlock; a second clause forbade owners from separating husbands and wives by sale. In the same year slaves gained the right to own property and bequeath it in their wills, and from 1813 the enslaved were allowed to give testimony against whites in court and also gained the right to trial by jury. Four years later an amendment to the Gradual Manumission Act decreed that all slaves born before July 4, 1799, were to be freed on July 4, 1827, thus paving the way for the absolute abolition of slavery in New York, a law which was finally passed in 1831. Even so, owners from other states were still permitted to bring their slaves into the state for up to nine months at a time, but in 1841 this permission was also repealed thus entirely extinguishing the practice of slavery from New York.[4]

Abolition did not bring equal rights. In 1815 a law was passed by the Republican-dominated legislature of New York which required Blacks to obtain special passes to vote in state elections. Six years later an amendment to the state constitution saw the property qualification abolished entirely for white voters yet increased for Blacks from $100 to $250. As a result, only sixteen Black votes were cast in New York City in the election of 1826. Concurrently, antipathy toward Blacks was growing among white working-class New Yorkers who saw the newly enfranchised ex-slaves as unwanted competition in the labor market. In July 1834 these tensions erupted as the city was hit by one of the longest riots in New York's history. Dozens of homes and businesses associated with the Black population or with white abolitionists were damaged or destroyed, particularly around the Five Points. At least seven churches were targeted, and order was only restored once the governor ordered the militia into the streets. Half a century after the first gradual abolition act had been passed in New York, the civil rights of African Americans appeared to be diminishing. As Alexis de Tocqueville, a French aristocrat who traveled widely through the country, noted in his 1834 work *Democracy in America*, "the prejudice of race appears to be stronger in the States which have abolished slavery, than in those where it still exists."[5]

In 1835, several Black abolitionists in New York, among them David Ruggles and William Johnson, set up the Committee of Vigilance, an organization aimed at resisting local cooperation with southern slaveholders. The committee, which met once a month in the Medical Hall on Crosby Street, aided recently arrived southern fugitives, as well as taking legal action against the slave catchers, or "blackbirds," who attempted to spirit runaways back to the plantation states. As a result, New York City became one of the principal hubs of the Underground Railroad, the network of secret routes and safe houses which led as many as 100,000 runaways from the southern states to freedom in the abolitionist North and Canada in the three decades preceding the Civil War. Perhaps the best-known of these escapees was Frederick Douglass. Having initially taken refuge in Ruggles's offices after his arrival from Baltimore in 1838, Douglass went on to become the leading Black advocate for abolition and the author of one of the principal "slave narratives," a genre which gave impetus to the cause. Another former slave and future author who was aided by the committee was the aforementioned Mahommah Gardo Baquaqua. Originally from Benin, Baquaqua had changed hands on numerous occasions before his arrival in New York harbor in 1847 as an enslaved sailor aboard the *Lembrança*, a ship transporting coffee from Brazil. Although Baquaqua was put in irons by his enslaver to prevent his escape after the *Lembrança* had been boarded by agents of the committee, he later managed to break free, only to be recaptured, before abolitionist lawyers eventually demanded he be released into their custody. Baquaqua's biography was published in 1854.[6]

In July 1863, seven months after Abraham Lincoln had issued the Emancipation Proclamation, New York City was struck by further race riots. Outraged by a law enabling wealthy young whites to avoid the draft, the city's working classes rioted. Although at first the destruction targeted the Ninth District's Marshal's Office where the draft had been scheduled to take place, the mob's wrath soon fell upon the Black population whom many of the rioters blamed for the war then raging throughout America. The rioters believed that working-class whites were paying for Black freedom with their lives. Adding further incentive was the fear that victory for the Union would result in increasing competition for jobs as free Blacks migrated north. The riots lasted for four days. The Colored Orphan Asylum was burned to the ground along with the homes of many Blacks, and by the time federal troops restored order, at least 105 people, the vast majority of whom were Black, had been beaten to death, shot, stabbed, or lynched.[7]

In the immediate aftermath of the Civil War, considerable progress was made toward racial equality in the southern states, and in 1870 the Fifteenth Amendment afforded African Americans equal voting rights nationwide. A white backlash soon followed. In the South the Ku Klux Klan emerged, while paramilitary groups such as the Red Shirts and White League used violence to suppress Black voting. Two decades later the so-called Jim Crow laws made racial segregation a de facto reality, a situation which was upheld by the Supreme Court in 1896 when it laid out its "separate but equal" doctrine in *Plessy v. Ferguson*. Meanwhile, in New York, Black emigration from the southern states and the Caribbean resulted in the city's Black population quadrupling in the two decades following 1890 and the establishment of Black neighborhoods in the Tenderloin district and San Juan Hill. Competition for jobs with an even larger wave of white European immigrants was intense. Irish and Italians displaced African Americans as domestics, while union segregation denied Blacks employment as longshoremen, street cleaners, baggage handlers, cement carriers, and garment workers. Blacks responded by taking these positions when the unions went on strike. Tensions increased and during a heat wave in 1900, yet another race riot broke out after a Black man fatally wounded a plainclothes policeman on the corner of 41st Street and 8th Avenue.[8]

The first decades of the twentieth century saw the emergence of two major national organizations aimed at promoting African American rights. In 1908 the National Association for the Advancement of Colored People (NAACP) was founded by W. E. B. Du Bois and Ida B. Wells-Barnett, among others, while the National League on Urban Conditions among Negroes (later known as the National Urban League or NUL) was established the following September. Both organizations were based in New York City. The NAACP focused on overturning the continuing disenfranchisement of Blacks and lobbied against the strengthening of segregation laws. In 1914 it helped secure the right of African Americans to serve as officers in World War I—six hundred were commissioned—and during the interwar years the NAACP sought federal legislation against the growing wave of lynching occurring throughout the United States. Meanwhile, the NUL worked to remove the barriers to Black employment. In 1916 the Jamaican-born Marcus Garvey set up a Pan-African movement, the Universal Negro Improvement Association (UNIA), whose offices were in Harlem, by then home to the largest Black urban community in the United States. In August 1920 the city hosted the first International Convention of Negro Peoples of the World which saw over 25,000 international delegates congregate in Madison Square Garden. The 1920s and 1930s also saw the rise of the Harlem Renaissance, which propelled numerous Black writers and artists to national and international prominence, one of the most notable being the poet, novelist, playwright, and social activist Langston Hughes.[9]

World War II led to increased employment opportunities for Black men and women in the city's war industries. Although these industries and the armed forces were still subject to racial segregation, when New Yorker A. Philip Randolph threatened to organize a march on Washington, President Roosevelt issued Executive Order 8802 banning discrimination in the defense industry and government. After the war, the victories African Americans had won against discrimination both in and out of the military boosted expectations of racial equality and the NAACP began to challenge segregation laws in education, housing, and employment. In 1954 the *Brown v. Board of Education* case ruled that racial segregation in public schools was unconstitutional, and between 1955 and 1968 numerous nonviolent protests and acts of civil disobedience led by figures such as Martin Luther King Jr. and Rosa Parks forced the state's recognition of the racial inequality still dominating the lives of African Americans one hundred years on from abolition. Further Supreme Court rulings followed bringing an end to the Jim Crow laws and resulting in legislated protection of equal rights in voting, employment practices, housing, and education. African Americans grew in political power and young people were inspired to take action. A wave of inner-city race riots followed in the 1960s and 1970s. Subsequently, racial tensions have periodically reignited, often triggered by instances of police brutality which highlight the institutionalized racism and use of racial profiling that still mars the legal and law enforcement systems. Despite the apparent sea change embodied by the presidential election of Barack Obama in 2008, the murder of George Floyd by police officers in Minneapolis twelve years later and the rise of the Black Lives Matter movement makes it all too evident that the struggle begun by the enslaved New York rebels of 1712 is still far from complete.[10]

Notes

The following abbreviations appear in the notes.

CNYHS   Collections of the New-York Historical Society
CO   Colonial Office
DRCHNY   John Romeyn Brodhead and E. B. O'Callaghan (eds.).
     Documents Relative to the Colonial History of New York:
     Produced in Holland, England and France, Volume 5.
     Albany, NY: Weed, Parsons and Company, 1855.
MCQS   Minutes of the Court of Quarter Sessions
NYGBR   New York Genealogical and Biographical Record
NYHS   New-York Historical Society
SPG   Society for the Propagation of the Gospel

PREFACE: IN SEARCH OF SILENT PROTAGONISTS

1. Kea, "'When I Die, I Shall Return to My Own Land': An 'Amina' Slave Rebellion in the Danish West Indies, 1733–1734," 159–160, in Wilks, *The Cloth of Many Colored Silks*; Konadu, *The Akan Diaspora in the Americas*, 19–20.
2. Konadu, *The Akan Diaspora in the Americas*, 3–6, 123; Thornton, *Warfare in Atlantic Africa, 1500–1800*, 57; Craton, *Testing the Chains*, 90; Midlo Hall, *Slavery and African Ethnicity in the Americas*, 122; Zoellner, *Island on Fire*, 66, 102–103.
3. *Boston News-Letter*, 14 April 1712.
4. John Sharpe letter, 23 June 1712, *NYGBR*, volume 21, 1809, 162–163; Midlo Hall, *Slavery and African Ethnicity in the Americas*, 47.
5. *MCQS*, 1704–1712, memorandum for Friday 30 May 1712.
6. On Akan oath taking and Obeah see Konadu, *The Akan Diaspora in the Americas*.
7. *MCQS*, 1704–1712, entries from April 1712 to October 1712.
8. *MCQS*, 1704–1712, entries from April 1712 to October 1712.

9. *MCQS*, 1704–1712, entries for Friday 11 April 1712.

10. T 70/956, f. 16; CO 157/1—Antigua Shipping Returns; T 70/8, f. 80; T 70/5, f. 48; T 70/956, f. 13; T 70/5, f. 56, 58–59, 70; *Boston News-Letter*, 11 June 1711; *Boston News-Letter*, 8 October 1711; CO 390/7, f. 1; Donnan, *Documents Illustrative of the History of the Slave Trade to America*, volume 3, 352, 466.

11. *MCQS*, 1704–1712, entries for 15 April 1712. For more on the possible connection between Rip Van Dam and Alan Jarrett see Chapter 8.

12. Craton, *Testing the Chains*, 90; Prince, *Maroon Societies*, 20; Konadu, *The Akan Diaspora in the Americas*, 3–6, 123; Zoellner, *Island on Fire*, 66; Brown, *Tacky's Revolt*, 130; Greenburg, *Crime and Punishment*, 150–151.

13. On ethnicity in colonial New York see Goodfriend, *Before the Melting Pot*; Archdeacon, *New York City, 1664–1710*.

14. https://en.wikipedia.org/wiki/Claus.

15. Davies, *The Royal African Company*, 224–225; Sparks, *Where the Negroes Are Masters*, 8–11; Bosman, *A New and Accurate Description of the Coast of Guinea*.

16. Rask, *Two Views*, 16–20; Rømer, *A Reliable Account*, x–xiii; Tilleman, *A Short Account of West Africa's Gold Coast*, i–iii.

17. Wilks, *Akwamu, 1640–1750*, 32–35; Gould, "The Shrine of Tutu Abo," *Research Review*, Institute of African Studies, 8, January 1972, 5–10; Dupuis, *Journal of a Residence in Ashantee*, 15–16, quoted in Wilks, *Forests of Gold*, 43.

18. Justeen (ed.), *Danish Source History of Ghana*, volume 1, 229–230. The Danish company ships which were trading on the Gold Coast in the period 1704 to 1715 were the *Cron Printzen*, the *Fredericus Quartus*, and the *Christianus Quintus*. The *Fredericus Quartus* and the *Christianus Quintus* were refitting in the Caribbean at the time of Jarrett's visit to the Gold Coast. Rask, *Two Views*, 220; Rømer, *A Reliable Account*, 135, footnote 80.

19. T 70/5, f. 56; Justeen (ed.), *Danish Source History of Ghana*, volume 1, 229–230.

20. Brown, *Tacky's Revolt*, 14; Hoffer, *Cry Liberty*, 159–164; Zoellner, *Island on Fire*, 87, 272–273.

21. *Acts of Assembly, Passed in the Province of New York, from 1691, to 1718*, 276; Horsmanden, *The New-York Conspiracy, or a History of the Negro Plot*, 72; *Boston News-Letter*, 14 April 1712. By comparison, in Tacky's Rebellion, which took place in Jamaica in 1760, 50 whites were killed and 400 slaves were executed.

PROLOGUE

1. Kammen, *Colonial New York*, 65; Peterson and Edward, *New York as an Eighteenth Century Municipality*, 169.

2. Walton, Puckett, Deskins, *The African-American Electorate*, 69–70.

3. Costello, *History of the New York Police*, 31; Peterson and Edward, *New York as an Eighteenth Century Municipality*, 178–181.

4. Greenburg, *Crime and Law Enforcement in the Colony of New York*, 44–45; *Coroner's Inquisition*, 9 April 1712 (NYHS Misc. Mss., NYC, Box 4, #13).

CHAPTER I: WHIPPED AT THE COMMON WHIPPING POST

1. Christoph, *The Freedmen of New Amsterdam*, 157; McManus, *A History of Negro Slavery in New York*, 4; Hodges, *Root and Branch*, 8–9.

2. Hodges, *Root and Branch*, 12–13; McManus, *A History of Negro Slavery in New York*, 17; Foote, *Black and White Manhattan*, 37–38.

3. Hodges, *Root and Branch*, 13–14; Christoph, *The Freedmen of New Amsterdam*, 157.

4. Kammen, *Colonial New York*, 57–58; McManus, *A History of Negro Slavery in New York*, 5.

5. Kruger, *Born to Run*, 36; Medford (ed.), *The New York African Burial Ground*, 43; Donnan (ed.), Documents Illustrative of the Slave Trade, Volume 3, 405, 411–413, 415, 417–419, 420–421; Goodfriend, "Burghers and Blacks," 128–129; Stokes, *The Iconography of Manhattan Island*, Volume 4, 106.

6. McManus, *A History of Negro Slavery in New York*, 6–8; Goodfriend, *Burghers and Blacks*, 134–136; Medford (ed.), *The New York African Burial Ground*, Volume 3, *Historical Perspectives*, 7; Foote, *Black and White Manhattan*, 36–38.

7. McManus, *A History of Negro Slavery in New York*, 11–22; *The Skeletal Biology, Archaeology, and History of the New York African Burial Ground: A Synthesis of Volumes 1, 2, and 3*, 19; Foote, *Black and White Manhattan*, 47–48; Christoph, *The Freedmen of New Amsterdam*, 157–158.

8. McManus, *A History of Negro Slavery in New York*, 22; Christoph, *The Freedmen of New Amsterdam*, 157–158, 167.

9. Goodfriend, "Burghers and Blacks," 138–141; Donnan (ed.), *Documents Illustrative of the Slave Trade*, volume 3, 428; McManus, *A History of Negro Slavery in New York*, 11.

10. Kammen, *Colonial New York*, 71–72; Shorto, *The Island at the Centre of the World*, 295–300.

11. Christoph, *The Freedmen of New Amsterdam*, 164–166; Kammen, *Colonial New York*, 88–89; Hodges, *Root and Branch*, 37; Peterson, *New York as an Eighteenth Century Municipality*, 198.

12. *Minutes of the Common Council of the City of New York*, volume I, 92–93.

13. O'Callaghan, *Calendar of Historical Manuscripts*, part 2, 135.

14. *An Abstract of the Evidence delivered before a Select Committee . . . for the Abolition of the Slave Trade*, 42; Rømer, *A Reliable Account*, 152.

15. Riddell, *The Slave in Early New York*, 67.

16. Hall, Leder, Kamman (eds.), *The Glorious Revolution in America*, 3–9, 109.

17. Kammen, *Colonial New York*, 118–127; Archdeacon, *New York City*, 97–123.

18. Medford (ed.), *The New York African Burial Ground*, volume 3, *Historical Perspectives*, 46; Hodges, *Root and Branch*, 38–40; Goodfriend, *Before the Melting Pot*, 47–48, 112–113, 141.

19. Bayles, *Old Taverns of New York*, 54–55.

20. Goodfriend, *Before the Melting Pot*, 112–113; Foote, *Black and White Manhattan*, 64; *The Skeletal Biology, Archaeology, and History of the New York African Burial Ground: A Synthesis of Volumes 1, 2, and 3*, 198, footnote 3; Archdeacon, *New York City*, 129–130.

21. *Minutes of the Common Council, 1675–1776*, volume I, 276–277.

22. Christoph, *The Freedmen of New Amsterdam*, 164–166.

23. *Minutes of the Common Council, 1675–1776*, volume II, 205–207.

24. Archdeacon, *New York City*, 143–145; Goodfriend, *Before the Melting Pot*, 134–135.

25. Chaplin, *Privateer Ships and Sailors*, 88–90, 226–227; *Boston News-Letter*, 31 July 1704; Weeks (ed.), *An Historical Digest of the Provincial Press*, 111–112.
26. Hunter to Board of Trade, New York, June 23, 1712, *DRCHNY*, 5:339; Albany Archives, Council Minutes, volume 10, 91–92, and volume 18, 25; O'Callaghan (ed.), *Calendar of Historical Manuscripts . . . Albany*, Part II, 108, 279, 409.
27. *Journal of the Legislative Council of the Colony of New York*, 1691 to 1743, 226; Riddell, *The Slave in Early New York*, 67–68.

CHAPTER 2: THE INEXORABLE RISE OF AKWAMU

1. Wilks, *Akwamu, 1640–1750*, 41–42; Rømer, *A Reliable Account*, 17.
2. Bosman, *A New and Accurate Description of the Coast of Guinea*, 61, 188–190, 193–194; Wilks, *Akwamu, 1640–1750*, 24, 68; Rask, *Two Views*, 103; Kea, *Settlements, Trade, and Polities*, 35, 69, 275; Justeen (ed.), *Danish Source History of Ghana*, Vol. 1, 163–164, 173; VKG: Dag–Journal 1699–1703, entry for 14 May 1701, quoted in Wilks, Akwamu, 1640–1750, 27; Gould, "The Shrine of Tutu Abo," *Research Review*, Institute of African Studies, 8, January 1972, 5–10.
3. Wilks, *Akwamu, 1640–1750*, 8.
4. Tilleman, *A Short Account*, 38.
5. Barbot, *A Description of the Coasts of North and South Africa*, 183.
6. Wilks, *Akwamu, 1640–1750*, 8–13; Rømer, *A Reliable Account*, 118.
7. Tilleman, *A Short Account*, 38–39.
8. Bosman, *A New and Accurate Description of the Coast of Guinea*, 70.
9. Rask, *Two Views*, 116.
10. Thornton, *Warfare in Atlantic Africa, 1500–1800*, 61–74.
11. Wilks, *Akwamu, 1640–1750*, 16–18; Barbot, *A Description of the Coasts of North and South Africa*, 185.
12. Wilks, *Akwamu, 1640–1750*, 19–21; Bosman, *A New and Accurate Description of the Coast of Guinea*, 63; Tilleman, Winsnes (ed.), *A Short Account of West Africa's Gold Coast*, 31.
13. Bosman, *A New and Accurate Description of the Coast of Guinea*, 65.
14. Wilks, *Akwamu, 1640–1750*, 22–25; Philips, *A Journal of a Voyage*, 211–212.
15. Wilks, *Akwamu, 1640–1750*, 25–32, 41–42.
16. Wilks, *Akwamu, 1640–1750*, 41.
17. Wilks, *Akwamu, 1640–1750*, 32–33.

CHAPTER 3: THE SUFFERING OF ELIAS NEAU

1. Jacobi, *A Short Account of the Life and Sufferings of Elias Neau*, 10; Sauter, *Elias Neau*, 1–3.
2. Jacobi, *A Short Account of the Life and Sufferings of Elias Neau*, 11.
3. Jacobi, *A Short Account of the Life and Sufferings of Elias Neau*, 36.
4. Jacobi, *A Short Account of the Life and Sufferings of Elias Neau*, 36.
5. Jacobi, *A Short Account of the Life and Sufferings of Elias Neau*, 36; Sauter, *Elias Neau*, 3–4.
6. Jacobi, *A Short Account of the Life and Sufferings of Elias Neau*, 38.
7. Jacobi, *A Short Account of the Life and Sufferings of Elias Neau*, 45.
8. Jacobi, *A Short Account of the Life and Sufferings of Elias Neau*, 39.
9. Sauter, *Elias Neau*, 4.

10. Jacobi, *A Short Account of the Life and Sufferings of Elias Neau*, 59–60.
11. Jacobi, *A Short Account of the Life and Sufferings of Elias Neau*, 40.
12. Sauter, *Elias Neau*, 6.
13. Jacobi, *A Short Account of the Life and Sufferings of Elias Neau*, 73.
14. Sauter, *Elias Neau*, 5.
15. Greenburg, *Crime and Law Enforcement*, 109.
16. Neau to the secretary of the SPG, 10 July 1703, letter books of the SPG.
17. Rask, *Two Views*, 124; Tilleman, *A Short Account*, 52.
18. *The Reverend John Sharpe's Proposals*, CNYHS, 1880, 350–355; Neau to the secretary of the SPG, 15 April 1704, letter books of the SPG.
19. Foote, *Black and White Manhattan*, 45–47, 125–128; Klein, "Anglicanism, Catholicism, and the Negro Slave," 156–159, in Foner and Genovese (eds.), *Slavery in the New World*, 138–169. Also see Haynes, *Noah's Curse: The Biblical Justification of American Slavery*.
20. Foote, *Black and White Manhattan*, 45–47; Hodges, *Root and Branch*, 22; Shorto, *The Island at the Centre of the World*, 305.
21. Foote, *Black and White Manhattan*, 47–49; *The Skeletal Biology, Archaeology, and History of the New York African Burial Ground: A Synthesis of Volumes 1, 2, and 3*, 200.
22. McManus, *A History of Negro Slavery in New York*, 68–69; Hodges, *Root and Branch*, 53–55; *The Skeletal Biology, Archaeology, and History of the New York African Burial Ground: A Synthesis of Volumes 1, 2, and 3*, 200.
23. Neau to Chamberlayne, 24 August 1708, letter books of the SPG.
24. Trinity Church Vestry Minutes, October 25, 1697, I:II.
25. *The Reverend John Sharpe's Proposals*, CNYHS, 1880, 357; Goodfriend, *Before the Melting Pot*, 126.
26. Kammen, *Colonial New York*, 158, 220; Foote, *Black and White Manhattan*, 93, 97; O'Connor, Three Centuries of Mission, 8–16; https://en.wikipedia.org/wiki/United_Society_Partners_in_the_Gospel.
27. Neau to Secretary of the SPG, 10 July 1703, letter books of the SPG.
28. Neau to Secretary of the SPG, 10 July 1703, letter books of the SPG.
29. Humphreys, *An Historical Account*, 237; *The Reverend John Sharpe's Proposals*, CNYHS, 1880, 348–350.
30. Humphreys, *An Historical Account*, 237.
31. *The Reverend John Sharpe's Proposals*, CNYHS, 1880, 350; Neau to Secretary of the SPG, 24 July 1707, letter books of the SPG.
32. Neau to Secretary of the SPG, 15 September 1704, letter books of the SPG.
33. Humphreys, *An Historical Account*, 237; *The Reverend John Sharpe's Proposals*, CNYHS, 1880, 348–350.
34. *The Reverend John Sharpe's Proposals*, CNYHS, 1880, 350–352; Foote, *Black and White Manhattan*, 128–131; Hodges, *Root and Branch*, 55–63.
35. Humphreys, *An Historical Account*, 237–238.
36. Neau to Secretary of the SPG, 18 April 1704, letter books of the SPG.
37. Humphreys, *An Historical Account*, 238–239; Rask, *Two Views*, 103.
38. Neau to Secretary of the SPG, 15 September 1704, letter books of the SPG.
39. Neau to Secretary of the SPG, 22 July 1707, letter books of the SPG.
40. Foote, *Black and White Manhattan*, 129.

41. Humphreys, *An Historical Account*, 239.

42. Neau to Secretary of the SPG, 24 July 1707, letter books of the SPG.

43. Neau to Secretary of the SPG, 5 October 1705, letter books of the SPG. On Van Dam see: Archdeacon, *Conquest and Change*, 64, 66–67, 73–74, 91, 136, 144; Goodfriend, *Before the Melting Pot*, 36; Matson, *Merchants and Empire*, 60–61, 86, 134–135, 144, 146,150, 153, 168.

44. Neau to Secretary of the SPG, 1 March 1706, letter books of the SPG; Neau to Secretary of the SPG, 5 October 1705, letter books of the SPG.

45. Neau to Secretary of the SPG, 24 July 1707, letter books of the SPG.

46. Neau to Secretary of the SPG, 30 April 1706, letter books of the SPG.

47. *Journal of the Legislative Council of the Colony of New York*, 1691 to 1743, 245.

48. Neau to Secretary of the SPG, 22 July 1707, letter books of the SPG.

49. *A List of the Slaves taught by Mr. Neau since the year 1704, Enclosed in his Letter of ye 16 Nov 1714*, letter books of the SPG.

50. *Journal of the Legislative Council of the Colony of New York*, 1691 to 1743, 245.

CHAPTER 4: AKWONNO'S FIRST CAMPAIGN

1. Wilks, *Akwamu, 1640–1750*, 33.

2. Gould, "The Shrine of Tutu Abo," *Research Review*, Institute of African Studies, 8, January 1972, 5–10; Hanserd, "Obayifo to Obeah"; Shumway, *The Fante*, 60, 101; Wilks, *Forests of Gold*, 216–217.

3. Wilks, *Akwamu, 1640–1750*, 2–3.

4. Finnegan, *Oral Literature in Africa*, 471; see also Nketia, *Drumming in Akan Communities of Ghana*.

5. Rask, *Two Views*, 80; Kea, *Settlements, Trade, and Polities*, 161–163; Bosman, *A New and Accurate Description*, 183; Thornton, *Warfare in Atlantic Africa*, 67; Tilleman, *A Short Account*, 38.

6. Bosman, *A New and Accurate Description*, 182.

7. Oldendorp, quoted in Konadu, *The Akan Diaspora*, 102.

8. Blakley and Rankin–Hill (eds.), *Skeletal Biology*, 105.

9. Bosman, *A New and Accurate Description*, 185.

10. Thornton, *Warfare in Atlantic Africa*, 61–64; Bosman, *A New and Accurate Description*, 184.

11. Bosman, *A New and Accurate Description*, 186.

12. Bosman, *A New and Accurate Description*, 185–187; Rask, *Two Views*, 81; Rømer, *A Reliable Account*, 166.

13. Rask, *Two Views*, 81.

14. Rask, *Two Views*, 133.

15. Bosman, *A New and Accurate Description*, 150.

16. Wilks, *Forests of Gold*, 215–217; Wilks, *Akwamu, 1640–1750*, 20, 41.

17. Konadu, *The Akan Diaspora*, 119, 136; John Sharpe letter, 23 June 1712, *NYGBR*, 21, 1809, 162–163; Rømer, *A Reliable Account*, 166.

18. Rømer, *A Reliable Account*, 18–19; Tilleman, *A Short Account*, 66; Wilks, *Akwamu, 1640–1750*, 33–34.

19. Rømer, *A Reliable Account*, 18.

20. Rask, *Two Views*, 58–61.

21. Rask, *Two Views*, 99.

22. Wilks, *Akwamu, 1640–1750*, 33–34; Oldendorp quoted in Konadu (ed.), *The Akan Reader*.

23. Bosman, *A New and Accurate Description*, 182–183.

24. Rask, *Two Views*, 80.

25. Bosman, *A New and Accurate Description*, 182–183; Thornton, *Warfare in Atlantic Africa*, 58–61.

26. Rask, *Two Views*, 80.

27. Rask, *Two Views*, 82.

28. Wilks, *Akwamu, 1640–1750*, 34.

CHAPTER 5: MARS, SAM, CAESAR, ROBIN, AND WILL

Epigraph: Speech of Nicolas Lejeune, St. Domingue, 1788. Quoted in Delle (ed.), *Mastery, Tyranny, and Desire*, 137.

1. *An Act for Settling a Ministry and Raising a Maintenance for Them in the City of New York*, 22 September 1693, *The Colonial Laws of New York*, Vol. 1, 328–329.

2. De Jong, *The Dutch Reformed Church*, 60.

3. Maynard, *The Huguenot Church of New York*, 63, 77; Greenburg, *Crime and Law Enforcement*, 26.

4. Goodfriend, *Before the Melting Pot*, 56–57; Kammen, *Colonial New York*, 216–217.

5. Goodfriend, *Before the Melting Pot*, 41, 84.

6. Kalm, *Travels in North America*, volume 2, 624.

7. *Sharpe's Proposals*, 357; Neau to Secretary of the PSG, 8 October 1719, letter books of the SPG.

8. Neau to the secretary of the SPG, 10 July 1703, letter books of the SPG.

9. *Minutes of the Common Council*, volume 1, 92–93.

10. Riddel, "The Slave in Early New York," *Journal of Negro History* 13, no. 1 (Jan. 1928), 68.

11. *MCQS*, 1704–1712, entries for June 1707.

12. *CNYHS*, volume 80, 1959, 173–175; *Will of Jacob Regnier*, written 8 November 1714; proved 20 November 1714; New York County, *NY Will Book*, volume 8, page 363.

13. Craton, *Testing the Chains*, 90; Prince, *Maroon Societies*, 20; Konadu, *The Akan Diaspora in the Americas*, 3–6, 123; Zoellner, *Island on Fire*, 66; Brown, *Tacky's Revolt*, 130; Greenburg, *Crime and Punishment*, 150–151.

14. *MCQS*, 1704–1712, entries for June 1707; https://www.wikitree.com/wiki/Pierson-1439.

15. Greenburg, *Crime and Law Enforcement*, 158–165.

16. *MCQS*, 1704–1712, entries for June 1707.

17. *Minutes of the Common Council*, volume 1, 134; Greenburg, *Crime and Law Enforcement*, 44.

18. *MCQS*, 1704–1712, entries for June 1707.

19. New York Colonial Muster Rolls, 1664–1775, roll for 26 June 1710; Archdeacon, *New York City, 1664–1710*, 72.

20. *Burghers and Freemen of New York*, *CNYHS*, 1885, 615.

21. Archdeacon, *New York City, 1664–1710*, 56; *MCQS*, 1704–1712, entries for June 1707.

22. *Census of the City of New York*, in O'Callaghan (ed.), *Documentary History of the State of New York*, volume 1, 395–405.

23. Hodges, *Root and Branch*, 53.

24. Hunter to Board of Trade, New York, June 23, 1712, *DRCHNY*, 5:339; Hunter to Board of Trade, New York, March 13, 1713, *DRCHNY*, 5:356–357; Stokes, *The Iconography of Manhattan Island*, volume 6, 87.

25. Stokes, *The Iconography of Manhattan Island*, volume 6, 87; *CNYHS*, volume 80, 1959, 173–175.

26. Smith, *The History of the Province of New York*, 111–113.

27. *MCQS*, 1704–1712, entries for June 1707; Greenburg, *Crime and Law Enforcement*, 74.

28. *MCQS*, 1704–1712, entries for June 1707.

29. *MCQS*, 1704–1712, entries for June 1707.

30. Mckee, Jr., *Labor in Colonial New York*, 155.

31. Goodfriend, "The Protestants of Colonial New York City," 246, in Van Ruymbeke and Sparks (eds.), *Memory and Identity*, 241–254; O'Callaghan, *Calendar of Historical Manuscripts*, part 2, 228.

32. Archdeacon, *Conquest and Change*, 64, 66–67, 73–74, 91, 136, 144; Goodfriend, *Before the Melting Pot*, 36; Matson, *Merchants and Empire*, 60–61, 86, 134–135, 144, 146, 150, 153, 168.

33. Valentine, *Manual of the Corporation of the City of New York*, 1845–1846, 126; https://www.geni.com/people/Walter-Thong/6000000006728257528.

34. Strum-Lind, *Actors of Globalization*, xix; Archdeacon, *Conquest and Change*, 91.

35. *MCQS*, 1704–1712, entries for 14 April 1712, and Memorandum for 14 and 15 April 1712; *MCQS*, 1704–1712, entry for 6 June 1712.

36. *MCQS*, 1704–1712, entries for June 1707.

37. Foote, *Black and White Manhattan*, 82; Hodges, *Root and Branch*, 108; De Voe, *The Market Book*, 344.

38. *MCQS*, 1704–1712, entries for June 1707.

39. O'Callaghan, *Calendar of Historical Manuscripts*, 59, 255.

40. https://www.wikitree.com/wiki/Hallett-130; *Ecclesiastical Records, State of New York*, volume 1, 360–361.

41. *CNYHS*, 1892, 332.

42. Riker, *The Annals of Newton*, 142.

43. *NYGBR*, 22 (1891), 128.

44. Riker, *The Annals of Newton*, 142–143.

45. Cornbury to the Council of Trade and Plantations, 10 Feb. 1707, New York. Calendar of State Papers, volume 23, 652–675, doc. 1333.

46. *The Colonial Laws of New York*, volume 1, 631–633.

47. Lustig, *Robert Hunter*, 49–50, 75–76; Kammen, *Colonial New York*, 157.

48. Lewis Morris to Secretary, quoted in Hills, *History of the Church in Burlington*, 81.

49. Neau to the secretary of the SPG, 27 February 1709, letter books of the SPG.

50. Lustig, *Robert Hunter*, 49–50, 75–76.

51. Lovelace to Council of Trade and Plantations, 18 December 1708, New York, *Calendar of State Papers Colonial*, volume 24, 182–193.

52. Lustig, *Robert Hunter*, 58.

53. Lustig, *Robert Hunter*, ix, xiv.

54. Lustig, *Robert Hunter*, 55–64.

55. Neau to the secretary of the SPG, 5 July 1710, letter books of the SPG.

56. *MCQS*, 1704–1712, entries for 14 April 1712; *The Reverend John Sharpe's Proposals*, *CNYHS*, 1880, 353; Humphreys, *An Historical Account*, 241; *A List of the Slaves taught by Mr. Neau since the year 1704, Enclosed in his Letter of ye 16 Nov 1714*, letter books of the SPG, 220–223; http://lynnesgenealogy.com/NorwoodDescendants/website/b917.htm; *Census of the City of New York*, in O'-Callaghan (ed.), *Documentary History of the State of New York*, volume 1, 395–405.

57. *MCQS*, 1704–1712, entries for 11 April 1712; *The Reverend John Sharpe's Proposals*, *CNYHS*, 1880, 353; Humphreys, *An Historical Account*, 241; *Census of the City of New York*, in O'Callaghan (ed.), *Documentary History of the State of New York*, volume 1, 395–405.

58. Goodfriend, *Before the Melting Pot*, 124–125.

CHAPTER 6: THE KWAHU STRIKE BACK

1. Wallis, "The Kwahus," *Transactions of the Gold Coast and Togoland Historical Society*, 1, no. 3 (1953), 10–26; Owusu, "A Case Study of the Easter Celebration Among the Kwahus."

2. Barbot, *A Description of the Coasts of North and South Africa*, 190; Bosman, *A New and Accurate Description*, 326.

3. Rask, *Two Views*, 84.

4. Oldendorp quoted in Konadu (ed.), *The Akan Reader*.

5. Wilks, *Akwamu, 1640–1750*, 33–35; Thornton, *Warfare in Atlantic Africa*, 69.

6. Wilks, *Akwamu, 1640–1750*, 34–35; Owusu, "A Case Study of the Easter Celebration among the Kwahus."

7. Wilks, *Akwamu, 1640–1750*, 34–35.

8. For details of Jarrett's voyage and the situation on the Gold Coast at the time see Chapter 4.

CHAPTER 7: THE SCOTTISH GOVERNOR

1. Hunter to Lords of Trade, 7 May 1711, *Calendar of State Papers Colonial, America and West Indies*, volume 25, 832.

2. Hunter to Commissioners of Customs, 7 May 1711, *Calendar of State Papers Colonial, America and West Indies*, volume 25, 832, iii; Hunter to secretary of the SPG, 7 May 1711, letter books of the SPG, A, 6, item 70.

3. McCusker, *Essays in the Economic History of the Atlantic World*, 125.

4. Lustig, *Robert Hunter*, 66.

5. *Minutes of the Common Council*, volume 2, 409.

6. Bayles, *Old Taverns of New York*, 49.

7. *Minutes of the Common Council*, volume 2, 410–411.

8. Otterness, *Becoming German*, 21–26.

9. Otterness, *Becoming German*, 37–41, 64.

10. Otterness, *Becoming German*, 71–75.

11. Otterness, *Becoming German*, 78–81; "Journal of Rev. John Sharpe," *Pennsylvania Magazine of History and Biography*, 40, no. 4 (1916), entries for 14 to 16 June 1710.

12. Council of Trade and Plantations to Lord Dartmouth, 19 July 1711, *Calendar of State Papers Colonial, America and West Indies*, volume 26, doc. 32; Lustig, *Robert Hunter*, 153.

13. Hunter to Lords of Trade, 24 July 1710, *DRCHNY* 5:166–167.

14. Hunter to Lords of Trade, 3 October 1710, *DRCHNY* 5:170–172.

15. Hunter to Lords of Trade, 24 July 1710, *DRCHNY* 5:166–167.

16. Matson, *Merchants and Empire*, 57; Davis, *Rumor of Revolt*, 22–23; Archdeacon, *New York City*, 125–126.

17. Archdeacon, *New York City*, 39–41.

18. Archdeacon, *New York City*, 138–139.

19. Goodfriend, *Before the Melting Pot*, 56–57; Kammen, *Colonial New York*, 216–217.

20. Archdeacon, *New York City*, 143–145.

21. Hunter to the secretary of the SPG, 25 February 1711, O'Callaghan, *The Documentary History of the State of New York*, volume III, 253; Hunter to Bishop of London, 1 March 1712, *DRCHNY* 5:311.

22. Hunter to the Lords of Trade, 14 November 1710, in Brodhead and O'Callaghan, *DRCHNY* 5:177–182; Lustig, *Robert Hunter*, 70–80.

23. Hunter to the Council of Trade and Plantations, 3 October 1710, *Calendar of State Papers Colonial, America and West Indies*, volume 25, 414; Otterness, *Becoming German*, 89–92.

24. Zabin, *Dangerous Economies*, 64; Goodfriend, *Before the Melting Pot*, 121.

25. "Journal of Rev. John Sharpe," entry for 5 November 1710; O'Callaghan, *Calendar of Historical Manuscripts . . . Albany*, part II, 374; Goodfriend, *Before the Melting Pot*, 124.

26. Clarendon to Lord Dartmouth, 8 March 1711, in Brodhead and O'Callaghan, *DRCHNY* 5:195–197; Lustig, *Robert Hunter*, 84–86.

27. Hunter to Lords of Trade, 7 May 1711, *Calendar of State Papers Colonial, America and West Indies*, volume 25, 832.

28. Pollhampton to the Lords of Trade, 6 March 1711, in Brodhead and O'Callaghan, *DRCHNY* 5:193–195; Lords of Trade to Governor Hunter, 10 April 1711, in Brodhead and O'Callaghan, *DRCHNY* 5:198.

29. It seems likely that the privateer in question was the *Castel del Rey* captained by Adrian Claver, which had taken two Spanish ships in 1704 while sailing off the coast of New Spain. See Chapter 1 of this volume for more details.

30. Hunter to Board of Trade, New York, June 23, 1712, *DRCHNY* 5:339; Albany Archives, Council Minutes, volume 10, 91–92.

31. Berrian, *An Historical Sketch of Trinity Church*, 321–324; *Boston News-Letter*, 11 June 1711.

32. Otterness, *Becoming German*, 99–103.

33. Secretary Clerk to the Lords of Trade, 28 May 1711, in Brodhead and O'Callaghan, *DRCHNY* 5:237–238.

34. "Journal of Rev. John Sharpe," entries for 1 to 8 June 1711; for birth of Maria Thong see https://www.geni.com/people/Sara-Thong/6000000006728344438; *Boston News-Letter*, 11 June 1711; Donnan, *Documents Illustrative of the History of the Slave Trade to America*, Volume 3, 444–445; Hershkowitz, "Anatomy of a Slave Voyage, New York 1721," in de Halve Maen, *Journal of The Holland Society of New York*, Fall 2003, 45–51.

CHAPTER 8: ALAN JARRETT AND THE NEW YORK SLAVE TRADE

1. T 70/956, f. 16; CO 157/1—Antigua Shipping Returns; T 70/8, f. 80; T 70/5, f. 48; T 70/956, f. 13; T 70/5, f. 56, 58–59, 70; *Boston News-Letter*, 11 June 1711; *Boston News-Letter*, 8 October 1711; CO 390/7, f. 1; Donnan, *Documents Illustrative of the History of the Slave Trade to America*, volume 3, 352, 466.
2. Lydon, "New York and the Slave Trade, 1700 to 1774," 390, *William and Mary Quarterly* 35, no. 2 (Apr. 1978), 375–394.
3. Quoted in Rediker, *Between the Devil and the Deep Blue Sea*, 49–50.
4. Rediker, *The Slave Ship*, 195–198, 291–301; Newton, *The Journal of a Slave Trader*, 81.
5. *CNYHS* 1893, 253.
6. Archdeacon, *New York City*, 49–57.
7. Pratt, *Annals of Public Education*, 98–99.
8. Rediker, *The Slave Ship*, 6–7, 217–221.
9. Pratt, *Annals of Public Education*, 98–99; Abstract of letters from Africa, Dalby to RAC, 23 March 1710, T 70/5, f. 5; T 70/956, f. 16; CO 157/1—Antigua Shipping Returns; T 70/8, f. 80; T 70/5, f. 48; T 70/956, f. 13; T 70/5, f. 56, 58–59, 70; *Boston News-Letter*, 11 June 1711; *Boston News-Letter*, 8 October 1711; CO 390/7, f. 1; Donnan, *Documents Illustrative of the History of the Slave Trade to America*, volume 3, 352, 466.
10. *CNYHS*, 1885, 606.
11. *Supplementary List of Marriage Licenses, State Library Bulletin, History No. 1*, April 1898, 31.
12. *Census of the City of New York*, published in O'Callaghan (ed.), *Documentary History of the State of New York*, volume 1, 395–405.
13. Oliver, *The History of the Island of Antigua*, 9; *CNYHS*, 1892, 424; Donnan, *Documents Illustrative of the History of the Slave Trade to America*, volume 3, 466.
14. T 70/956, f. 16; CO 157/1—Antigua Shipping Returns 1708; T 70/5, f. 48; T 70/8, f. 80.
15. Davies, *The Royal African Company*, 9–46.
16. T 70/956, f. 16; CO 157/1—Antigua Shipping Returns 1708; T 70/5, f. 48; T 70/8, f. 80; Hughes, *Apocalypse 1692*, 101–105.
17. T 70/8, f. 80; T 70/956, f. 13; T 70/5, f. 56, 58–59.
18. T 70/5, f. 70; *Boston News-Letter*, 11 June 1711; Donnan, *Documents Illustrative of the History of the Slave Trade to America*, volume 3, 444–445; *Boston News-Letter*, 23 June 1712.
19. Johnson to the Council of Trade, Antigua, 13 March 1706, *Calendar of State Papers Colonial, America and West Indies*, volume 23, 168; Crouse, *French Struggle for the West Indies*, 48–52; Miller, *Colonel Parke of Virginia*, 183.
20. Gaspar, *Bondsmen and Rebels*, 185–189.

21. Dunn, *Sugar and Slaves*, 185, 264, 277–280.

22. Miller, *Colonel Parke of Virginia*, 83, 155–161, 185–189, 194, 196, 198–204.

23. Davies, *The Royal African Company*, 114, 117, 259; Galenson, *Traders, Planters and Slaves*, 18.

24. Davies, *The Royal African Company*, 143; Gaspar, *Bondsmen and Rebels*, 84–86; T 70/956, f. 16; CO 157/1—Antigua Shipping Returns 1708; T 70/5, f. 48; T 70/8, f. 80; Donnan, *Documents Illustrative of the History of the Slave Trade to America*, volume 3, 444–445.

25. Quoted in O'Malley, *Final Passages*, 23.

26. Dudley to the Council of Trade, 1 October 1708, *Calendar of State Papers Colonial, America and West Indies*, volume 24, 151.

27. Darold D. Wax, "Preferences for Slaves in Colonial America," *Journal of Negro History* 58, no. 4 (1973): 375–378.

28. *The Colonial Laws of New York*, volume 1, 675–677.

29. Rediker, *The Slave Ship*, 190–199, 390 n. 18; Lydon, "New York and the Slave Trade, 1700 to 1774," 388.

30. Lydon, "New York and the Slave Trade, 1700 to 1774," 390; Donnan, *Documents Illustrative of the History of the Slave Trade to America*, volume 3, 462–491.

31. Archdeacon, *Conquest and Change*, 64, 66–67, 73–74, 91, 136, 144; Goodfriend, *Before the Melting Pot*, 36; Matson, *Merchants and Empire*, 60–61, 86, 134–135, 144, 146, 150, 153, 168.

32. *Slave Voyages Database*—70202. https://www.slavevoyages.org/voyage/70202/variables.

33. Donnan, *Documents Illustrative of the History of the Slave Trade to America*, Volume 3, 462–463, 475; Lydon, "New York and the Slave Trade, 1700 to 1774," 391n. 50.

34. Lydon, "New York and the Slave Trade, 1700 to 1774," 390.

35. *MCQS*, 1704–1712, entries for 14 and 15 April 1712, and 27 May 1712; Hunter to Board of Trade, New York, June 23, 1712, *DRCHNY*, 5:339.

36. Donnan, *Documents Illustrative of the History of the Slave Trade to America*, volume 3, 444.

37. *Journal of the Legislative Council of the Colony of New York*, 288–289.

38. *Slave Voyages Database*—20918. https://www.slavevoyages.org/voyage/20918/variables; CNYHS 1885, 89; T 70/5, f. 5.

39. T 70/5, f. 5.

40. Donnan, *Documents Illustrative of the History of the Slave Trade to America*, volume 3, 444.

41. *An Essay Towards An Improved Register of Deeds*, 79.

42. Craton, *Testing the Chains*, 90; Prince, *Maroon Societies*, 20; Konadu, *The Akan Diaspora in the Americas*, 3–6, 123; Zoellner, *Island on Fire*, 66; Brown, *Tacky's Revolt*, 130; Greenburg, *Crime and Punishment*, 150–151. On slave mortality see Kalm, *Travels in North America*, volume 2, 207; Neau to SPG, 27 February 1708, letter books of the SPG, Box A, 4, item 121; McManus, *Bondage in the North*, 94–95.

43. Phipps, Cape Coast Castle, 26 January 1711, C 113/282.

CHAPTER 9: THE MIDDLE PASSAGE

Epigraph: Zachary Macaulay, abolitionist, quoted in Adam Hochschild, *Bury the Chains*, 254.

1. ADM 51/49; ADM 51/374, entries for September 1710 to 1 January 1711.
2. ADM 51/49; ADM 51/374, entries for 2 January to 5 January 1711.
3. ADM 51/49; ADM 51/374, entries for 5 January to 23 January 1711; Bosman, *A New and Accurate Description*, 485–486, 490–493.
4. ADM 51/49; ADM 51/374, entries for 24 January to 25 January 1711.
5. ADM 51/49; ADM 51/374, entries for 26 January to 13 February 1711; Bosman, *A New and Accurate Description*, 45–54, 490–493; Phillips, *A Journal of a Voyage*, 204–205.
6. Phipps and Grosvenor to RAC, Cape Coast Castle, 8 March 1711, T 70/5; Phipps, Cape Coast Castle, 11 January 1711 and 30 April 1711, C 113/282; C 113/292, f. 37–38.
7. Phipps and Grosvenor to RAC, Cape Coast Castle, 10 January 1711, T 70/5; Phipps, Cape Coast Castle, 26 January 1711, C 113/282.
8. Thomas at RAC, 23 August 1710, T 70/5; Hickes to Thomas, Ouidah, 18 October 1710, T 70/5.
9. Phipps, Cape Coast Castle, 30 April 1711, C 113/282.
10. Uring, *The Voyages and Travels*, 98–99.
11. Galenson, *Traders, Planters and Slaves*, 18.
12. Thomas to RAC, 19 November 1708, Cape Coast Castle, T 70/5, f. 56.
13. Thomas to RAC, Cape Coast Castle, 19 November 1710, T 70/5; Grosvenor and Phipps to RAC, 10 January 1711, Cape Coast Castle, T 70/5.
14. Davies, *The Royal African Company*, 139–140, 312–315.
15. Shumway, *The Fante and the Transatlantic Slave Trade*, 96.
16. Thomas to RAC, Cape Coast Castle, 3 and 16 August 1710, and 28 October 1710, T 70/5.
17. Grosvenor and Phipps to RAC, Cape Coast Castle, 10 January 1711, T 70/5.
18. Wilks, *Akwamu, 1640-1750*, 34–35; Wilks, *Forests of Gold*, 119, 252–253.
19. Davies, *The Royal African Company*, 278–279.
20. Thomas to RAC, Cape Coast Castle, 9 April 1710 and 28 May 1710, T 70/5; Lygaard to Director of the Guinea Company, Christiansborg, 12 May 1710 and 2 August 1710, reproduced in Justesen, *Danish Source History of Ghana*, volume 1, 229–230; Grosvenor and Phipps, 24 January 1711 and 8 March 1711, Cape Coast Castle, T 70/5.
21. ADM 51/49, entries for 18 March, 23 March, 6 April 1711.
22. *Boston News-Letter*, 4 June 1711.
23. Thomas to RAC, Cape Coast Castle, 23 March 1710, T 70/5.
24. ADM 51/49, entries for 18 March, 23 March, 6 April 1711.
25. Lydon, "New York and the Slave Trade, 1700 to 1774," *William and Mary Quarterly*, 35, no. 2 (1978), 391; *Slave Voyages Database*—nos. 20918 and 9767; Donnan, *Documents Illustrative of the History of the Slave Trade to America*, volume 3, 466; Phipps, Cape Coast Castle, 26 January 1711, C 113/282.
26. Rediker, *The Slave Ship*, 68–72.
27. Lydon, "New York and the Slave Trade, 1700 to 1774," 391.

28. Rediker, *The Slave Ship*, 57.

29. T 70/956, f. 13.

30. Rediker, *The Slave Ship*, 59.

31. Rediker, *The Slave Ship*, 225–230.

32. ADM 51/49, entries for 18 March, 23 March, 6 April 1711; *Boston News-Letter*, 4 June 1711; T 70/1199.

33. Thomas to RAC, 16 April 1709 and 6 May 1709, Cape Coast Castle, T 70/5, f.56; Thomas to RAC, 15 August 1710, Cape Coast Castle, T 70/5, f. 70.

34. John Sharpe letter, 23 June 1712, *NYGBR*, Volume XXI, 1809, 162–163; Midlo Hall, *Slavery and African Ethnicities*, 47, 112, 115; Konadu, *The Akan Diaspora*, 123–124.

35. Bosman, *A New and Accurate Description*, 70.

36. Tilleman, *A Short Account*, 49.

37. Wilks, *Akwamu*, 1640–1750, 34–35.

38. Thornton, *Warfare in Atlantic Africa*, 133.

39. Lygaard to Director, 2 August 1710, Christiansborg, Justesen, *Danish Source History of Ghana*, volume 1, 229–230.

40. Chester to RAC, Saint John's, Antigua, November 1708, T 70/8, f. 80.

41. Sparks, *Where the Negroes are Masters*, 164–165.

42. That Kwahu captives would have been sold out of Accra and its environs is given credence by the fact that when Akwamu itself was conquered in 1730 many of those who were subsequently enslaved were sold out of Fort Christainsborg and taken to the island of Saint Johns. The time frame of these sales also suggests that Kwahu slaves may have been available to Jarrett in late 1710 and early 1711. When the Akwamu were sold out of Christiansborg following the collapse of their polity in 1730, sales continued from at least 1730 until 1733. For more details on this see Chapter 12 below, and Ray A. Kea, "When I Die, I Shall Return to My Own Land: An 'Amina' Slave Rebellion in the Danish West Indies, 1733–1734," in John Hunwick and Nancy Lawler (eds.), *The Cloth of Many Colored Silks: Papers on History and Society, Ghanaian and Islamic in Honor of Ivor Wilks* (Evanston: Northwestern University Press, 2012), 159–193.

43. *The Skeletal Biology, Archaeology and History of the New York African Burial Ground*, volume 4, 127.

44. Hickes to Thomas, Ouidah, 10 December 1710, T 70/5.

45. Hickes to Thomas, Ouidah, 15 March 1711, T 70/5.

46. Midlo Hall, *Slavery and African Ethnicities*, 24–31, 112–113.

47. Tilleman, *A Short Account*, 50; Bosman, *A New and Accurate Description*, 365; Equiano, *The Interesting Narrative*, 52–55.

48. Thomas, *The Slave Trade*, 382; Equiano, *The Interesting Narrative*, 52–55.

49. Moore, *Biography of Mahommah G. Baquaqua*, 35–40.

50. Konadu, *The Akan Diaspora*, 124–127.

51. Thomas, *The Slave Trade*, 384–385.

52. Bosman, *A New and Accurate Description*, 246; Phillips, *Journal of a Voyage*, 211.

53. Moore, *Biography of Mahommah G. Baquaqua*, 35–40.

54. Davies, *The Royal African Company*, 170–179.

55. Donnan, *Documents Illustrative of the History of the Slave Trade to America*, Volume 3, 444.

56. Rediker, *The Slave Ship*, 5–6, 274–276, 347.

57. T 70/956, f. 13; T 70/956, f. 16.

58. *Census of the City of New York*, published in O'Callaghan (ed.), *Documentary History of the State of New York*, volume 1, 395–405; Walton Jr., Puckett, Deskins Jr., *The African American Electorate*, 70; Donnan, *Documents Illustrative of the History of the Slave Trade to America*, volume 3, 444.

59. Bosman, *A New and Accurate Description*, 279–280; Rømer, *A Reliable Account*, 192.

60. Equiano, *The Interesting Narrative*, 55.

61. ADM 51/49, entries for 18 March, 23 March, 6 April 1711; *Boston News-Letter*, 4 June 1711.

62. David Richardson, "Shipboard Revolts: African Authority, and the Atlantic Slave Trade," *William and Mary Quarterly*, 58, no. 1 (2001), 73–74.

63. Phillips, *Journal of a Voyage*, 229.

64. Slave Voyages Database no. 15215; Phipps and Grosvenor to RAC, Cape Coast Castle, 8 March 1711, T 70/5.

65. Slave Voyages Database no. 21015; Law, *The English in West Africa*, 1685–1688, 268, 352, 379.

66. Equiano, *The Interesting Narrative*, 58.

67. *An Abstract of the Evidence delivered before a Select Committee . . . for the Abolition of the Slave Trade*, 35–36.

68. Newton, *The Journal of a Slave Trader*, 105.

69. Rediker, *The Slave Ship*, 152.

70. Phillips, *Journal of a Voyage*, 229.

71. Equiano, *The Interesting Narrative*, 56.

72. Rediker, *The Slave Ship*, 17.

73. Phillips, *Journal of a Voyage*, 230; *An Abstract of the Evidence delivered before a Select Committee . . . for the Abolition of the Slave Trade*, 39.

74. Phillips, *Journal of a Voyage*, 237.

75. Hochschild, *Bury the Chains*, 118.

76. Equiano, *The Interesting Narrative*, 111.

77. *An Abstract of the Evidence delivered before a Select Committee . . . for the Abolition of the Slave Trade*, 39–40.

78. Equiano, *The Interesting Narrative*, 59.

79. Rømer, *A Reliable Account*, 125.

80. *An Abstract of the Evidence delivered before a Select Committee . . . for the Abolition of the Slave Trade*, 42.

81. Rediker, *The Slave Ship*, 290–291.

82. Cugoano, *Narrative of the Enslavement*, 124.

83. Hochschild, *Bury the Chains*, 254.

84. Rediker, *The Slave Ship*, 305–307.

85. Sloane, *A Voyage to the Islands*, volume 1, liii.

86. Equiano, *The Interesting Narrative*, 59–61.

87. Hodges, *Root and Branch*, 105.

88. Governor Coddrington to the Council of Trade and Plantations, 30 December 1701, *Calendar of State Papers Colonial, America and West Indies*: volume 19, 1701, 696–729.

89. Phillips, *Journal of a Voyage*, 214.

90. McManus, *Black Bondage in the North*, 25.

91. *An Abstract of the Evidence delivered before a Select Committee . . . for the Abolition of the Slave Trade*, 46–47.

92. T 70/956, f. 16.

93. Galenson, *Traders, Planters and Slaves*, 80.

94. *Address of the Council and Assembly of Jamaica to the King, James II*, Calendar of State Papers Colonial, America and West Indies, 12 July 1689, 100–113.

95. Davies, *The Royal African Company*, 296.

96. Galenson, *Traders, Planters and Slaves*, 81–85; *An Abstract of the Evidence delivered before a Select Committee . . . for the Abolition of the Slave Trade*, 148.

97. *An Abstract of the Evidence delivered before a Select Committee . . . for the Abolition of the Slave Trade*, 46.

98. Equiano, *The Interesting Narrative*, 54–55; Burnard, *Mastery, Tyranny and Desire*, 134.

99. *An Abstract of the Evidence delivered before a Select Committee . . . for the Abolition of the Slave Trade*, 46.

100. Equiano, *The Interesting Narrative*, 57.

101. For the identities of the owners of the future rebels see *MCQS*, 1704–1712, entries for April and May 1712. On Van Dam see Archdeacon, *Conquest and Change*, 64, 66–67, 73–74, 91, 136, 144; Goodfriend, *Before the Melting Pot*, 36; Matson, *Merchants & Empire*, 60-61, 86, 134–135, 144, 146, 150, 153, 168 etc.; Rothschild, *New York City Neighborhoods*, 201. On Thong see Valentine, *Manual of the Corporation of the City of New York*, 1845–1846, 126; https://www.geni.com/people/Walter-Thong/6000000006728257528; Rothschild, *New York City Neighborhoods*, 201. On Morin and Barberie see *Census of the City of New York*, published in O'Callaghan (ed.), *Documentary History of the State of New York*, volume 1, 395–405; Rothschild, *New York City Neighborhoods*, 186, 197. Also on Barberie see Matson, *Merchants and Empire*, 63, 84, 140, 154, 209, 222–223.

102. T 70/956, f. 13, 16.

103. *MCQS*, 1704–1712, entry for 11 April 1712.

104. *MCQS*, 1704–1712, entry for 27 May 1712; Archdeacon, *New York City*, 136.

105. *Boston News-Letter*, 14 April 1712; *CNYHS*, 1910, 195; *Census of the City of New York*, published in O'Callaghan (ed.), *Documentary History of the State of New York*, volume 1, 395–405; Rothschild, *New York City Neighborhoods*, 190.

106. On Lyell see *MCQS*, 1704–1712, entry for 16 April 1712; Rothschild, *New York City Neighborhoods*, 196; Archdeacon, *New York City*, 53; Goodfriend, *Before the Melting Pot*, 142. On Roosevelt see *MCQS*, 1704–1712, entry for 12 April 1712; Rothschild, *New York City Neighborhoods*, 199; Matson, *Merchants and Empire*, 147, 261; Archdeacon, *New York City*, 133–134, 138, 142, 145.

107. On Cure and Sheppard see *MCQS*, 1704–1712, entry for 11 April 1712; Rothschild, *New York City Neighborhoods*, 200; *Census of the City of New York*, published in O'Callaghan (ed.), *Documentary History of the State of New York*, volume 1, 395–405; *CNYHS*, 1894, 212.

108. On Provoost see *CNYHS*, 1961, 65; https://www.wikitree.com/wiki/Provoost-44; *MCQS*, 1704–1712, entry for 11 April 1712. On Burger see *MCQS*,

1704–1712, entry for 11 April 1712; *CNYHS*, 1961, 63; Goodfriend, *Before the Melting* Pot, 119; Rothschild, *New York City Neighborhoods*, 188. On Vantilborough see *MCQS*, 1704–1712, entry for 11 April 1712; *CNYHS*, 1961, 63.

109. On Pels see *MCQS*, 1704–1712, entry for 17 April 1712; *CNYHS*, 1961, 66; *CNYHS*, 1911, 267; Rothschild, *New York City Neighborhoods*, 198. On Ray see *MCQS*, 1704–1712, entry for 16 April 1712; *CNYHS*, 1884, 236; Matson, *Merchants and Empire*, 148, 211, 267. On Fauconnier see *MCQS*, 1704–1712, entry for 12 April 1712; *CNYHS*, 1961, 66.

110. On slaves meeting at water pumps in New York City see Horsmanden, *The New-York Conspiracy*, 75, 147.

CHAPTER IO: ENSLAVED IN NEW YORK

1. For details on all of these statements see the paragraphs that follow and their sources.

2. Hodges, *Root and Branch*, 43; *Minutes of the Common Council, 1675–1776*, 6.

3. *The Letters and Papers of Cadwallader Colden*, Volume I, *CNYHS*, 1917, 51.

4. On Roosevelt see *MCQS*, 1704–1712, entry for 12 April 1712; Rothschild, *New York City Neighborhoods*, 199; Matson, *Merchants & Empire*, 147, 261; Archdeacon, *New York City*, 133–134, 138, 142, 145. On Sheppard see *MCQS*, 1704–1712, entry for 11 April 1712; Rothschild, *New York City Neighborhoods*, 200; *Census of the City of New York*, published in O'Callaghan (ed.), *Documentary History of the State of New York*, volume 1, 395–405; *CNYHS*, 1894, 212.

5. Horsmanden, *The New-York Conspiracy*, 344.

6. On Provoost see *CNYHS*, 1961, 65; https://www.wikitree.com/wiki/Provoost-44; *MCQS*, 1704–1712, entry for 11 April 1712.

7. Uring, *Voyages and Travels*, 96.

8. O'Callaghan (ed.), *Calendar of Historic Manuscripts*, Albany, N.Y., 375.

9. Bosman, *A New and Accurate Description*, 343.

10. *The Skeletal Biology, Archaeology, and History of the New York African Burial Ground: A Synthesis of Volumes 1, 2, and 3*, 166–173; *The New York African Burial Ground*, volume I, part 2: *Burial Descriptions and Appendices*, 13, 69.

11. *An Act for the more effective preservation of Deer and other game and the destruction of Wolves Wild Catts and other vermin*, CO 5/1147, f.7; Oldendorp quoted in Konadu (ed.), *The Akan Reader*.

12. Foote, *Black and White Manhattan*, 73–74, 257.

13. *MCQS*, 1704–1712, entry for 16 April 1712; Thompson, *History of Long Island*, 369.

14. That slaves worked in this trade in the city is revealed by an advertisement placed in the *New York Mercury* in 1756 when Duke, a slave who "work[ed] at the goldsmith business" and belonged to the goldsmith Thomas Hamersley, ran away.

15. McManus, *A History of Negro Slavery*, 61–62.

16. Paschal Nelson to Henry Lloyd, February 1726, 1687–1787 Lloyd Manor PDF, https://robcanobbio.files.wordpress.com/2020/01/1687-1787.lloyd-manor.pdf.

17. Henry Lloyd to Mrs. Smith, 1725, 1687–1787 Lloyd Manor PDF, https://robcanobbio.files.wordpress.com/2020/01/1687-1787.lloyd-manor.pdf

18. *The Skeletal Biology, Archaeology, and History of the New York African Burial Ground: A Synthesis of Volumes 1, 2, and 3*, 166–173.

19. *MCQS*, 1704–1712, entry for 17 April 1712; *CNYHS*, 1961, 66; *CNYHS*, 1911, 267; Rothschild, *New York City Neighborhoods*, 198; *Census of the City of New York*, published in O'Callaghan (ed.), *Documentary History of the State of New York*, volume 1, 395–405; https://www.ancestry.com/search/categories/cen_1780/?name=_Pelz&_phsrc=hkC1&_phstart=successSource; *Acts of Assembly in the Province of New York, from 1691 to 1718*, 275–276; Hunter to Popple, 10 September 1713, New York, in O'Callaghan, *DRCHNY*, volume 5, 871.

20. *The Skeletal Biology, Archaeology, and History of the New York African Burial Ground: A Synthesis of Volumes 1, 2, and 3*, 166–173.

21. Medford (ed.), *The New York African Burial Ground*, Volume 3, *Historical Perspectives*, 60.

22. *The Letters and Papers of Cadwallader Colden*, volume I, *CNYHS*, 1917, 51.

23. *The Letters and Papers of Cadwallader Colden*, volume I, *CNYHS*, 1917, 39.

24. Mckee, Jr., *Labor in Colonial New York*, 123–124.

25. Grant, *Memoirs of an American Lady*, 42.

26. Gronniosaw, *A Narrative of the Most Remarkable Particulars*, 10–11.

27. Davis, *Rumor of Revolt*, 43–44; Horsmanden, *The New-York Conspiracy*, 127, 196; Matson, *Merchants and Empire*, 179.

28. On Stuckey/Stukey see Bosher, "Huguenot Merchants and the Protestant International in the Seventeenth Century," *William and Mary Quarterly*, Vol. 52, no. 1 (January 1955), 81–83, 98. On Walton see *Census of the City of New York*, published in O'Callaghan (ed.), *Documentary History of the State of New York*, volume 1, 395–405; Matson, *Merchants and Empire*, 179, 202, 244, 298; Goodfriend, *Before the Melting Pot*, 117, 160; Foote, *Black and White Manhattan*, 148.

29. *Census of the City of New York*, published in O'Callaghan (ed.), *Documentary History of the State of New York*, volume 1, 395–405.

30. Hodges, *Root and Branch*, 112–114; Singleton, *Social New York under the Georges*, 66.

31. *CNYHS*, 1903, 1–2; Sill, *A Notable Example of Longevity*, 1737-1852, *NYGBR*, 56, 1925, 67.

32. Gilbert, *Narrative of Sojourner Truth*, 14.

33. *The Reverend John Sharpe's Proposals*, *CNYHS*, 1880, 350; Gilbert, *Narrative of Sojourner Truth*, 14.

34. Horsmanden, *The New-York Conspiracy*, 22.

35. Wall, "Twenty Years After," *African Diaspora Archaeology Newsletter*, 7, no. 2, April 2000, Article 2; *The Skeletal Biology, Archaeology, and History of the New York African Burial Ground: A Synthesis of Volumes 1, 2, and 3*, 67.

36. *The Skeletal Biology, Archaeology, and History of the New York African Burial Ground: A Synthesis of Volumes 1, 2, and 3*, 114–116; Leone and Fry, *Conjuring in the Big House Kitchen*, *The Journal of American Folklore*, Vol. 112, No. 445, Summer 1999, 372–403.

37. Neau to SPG, 27 February 1709, SPG a, 4, item 121.

38. Horsmanden, *The New-York Conspiracy*, 158.

39. *The Skeletal Biology, Archaeology, and History of the New York African Burial Ground: A Synthesis of Volumes 1, 2, and 3*, 155–156; Goodfriend, *Before the Melting Pot*, 113.
40. *The New York African Burial Ground*, Volume I, Part 2: *Burial Descriptions and Appendices*, 75.
41. *The Skeletal Biology, Archaeology, and History of the New York African Burial Ground: A Synthesis of Volumes 1, 2, and 3*, 179, 185, 187, 190–191.
42. On slaves and suicide see Snyder, Terri L., *The Power to Die: Slavery and Suicide in British North America*.
43. Goodfriend, *Before the Melting Pot*, 123.
44. Horsmanden, *The New-York Conspiracy*, 78.
45. McManus, *A History of Negro Slavery in New York*, 64–66.
46. *The Skeletal Biology, Archaeology, and History of the New York African Burial Ground: A Synthesis of Volumes 1, 2, and 3*, 174–176.
47. Humphreys, *An Historical Account*, 237–238; Klingberg, *Anglican Humanitariansim in Colonial New York*, 154.
48. *The Reverend John Sharpe's Proposals*, CNYHS, 1880, 355.
49. CNYHS, 1893, *Abstract of Wills*, volume 2, 176; CNYHS, 1917, *Colden Letters*, volume 1, 39.
50. Horsmanden, *The New-York Conspiracy*, 90.
51. Bernard, *Journey Towards Freedom*, 47-48.
52. Goodfriend, *Before the Melting Pot*, 118.
53. *The Skeletal Biology, Archaeology, and History of the New York African Burial Ground: A Synthesis of Volumes 1, 2, and 3*, 199; Horsmanden, *The New-York Conspiracy*, 66; Davis, *Rumor of Revolt*, 259, 227; Thomas Sutton's Will, PROB 11/520.
54. Horsmanden, *The New-York Conspiracy*, 93.
55. Gronniosaw, *A Narrative of the Most Remarkable Particulars*, 10-11; *New-York Weekly Journal*, 15 April 1734.
56. *Boston News-Letter*, 3 July 1704, Weeks (ed.), *An Historical Digest of the Provincial Press*, 97.
57. *Boston News-Letter*, 9 October 1704, Weeks (ed.), *An Historical Digest of the Provincial Press*, 129.
58. *Boston News-Letter*, 10 December 1705, and 22 July 1706, Weeks (ed.), *An Historical Digest of the Provincial Press*, 276, 362.
59. Horsmanden, *The New-York Conspiracy*, 93.
60. Hodges, *Root and Branch*, 134.
61. Kalm, *Travels in North America*, volume 2, 208.
62. Medford (ed.), *The New York African Burial Ground*, Volume 3, *Historical Perspectives*, 82.
63. CNYHS, 1903, 1–2.
64. *The Skeletal Biology, Archaeology, and History of the New York African Burial Ground: A Synthesis of Volumes 1, 2, and 3*, 130, 155–156.
65. Horsmanden, *The New-York Conspiracy*, 344; NYPL Archives, *Adolph Philipse Estate Eecord*, ID 5429756, https://www.nypl.org/blog/2016/04/12/slavery-early-nyc.
66. Foote, *Black and White Manhattan*, 199.

67. *The New York African Burial Ground*, Volume I, Part 2: *Burial Descriptions and Appendices*, 64, 76, 14; *The Skeletal Biology, Archaeology, and History of the New York African Burial Ground: A Synthesis of Volumes 1, 2, and 3*, 210–211.

68. McManus, *A History of Negro Slavery*, 48–49.

69. Hodges, *Root and Branch*, 132–133; Horsmanden, *The New-York Conspiracy*, 259.

70. Hodges, *Root & Branch*, 132–133.

71. Foote, *Black and White Manhattan*, 163, 171, 203–204.

72. Horsmanden, *The New-York Conspiracy*, 114–115.

73. Horsmanden, *The New-York Conspiracy*, 256.

74. Horsmanden, *The New-York Conspiracy*, 39, 54.

75. Horsmanden, *The New-York Conspiracy*, 16–17.

76. Greenburg, *Crime and Law Enforcement*, 113–114.

77. Horsmanden, *The New-York Conspiracy*, 123.

78. Defoe, *An Effectual Scheme for the Immediate Preventing of Street Robberies*, 31.

79. Scott (ed.), *New York City Court Records, 1684–1760*, 33.

80. Zabin, *Dangerous Economies*, 64.

81. Zabin, *Dangerous Economies*, 61; Scott (ed.), *New York City Court Records, 1684–1760*, 8, 10, 12; Mckee, Jr., *Labor in Colonial New York*, 147.

82. Foote, *Black and White Manhattan*, 155; McManus, *A History of Negro Slavery*, 66–67.

83. Foote, *Black and White Manhattan*, 155, 276 n.183.

84. *CNYHS, 1893, Abstract of Wills*, volume 1, 75–76; Pulis (ed.), *Moving on: Black Loyalists in the Afro-Atlantic World*, 192.

85. Grant, *Memoirs of an American Lady*, 39.

86. *CNYHS, 1912, Minutes of the Supreme Court of Judicature, 1693 to 1701*, 161.

87. O'Callaghan (ed.), *Calendar of Historical Manuscripts . . . Albany*, Part II, 366.

88. Foote, *Black and White Manhattan*, 154.

89. Mckee, Jr., *Labor in Colonial New York*, 130–131.

90. O'Callaghan (ed.), *Calendar of Historical Manuscripts . . . Albany*, Part II, 263, 265; Greenburg, *Crime and Law Enforcement*, 131; Banner, *The Death Penalty: an American History*, 55.

91. Horsmanden, *The New-York Conspiracy*, 227.

92. *The Skeletal Biology, Archaeology, and History of the New York African Burial Ground: A Synthesis of Volumes 1, 2, and 3*, 132.

93. Olson, "The Slave Code in Colonial New York," *Journal of Negro History*, 29, no. 2 (1944), 147–165; Goodfriend, *Before the Melting Pot*, 118; *The Skeletal Biology, Archaeology, and History of the New York African Burial Ground: A Synthesis of Volumes 1, 2, and 3*, 100–101, 131–132.

94. Hodges, *Root and Branch*, 116.

95. Medford (ed.), *The New York African Burial Ground*, Volume 3, *Historical Perspectives*, 83–84.

96. Hair, *Barbot on Guinea*, 84–86; Bosman, *A New and Accurate Description*, 125.

97. Neau to the secretary of the SPG, 10 July 1703, letter books of the SPG.

98. Skemer, "New Evidence on Black Unrest in Colonial Brooklyn," *Journal of Long Island History*, 12, no. 1 (1975), 48.

99. Riker, *The Annals off Newton*, 142.

100. Earle, *Colonial Days in Old New York*, 209.

101. Horsmanden, *The New-York Conspiracy*, 180, 199–200, 255, 259.

102. *The Skeletal Biology, Archaeology, and History of the New York African Burial Ground: A Synthesis of Volumes 1, 2, and 3*, 56–61; Leone, Polter (eds.), *Historical Archaeologies of Capitalism*, 81–83.

103. Rucker, *Gold Coast Diasporas*, 142–143; Dewulf, *The Pinkster King*, 141–142; Earle, *Colonial Days in Old New York*, 196–201.

104. Dewulf, *The Pinkster King*, 141–142.

105. *Pinkster Festival, Albany Morning Express*, 1880, https://www.flickr.com/photos/albanygroup/32218500442/in/photostream/lightbox/

106. Konadu, *The Akan Diaspora*, 133–136, 150; *The Skeletal Biology, Archaeology, and History of the New York African Burial Ground: A Synthesis of Volumes 1, 2, and 3*, 108–110; Midlo Hall, *Slavery and African Ethnicities*, 49–50, 168–170; Thornton, *Africa and Africans in the Making of the Atlantic World, 1400–1800*, 5–7; Bostoen, Brinkman (eds.), *The Kongo Kingdom*, 260.

107. Trial of William Hunt's Quawcoo, December 11, 1736. Minutes of the Antiguan Council, January 12, 1737, CO9/10. Quoted in Craton, *Testing the Chains*, 123.

108. *The Skeletal Biology, Archaeology, and History of the New York African Burial Ground: A Synthesis of Volumes 1, 2, and 3*, 108–110; Midlo Hall, *Slavery and African Ethnicities*, 49–50, 168–170.

109. *The Skeletal Biology, Archaeology, and History of the New York African Burial Ground: A Synthesis of Volumes 1, 2, and 3*, 46–66; Cantwell and Wall, *Unearthing Gotham*, 54, 279; Foote, *Report on Site-Specific History of Block 154*, 6, http://s-media.nyc.gov/agencies/lpc/arch_reports/861.pdf; Bankoff and Loorya, *The History and Archaeology of City Hall Park*, 133–139; *The Reverend John Sharpe's Proposals, CNYHS*, 1880, 355; *Minutes of the Common Council of the City of New York*, volume 3, 296–297.

110. Buisseret (ed.), *1687*, 272.

111. Sloane, *A Voyage to the Islands*, volume 1, xlviii.

112. *The Skeletal Biology, Archaeology, and History of the New York African Burial Ground: A Synthesis of Volumes 1, 2, and 3*, 115; *The New York African Burial Ground*, volume I, part 2: *Burial Descriptions and Appendices*, 123.

113. Shumway, *The Fante and the Transatlantic Slave Trade*, 134–137.

114. Hunter to Board of Trade, New York, June 23, 1712, *DRCHNY*, volume 5, 339.

CHAPTER II: A BACKDROP OF WAR

1. Lyons, *The 1711 Expedition to Quebec*, 9, 38–41, 84–85, 136; Peckham, *The Colonial Wars, 1689–1762*, 63–72.

2. Lyons, *The 1711 Expedition to Quebec*, 45–107; Peckham, *The Colonial Wars, 1689–1762*, 71–73.

3. Council Minutes, entries for 16 June and 27 June 1711, volume 10, 597, 598; "Journal of Rev. John Sharpe," entries for 17 June to 27 June 1711; Hunter to Rensselaer, New York, 22 June 1711, Council Docs., volume 55, 38.

4. *Boston News-Letter*, 9 July 1711.

5. *Petition from the Inhabitants of New York*, 30 June 1711, *Council Docs.*, volume 55, 78.

6. Hunter to Hill, New York, 9 July 1711, Council Docs., volume 55, 107.

7. Hunter to Rensselaer, New York, 22 June 1711, Council Docs., volume 55, 38; Lustig, *Robert Hunter*, 90-93; *Instructions for the proper defense of the city of New York*, 4 July 1711, Council Docs., volume 55, 84; Council Minutes, 10 July 1711, volume 10, 608.

8. *Boston News-Letter*, 30 July 1711.

9. *Petition of the Merchants of New York*, 23 July 1711, Council Docs., volume 55, 180.

10. Rensselaer, Wessels, and Schuyler to Hunter, Albany, 24 July 1711, Council Docs., volume 55, 182.

11. "Journal of Rev. John Sharpe," entry for 31 July 1711; *Boston News-Letter*, 13 August 1711.

12. "Journal of Rev. John Sharpe," entries for 5 to 9 August 1711.

13. Lyons, *The 1711 Expedition to Quebec*, 136-137; Hunter to St. John, New York, 12 September 1711, *Calendar of State Papers Colonial, America and West Indies*, volume 26, 96.

14. Acorn Club, *Roll and Journal of Connecticut Service in Queen Anne's War, 1710–1711*, 33–34.

15. Hunter to St. John, New York, 12 September 1711, O'Callaghan (ed.), *DRCHNY*, volume 5, 252–256.

16. *Boston News-Letter*, 1 October 1711; Lustig, *Robert Hunter*, 45.

17. *Boston News-Letter*, 17 September 1711.

18. Lyons, *The 1711 Expedition to Quebec*, 132–135.

19. Hunter to Nicholson, New York, 18 September 1711, Council Docs., volume 56, 95; Hunter to Dudley, New York, 18 September 1711, Council Docs., volume 56, 95.

20. Acorn Club, *Roll and Journal of Connecticut Service in Queen Anne's War, 1710–1711*, 40.

21. *Boston News-Letter*, 1 October 1711.

22. Hunter to Hill, New York, 1 October 1711, Council Docs., volume 56, 109.

23. *Boston News-Letter*, 8 October 1711; *Proposition made by the Sachems of the Five Nations*, Albany, 9 October 1711, Council Docs., volume 56, 122; *Boston News-Letter*, 15 October 1711.

24. Commissioners of Indian Affairs to Hunter, Albany, 22 October 1711, Council Docs., volume 56, 131; *Account of the . . . outrages as furnished by an Indian*, 20 October 1711, Council Docs., volume 56, 131.

25. Aptheker, *American Negro Slave Revolts*, 18–53; Dunlap, *History of the New Netherlands, Province of New York*, volume 1, 277.

26. Lockley (ed.), *Maroon Communities in South Carolina: A Documentary Record*, 8–9; Coffin, *An Account of Some of the Principal Slave Insurrections*, 10; Aptheker, *American Negro Slave Revolts*, 171.

27. "Journal of Rev. John Sharpe," entry for 6 November 1711; Lyons, *The 1711 Expedition to Quebec*, 144–145; *Boston News-Letter*, 19 November 1711; MacKinnon and Murphy, *Treasure Hunter: Diving for Gold on North America's Death Coast*, chapter 10; Courtin de St. Aignan, *Affidavit*, Council Docs., volume 56, 151.

28. Hunter to Dartmouth, New York, 12 November 1711, *Calendar of State Papers Colonial, America and West Indies,* volume 26, 162.

29. Hunter to Matthews, New York, 24 December 1711, Council Docs., volume 57, 36; Matson, *Merchants and Empire,* 219–220.

30. Otterness, *Becoming German,* 108.

31. "Journal of Rev. John Sharpe," entries for 26 November, 26 and 31 December 1711.

32. *Boston News-Letter,* 21 January 1712.

33. *Boston News-Letter,* 4 February 1712.

34. Hodges, *Root and Branch,* 74–75.

35. Horsmanden, *The New-York Conspiracy,* 158.

36. Horsmanden, *The New-York Conspiracy,* 41.

37. Kalm, *Travels in North America,* 207.

38. McManus, *Black Bondage in the North,* 52.

39. Hunter to Board of Trade, New York, June 23, 1712, *DRCHNY,* 5:339.

40. Kea, "When I die, I shall return to my own land," 172, in Wilks, *The Cloth of Many Colored Silks,* 159–193.

41. Gaspar, *Bondmen and Rebels,* 142–143, 224–225.

42. On Grassett see Goodfriend, "The Protestants of Colonial New York City," 246, in Van Ruymbeke and Sparks (eds.), *Memory and Identity,* 241–254; O'Callaghan, *Calendar of Historical Manuscripts,* part 2, 228; On Dehonneur see *Boston News-Letter,* 14 April 1712; *CNYHS,* 1910, 195; *Census of the City of New York,* published in O'Callaghan (ed.), *Documentary History of the State of New York,* volume 1, 395–405; Rothschild, *New York City Neighborhoods,* 190. On Vaninburgh see *MCQS,* 1704–1712, entry for 27 May 1712; Archdeacon, *New York City,* 136; Baker, *Women and Capital Punishment,* 87.

43. John Sharpe letter, 23 June 1712, *NYGBR,* volume 21, 1809, 162–163.

44. Horsmanden, *The New-York Conspiracy,* 352.

45. See Preface for details.

46. *Boston News-Letter,* 21 April 1712.

47. John Sharpe letter, 23 June 1712, *NYGBR,* Volume 21, 1809, 162–163.

48. T 70/5, f. 5; Donnan, *Documents Illustrative of the History of the Slave Trade to America,* volume 3, 444.

49. *MCQS,* 1704–1712, entry for 11 April 1712.

50. *MCQS,* 1704–1712, entries for 14 and 15 April 1712.

51. On Peter the Doctor, see John Sharpe letter, 23 June 1712, *NYGBR,* Volume XXI, 1809, 162–163; *Census of the City of New York,* published in O'Callaghan (ed.), *Documentary History of the State of New York,* volume 1, 395–405; Foote, *Black and White Manhattan,* 142, 204, 271; Rucker, *The River Flows on,* 38; *CNYHS,* 1961, 65. On Obeah see Konadu, *The Akan Diaspora,* 139–140.

52. Craton, *Testing the Chains,* 109.

53. Craton, *Testing the Chains,* 121.

54. John Sharpe letter, 23 June 1712, *NYGBR,* Volume 21, 1809, 162–163.

55. Craton, *Testing the Chains,* 101–104.

56. John Sharpe letter, 23 June 1712, *NYGBR,* Volume 21, 1809, 162–163.

57. Hunter report, 1 March 1712, N.Y. Col. Docs., volume 5, 311.

58. "Journal of Rev. John Sharpe," entry for 4 March 1712.

59. *Registers of the French Church of New York*, volume 1, 129; *Boston News-Letter*, 17 March 1712.

60. *Boston News-Letter*, 24 March 1712; Bass to Hunter, Burlington, 19 March 1712, Council Docs., volume 57, 115.

61. John Sharpe letter, 23 June 1712, *NYGBR*, volume 21, 1809, 162–163.

62. Konadu, *The Akan Diaspora*, 195.

63. Gould, "The Shrine of Tutu Abo," 9–10, *Michigan State University African e-Journals Project*.

64. Rask, *Two Views*, 133.

CHAPTER 12: THE REVOLT

1. Valsecchi, "Calendar and the Annual Festival in Nzema," *Africa: Rivista trimestrale* 54, no. 4 (December 1999), 497; Wilks, *Forests of Gold*, 198–199.

2. http://astropixels.com/ephemeris/phasescat/phases1701.html.

3. Valsecchi, "Calendar and the Annual Festival in Nzema," 497, 505; Habel, *Earth Story*, 103–104.

4. Rømer, *A Reliable Account*, 107.

5. Habel, *Earth Story*, 103–104; Achebe, *Things Fall Apart*, 165.

6. Hunter to Board of Trade, New York, June 23, 1712, *DRCHNY*, 5:339; *MCQS*, 1704–1712, entry for 16 April 1712; Coroner's Inquest, 9 April 1712, Manuscripts, CNYHS.

7. *MCQS*, 1704–1712, entries for 11 April 1712 to 14 April 1712; Coroner's Inquest, 9 April 1712, Manuscripts, CNYHS.

8. Horsmanden, *The New-York Conspiracy*, 129, 196, 65.

9. "Journal of Rev. John Sharpe," entry for 6 April 1712.

10. Grier (ed.), *CNYGBS*, volume 2, *Baptisms from 1639 to 1730 in the Reformed Dutch Church*, 359.

11. *The Boston News-Letter*, 14 April 1712.

12. Neau to SPG, 10 July 1703, Collections of the SPG, Box A, 1, item 106.

13. On the numbers involved in the revolt see Hunter to Board of Trade, New York, June 23, 1712, *DRCHNY*, volume 5, 339; *Boston News-Letter*, 14 April 1712; Coroner's Inquest, 9 April 1712, Manuscripts, CNYHS. On slaves' means of leaving their masters' property at night see Horsmanden, *The New-York Conspiracy*, 155, 193.

14. Rothschild, *New York City Neighborhoods*, 184–204; *Census of the City of New York*, published in O'Callaghan (ed.), *Documentary History of the State of New York*, volume 1, 395–405.

15. Hunter to Board of Trade, New York, June 23, 1712, *DRCHNY*, 5:339.

16. Horsmanden, *The New-York Conspiracy*, 55, footnote, mentions that several rebels "shot themselves"—presuming that these suicides were the Akan leaders (as was a common pattern in other revolts such as the 1736 revolt in Antigua), then it seems likely that the Akan leaders were armed with guns.

17. John Sharpe letter, 23 June 1712, *NYGBR*, volume 21, 1809, 162–163; Konadu, *The Akan Diaspora*, 195.

18. Rømer, *A Reliable Account*, 107.

19. *Boston News-Letter*, 14 April 1712.

20. John Sharpe letter, New York, 23 June 1712, *NYGBR*, volume 21, 1809, 162–163.

21. Hunter to Board of Trade, New York, June 23, 1712, *DRCHNY,* volume 5, 339.

22. Humphreys, *An Historical Account,* 240; *Boston News-Letter,* 14 April 1712.

23. Costello, *History of the New York Police,* 31; Peterson and Edwards, *New York as an Eighteenth Century Municipality,* 178–181.

24. O'Callaghan, *Calendar of Historical Manuscripts,* Part II, 236.

25. *Boston News-Letter,* 14 April 1712; *Coroner's Inquisition,* 9 April 1712, NYHS Misc. Mss., NYC, Box 4, document 13; *MCQS,* 1704–1712, entries from April 1712 to October 1712; Goodfriend, *Before the Melting Pot,* 49; https://www.my heritage.es/names/augustus_grasset; O'Callaghan, *Calendar of Historical Man-uscripts,* Part II, 218, 228, 236; *CNYHS, 1911,* 225; *NYGBR,* volume 21, 1809, 162–163; https://www.geni.com/people/Joris-Marschalk/6000 000001692130 942; *CNYHS, 1885,* 71, 606; https://www.myheritage.es/names/ william_echt; O'Callaghan, *Lists of Inhabitants of Colonial New York,* 20; https://www.myheri-tage.com/names/henry_breser; Goodfriend, *Before the Melting Pot,* 182; https://www.wikitree.com/wiki/Beekman-92; Archdeacon, *New York City, 1664–1710,* 120, volume 21, 1809, 162–163; 124.

26. John Sharpe letter, 23 June 1712, *NYGBR,* volume 21, 1809, 162–163; Hunter to Board of Trade, New York, June 23, 1712, *DRCHNY,* 5:339.

27. *Boston News-Letter,* 14 April 1712.

28. *CNYHS,* 1961, 56; Hunter to Board of Trade, New York, June 23, 1712, *DRCHNY,* 5:339.

29. Hunter to Board of Trade, New York, June 23, 1712, *DRCHNY,* 5:339; John Sharpe letter, 23 June 1712, *NYGBR,* volume 21, 1809, 162–163.

30. *Coroner's Inquisition,* 9 April 1712, NYHS Misc. Mss., NYC, Box 4, docu-ment 13; *MCQS,* 1704–1712, entry for 15 April 1712 (including Memorandum for this date).

31. *Coroner's Inquisition,* 9 April 1712, NYHS Misc. Mss., NYC, Box 4, docu-ment 13; *MCQS,* 1704–1712, entry for 16 April 1712 (including Memorandum for this date).

32. *Boston News-Letter,* 14 April 1712; *MCQS,* 1704–1712, entry for 30 May 1712 (including Memorandum for this date); *Coroner's Inquisition,* 9 April 1712, NYHS Misc. Mss., NYC, Box 4, document 13.

33. *Boston News-Letter,* 14 April 1712; *MCQS,* 1704–1712, entry for 11 April 1712 (including Memorandum for this date).

34. *MCQS,* 1704–1712, entry for 12 April 1712 (including Memorandum for this date); https://www.wikitree.com/wiki/Beekman-92; https://www.finda-grave.com/memorial/183862639/hendrick-jansz-hoogland.

35. *Boston News-Letter,* 14 April 1712; *CNYHS,* 1961, 49; Rothschild, *New York City Neighborhoods,* 198; Goodfriend, *Before the Melting Pot,* 60; CNYHS, 1885, 64; http://www.jakehannam.com/web/cossart_descendants/d1.htm.

36. Hunter to Board of Trade, New York, June 23, 1712, *DRCHNY,* 5:339; Humphreys, *An Historical Account,* 240.

37. Hunter to Board of Trade, New York, June 23, 1712, *DRCHNY,* 5:339; John Sharpe letter, 23 June 1712, *NYGBR,* volume 21, 1809, 162–163.

38. Horsmanden, *The New-York Conspiracy,* 55, footnote; John Sharpe letter, 23 June 1712, *NYGBR,* volume 21, 1809, 162–163.

39. John Sharpe letter, 23 June 1712, *NYGBR*, volume 21, 1809, 162–163.

40. Kea, "When I Die, I Shall Return to My Own Land," 187, in Wilks, *The Cloth of Many Colored Silks*, 159–193.

41. John Sharpe letter, 23 June 1712, *NYGBR*, volume 21, 1809, 162–163; Horsmanden, *The New-York Conspiracy*, 55, footnote; Humphreys, *An Historical Account*, 240.

42. Rømer, Winsnes (ed.), *A Reliable Account*, 152, footnote 139.

43. Rømer, *A Reliable Account*, 152.

44. *Boston News-Letter*, 14 April 1712.

45. Hunter to Board of Trade, New York, June 23, 1712, *DRCHNY*, 5:339.

46. Horsmanden, *The New-York Conspiracy*, 251.

47. Riker, *The Annals of Newton*, 142–143.

48. *The Colonial Laws of New York*, volume 1, 631–633.

49. Hunter to Board of Trade, New York, June 23, 1712, *DRCHNY*, 5:339; Council Minutes, Fort Anne, 7 April 1712, Albany Archives, Vol. 11, 70; *Boston News-Letter*, 14 April 1712; John Sharpe letter, 23 June 1712, *NYGBR*, volume 21, 1809, 162–163.

50. *Boston News-Letter*, 21 April 1712; Hunter to Board of Trade, New York, June 23, 1712, *DRCHNY*, 5:339.

51. Hart, *Slaves who Abolished Slavery*, 13–14; Price (ed.), *Maroon Societies*, 256; Craton, *Testing the Chains*, 75–76.

52. Inchiquin to Lords of Trade, 31 August 1690, CO 138/7, folios 1–6; John Helyar letter, 7 August 1690, Helyar Papers, Jamaican letters, 17th Century, DD/WHh/1151–1153, Somerset Heritage Centre.

53. Gaspar, *Bondsmen and Rebels*, 185–189.

54. Craton, *Testing the Chains*, 108–110.

55. Kea, "When I Die, I Shall Return to My Own Land," 187.

56. Kea, "When I Die, I Shall Return to My Own Land."

57. Kilson, "Towards Freedom: An Analysis of Slave Revolts in the United States," *Phylon*, 25, no. 2 (1960), 175–187.

58. Although Kilson believed the New York revolt of 1712 was a "Systematic Revolt" aimed at "establishing a Negro state," there are several reasons to doubt this conclusion as outlined in the main body of the text.

59. *Census of the City of New York*, in O'Callaghan (ed.), *Documentary History of the State of New York*, volume 1, 395–405.

60. *An Act for the more effective preservation of Deer and other game and the destruction of Wolves Wild Catts and other vermin*, CO 5/1147, f. 7.

61. Lockley (ed.), *Maroon Communities in South Carolina: A Documentary Record*, 8–9; Coffin, *An Account of Some of the Principal Slave Insurrections*, 10; Aptheker, *American Negro Slave Revolts*, 171.

62. Robinson, "The Outlaw Fort Canisteo Castle," *Crooked Lake Review*, November 1995, https://www.crookedlakereview.com/articles/67_100/92nov1995/92robinson.html; Robinson, "Canisteo Castle Builders Found," *Crooked Lake Review*, February 1996, https://www.crookedlakereview.com/articles/67_100/95feb1996/95robinson.html; Dickey, "More on Canisteo Castle," *Crooked Lake Review*, May 1996, https://www.crookedlakereview.com/articles/67_100/98may1996/98dickey.html.

63. See the prologue for details of contemporary precedents.

64. *Boston News-Letter*, 21 April 1712; Hunter to Board of Trade, New York, June 23, 1712, *DRCHNY*, 5:339; John Sharpe letter, 23 June 1712, *NYGBR*, volume 21, 1809, 162–163; "Journal of Rev. John Sharpe," entry for 6 April 1712; Horsmanden, *The New-York Conspiracy*, 55, footnote.

65. Neau to SPG, New York, 15 October 1712, SPG letter books, box A, 7, 227–228.

CHAPTER 13: BROKEN ON THE WHEEL

1.*Boston News-Letter*, 21 April 1712.

2. Peterson, *New York as an Eighteenth Century Municipality*, 193–194.

3. Hunter to Popple, 10 September 1713, New York, *DRCNHY*, volume 5, 871.

4. Greenburg, *Crime and Law Enforcement*, 125–127.

5. *Coroner's Inquisition*, 9 April 1712, NYHS Misc. Mss., NYC, Box 4, document 13.

6. "Journal of Rev. John Sharpe," entry for 9 April 1712. When the ninth victim's body was interred is unrecorded. It seems plausible that it belonged to Lieutenant John Corbet, the English career soldier who had been promoted from the ranks in exchange for accepting a command in General Francis Nicholson's ill-fated Montreal expedition. Having only arrived in New York from England on 11 July 1711, it is unlikely that Corbet had any friends or family in the city to mourn him. Perhaps no funeral was conducted for the lieutenant at all.

7. Earle, *Colonial Days in Old New York*, 293–297; Cohen, *The Dutch-American Farm*, 165–166; Wees, Carver Harvey, Higgins, *Early American Silver*, 138–139.

8. Humphreys, *An Historical Account*, 242.

9. *The Reverend John Sharpe's Proposals*, CNYHS, *1880*, 352–353.

10. John Sharpe letter, 23 June 1712, *NYGBR*, volume 21, 1809, 162–163.

11. *Coroner's Inquisition*, 9 April 1712, NYHS Misc. Mss., NYC, Box 4, document 13; *MCQS*, 1704–1712, entry for 11 April 1712; John Sharpe letter, 23 June 1712, *NYGBR*, Volume XXI, 1809, 162–163.

12. Hunter to Board of Trade, New York, June 23, 1712, *DRCHNY*, 5:339; Albany Archives, Council Minutes, volume 10, 91–92.

13. John Sharpe letter, 23 June 1712, *NYGBR*, Volume XXI, 1809, 162–163.

14. *Coroner's Inquisition*, 9 April 1712, NYHS Misc. Mss., NYC, Box 4, document 13.

15. John Sharpe letter, 23 June 1712, *NYGBR*, volume 21, 1809, 162–163; Hunter to Board of Trade, New York, June 23, 1712, *DRCHNY*, 5:339.

16. *CNYHS*, 1961, 56; *MCQS*, 1704–1712, entries from April 1712 to October 1712.

17. *The Colonial Laws of New York*, volume 1, 631–633.

18. *CNYHS*, 1961, 53–54; Horsmanden, *The New-York Conspiracy*, 72.

19. *The Reverend John Sharpe's Proposals*, CNYHS, 1880, 353.

20. Hunter to Board of Trade, New York, June 23, 1712, *DRCHNY*, 5:339.

21. Hunter to Earl of Dartmouth, New York, 23 June 1712, *Calendar of State Papers Colonial, Amrica and West Indies*, volume 26, 456.

22. Archdeacon, *New York City*, 114–145; Kammen, *Colonial New York*, 141–142; Lustig, *Robert Hunter*, 110–111.

23. Hunter to Board of Trade, New York, June 23, 1712, *DRCHNY*, 5:339.

24. See Chapter 2 for details and references.

25. *MCQS*, 1704–1712, entry for 12 April 1712.

26. *MCQS*, 1704–1712, entry for 11 April 1712; *CNYHS*, 1961, 51–58; Archdeacon, *New York City*, 126; Kammen, *Colonial New York*, 252; Peterson, *New York as an Eighteenth Century Municipality*, 24–26; *The Colonial Laws of New York*, volume 1, 387–388; Johnson, "Civil Procedure in John Jay's New York," *American Journal of Legal History*, 11, no. 1, Jan. 1967, 75; "Law in Colonial New York," *Harvard Law Review*, 80, no. 8 (June 1967), 1762. For a background on the legal process in colonial New York see Greenburg, *Crime and Law Enforcement*, and Goebel and Naughton, *Law Enforcement in Colonial New York*.

27. On Harrison see *Minutes of the Common Council of the City of New York*, Vol. 3, 27.

28. *CNYHS*, 1961, 54–56; Rothschild, *New York City Neighborhoods*, 196; *Census of the City of New York*, published in O'Callaghan (ed.), *Documentary History of the State of New York*, volume 1, 395–405.

29. *MCQS*, 1704–1712, entry for 11 April 1712.

30. "Journal of Rev. John Sharpe," entries for 11 and 12 April, 1712.

31. Horsmanden, *The New-York Conspiracy*, 60.

32. Horsmanden, *The New-York Conspiracy*, 96, 143, 235, 277, 384; Mckee, Jr., *Labor in Colonial New York*, 155.

33. *MCQS*, 1704–1712, entry for 11 April 1712.

34. Brown, *Tacky's Revolt*, 155.

35. John Sharpe letter, 23 June 1712, *NYGBR*, volume 21, 1809, 162–163.

36. *MCQS*, 1704–1712, entry for 12 April 1712; *CNYHS*, 1961, 54–56.

37. *MCQS*, 1704–1712, entry for 12 April 1712.

38. Hunter to Board of Trade, New York, June 23, 1712, *DRCHNY*, 5:339.

39. *MCQS*, 1704–1712, entry for 12 April 1712.

40. "Journal of Rev. John Sharpe," entry for 12 April, 1712.

41. Young, *The Historical Cabinet*, 481–482; Bailey, *An Universal Etymological English Dictionary*, entry for "Wheel."

42. Mckee, Jr., *Labor in Colonial New York*, 155.

43. Horsmanden, *The New-York Conspiracy*, 96–100.

44. Horsmanden, *The New-York Conspiracy*, 237.

45. Evans (ed.), *Records of the Reformed Dutch Church, Baptisms 1639 to 1730*, 359.

46. *Boston News-Letter*, 21 April 1712.

47. *Boston News-Letter*, 21 April 1712; Hunter to Board of Trade, New York, 23 June 1712, *DRCHNY*, 5:339.

48. Greenburg, "The Effectiveness of Law Enforcement in Eighteenth Century New York," *American Journal of Legal History*, 19, no. 3 (July 1975), 181.

49. *MCQS*, 1704–1712, entry for 14 April 1712; *CNYHS*, 1961, 54–56.

50. John Sharpe letter, 23 June 1712, *NYGBR*, volume 21, 1809, 162–163; Barclay to Secretary of the SPG, 31 May 1712, SPG Letter books, Box A, 7, 206.

51. *MCQS*, 1704–1712, entry for 14 April 1712.

52. "Journal of Rev. John Sharpe," entry for 16 April 1712.

53. *MCQS*, 1704–1712, entry for 14 April 1712.

54. Sloane, *A Voyage to the Islands*, volume 1, lvii.

55. Buisseret (ed.), *1687*, 278.
56. John Sharpe letter, 23 June 1712, *NYGBR*, volume 21, 1809, 162–163.
57. *MCQS*, 1704–1712, entries for 17, 18, 19 April 1712; *CNYHS*, 1961, 54–56.
58. "Journal of Rev. John Sharpe," entry for 21 April, 1712.
59. *MCQS*, 1704–1712, entries for 17, 18, 19 April 1712.
60. Hunter to Popple, 10 September 1713, New York, *DRCNHY*, 5:871.
61. *MCQS*, 1704–1712, entries for 22 April 1712 and 6 August 1712; *CNYHS*, 1961, 54–56.
62. Hunter to Popple, 10 September 1713, New York, *DRCNHY*, 5:871.
63. "Journal of Rev. John Sharpe," entry for 21 April 1712.
64. Journal of the General Assembly of New York, CO 5/1185, folio 197.
65. *MCQS*, 1704–1712, entries for 20 to 30 May, 1712; Hunter to Popple, 10 September 1713, New York, *DRCNHY*, 5:871.
66. Hunter to the Lords of Trade, New York, 14 March 1713, *DRCHNY*, 5:357.
67. *MCQS*, 1704–1712, entries for 4 and 7 June 1712; *CNYHS*, 1961, 54–56; John Sharpe letter, 23 June 1712, *NYGBR*, volume 21, 1809, 162–163; Hunter to Board of Trade, New York, June 23, 1712, *DRCHNY*, 5:339.
68. Hunter to the Lords of Trade, New York, 14 March 1713, *DRCHNY*, 5:357.
69. John Sharpe letter, 23 June 1712, *NYGBR*, volume 21, 1809, 162–163.
70. Hunter to the Lords of Trade, New York, 14 March 1713, *DRCHNY*, 5:357.

CHAPTER 14: REPRIEVE

1. McCusker, *Essays in the Economic History of the Atlantic World*, 126.
2. Hunter to the Lords of Trade, New York, 14 March 1713, *DRCHNY*, 5:357; Lustig, *Robert Hunter*, 106.
3. Bonomi, *The Lord Cornbury Scandal*, 47-49, 196.
4. McCusker, *Essays in the Economic History of the Atlantic World*, 126.
5. Hunter to the Lords of Trade, New York, 14 March 1713, *DRCHNY*, 5:357.
6. Lords of Trade to the Earl of Dartmouth, Whitehall, 27 August 1712, *DRCHNY*, 5:346.
7. *Order of Queen in Council*, Windsor, 20 October 1712, *Calendar of State Papers Colonial, America and West Indies*, volume 27, 102.
8. *MCQS*, 1704–1712, entry for 6 August 1712; Hunter to the Lords of Trade, New York, 14 March 1713, *DRCHNY*, 5:357.
9. *MCQS*, 1704–1712, entries for 14 and 18 October 1712.
10. *The Colonial Laws of New York*, volume 1, 761–767.
11. Hunter to the Council of Trade, New York, 12 November 1715, *Calendar of State Papers Colonial, America and West Indies*, volume 28, 673.
12. Wax, "Negro Import Duties in Colonial Pennsylvania," *Pennsylvania Magazine of History and Biography*, 97, 1973, 46; Rugemer, *Slave Law and the Politics of Resistance*, 90.
13. Hunter to the Council of Trade, New York, 18 July 1713, *Calendar of State Papers Colonial, America and West Indies*, volume 27, 404.
14. Hunter to Popple, 10 September 1713, New York, *DRCNHY*, 5:871.
15. Hunter to Popple, 10 September 1713, New York, *DRCNHY*, 5:871.
16. Basker, *Acts of Assembly, Passed in the Province of New York, from 1691, to 1718*, 275–276.

17. *The Reverend John Sharpe's Proposals*, CNYHS, *1880*, 353.

18. Hunter to Board of Trade, New York, June 23, 1712, *DRCHNY*, 5:339.

19. Horsmanden, *The New-York Conspiracy*, 59, 72, 390; *Abstract of Wills*, volume IV, CNYHS 1895, 44; Hodges, *Root and Branch*, 134.

20. *MCQS*, 1704–1712, entry for 1 February 1715.

21. Lustig, *Robert Hunter*, ix.

22. Lustig, *Robert Hunter*, 163–164, 174.

23. Craton, *Testing the Chains*, 67–96.

24. Craton, *Testing the Chains*, 81–85; Price (ed.), *Maroon Societies*, 263–266; Lustig, *Robert Hunter*, 214–215.

25. *Boston News-Letter*, 15 October 1711; *Boston News-Letter*, 30 June 1712.

26. Pratt, *Annals of Public Education*, 98–99.

27. *A List of Ships Ashore Cleared for Africa*, 1717, CO 390/7; Slave Voyages Database no. 25365; Donnan, *Documents Illustrative of the Slave Trade*, volume 3, 466.

28. Lydon, "New York and the Slave Trade, 1700 to 1774," *William and Mary Quarterly*, 35, no. 2 (April 1978) 390–391, footnote 50; Donnan, *Documents Illustrative of the Slave Trade*, volume 3, 445, 446.

29. Kea, "When I Die, I Shall Return to My Own Land," 167–168.

30. Rømer, *A Reliable Account*, 136–137.

31. Kea, "When I Die, I Shall Return to My Own Land," 168–169, 180–189.

32. McManus, *A History of Negro Slavery*, 126–128.

33. McManus, *A History of Negro Slavery*, 128–130.

34. McManus, *A History of Negro Slavery*, 130–132.

35. McManus, *A History of Negro Slavery*, 132–139. For more on the 1741 plot see Davis, *Rumor of Revolt*; and Horsmanden, *The New-York Conspiracy*; McManus, *Black Bondage in the North*, 152–159.

EPILOGUE

1. McManus, *A History of Negro Slavery*, 139–140, 151.

2. McManus, *A History of Negro Slavery*, 151–153.

3. McManus, *A History of Negro Slavery*, 153–159; *The Skeletal Biology, Archaeology, and History of the New York African Burial Ground: A Synthesis of Volumes 1, 2, and 3*, 208; Hodges, *Root and Branch*, 139–162.

4. McManus, *A History of Negro Slavery*, 161–179; Hodges, *Root and Branch*, 162–227.

5. McManus, *A History of Negro Slavery*, 186–188; Foner, *Gateway to Freedom*, 47, 59–60; Kerber, "Abolitionists and Amalgamators: The New York City Race Riots of 1834," *New York History*, 48, no. 1, January 1967, 28–39; Finkelman, *The Age of Jim Crow*, 69.

6. Hodges, *Root and Branch*, 245–247; Douglas and Baker (ed.), *Narrative of the Life*, 8–18; Rudisel and Blaisdell (eds.), *Slave Narratives of the Underground Railroad*, viii.

7. Man, Jr., "Labor Competition and the New York Draft Riots of 1863," *Journal of Negro History*, 36, no. 4, October 1951, 375–401; Hodges, *Root and Branch*, 267. Also see Cook, *The Armies of the Streets: The New York City Draft Riots of 1863*.

8. Halpin, *A Brotherhood of Liberty*, 1–6; Martinez, *Carpetbaggers, Cavalry, and the Ku Klux Klan*, 202–203; Brown and Stentiford, *The Jim Crow Experience*, xviii; Sacks, *Before Harlem*, 5–6, 40–42, 107–137.

9. Amessen, *Encyclopedia of U.S. Labor and Working-Class History*, 82–84, 939–941; Wintz, Finkelman, *Encyclopedia of the Harlem Renaissance*, 420–421, 590–592.

10. Anderson, *A. Philip Randolph*, 259; Kirk, *Martin Luther King, Jr.*, 27–29, 136–137.

Bibliography

MANUSCRIPT SOURCES

National Archives, Kew, London

ADM 51/49—Admiralty Records, Captain's Log, *HMS Anglesea*, 1695–1739.

ADM 51/374—Admiralty Records, Captain's Log, *HMS Fowey*, 1690–1716.

C 113/282—Chancery Records, Letters to England from James Phipps, Chief Factor, Royal African Company, Cape Coast Castle, 1709–1716.

C 113/292—Chancery Records, Administrative records of Peter Holt, Royal African Company, Cape Coast Castle, 1710–1711.

CO 5/1147—Colonial Office, Board of Trade and Secretaries of State: America and West Indies, Original Correspondence. New York. Acts. 1708–1713.

CO 157/1—Colonial Office, Naval Office Returns (shipping returns) for Leeward Islands including Antigua, 1704–1720.

CO 390/7—Colonial Office, Customs House Accounts and Statistics, Shipping Returns, 1690–1729.

T 70/5—Company of Royal Adventurers Trading with Africa and Successors: Records, Letters Received from Africa. Abstracts. 1705–1714.

T 70/8—Company of Royal Adventurers Trading with Africa and Successors: Records, Letters Received from the West Indies. Abstracts. 1706–1719.

T 70/355—Company of Royal Adventurers Trading with Africa and Successors: Records, Duty Journals. 1708–1715.

T 70/956—Company of Royal Adventurers Trading with Africa and Successors: Records, Records, Accounts: Invoice Books. HOMEWARDS. 1709–1711.

T 70/1199—Company of Royal Adventurers Trading with Africa and Successors: Records, Customs. Sworn value of cargoes and amounts levied. 1702–1712.
New York State Archives, Albany
A1895—New York Colony Council Minutes, 1668–1783, Volumes 10 and 55.
New York City Municipal Archives, NYC
Minutes of the Court of Quarter Sessions, 1704–1712, entries for May 1708, from April 1712 to October 1712, and February 1715.
Lambeth Palace Library Archives, London
SPG XIII—Letter Books of the Society for the Propagation of the Gospel, New York Correspondence, 1700–1706.
SPG XIV—Letter Books of the Society for the Propagation of the Gospel, New York Correspondence, 1707-undated.
New-York Historical Society Archives, New York City
Coroner's Inquisition and Jury Findings on the Death of Augustus Grasset; Coroner's Inquisition and Jury Findings on the Death of William Asht; both 9 April 1712 (NYHS Misc. Mss., NYC, Box 4, 13, 14).

PUBLISHED PRIMARY SOURCES

An Abstract of the Evidence delivered before a Select Committee of the House of Commons in the Years 1790, and 1791, on the Part of the Petitioners for the Abolition of the Slave Trade. London: James Phillips, 1791.
Abstract of Wills on File in the Surrogate's Office, City of New York, Volume II, 1708–1728, Volume III, 1730–1744, Volume IV, 1744–1754, Volume V, 1754–1760. New York: Collections of the New-York Historical Society, 1893, 1894, 1895, 1896.
Acorn Club (ed.). *Roll and Journal of Connecticut Service in Queen Anne's War, 1710–1711.* Connecticut: Duke University Library, 1916.
Baquaqua, Mahommah, and Samuel Moore, (eds.). *An Interesting Narrative: Biography of Mahommah G. Baquaqua, A Native of Zoogoo, in the Interior of Africa.* Detroit, 1854.
Barbot, Jean. *A Description of the Coasts of North and South-Guinea; and of Ethiopia inferior, vulgarly Angola: Being A New and Accurate Account of the Western Maritime Countries of Africa.* London: A. & J. Churchill, 1732.
Basker, J. (ed.). *Acts of Assembly, Passed in the Province of New York, from 1691, to 1718.* London: John Baskett, 1719.

Blakely, Michael L., and Lesley M. Rankin-Hill (eds.). *Skeletal Biology, Archaeology and History of the New York African Burial Ground*, Part 1. Washington, D.C.: Howard University Press, 2009.

Bosman, Willem. *A New and Accurate Description of the Coast of Guinea Divided into the Gold, the Slave, and the Ivory Coasts*. London: James Knapton, 1705.

Brodhead, John Romeyn, and E. B. O'Callaghan (eds.). *Documents Relative to the Colonial History of New York: Produced in Holland, England and France*, Volume 5. Albany: Weed, Parsons and Company, 1855.

Buisseret, David (ed.). *Jamaica in 1687: The Taylor Manuscript at the National Library of Jamaica*. Kingston: University of the West Indies Press, 2010.

Calendar of State Papers Colonial, America and West Indies, Edited by Cecil Headlam. Volumes 19, 1701; 23, 1706–1708; 24, 1708–1709; 25, 1710–1711; 26, 1711–1712; 27, 1712–1714. London: University of London, 1910, 1916, 1922, 1924, 1925, 1926.

Colden, Cadwallader. *The Letters and Papers of Cadwallader Colden*, Volume I. New York: Collections of the New-York Historical Society, 1917.

The Colonial Laws of New York from the Year 1664 to the Revolution, Volume 1. Albany: James B. Lyon, 1894.

Cugoano, Ottobah. *Narrative of the Enslavement of Ottobah Cugoano, a Native of Africa, published by himself, in the Year 1787*. In Anon, *The Negro's memorial, or, Abolitionist's Catechism by an Abolitionist*. London: Hatchard and Co., 1825.

Defoe, Daniel. *An Effectual Scheme for the Immediate Preventing of Street Robberies and Suppressing All Other Disorders of the Night: With a Brief History of the Night-houses, and an Appendix Relating to Those Sons of Hell, Call'd Incendiaries*. London: J. Wilford, 1731.

Donnan, Elizabeth. *Documents Illustrative of the History of the Slave Trade to America*, Volume 3, *New England and the Middle Colonies*. Washington, D.C.: Carnegie Institution, 1932.

Douglass, Frederick, and Houston A. Baker, Jr. (ed.). *Narrative of the Life of Frederick Douglass, an America Slave Written by Himself*. Harmondsworth: Penguin, 1986.

Dupuis, Joseph. *Journal of a Residence in Ashantee*. London: Henry Colburn, 1824.

Ecclesiastical Records, State of New York, Volume 1. New York: J. B. Lyon, 1901.

Equiano, Olaudah. *The Interesting Narrative and Other Writings*. New York: Penguin, 1995.

Evans, Thomas Grier, and Tobias Alexander Wright (eds.). *Records of the Reformed Dutch Church in New Amsterdam and New York*, Volume II, *Baptisms 1639 to 1730*. New York: New York Genealogical and Biographical Society, 1901.

Franks, Abigaill. *The Letters of Abigaill Levy Franks*. New Haven: Yale University Press, 2004.

Gilbert, Olive. *Narrative of Sojourner Truth, a Northern Slave, Emancipated from Bodily Servitude by the State of New York, in 1828*. Boston: Olive Gilbert, 1850.

Grant, Anne MacVicar. *Memoirs of an American Lady: with Sketches of Manners and Scenery in America, as they Existed Previous to the Revolution*. New York: D. and G. Bruce, 1809.

Grim, Charles Frederick. *An Essay Towards An Improved Register of Deeds, City and County of New York, to Dec. 31, 1799. Inc.* New York: Gould, Banks & Company, 1832.

Gronniosaw, James Albert Ukawsaw. *A Narrative of the Most Remarkable Particulars in the Life of James Albert Ukawsaw Gronniosaw, an African Prince, as Related by Himself*. Bath: W. Gye, 1772.

Horsmanden, Daniel. *The New-York Conspiracy, or a History of the Negro Plot, with the Journal of the Proceedings against the Conspirators at New-York in the Years 1741–2*. New York: Southwick & Pelsue, 1810.

Humphreys, David. *An Historical Account of the Incorporated Society for the Propagation of the Gospel in Foreign Parts*. London: Joseph Downing, 1730.

Journal of the Legislative Council of the Colony of New York, Began the 9th Day of April, 1691; and Ended the 27 of September, 1743. Albany: Weed, Parsons & Company, 1861.

Justeen, Ole (ed.). *Danish Sources for the History of Ghana, 1657–1754*, Volume 1: *1657–1735*. Viborg: Royal Danish Academy of Science and Letters, 2005.

Kalm, Peter, and Adolph B. Benson (trans./ed.). *Peter Kalm's Travels in North America, The English Version of 1770*. New York: Dover, 1987.

Knight, Sarah Kemble. *The Journal of Madam Knight*. Boston: Small, Maynard & Company, 1920.

Konadu, Kwasi (ed.). *The Akan People: A Documentary History*. Volume 1. Princeton: Markus Wiener Publishers, 2016.

Konadu, Kwasi, and Clifford C. Campbell (eds.). *The Ghana Reader: History, Culture, Politics*. Durham: Duke University Press, 2016.

Law, Robin (ed.). *The English in West Africa, 1685–1688: The Local Correspondence of the Royal African Company of England, 1681–1699, Part 2*. Oxford: Oxford University Press, 2001.

Lockley, Timothy James (ed.). *Maroon Communities in South Carolina: A Documentary Record.* Columbia: University of South Carolina Press, 2009.

Minutes of the Common Council of the City of New York, 1675–1776, Volumes 1 and 2. New York: Dodd, Mead and Company, 1905.

Morin, J., and John Christian Jacobi (trans.). *A Short Account of the Life and Sufferings of Elias Neau, upon the Gallies, and in the Dungeons of Marseilles; for the Constant Profession of the Protestant Religion.* London: John Lewis, 1749.

Nelson, William. *Some Account of American Newspapers, particularly of the Eighteenth Century, and Libraries in which they may be found.* Patterson, N. Y: Press Printing and Publishing Co., 1894.

Newton, John, and Martin Bernard, and Mark Spurrell (eds.). *The Journal of a Slave Trader, 1750–1754.* London: Epworth Press, 1962.

New York Colonial Muster Rolls, 1664–1775: Report of the State Historian of the State of New York, Volume II. New York: Genealogical Publishing Company, 2000.

O'Callaghan, E. B. (ed.). *Calendar of Historical Manuscripts in the Office of the Secretary of State, Albany N. Y.*, Part II. Albany: Weed, Parsons and Company, 1866.

———. *The Documentary History of the State of New York*, volumes 1, 2, 3. Albany: Weed, Parsons & Company, 1850, 1851.

Phillips, Thomas. *A Journal of a Voyage Made in the Hannibal of London, Ann. 1693, 1694, from England, to Cape Monseradoe, in Africa, and Thence along the Coast of Guiney...* In *A Collection of Voyages and Travels, Some Now First Printed from Original Manuscripts Others Now First Published in English. In Six Volumes.* Volume VI. Walthoe, 1732.

Pratt, Daniel J. *Annals of Public Education of the State of New York, from 1626 to 1746.* Albany: Argus Company, 1872.

Rask, Johannes, and Selena Axelrod Winsnes (ed.). *Two Views From Christiansborg Castle, Volume I, A Brief and Truthful Description of a Journey to and from Guinea.* Accra: Sub-Saharan Publishers, 2009.

Rattray, R. Sutherland. *Akan Proverbs (the Primitive Ethics of a Savage People), Translated from the Original with Grammatical and Anthropological Notes.* Oxford: Clarendon Press, 1916.

Rømer, Ludewig Ferdinand, and Selena Axelrod Winsnes (ed.). *A Reliable Account of the Coast of Guinea [1760].* New York: Diasporic Africa Press, 2013.

Rudisel, Christine, and Bob Blaisdell (eds.). *Slave Narratives of the Underground Railroad.* New York: Dover, 2014.

Scott, Kenneth (ed.). *New York City Court Records, 1684–1760: Genealogical Data from the Court of Quarter Sessions.* New York: National Genealogical Society, 1982.

Sharpe, John."Journal of Rev. John Sharpe." *Pennsylvania Magazine of History and Biography,* 40, nos. 3–4 (1916), 257–297 and 412–425.

———. "Letter to the Secretary of the Society for the Propagation of the Gospel, 23 June 1712, New York." *New York Genealogical and Biographical Record,* Volume 19. New York City: Genealogical Society, 1888.

———. *The Reverend John Sharpe's Proposals.* New York: Collections of the New-York Historical Society, 1880, 350–355.

Sloane, Hans. *A Voyage to the Islands of Madera, Barbados, Nieves, S. Christophers and Jamaica . . . in Two Volumes.* London, 1707.

"Supplementary List of Marriage Licenses." *History Bulletin, Issue 1,* April 1898. New York: New York State Library, 1898.

Tax Lists of the City of New York, December, 1695 to July, 1699. Collections of the New-York Historical Society: New York, 1910, 1911.

Tilleman, Erick, and Selena Axelrod Winsnes (eds.). *A Short Account of West Africa's Gold Coast and Its Nature.* New York: Diasporic Africa Press, 2013.

Uring, Nathaniel. *The Voyages and Travels of Captain Nathaniel Uring with Introduction and Notes by Captain Alfred Dewar.* London: Cassell and Company, 1928.

Weeks, Lyman Horace, and Edwin M. Bacon (eds.). *An Historical Digest of the Provincial Press; Being a Collation of All Items of Personal and Historic Reference Relating to American Affairs Printed in the Newspapers of the Provincial Period . . .* Volume 1. Boston: Society for Americana, 1911.

NEWSPAPERS

Albany Morning Express, Albany, New York State, 1880.
Boston News-Letter, Boston, Massachusetts, 1704, 1705, 1711–1712
New York Mercury, New York, 1756.
New-York Weekly Journal, New York, 1734.
Weekly Rehearsal, Boston, 1734.

SECONDARY SOURCES

Achebe, Chinua. *Things Fall Apart.* Oxford: Heinemann, 2000.

Amessen, Eric (ed.). *Encyclopedia of U.S. Labor and Working-Class History.* New York: Routledge, 2007.

Anderson, Jervis. *A. Philip Randolph: A Biographical Portrait.* Berkeley: University of California Press, 1986.

Aptheker, Herbert. *American Negro Slave Revolts*. New York: International Publishers, 1978.

Archdeacon, Thomas J. *New York City, 1664–1710: Conquest and Change*. Ithaca: Cornell University Press, 1976.

Bailey, Nathan. *An Universal Etymological English Dictionary...* London: R. Ware, W. Innys, J. Richardson, 1775.

Baker, David V. *Women and Capital Punishment in the United States: An Analytical History*. Jefferson: McFarland & Company, 2015.

Bankoff, H. Arthur, and Alyssa Loorya (eds.). *The History and Archaeology of City Hall Park*. New York: Brooklyn College Archaeological Research Center, 2008.

Banner, Stuart. *The Death Penalty: An American History*. Cambridge: Harvard University Press, 2009.

Bayles, William Harrison. *Old Taverns of New York*. New York: Frank Allaben Genealogical Company, 1915.

Bernard, Jacqueline. *Journey Towards Freedom: The Story of Sojourner Truth*. New York: Feminist Press at the City University of New York, 1990.

Berrian, William. *An Historical Sketch of Trinity Church, New York*. New York: Stanford and Swords, 1847.

Bolster, W. Jeffrey. *Black Jacks: African American Seamen in the Age of Sail*. Cambridge: Harvard University Press, 1997.

Bonomi, Patricia U. *The Lord Cornbury Scandal: The Politics of Reputation in British America*. Chapel Hill: University of North Carolina Press, 1998.

Bosher, J. F. "Huguenot Merchants and the Protestant International in the Seventeenth Century." *William and Mary Quarterly*, 52, no. 1 (Jan. 1995), 77–102.

Bostoen, Koen, and Inge Brinkman (eds.) *The Kongo Kingdom: The Origins, Dynamics and Cosmopolitan Culture of an African Polity*. Cambridge: Cambridge University Press, 2018.

Brown, Nikki, and Barry M. Stentiford. *The Jim Crow Encyclopedia: Greenwood Milestones in African American History*. Westport: Greenwood Press, 2008.

Brown, Vincent. *Tacky's Revolt: The Story of an Atlantic Slave War*. Cambridge: Belknap Press, 2020.

Burnard, Trevor. *Mastery, Tyranny, and Desire: Thomas Thistlewood and His Slaves in the Anglo-Jamaican World*. Chapel Hill: University of North Carolina Press, 2004.

Candy, Nicholas (ed.). *The Oxford History of the British Empire*, Volume 1, *The Origins of Empire: British Overseas Enterprise at the Close of the Seventeenth Century*. Oxford: Oxford University Press, 1998.

Cantwell, Anne-Marie, and Diana diZerega Wall. *Unearthing Gotham: The Archaeology of New York City*. New Haven: Yale University Press, 2001.

Chaplin, Howard M. *Privateer Ships and Sailors: The First Century of American Colonial Privateering, 1625–1725*. Connecticut: Martino Fine Books, 2017.

Christoph, Peter R. "The Freedmen of New Amsterdam." In Nancy Anne McClure Zeller (ed.), *A Beautiful and Fruitful Place: Selected Rensselaerswijck Seminar Papers*, 157–170. New York: New Netherland Publishing, 1991.

Coffin, Joshua. *An Account of Some of the Principal Slave Insurrections, and Others, which have Occurred, or been Attempted, in the United States and Elsewhere, during the Last Two Centuries*. New York: American Anti-Slavery Society, 1860.

Cohen, David S. *The Dutch-American Farm*. New York: New York University Press, 1992.

Cook, Adrian. *The Armies of the Streets: The New York City Draft Riots of 1863*. Lexington: University Press of Kentucky, 1974.

Costello, A. E. *Our Police Protectors: History of the New York Police from the Earliest Period to the Present Time*. New York: Costello, 1885.

Craton, Michael. *Testing the Chains: Resistance to Slavery in the British West Indies*. Ithaca: Cornell University Press, 1982.

Crouse, Nellis M. *The French Struggle for the West Indies, 1665–1713*. New York: Octagon Books, 1966.

Davies, K. G. *The Royal African Company*. New York: Octagon Books, 1975.

Davis, T. J. *Rumor of Revolt: The "Great Negro Plot" in Colonial New York*. New York: Free Press, 1985.

De Jong, Gerald F. *The Dutch Reformed Church and Negro Slavery in Colonial American*. Cambridge: Cambridge University Press, 1978.

De Voe, Thomas F. *The Market Book, Containing a Historical Account of the Public Markets in the Cities of New York, Boston, Philadelphia, and Brooklyn*...Volume I. New York: De Voe, 1862.

Dewulf, Jeroen. *The Pinkster King and the King of Kongo: The Forgotten History of America's Dutch-Owned Slaves*. Jackson: University Press of Mississippi, 2017.

Du Bois, W. E. B. *The Negro*. New York: H. Holt, 1915.

Du Bois, W. E. B. *The Souls of Black Folk*. New York: Pocket Books, 2005.

Dunlap, William. *History of the New Netherlands, Province of New York, and State of New York*, Volume 1. New York: Carter & Thorp, 1840.

Dunn, Richard S. *Sugar and Slaves: The Rise of the Planter Class in the English West Indies, 1624–1713*. New York: Norton Library, 1973.

Earle, Alice Morse. *Colonial Days in Old New York*. New York: I. J. Fredman, 1962.

Faucquez, Anne-Claire. *"A Bloody Conspiracy": Race, Power and Religion in New York's 1712 Slave Insurrection*. In Lauric Henneton, and Louis Roper (eds.). *Fear and the Shaping of Early American Societies*. Leiden: Brill, 2016. 204–225.

Finkelman, Paul. *The Age of Jim Crow: Segregation from the End of Reconstruction to the Great Depression*. New York: Garland, 1992.

Finnegan, Ruth. *Oral Literature in Africa*. Cambridge: Open Book Publishers, 2012.

Foner, Eric. *Gateway to Freedom: The Hidden History of America's Fugitive Slaves*. Oxford: Oxford University Press, 2015.

Foner, Laura, and Genovese, Eugene D. (eds.) *Slavery in the New World: A Reader in Comparative History*. Englewood, NJ: Prentice Hall, 1969.

Foote, Thelma. *Black and White Manhattan: The History of Racial Formation in Colonial New York City*. Oxford: Oxford University Press, 2004.

———. "Some Hard Usage: The New York City Slave Revolt of 1712." *New York Folklore*, 18 (2001), 147–160.

Foote, Thelma, M. Carey, J. Giesenberg-Haag, J. Gray, K. McKoy, and C. Todd. *Report on Site-Specific History of Block 154*. Written for the African Burial Ground Research Project New York. http://s-media.nyc.gov/agencies/lpc/arch_reports/861.pdf.

Fox, Caleb Heathcote. *Gentleman Colonist: The Story of a Career in the Province of New York, 1692–1721*. New York: Cooper Square Publishers, 1971.

Galenson, David W. *Traders, Planters and Slaves: Market Behavior in Early English America*. Cambridge: Cambridge University Press, 2002.

Gaspar, David Barry. *Bondsmen and Rebels: A Study of Master-Slave Relations in Antigua, with Implications for Colonial British America*. Baltimore: Johns Hopkins University Press, 1983.

Goebel, Julius, and Thomas Raymond Naughton. *Law Enforcement in Colonial New York: A Study in Criminal Procedure (1664–1776)*. New York: Patterson Smith, 1970.

Goodfriend, Joyce D. *Before the Melting Pot: Society and Culture in Colonial New York City, 1664–1730*. Princeton: Princeton University Press, 1992.

Goodfriend, Joyce D. "Burghers and Blacks: The Evolution of a Slave Society at New Amsterdam." *New York History*, 59, no. 2 (April 1978), 125–144.

———. "The Protestants of Colonial New York City." In Bertrand Van Ruymbeke and Randy J. Sparks (eds.), *Memory and Identity: The Huguenots in France and the Atlantic Diaspora*, 241–254. Columbia: University of South Carolina Press, 2003.

Gould, C. "The Shrine of Tutu Abo, Akwamu War God." *Research Review, Institute of African Studies*, 8, January 1972, 5–10.

Greenburg, Douglas. *Crime and Law Enforcement in the Colony of New York*. Ithaca: Cornell University Press, 1974.

———. "The Effectiveness of Law Enforcement in Eighteenth Century New York." *American Journal of Legal History*, 19, no. 3 (July 1975), 173–207.

Habel, Norman C. (ed.). *Earth Story in the Psalms and the Prophets*. Bodmin: Sheffield Academic Press, 2001.

Hair, Paul Edward Hedley, Adam Jones, and Robin Law. *Barbot on Guinea: The Writings of Jean Barbot on West Africa 1678–1712*. London: Hakluyt Society, 1992.

Hall, Michael G., Lawrence H. Leder, and Michael Kammen (eds.). *The Glorious Revolution in America: Documents on the Colonial Crisis of 1689*. Chapel Hill: University of North Carolina Press, 1964.

Halpin, Dennis Patrick. *A Brotherhood of Liberty: Black Reconstruction and its Legacies in Baltimore, 1865–1920*. Philadelphia: University of Pennsylvania Press, 2019.

Hanes, Walton Jr., Sherman Puckett, and Donald R. Deskins Jr. *The African American Electorate: A Statistical History*. Los Angeles: Sage, 2012.

Hanserd, Robert. "Obayifo to Obeah: Priestly Power and Other Elements of Afro-Atlantic Akan Identity." Paper presented at the American Historical Association, 2012.

Hart, Richard. *Slaves who Abolished Slavery: Blacks in Rebellion*. 1980. Mona: University of the West Indies Press, 2002.

Haynes, Stephen R. *Noah's Curse: The Biblical Justification of American Slavery*. Oxford: Oxford University Press, 2002.

Hershkowitz, Leo. "Anatomy of a Slave Voyage, New York 1721." In de Halve Maen, *Journal of The Holland Society of New York*, Fall 2003, 45–51.

Hills, George Morgan. *History of the Church in Burlington, New Jersey; Comprising the Facts and Incidents of Nearly Two Hundred Years, from Original, Contemporaneous Soucres*. Trenton: William S. Sharp, 1876.

Hochschild, Adam. *Bury the Chains: The British Struggle to Abolish Slavery*. London: Pan, 2012.

Hodges, Graham Russell Gao. *Root and Branch: African Americans in New York and East Jersey, 1613–1863*. Chapel Hill: University of North Carolina Press, 1999.

Hoffer, Peter Charles. *Cry Liberty: The Great Stono River Slave Rebellion of 1739*. Oxford: Oxford University Press, 2010.

Hughes, Ben. *Apocalypse 1692: Empire, Slavery, and the Great Port Royal Earthquake*. Yardley: Westholme Publishing, 2017.

Johnson, Herbert A. "Civil Procedure in John Jay's New York." *American Journal of Legal History*, 11, no. 1 (Jan. 1967), 69–80.

Kammen, Michael. *Colonial New York: A History*. New York: Charles Scribner's Sons, 1975.

Kea, Ray A. *Settlements, Trade, and Polities in the Seventeenth Century Gold Coast*. Baltimore: Johns Hopkins University Press, 1982.

———. "'When I Die, I Shall Return to My Own Land': An 'Amina' Slave Rebellion in the Danish West Indies, 1733–1734," in John Hunwick and Nancy Lawler (eds.), *The Cloth of Many Colored Silks: Papers on History and Society, Ghanaian and Islamic, in Honor of Ivor Wilks*. Evanston: Northwestern University Press, 1996.

Kerber, Linda K. "Abolitionists and Amalgamators: The New York City Race Riots of 1834." *New York History*, 48, no. 1 (January 1967), 28–39.

Kilson, Marion D. deB. "Towards Freedom: An Analysis of Slave Revolts in the United States." *Phylon*, 25, no. 2 (1960), 175–187.

Kirk, John A. *Martin Luther King, Jr: Profiles in Power*. Abingdon: Routledge, 2014.

Klingberg, Frank Joseph. *Anglican Humanitarianism in Colonial New York, Issue 11*. New York: Church Historical Society, 1940.

Konadu, Kwasi. *The Akan Diaspora in the Americas*. New York: Oxford University Press, 2010.

Kruger, Vivienne L. "Born to Run: The Slave Family in Early New York, 1626 to 1827." Ph.D. diss., Columbia University, 1985.

Law, Robin. *Ouidah: The Social History of a West African Slaving "Port," 1727–1892*. Athens: Ohio University Press, 2004.

"Law in Colonial New York: The Legal System of 1691." *Harvard Law Review*, 80, no. 8 (June 1967), 1757–1772.

Leone, Mark, and G. Fry. "Conjuring in the Big House Kitchen." *Journal of American Folklore*, 112, no. 445 (Summer 1999), 372–403.

Leone, Mark P., Parker B. and Potter (eds.), *Historical Archaeologies of Capitalism*. 2nd edition. New York: Springer, 2015.

Lustig, Mary Lou. *Robert Hunter 1664–1734: New York's Augustan Statesman.* Syracuse: Syracuse University Press, 1983.

Lydon, James G. "New York and the Slave Trade, 1700 to 1774." *William and Mary Quarterly*, 35, no. 2 (April 1978), 375–394.

Lyons, Adam. *The 1711 Expedition to Quebec: Politics and the Limitations of British Global Strategy.* London: Bloomsbury, 2014.

MacKinnon, Robert, and Dallas Murphy. *Treasure Hunter: Diving for Gold on North America's Death Coast.* New York: Berkley Books, 2012.

Man, Jr., Albon P. "Labor Competition and the New York Draft Riots of 1863." *Journal of Negro History*, 36, no. 4 (October 1951), 375–401.

Martinez, James Michael. *Carpetbaggers, Cavalry, and the Klu Klux Klan: Exposing the Invisible Empire During Reconstruction.* Lanham: Rowman & Littlefield, 2007.

Matson, Cathy. *Merchants and Empire: Trading in Colonial New York.* Baltimore: Johns Hopkins University Press, 1998.

Maynard, John Albert. *The Huguenot Church of New York: A History of the French Church of Saint Espirit.* New York: French Church of Saint Esprit, 1938.

McCusker, John. *Essays in the Economic History of the Atlantic World.* London: Routledge, 1997.

Mckee, Jr., Samuel. *Labor in Colonial New York, 1664–1776.* New York: Columbia University Press, 1935.

McKnight, Kathryn Joy and Leo J. Garofalo. *Afro-Latino Voices: Narratives from the Early Modern Ibero-Atlantic World, 1550–1812.* Indianapolis: Hackett Publishing, 2009.

McManus, Edgar J. *Bondage in the North.* Syracuse: Syracuse University Press, 1973.

———. *A History of Negro Slavery in New York.* Syracuse: Syracuse University Press, 1966.

Medford, Edna Greene (ed.). *The New York African Burial Ground*, Volume 3, *Historical Perspectives of the African Burial Ground: New York Blacks and the Diaspora.* Washington: Howard University Press, 2009.

Midlo Hall, Gwendolyn. *Slavery and African Ethnicity in the Americas: Restoring the Links.* Chapel Hill: University of North Carolina Press, 2005.

Miller, Helen Hill. *Colonel Parke of Virginia: "The Greatest Hector in the Town."* Chapel Hill: Algonquin Books, 1989.

Nketia, J. H. Kwabena. *Drumming in Akan Communities of Ghana.* Accra: University of Ghana, 1963.

O'Connor, Daniel. *Three Centuries of Mission: The United Society for the Propagation of the Gospel, 1701–2000.* London: Continuum, 2000.

Oliver, V. Langford. *The History of the Island of Antigua, One of the Lee-ward Caribbees in the West Indies*. London: Mitchell and Hughes, 1894.

Olson, Edwin. "The Slave Code in Colonial New York." *Journal of Negro History*, 29, no. 2, (1944), 147–165.

O'Malley, Gregory E. *Final Passages: The Intercontinental Slave Trade of British America, 1619–1807*. Chapel Hill: University of North Carolina Press, 2014.

Otterness, Philip L. *Becoming German: The 1709 Palatine Migration to New York*. Ithaca: Cornell University Press, 2013.

Owusu, Effah. "A Case Study of the Easter Celebration among the Kwahus." A Dissertation submitted to the Faculty of Theology in partial fulfillment of the Requirements for a certificate in Theology. St. Victor's Major Seminary Tamale, Ghana, Retrieved from: https://www.academia.edu/29414101/A_Case_Study_Of_Easter_Celebration_Am ong_The_Kwahus_Kwahu_Ooo_Kwahu_

Pares, Richard. *Yankees and Creoles: The Trade Between North America and the West Indies before the American Revolution*. Cambridge: Harvard University Press, 1956.

Peckham, Howard H. *The Colonial Wars, 1689–1762*. Chicago: University of Chicago Press, 2014.

Peterson, Arthur Everett, and George William Edward. *New York as an Eighteenth-Century Municipality*. New York: Columbia University, 1917.

Prince, Richard. *Maroon Societies: Rebel Slave Communities in the Americas*. 3rd edition. Baltimore: Johns Hopkins University Press, 1996.

Pulis, John W. (ed.). *Moving on: Black Loyalists in the Afro-Atlantic World*. New York: Garland, 1999.

Rediker, Marcus. *Between the Devil and the Deep Blue Sea: Seamen, Pirates and the Anglo-American Maritime World, 1700–1750*. Cambridge: Cambridge University Press, 1993.

———, *The Slave Ship: A Human History*. London: John Murray, 2007.

Richardson, David. "Shipboard Revolts, African Authority, and the Atlantic Slave Trade." *William and Mary Quarterly*, 58, no. 1 (2001), 69–92.

Riddell, William Renwick. "The Slave in Early New York." *Journal of Negro History*, 13, no. 1 (Jan. 1928), 53–86.

Riker, James. *The Annals of Newton, in Queens County, New York: Containing Its History from Its First Settlement*. New York: D. Fanshaw, 1852.

Rock, Howard B. *The New York City Artisan, 1789–1825: A Documentary History*. New York: State University of New York Press, 1989.

Rothschild, Nan A. *New York City Neighborhoods: The 18th Century*. New York: Percheron Press, 1990.

Rucker, Walter C. *Gold Coast Diasporas: Identity, Culture, and Power*. Bloomington: Indiana University Press, 2015.

———. *The River Flows on: Black Resistance, Culture, and Identity in Early America*. Baton Rouge: Louisiana State University Press, 2006.

Rugemer, Edward B. *Slave Law and the Politics of Resistance in the Early Atlantic World*. Cambridge: Harvard University Press, 2018.

Sacks, Marcy S. *Before Harlem: The Black Experience in New York City Before World War I*. Philadelphia: University of Pennsylvania Press, 2013.

Sauter, Suzanne Van H. *Elias Neau (c. 1662–1722): Also known as Elie Naud: Huguenot, Refugee, Ship Captain, Prisoner, Poet, Merchant, Catechist, Teacher*. Presentation to the Huguenot Society of North Carolina. 14 April 2012. Retrieved from http://www.huguenot.netnation.com/states/nc/documents/Life_of_Elias_Neau_by_S_Sauter.pdf.

Scott, Kenneth. "The Slave Insurrection in New York in 1712." *New-York Historical Society Quarterly*, 45, 1961, 43–74.

Shorto, Russel. *The Island at the Centre of the World: The Untold Story of Dutch Manhattan and the Founding of New York*. Chatham: Doubleday, 2004.

Shumway, Rebecca. *The Fante and the Transatlantic Slave Trade*. Rochester: University of Rochester Press, 2014.

Sill, Dunkin H. "A Notable Example of Longevity, 1737–1852." *New York Genealogical and Biographical Record*, 56, no. 1 (1925), 65–67.

Singleton, Esther. *Social New York under the Georges, 1714–1776: Houses, Streets and Country Homes, with Chapters on Fashions, Furniture, China, Plates and Manners*. New York: D. Appleton and Company, 1902.

Skemer, Don C. "New Evidence on Black Unrest in Colonial Brooklyn." *Journal of Long Island History*, 12, no. 1 (1975), 46–49.

Smith, William. *The History of the Province of New York, from the First Discovery to the Year 1732: With a Description of the Country, with a Short Account of the Inhabitants, their Trade, Religious and Political State, and the Constitution of the Courts of justice in that Colony*. London: Thomas Wilcox, 1757.

Snyder, Terri L. *The Power to Die: Slavery and Suicide in British North America*. Chicago: University of Chicago Press, 2015.

Sparks, Randy J. *Where the Negroes Are Masters: An African Port in the Ear of the Slave Trade*. Cambridge: Harvard University Press, 2014.

Stokes, I. N. Phelps. *The Iconography of Manhattan Island, 1498–1909: Compiled from Original Sources and Illustrated by Photo Intaglio Reproductions of Important Maps, Plans, Views and Documents in Public and Private Collections*. New York: Robert H. Dodd, 1915.

Strum-Lind, Lisa. *Actors of Globalization: New York Merchants in Global Trade*. Leiden: Brill, 2018.

Thomas, Hugh. *The Slave Trade: The History of the Atlantic Slave Trade, 1440–1870*. London: Picador, 1997.

Thornton, John K. *Warfare in Atlantic Africa, 1500–1800*. London: University College London Press, 1999.

——. *Africa and Africans in the Making of the Atlantic World, 1400–1800*. Cambridge: Cambridge University Press, 1998.

Valentine, D. T. *Manual of the Corporation of the City of New York, for the Years 1845–6*. New York: Levi D. Slamm & C. C. Childs, 1846.

Valsecchi, Pierluigi. "Calendar and the Annual Festival in Nzema: Notes on Time and History." *Africa: Rivista trimestrale*, 54, no. 4 (December 1999), 489–513.

Van Ruymbeke, Bertrand, and Sparks, Randy J. (eds.). *Memory and Identity: The Huguenots in France and the Atlantic Diaspora*. Columbia: University of South Carolina Press, 2003.

Various. *The Skeletal Biology, Archaeology, and History of the New York African Burial Ground: A Synthesis of Volumes 1, 2, and 3*. Washington D.C.: Howard University Press, 2009.

Wall, Diana diZerega. "Twenty Years After: Re-examining Archaeological Collections for Evidence of New York City's Colonial African Past." *African Diaspora Archaeology Newsletter*, Volume 7, Issue 2, April 2000, Article 2.

Wallis, J. R. "The Kwahu—their Connexion with the Afram Plains." *Transactions of the Gold Coast & Togoland Historical Society*, 1, no. 3 (1953), 10–26.

Wax, Darold D. "Negro Import Duties in Colonial Pennsylvania." *Pennsylvania Magazine of History and Biography*, 97, no. 1 (1973), 22–44.

——. "Preferences for Slaves in Colonial America." *Journal of Negro History*, 58, no. 4 (1973), 375–378.

Wees, Beth Carver. *Early American Silver in the Metropolitan Museum of Art*. New York: Metropolitan Museum of Art, 2013.

Wilks, Ivor. *Akwamu, 1640–1750: A Study of the Rise and Fall of a West African Empire*. Trondheim: Department of History, Norwegian University of Science and Technology, 2001.

——. *Forests of Gold: Essays on the Akan and the Kingdom of Asante*. Athens: Ohio University Press, 1993.

Wintz, Cary D., and Paul Finkelman (eds.). *Encyclopedia of the Harlem Renaissance*, Volume 1 A-J. New York: Routledge, 2004.

Young, L. H. *The Historical Cabinet: Containing Authentic Accounts of Remarkable and Interesting Events which Have Taken Place in Modern Times: Carefully Collected and Compiled from Various and Authentic Sources . . .* New Haven: L. H. Young, 1835.

Zabin, Serena R. *Dangerous Economies: Status and Commerce in Imperial New York.* Philadelphia: University of Pennsylvania Press, 2011.

Zoellner, Tom. *Island on Fire: The Revolt that Ended Slavery in the British Empire.* Cambridge: Harvard University Press, 2020.

WEBSITES

"1687–1787. Slave Life at Lloyd Manor." PDF, https://robcanobbio.files.wordpress.com/2020/01/1687-1787.lloyd-manor.pdf.

Dickey, George. "More on Canisteo Castle," *Crooked Lake Review*, May 1996, https://www.crookedlakereview.com/articles/67_100/98may1996/98dickey.html.

"Phases of the Moon 1701–1800." http://astropixels.com/ephemeris/phasescat/phases1701.html.

Robinson, David D. "The Outlaw Fort Canisteo Castle," *Crooked Lake Review*, November 1995, https://www.crookedlakereview.com/articles/67_100/92nov1995/92robinson.html.

———. "Canisteo Castle Builders Found," *Crooked Lake Review*, February 1996, https://www.crookedlakereview.com/articles/67_100/95feb1996/95robinson.html.

"Slave Voyages." https://www.slavevoyages.org.

"Walter Thong." Geni. https://www.geni.com/people/Walter-Thong/6000000006728257528.

"William Hallett Sr." https://www.wikitree.com/wiki/Hallett-130.

Acknowledgments

I WOULD LIKE TO ACKNOWLEDGE the help provided by the archivists at the National Archives in Kew, London, and the New-York Historical Society Library. The staff of the reading rooms of the Surrogate's Court Building in New York and those of the State Archives in Albany were particularly friendly and accommodating.

I thank Bruce H. Franklin, my publisher, who suggested that I write about the 1712 New York City slave revolt, and provided support and encouragement. I also thank Noreen O'Connor Abel, my copyeditor, for her hard-work, and professionalism. I must also thank Tracy Dungan, the cartographer, for producing the high-quality maps that accompany this book and Trudi Gershenov for her striking cover design.

Finally, I would like to thank my wife Vanessa and our daughter Emily for their patience and support. I dedicate this book to the rebels who instigated the revolt of 1712. Their courage and determination to resist are inspiring.

Index

Westholme Titles of Related Interest

Apocalypse 1692: Empire, Slavery, and the Great Port Royal Earthquake by Ben Hughes

Carrying the Colors: The Life and Legacy of Medal of Honor Recipient Andrew Jackson Smith by W. Robert Beckman and Sharon S. McDonald

From Slaves to Soldiers: The 1st Rhode Island Regiment in the American Revolution by Robert A. Geake with Lorén M. Spears

The Involuntary American: A Scottish Prisoner's Journey to the New World by Carol Gardner

King William's War: The First Contest for North America, 1689–1697 by Michael G. Laramie

The Man with the Branded Hand: The Life of Jonathan Walker, Abolitionist by Alvin F. Oickle

Queen Anne's War: The Second Contest for North America, 1702–1712 by Michael G. Laramie

Revolt at Taos: The New Mexican and Indian Insurrection of 1847 by James A. Crutchfield

Settling the Frontier: Urban Development in America's Borderlands, 1600–1830 by Joseph P. Alessi

To Raise Up a Nation: John Brown, Frederick Douglass, and the Making of a Free Country by William S. King

Wives, Slaves, and Servant Girls: Advertisements for Female Runaways in American Newspapers, 1770–1783 by Don N. Hagist